ALSO BY JONATHAN C. RANDAL

Going All the Way: Christian Warlords,
Israeli Adventurers, and the War in Lebanon

After Such Knowledge, What Forgiveness?

AFTER SUCH KNOWLEDGE, WHAT FORGIVENESS?

My Encounters with Kurdistan

Jonathan C. Randal

Farrar, Straus and Giroux

NEW YORK

Library of Congress Cataloging-in-Publication Data
Randal, Jonathan C., 1933–
    After such knowledge, what forgiveness? : my encounters with
Kurdistan / Jonathan C. Randal. — 1st ed.
        p.   cm.
    Includes bibliographical references (p.   ) and index.
    ISBN 0-374-10200-7 (alk. paper)
        1. Kurds—Politics and government.   2. Middle East—Ethnic
relations.   3. Randal, Jonathan C., 1933–   . I. Title.
    DS59.K86R43   1997
956'.00491597—dc21   *96-48612*
                                                        CIP

For Geneviève and Julie

and for Fred Cuny and other Absent Friends,

many of them Kurds

Contents

After such knowledge, what forgiveness? Think now

History has many cunning passages, contrived corridors

And issues, deceives with whispering ambitions,

Guides us by vanities . . .

Think

Neither fear nor courage saves us. Unnatural vices

Are fathered by our heroism. Virtues

Are forced upon us by our impudent crimes.

These tears are shaken from the wrath-bearing tree.

T. S. ELIOT, *"Gerontion"*

After Such Knowledge,

What Forgiveness?

"Have You Notified
Your Next of Kin?"

*To those born under an elaborate social order few such moments of
exhilaration can come as that which stands at the threshold of wild
travel.*

GERTRUDE BELL, *The Desert and the Sown* (1907)

The idea for a book about the Kurds and Kurdistan came
to me on a near-empty South Beach on Martha's Vineyard
on a clear August afternoon in 1986. Even now I can hear
myself telling my doubting wife, between rapidly replenished plastic cups of passable white wine, "Here's my idea: throw a spotlight
on one of the Middle East's forgotten corners, a nineteenth-century
kind of walking tour through a country that does not exist, three
months in and out." The project was a holiday fantasy. I should
have known better. In fact, I knew pitifully little about the
Kurds—few Westerners did. My only firsthand Kurdish experi-
ences had not been outwardly happy, but they had piqued my
curiosity amid more immediately compelling happenings in Beirut,
where I was then the *Washington Post*'s correspondent. In the
early days of the Lebanese civil war in 1975, Kurdish gunsels in
the temporary employ of local self-styled Maoists had forcibly
evicted me from my office apartment.

They meant me no particular harm: I had simply been in the
way during a neighborhood offensive. I lost everything I owned,
and was delivered once and for all of any desire for possessions. A
few months later I watched Maronite Christian militiamen force
wretched Kurds as well as Palestinian and Lebanese Shia residents
at gunpoint from their slum homes in the old quarantine section
of Beirut to clear a perimeter around their headquarters. Finally,

on the eve of Israel's invasion of Lebanon in 1982, other Kurds working for obscure patrons used rocket-propelled grenades to destroy the home of Beirut friends who had sheltered me while I was writing a book on the Lebanese crisis.

What passed for a deeper knowledge of the Kurds could be summed up in a few banalities. A century earlier, Europeans considered Kurdistan as remote and dangerous as the American Wild West (indeed the imaginative Karl May, a great German inventor of adventure stories, wrote both of cowboys and Indians and of what he called "wildest Kurdistan"). A character in Anthony Trollope's 1864 novel *Can You Forgive Her?* talks of Kurdistan as if it were a violent Ultima Thule. During World War I President Woodrow Wilson's Fourteen Points promised Kurds a vaguely defined country of their own, to be carved out of the carcass of the defeated Ottoman Empire. Subsequently, such undertakings were rejected by Mustafa Kemal Ataturk's resurgent Turkey, which first manipulated the Kurds against its foreign enemies, then crushed their nationalist ambitions. The British, entrusted with a League of Nations mandate for Ottoman territory in what was to be called Iraq, were also bent on thwarting Kurdish nationalist aspirations. Determined to control the oil in territory Kurds claimed as theirs, Britain forced them into a blood-spattered union with its freshly minted Iraqi state, dominated by its Sunni Arab minority.

Ever since, various Middle Eastern governments have invoked Western notions of the modern centralized nation-state to crush repeated Kurdish revolts, leaguing together when necessary lest the restive Kurdish subjects succeed in organizing themselves across artificial political frontiers. For the Kurds were—and still are—the fourth largest group in the Middle East and, arguably, its prize losers. No one disputes that they are the world's largest ethnic group without a state of their own. Such has been their various foreign rulers' abiding fear of them that no reliable census has been conducted in decades, and their numbers can only be estimated, the best guess being 25 million. Outside inquiry has been discouraged.

Eternal outsiders, who in this century can only have marveled at the wasted fortunes that the Arab world lavished on Palestinian nationalism, the Kurds are the Middle East's essential poor boys. Deprived even of their own oil and kept on short rations in one state, their national dress banned in another, their language in still a third, their most basic human and civil rights denied to differing, but often extreme, degrees at various times in various places, the Kurds have resisted assimilation with a constancy confounding their would-be masters. They have survived the first aerial bombing in the Third World, poison gas, the deliberate leveling of their rural society in Iraq, mass destruction of villages and forced deportation to the western cities of Turkey, and the assassination of their leaders in Iran. The Royal Air Force bombed Iraqi Kurds in January 1919 in what is believed to be the first use of air power to put down revolts; bombing was cheaper than garrisoning troops. Later that year, in Britain's third Afghan War, the RAF based in India bombed Afghan cities, forcing the emir, Amanullah Khan, to sue for peace. Winston Churchill, as Colonial Secretary in 1921, formally gave the RAF responsibility for maintaining law and order in the British-mandated parts of the Middle East. Among the RAF officers who served in Iraq was Arthur Harris, known in World War II as Bomber Harris for his ruthless championing of saturation bombing against German civilian and military targets.

Kurds living in Baghdad, Damascus, Istanbul, or Tehran keep alive a secret Kurdish garden, nurturing it despite the homogenizing erosion of life in these cosmopolitan capitals. A generation ago a French journalistic colleague of mine was amazed at the determined Kurdishness of a young interpreter he met in wartime Iraqi Kurdistan who had been brought up in Baghdad and spoke little Kurdish. Despite the outward evidence, he insisted he felt Kurd, explaining, "There's nothing I can do about it." I myself have marveled at the bedrock nationalism of young Turkish Kurds who speak, read, and write Turkish effortlessly but are prepared to die for a Kurdistan whose language they barely know. So, too, are Kurds as far away as Australia.

History is said to be written by the victors, and that has meant the Kurds' enemies. But thanks to their mountains and remoteness from the centers of imperial power in Constantinople and Tehran, Kurds have from time to time enjoyed a sense of freedom which has waxed and waned with the strength of their overlords. Before World War I, with the decline of the Ottoman Empire, where the overwhelming majority of Kurds then lived, notions of modern nationalism awakened both Kurds and Arabs, but the Kurds' unquenchable craving for independence from alien rule was never matched by political gifts capable of overcoming the determination to keep them divided. In the Middle East their travail in this century alone remains unmatched even in a region given over to terror, treachery, and repression on a grand scale. The "modern-izing" handiwork that did such harm to the Kurds as often as not was carried out with the tolerant complicity of foreign powers, ranging from their immediate neighbors to Israel, Britain, and the United States. This international meddling has not been gratuitous. Kurdistan is blessed—or, as some Kurds maintain, cursed—with the parched Middle East's major sources of water, and it has abun-dant oil as well.

The Kurds' almost unbroken record of revolt and punishment has also been unrivaled over the past century. Alas for the Kurds, so, too, is their lack of organization and effective leadership. In the age of the helicopter and modern counterinsurgency weapons, their favorite adage—"The Kurds have no friends but the mountains"—has lost much if not all of its age-old validity. For even the mountains no longer provide the protection that once earned Kurdistan its reputation as "the land of insolence."

For me, just getting to Kurdistan, which at the time I construed as being in either Iran or Iraq, was the immediate problem. In times past, Kurdistan was often no more than at the end of a long car trip or, at worst, several days on muleback. But neither state, in the midst of an already six-year-old war, welcomed foreigners. The traditional illicit access to Kurdistan was through Turkey, but no longer; an ever more serious uprising among Turkey's own Kurds, starting in 1984, had prompted Ankara to send troop re-inforcements to its officially closed mountain border with Iraq, making a crossing there risky. Entry from Syria was more iffy still, involving crossing the Tigris River at night on inflated sheepskins or inner tubes, evading Iraqi patrols and trip wires set to unleash enfilading fire, before negotiating a wide no-man's-land—all be-fore sunup. I was fifty-three years old at the time, and after three decades of covering wars I had no more coupons left in my ration book for taking on such odds. As for Iran, my many visits chronicling the fall of the Shah and the early days of the Islamic Republic had landed me on Ayatollah Ruhollah Khomeini's gray, if not black, list. Even if I was somehow blessed with a three-day visa, such as was then the rule in Tehran, no foreign journalists were allowed into Iranian Kurdistan because of the war with Iraq.

Yet so taken was I by the project that before leaving Martha's Vineyard for my base in Paris I purchased Italian hiking boots and other camping paraphernalia. At times suspension of disbelief can be as essential to the reporter's trade as luck. And I soon got lucky—or so I thought. Upon my return to Paris in September, I won over Abdul Rahman Qassemlou, the urbane and genuinely democratic leader of the Iranian Kurds, who was passing through on one of his irregular European outings. We had known each other since the Iranian revolution nearly a decade earlier, when we'd become friendly in Tehran and, especially, in Iranian Kurdistan, where he made it a point of honor to provide whiskey for his guests—and himself—in a calculated act of defiance to the Ayatollah's teetotaling Islamic Republic. Now we agreed to meet in a nondescript Left Bank café. When I showed up, his Paris representative apologized, led me to an old Peugeot, drove around the block, and deposited me at the Closerie des Lilas, where Qassemlou was waiting. At the time I thought this was all a bit melodramatic. But I discarded this view long before both men imprudently abandoned their precautions and were assassinated in Vienna in 1989 by Iranian agents.

Qassemlou proposed to persuade the Iraqi government, which, in a classic example of Kurdish contrariness, was his ally, to remove me from Saddam Hussein's long-standing blacklist and give me not a visa but a laissez-passer, a lesser document that would allow me to travel from, but not linger in, Baghdad and thence go to the Iranian border. There Qassemlou would hand me over to a set of Iraqi Kurds headed by one Jalal Talabani, with whom he, but not Baghdad, was on good terms. They in turn might just pass me on to another Iraqi Kurdish group, Massoud Barzani's Kurdistan Democratic Party. Qassemlou's hesitation was prompted by bad blood between him and Barzani, who had sided with Tehran in its war with Iraq and fought against the Iranian Kurds. Relations between Barzani and Talabani were scarcely better.

In light of these obstacles, how I was to exit Kurdistan was problematic, since retracing my footsteps seemed out of the question once the Iraqis discovered that I had strayed from Qassemlou's reservation. Qassemlou made it plain that I had to assume Iraqi and Iranian intelligence would be tracking everything I did everywhere I went. Had I known then just how accurate that estimation was—Iraqi agents did indeed report back about foreigners' whereabouts and placed an all too attractive price on their heads—I might have demurred.

But the next day I went round to Qassemlou's Paris office and filled out forms, complete with photographs, for myself and a photographer friend. The paperwork, I was told, was destined for Iraqi intelligence agents, who would decide if we were worthy of their indulgence. Within days I took the overnight train to Berlin, where I attended a conference of pro-Barzani Kurdish students in a seedy hotel in Kreuzberg near the still very much standing wall dividing the city. With the exception of a Libyan diplomat from East Berlin, I was the only non-Kurd present. Only a few of the several dozen participants appeared to be under forty. Many were fat, gray, or balding.

I spent two days listening to Barzani operatives explain why oil, water, and geopolitics ruled out any hope of winning Western or regional support for Kurdish rights, much less autonomy or independence. Only the Soviet Union would ever help the Kurds, they argued. That, too, seemed a dim prospect. To buck up their spirits they fell back on the Kurds' galloping birth rate (an argument Palestinians also dredged up when everything else was going wrong for them). I told anyone who would listen to me about my book idea, hoping my enthusiasm would disarm these old revolutionaries' innate suspicion of Westerners, especially Americans. Ever polite, the Kurds promised to help—if I could reach Kurdistan on my own.

Back in Paris, I read about the Kurds at the Kurdish Institute and waited week after week, but I heard nothing from Qassemlou's Paris office. When eventually I inquired, I was told that no application had ever been received. They had wondered where I had gone but hadn't bothered to telephone me. I protested my good faith. Such was my introduction to Kurdish notions of administration. Nothing was to be gained from arguing. I resubmitted the applications. Another month dragged by and in early November, when the green light was flashed, Kurdish friends discouraged me from making the trip. Kurdish winters are often late but just as often severe, and I had no desire to remain snowbound in the mountains until the following spring. I blithely assumed, incorrectly it turned out, that the Iraqi laissez-passer would again be forthcoming.

In Washington just before Christmas, I sought out William Eagleton, the State Department's senior Kurdish specialist. Many Kurds are indebted to him for writing a history of the Mahabad Republic, the Iranian Kurds' brief, futile experience with trying to establish a state at the end of World War II. Since we were old friends Eagleton heard me out, but his disapproval was unequivocal. His only comment was to ask, "Have you notified your next of kin?" I took the advice to heart, knowing that in the foreseeable future there was nothing I could do to get to Kurdistan.

As it turned out, all I had to do was wait. The vagaries of a foreign correspondent's life are such that I was assigned to cover the Kurds in 1991 when the United States led a coalition army that drove the Iraqis out of Kuwait after a seven-month occupation. It was a case of answered prayers, with all that bittersweet phrase connotes. Kurdistan turned out to be an abiding, if often unorthodox, fascination.

Over the years I've walked in and out of Kurdistan's Zagros Mountains, crossing borders without benefit of visa, passport, or armed guard in countryside so wild that three British journalists were murdered nearby for their money only days before one of my passages. I've trudged along highways with exhausted Kurdish refugees reduced to burying their children and grandparents by the roadside for fear of setting off land mines if they ventured farther afield to provide a proper sepulcher. I've also flown in helicopters through the jagged teeth of the snowcapped 12,000-foot mountains that form the Iraqi-Turkish border, effortlessly surveying some of the late twentieth century's most isolated real estate, discovering high plateaus, valleys of sheer-faced rock, and rushing white water, then following the meandering Tigris River through endless plains to Diyarbakir, the unofficial capital of Turkish Kurdistan. In Iraqi Kurdistan I've watched hawks, bustards, and eagles ride the thermals high over scrub oak and bald hills and mountains, waiting to zero in on their prey.

For my own good I've also been forced by friendly Kurds to hire guards when traveling on Iraqi Kurdistan's main roads—and I do that only during daylight. I've coughed dust and baked in 120-degree summers, and I've frozen alongside Kurds so destitute they were reduced to burning scavenged asphalt for heating only a few miles from some of the world's richest oil fields. I've drunk tea as well as whiskey with Kurdish tribal leaders in Iraq and Iran, listened to Kurdish human-rights activists under constant threat of death in Turkey, and talked politics with Kurds of every station everywhere. In Iraq I've run into peasants harvesting thistles with odd implements designed in some dateless antiquity, talked wheat prices with tractor-owning farmers, commiserated with the urban middle class reduced to selling land, jewelry, silver, cars, radios, television sets, doors, beds, windows, homes to stay alive.

I've cried listening to stories of the wrecks of Kurdish lives, stories even more depressing than the intended lessons imparted by those who caused the endless ruins of thousands of small Kurdish villages, once the very essence of Kurdistan. I've been awakened at dawn in a cheap city hotel in Turkish Kurdistan by sustained shooting only a few hundred yards away, then watched Turkish security forces go through neighborhood after neighborhood with all the violent efficiency of colonial troops answerable to no one. I've trudged through winter snows along smugglers' mountain paths to listen to the nationalist fervor lurking beneath the relentlessly inculcated, half-baked Marxism of young, jejune Turkish Kurds who would have died by the thousands for an independent state. I have also come to understand the more limited goals of autonomy or federalism within existing borders, which Iranian and Iraqi Kurds have accepted after many shattered dreams and much destruction over many decades.

I've argued with Kurds in Western hotels, in tents, in rudimentary shelters made of leafy branches, and on long drives in broken-down vehicles. Perhaps because of my age, I personally have never been treated with anything but respect, generosity, and friendship no matter how heated the arguments. I've often wondered at a peculiarly Kurdish mixture of forbearance and bloody-mindedness, especially when I recall a scene high up in the mountains during the very heavy snows in the winter of 1992. Two busloads of Kurds coming from opposite directions met on the narrow road cleared by the region's only snowplow. I was in a Land Rover. Neither bus would give way or back up. There was not enough room for a vehicle to get by. Minutes passed. Suddenly the passengers poured out onto the snow and started pummeling one another, remembering, or feigning to remember, ancient slights. The fisticuffs showed no sign of abating, and, like all self-respecting Kurds, the men were armed with Kalashnikovs. To control my fears of impending general slaughter, I finally took a shovel out of the car and dug out enough snow alongside the road to allow my vehicle and one bus to pass. I yelled at the Kurds in English that I was in a hurry. They understood not a word of what I was howling.

I doubtless seemed quite mad to them, so much so, indeed, that they stopped abruptly and somewhat sheepishly, it seemed to me, climbed back aboard their buses. I directed traffic, guiding one bus into the spot I'd cleared while the other went on its way.

The incident pleases me because for once a foreigner helped solve—rather than complicate—a Kurdish problem, albeit a minor one. It also illustrates why I suspect a rogue chromosome in Kurdish genetics causes what Indians, with their love of fancy words, would call "fissiparous tendencies."

2

After Such Knowledge,
What Forgiveness?

In a hoary Oriental punishment the Ottomans in the late nineteenth century deported the entire Hamawand tribe from what is present-day Iraqi Kurdistan to Libya as punishment for its boundless truculence and unbridled highway robbery. Within seven years the tribe fought its way home across the Middle East and went back to its wicked old ways. There's something of the Hamawand in nearly every Kurd, at least when it comes to bouncing back from adversity imposed by outside authority. And yet it is the ever-fresh scars of relentlessly repeated calamity that strike the outsider as the Kurds' enduring legacy. An old poem insists that a Kurd's lot is one of "a thousand sighs, a thousand tears, a thousand revolts, a thousand hopes."

At first glance, many Kurdish acts of resistance and heroism by themselves impress; then, all too often, detailed examination reveals repeated fault lines that, one can see in retrospect, doomed the Kurds' revolts from the start. Kurdish nationalists confess amazement at their lack of success either in a single country or in combination with Kurds of other states. Never a politically unified people, they have suffered greatly from deep divisions and an entrenched penchant for treachery in their own ranks. Faced with increasingly well-armed, ruthless, and oppressive governments, the Kurds give only scant signs of learning from past errors. They cannot but rue the escalating human price of rebellion, especially in Iraq and Turkey, where their ancient, essentially rural society has been uprooted.

In a classic case of underdevelopment, the Kurds' often-maladroit politics reflect the effectiveness of constant official repression. The Kurds have experimented with various leaders, but none has succeeded in transforming their nationalism into independence or even sustainable autonomy—and this in a century when even tiny islands boast United Nations membership. Time and again, Kurdish nationalists have cooperated with foreign governments only too delighted to use them as pawns against neighboring states or even their own Kurds.

The Kurds' foreign overlords have historically followed a "dumbing down" strategy, rooting out anything smacking of a Kurdish elite able to generate first-rate leadership. They have co-opted, jailed, exiled, and assassinated educated Kurds and deprived them of incipient leaders and experienced politicians. In this century, with rare exceptions, Kurdish leaders have proved clumsy, provincial, and untutored in the ways of the outside world, where the fate of nations is decided beyond the confines of the Middle East and the often-paranoid mindsets there. At times Kurdish leadership was broadly traditional, as in Iraq, at others newly minted from the deracinated underclass, as in contemporary Turkey.

At one recent point, Kurds in Iran, Iraq, and Turkey were all in simultaneous, but uncoordinated, revolt. No sooner did cautious Kurds in one country appear to apply the dearly paid lessons of disastrous past errors than they were undercut by those next door trumpeting maximalist demands. Even those who had grown prudent over the decades threw caution to the winds in furtherance of narrow personal quarrels and ambitions. In 1991, the first Kurds in seven decades were elected to Turkey's parliament as genuine representatives of Kurdish interests. Unsurprisingly, they lacked sufficient political skills to avoid isolation, arrest, and imprisonment at the hands of a government dominated by Turkey's armed forces. Their inexperience inadvertently helped prolong the very conflict in Turkish Kurdistan that they had hoped to end.

Considering the lack of a Kurdish state and the sorry record of constantly repressed revolt, the very fact that most Kurds still inhabit a large contiguous geographic core area as a recognizable ethnic community reaching across five countries is remarkable. "Recognizable" requires amplification, but Kurds certainly do know who they are.

Although Kurdish society is multilingual, multiracial, and multireligious, Kurds nonetheless share a long common historical experience and collective aspirations. First and foremost, that means Kurds know they are not Arabs, not Turks, and not Iranians. Kurds also certainly know where Kurdistan is, notwithstanding the euphemistic contortions of those who govern to obscure its existence.

Modern Turkey has pursued policies aimed at obliterating the Kurds' cultural as well as political identity for more than seventy years. In March 1924, less than a year after the creation of Mustafa Kemal Ataturk's Turkish Republic, Kurdish culture, language, and even place-names were banned. Elevated to dogma was the assimilationist credo that any Kurd outside physical Kurdistan accepted the regime's central ideological objective of "turkification" and in effect ceased being a Kurd, or, at least, a nationalist Kurd. Iran and Iraq have never denied the Kurds' existence but have consciously tried to play down their numbers.

Even Iraq, which whatever its crimes against the Kurds has accepted formal autonomy for them, refuses to use the word "Kurd" to describe the far from perfect status granted the "Northern Region." For decades Turkey insisted that the Kurds were "mountain Turks" who lived in the "east and southeast," not in any Kurdistan. Such circumlocution was part of officially induced amnesia. So although "Kurdistan" has been a recognized geographical expression since the thirteenth century, today it enjoys official status solely in one Iranian province of that name, representing only a fraction of that country's Kurds, and in Iraq, where it figures in the official title of the truncated regional autonomy zone.

For everyone except regional bureaucrats, Kurdistan covers an area of some 200,000 square miles—roughly as large as France or as California and Pennsylvania combined. Its climates vary from the mild weather of the foothills and plains of Mesopotamia to mountainous northeastern Turkey, often snowbound for as much as five months a year. Unlike most of the parched Middle East, much of Kurdistan is well watered, and it was once heavily forested. Now much of Kurdistan is a treeless illustration of the evils of wartime and peacetime ecological destruction—erosion caused by napalm, defoliants, and overgrazing. Among the snow-covered peaks of Turkish Kurdistan, Kurds claim two places where Noah's ark might have come to rest—Mount Cudi, just north of Turkey's border with Iraq and Syria, and its highest mountain, 16,946-foot Mount Ararat, close to Turkey's Armenian and Iranian frontiers.

Current maps show most Kurds living inside an imperfect upside-down triangle, whose sides run in northwestern Iran from the borders with Turkey and Azerbaijan south along the Zagros mountain chain to almost the same parallel as Baghdad; in Iraq in a deep arc along the Iranian and Turkish borders, and on into the extreme northeastern corner of Syria; and in southeastern Turkey in a solid mass increasingly diluted at its northern and western edges, along the Iranian and Armenian borders to well west to the Euphrates River. Large additional islands of Kurdish population are found, too, notably in eastern Iran—in Khorasan, along the border with Turkmenistan, and in Baluchistan, near Pakistan in the south; in Turkey's Anatolian plateau, both west and northeast of Ankara; and in Syria, north of Aleppo and south from Mount Afrin, near the Turkish border and a few miles from the Mediterranean Sea.

Smaller, isolated Kurdish communities spread out in an uneven and often unconnected northeasterly arc from just north of this pocket, in Turkey. Other clumps of Kurds can be found in Armenia, Georgia, and especially Azerbaijan, as well as elsewhere in the ex-Soviet Union, where Stalin's paranoid fear of betrayal scattered them; and in Iran, on and inland from the Caspian Sea. Turkey's great western cities—Ankara, Adana, Antalya, Istanbul, and Izmir—teem with Kurds, many of them recent arrivals forced from their villages by Turkish security forces, which have emptied great swaths since the current Kurdish rebellion erupted in 1984. Syria's capital, Damascus, has had a Kurdish quarter on the hills overlooking the city center for centuries. Tehran, Tabriz, and the oil centers of southern Iran harbor large Kurdish minorities, as does Baghdad. So do Germany, Sweden, and other Western European countries.

Such concentrations of Kurds should facilitate nose counting, but no reliable population statistics exist. Kurdish nationalists have understandably exaggerated the numbers, much as their elders claimed uninterrupted territorial continuity from the Mediterranean Sea to the Persian Gulf in a map prepared to impress the inaugural San Francisco session of the United Nations in 1945. Without a state of their own, the Kurds lack the means to carry out a census. Other governments, once scrupulous in counting their Kurds and other minorities in census-taking, gradually found it politic to stop publishing or to blur that data. That way they disguised the Kurds' growing numbers, often the poor and downtrodden's only revenge against their masters. The Kurds' proportionally increasing demographic weight, in turn, justified denying them an equitable share of oil revenues and economic development funds, for without an ethnic breakdown, governments could trumpet official claims of successful assimilation. In Iraq Saddam Hussein repeatedly refused a new census, not wanting to give the Kurds their pro-rated share of the country's oil, much of which they claim as rightfully theirs. Turkish denial of the Kurds' very identity may turn out to be self-deluding woolgathering, in light of the growing evidence that in Turkey at least the Kurds' birthrate is markedly higher than others'. In 1989 official statistics showed that the average gross reproductive rate was 2.75 percent in Turkish Kurdistan, only 1.49 percent in the rest of Turkey, with the proportion of those under fifteen roughly 50 percent and 35 percent, respectively.

Consensus rather than census has convinced Western specialists that there are 25 million Kurds, maybe considerably more. Now the Middle East's fourth largest community—after Arabs, Iranians, and Turks—Kurds, if current demographic projections remain unchanged, seem destined to outnumber Turks regionally and even within Turkey itself in another fifty years. Such is their recovered fecundity after the most devastating century of all. Slightly more than half of all Kurds live in Turkey, where their demographic center has shifted ever westward. The Kurdish migration out of Kurdistan itself is producing sizable Kurdish communities in some western Turkish cities for the first time since the Byzantines expelled them. If, as is widely but unprovably believed, Kurds make up more than 20 percent of Turkey's 60-plus million inhabitants, they would number roughly 13 million now. Roughly half that many Kurds are believed to live in Iran, where they account for 10 percent of the population. In Iraq the 4.2 million or so Kurds account for about 23 percent of the country's 18 million inhabitants, traditionally the largest proportion of any state in the region. This high proportion, plus rugged mountain terrain, foreign intervention, and tensions between Muslim Sunnis and the Muslim Shia majority in this artificially created state, help to explain why Iraq has seen more sustained Kurdish rebellion than the other countries. Syria's Kurds number more than a million, roughly 9 percent of the country's 13 million citizens. And Kurds in Azerbaijan and Armenia add another 300,000 to the total; as many as 700,000 live in Western Europe, with Germany alone accounting for some 400,000.

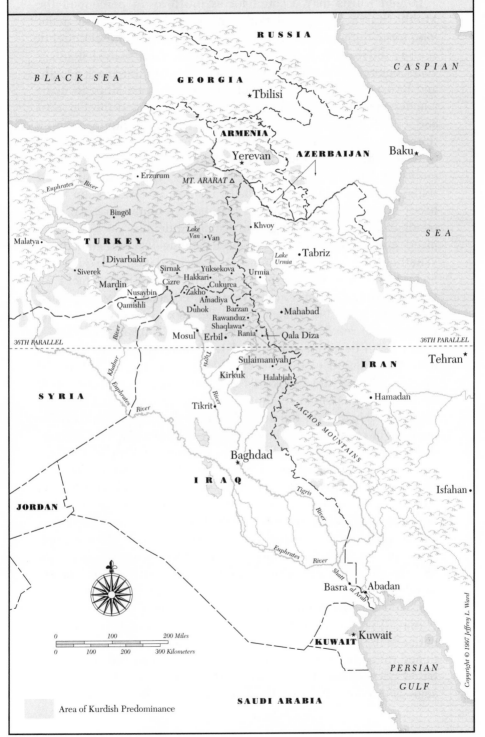

KURDISTAN

RUSSIA

GEORGIA

BLACK SEA

★Tbilisi

CASPIAN

ARMENIA

AZERBAIJAN

Baku★

Yerevan

•Erzurum

MT. ARARAT △

SEA

Euphrates River

Bingöl

•Khvoy

Malatya•

TURKEY

Lake Van

•Van

Lake Urmia

•Tabriz

Diyarbakir

•Siverek

Şirnak Yüksekova

Hakkari

Urmia

Mardin

Cizre Cukurca

•Zakho Amadiya

Nusaybin

•Qamishli

Duhok Barzan

Rawanduz

•Mahabad

Shaqlawa

Mosul Erbil• Rania Qala Diza

36TH PARALLEL

36TH PARALLEL

SYRIA

Sulaimaniyah

IRAN

Tehran★

Kirkuk Halabjah

•Hamadan

Khabur

Euphrates

River

Tikrit•

River

ZAGROS MOUNTAINS

Baghdad
★

IRAQ

Tigris River

Isfahan •

JORDAN

Euphrates River

Tigris

Basra• Abadan

Shatt al Arab

0   100   200 Miles

0   100   200   300 Kilometers

KUWAIT ★Kuwait

PERSIAN

GULF

SAUDI ARABIA

Copyright © 1997 Jeffrey L. Ward

Area of Kurdish Predominance

Indeed Kurds may account for as much as 15 percent of the Middle East's total population, which would represent a major long-term demographic comeback. Only in the mid-eighteenth century did the Kurds' numbers approximate those of the legendary years before the devastation of repeated wars, the Black Death, and Vasco da Gama's rounding of the Cape of Good Hope in 1497, which ushered in sea transport between Europe and the Far East and ended the usefulness of the overland Silk Route running through Kurdistan. Together with the other calamities, this helped to turn a once reasonably cultivated and prosperous region into an enduring economic and political backwater. Absent the overland trade, there was no need for roads, for bureaucrats to keep them fixed, or, indeed, for a state to maintain an administration. As a result of incessant fighting, Kurdistan's sedentary society, organized around agriculture, collapsed, giving way to nomadism. Whether the Kurds have completely recovered is open to question. So backward were they in the nineteenth century that contact with the expanding Russian empire represented access to what passed for them as a highly civilized and modern society, notwithstanding Russia's own retard compared with Western Europe.

Kurdistan declined into an isolated "mountainous irrelevancy" until the collapse of the Ottoman Empire at the end of World War I. Not only did the Kurds then miss their best chance ever to achieve independence, but they were tarred with blame for active participation in the annihilation of more than a million Armenians in 1915, though they themselves had lost "nearly 400,000 dead" in the fighting in Turkey alone, according to Kurdish sources, a fact virtually ignored in the West. As many as 700,000 Turkish Kurds were deported to remove them from the ebb and flow of fighting with Russian troops in eastern Turkey, "of whom all but half perished." Many other Kurds died because of war-caused starvation in technically neutral Iran, as well as in the Ottoman provinces of what became Iraq. When peace returned in 1918, "Kurdistan was a land with its infrastructure wrecked, its society in utter disarray, its intelligentsia dispersed, and the tribal chieftains and sheikhs in full control of what was left."

Iran, Iraq, and especially Turkey—new, highly centralized nation-states structured on Western European criteria—abandoned the old imperial multiethnic tolerance in favor of a narrowly based nationalism. In the face of these governments' continued aggressive efforts to break their attachment to their language, tra-

ditional dress, and culture, Kurds give every impression of remaining remarkably themselves, even when moved a thousand or
more miles away from their often-idealized mountain roots.

Strewn from Baluchistan and Turkmenistan in the east to Istanbul's slums and German and Swedish cities in the West, casualties
of deportation or economic migration, the Kurds over the centuries
have not harbored existential doubts about their identity. Regional
states as ideologically varied as the Soviet Union under Stalin,
Saddam Hussein's Iraq, Turkey today, Ba'athist Syria in the 1960s,
and Iran in 1925–41 have uprooted them and spread them around
in faraway villages in small groups, all of these states hoping that
once removed from their mountains and plateaus the Kurds would
cease being Kurds, or at least nationalists. Their success seems far
from assured.

Kurds are not much given to the ideological straining that more
outwardly pushy people favor for tricking out real or imagined past
glory and vouchsafing a brighter tomorrow for themselves. Theirs
is not a culture rooted in ancient texts comparable to other Middle
Eastern peoples', such as the Jews' Old Testament, the Assyrian
Christians' New Testament, or the Armenians' rich church archives. Unlike their Muslim neighbors, the Kurds have nothing
comparable to the Koran for the Arabs.

Nor do they have the accumulated weight of Persian and Turkish
culture and administration to buttress their sense of historical self.
But like many of history's losers, Kurds must put their past into
some meaningful continuum in the odd niche or two overlooked
by the victors' pat, all-encompassing versions. Kurdish intellectuals
are sometimes reduced to pawing over obscure cultural potsherds
uncovered by others to put Kurdish identity in perspective. "Reconstruction of Kurdish history is difficult," one scholar noted rue-
fully. "It frequently involves interpolation and extrapolation among
the variety of sources written neither for nor about Kurds."

And even when the sources of inspiration are Kurdish, the message is not always unambiguous. Many a culture has a legend
explaining its origins; the Kurds have at least two. One would have
them descended from young men and women who escaped the
murderous clutches of a usurper King of Persia, a giant mythological
tyrant named Zohhak. Snakes growing out of his shoulders required
a daily meal of young men's brains. Ingenious ministers, determined to save the race, substituted calves' brains, and the few
surviving boys and girls were smuggled to the mountains, where

they begat the Kurds. The other myth involves King Solomon, who ruled over the supernatural world inhabited by jinns. He ordered them to fly off to Europe and bring back five hundred fair damsels for the royal harem. But upon their return, the jinns found their master had died, and they kept the damsels for themselves; their offspring were the Kurds.

Kurds feel no more embarrassment over these differing versions than they do about the multiplicity of peoples who have crossed or settled Kurdistan and contributed to the gene pool. Physical evidence abounds that many peoples have migrated to, more often through, Kurdistan. Small, dark Kurds are virtually indistinguishable from southern Europeans, Levantines, Arabs, or Persians. A sizable minority of often tall, blond, blue- or gray-eyed Kurds living in a band running from Lake Urmia in western Iran across northern Iraq to the Syrian border are clearly descended from northern tribes known to have invaded from Europe in centuries past. Even so, William Lynn Westermann half a century ago, noting that the Kurds had been nomads and herdsmen since 2400 B.C., argued that "the Kurds can present a better claim to 'race purity,' meaning ethnic purity, and to a continuity of their cultural pattern for a much longer period than can any people now living in Europe."

Other academics credit the inhabitants of the Kurdish mountains with pioneering agriculture as early as 12,000 B.C., by domesticating goats, sheep, and pigs and common crops such as wheat, barley, rye, oats, and lentils. The first copper metallurgy is thought to have started near Diyarbakir, in Turkish Kurdistan, in the seventh millennium B.C., and bronze instruments made their appearance there early in the fourth millennium B.C. Despite these estimable contributions, the center of civilization shifted south to the plains of Mesopotamia. There the land's flat expanses required for survival the appurtenances of a disciplined state—taxes, a large standing army, administration, and writing—which were unnecessary for independence in the mountains.

Invaders galore passed through Kurdistan. Indo-European nomadic westward migration in 1200–900 B.C. destroyed and disrupted Kurdistan and much of southwestern Asia. One such intruder, Cyaxares the Great, occupied Nineveh in 612 B.C., ending the Assyrian empire and fifteen hundred years of Mesopotamian domination of the highlands. By then the Kurds were well known for their military prowess, especially in guerrilla warfare. Throughout the ages Kurds went on to serve in any number of armies other than their own, including a special Kurdish regiment of the Red Army which liberated Minsk from the Nazis in World War II.

The Kurds' reputation as fearsome warriors was immortalized by Xenophon in his *Anabasis*, which chronicled their exploits, or those of the people he called the Karduchoi. That epic account of the retreat, in 401 B.C., to the Black Sea of ten thousand Greek mercenaries in the pay of a Persian royal pretender notes, "The Greeks spent a happy night with plenty to eat. Talking about the struggle now past. For they passed through the country of the Karduchoi, fighting all the time and they had suffered worse things at the hands of the Karduchoi than all that the King of Persia and his general, Tissaphernes, could do to them."

Shortly thereafter, another Greek historian, Diodorus, came to a conclusion that many others down through the ages were to endorse. The Kurds "in their mountain fastnesses were more trouble than they were worth to foreign armies and empires," he wrote. It was "sufficient to keep them by force or agreement from troubling the plain." That was not always easy, given, in Westermann's words, that "the predilection of the Kurds for shooting at moving objects, preferably human beings, hasn't altered much since Xenophon's time." The Kurds, he also noted, were recalcitrant about "taxmen and conscription for the military purposes of their nominal rulers."

The Kurds' fate often depended on their success in fending off forces—starting with Assyrian kings Shalmaneser III and Sargon II in the ninth and eighth centuries B.C., respectively—who mounted punitive expeditions across Kurdistan. When the going was good, Kurds lived far and wide, from the shores of the Mediterranean almost to the Persian Gulf. In what Kurds sometimes call the Kurdish centuries of Islam—from the tenth to the twelfth centuries A.D.—their political rule, or that which Kurdish soldiers defended, went from central Asia through the Fertile Crescent to Libya and Yemen. And thanks to their military skill and emigration, the Kurds helped protect the Middle East's heartland against invaders, most famously the Crusaders. Theirs was a role not unlike that which Scots played for centuries in the British army. Kurds shone in architecture, astronomy, history, mathematics, philosophy, and music. Their most famous son, Saladin, was born in the Tigris River city of Tikrit (also Saddam Hussein's birthplace), where his aristocratic family was in the service of a non-Kurdish dynasty. Whether Saladin considered himself a Kurd first or foremost, or indeed at all, is questioned by historians who believe he never set foot in Kurdistan. But mercenary service outside Kurdistan itself was then a frequent calling for Kurds of his class, although some historians believe that Saladin thought of himself less as a Kurd than as a soldier defending Islam.

Saladin, his father, and his uncle all originally served a Turkish prince in Syria, and many of their troops were Turks. The Sunni Ayyubid dynasty (named after his father) ended two centuries of rival Shia rule in Egypt under the Fatimids, and the Sunni caliphate in Baghdad was restored. Saladin beat the Crusaders at the battle of Hattin in 1187, won back Jerusalem from them the following year, and defeated Richard the Lionhearted. Known as the Prince of Chivalry for his equitable treatment of his defeated Christian and Jewish foes, Saladin reigned from 1174 to 1193, expanding Ayyubid rule, which held on in one form or another until the end of the fifteenth century. Other Kurdish dynasties ruled in the Caucasus and in central and southern Kurdistan.

By the early thirteenth century, Turkic nomads began inundating western Asia. Mongol invaders wrought such massive destruction to agriculture there that Kurdistan a century later produced only a tenth of the revenues prior to their devastating appearance. Tamerlane's son in 1393 sacked Diyarbakir, Mardin, and other Kurdish centers in what today is Turkey. Following a Kurdish revolt, Tamerlane himself sacked Erbil, Mosul, and Cizre in 1401.

Barely a century later, wars between the Ottoman and Persian empires turned much of Kurdistan into a wasteland after the battle of Chaldiran in 1514, when the Ottomans defeated the Safavids near Lake Van, in present-day eastern Turkey. Fighting and attendant massive destruction in Kurdistan continued for more than a century, with the Ottomans relentlessly pushing the Persians ever eastward until they agreed on a border, which remained in force for some three hundred years. Not content with turning Kurdistan into a battlefield, both empires adopted scorched-earth tactics and, to deprive each other of military manpower, deported Kurds.

Deportation has been a firmly entrenched practice in Middle Eastern tradition since antiquity. The victor at Chaldiran, Sultan Selim the Grim, deported entire Kurdish tribes to central and northern Anatolia, notably to areas south of Ankara where many of their descendants still live, and as far away as Bulgaria. But his endeavors were dwarfed by the Safavids. Hundreds of thousands of Kurds—plus Armenians, Azeris, and Turkomans—were forced to move inside the Safavid empire. In 1534–35, retreating ahead of advancing Ottoman troops, the Safavids systematically destroyed Kurdish cities and countryside, burning crops, filling in qanats (underground water channels) and wells, and wrecking irrigation works.

Shah Abbas I later in the century stepped up the process. The uprooted Kurds were dispatched eastward, first across the border to Azerbaijan, then to Khorasan, facing Turkmenistan, where they remain today, some one thousand miles east of their original homes. The Safavids thus removed unruly Kurdish tribes from their western marches, curiously setting the same Kurds up as border guards on another critical frontier. Other Kurdish tribes were sent even farther afield, to Afghanistan's Hindu Kush mountains and in present-day Baluchistan.

The nomads' ascendancy over settled society also changed the linguistic patterns within Kurdistan. The Kurdish language belongs to the Aryan branch of Indo-European tongues and is as closely linked to Persian, specialists say, as Danish is to German. The earliest Kurds spoke a language called Pahlawani, which held sway in the original Kurdish heartland of the Zagros Mountains, which now mark part of the Iran-Iraq border. Over the centuries migration northwest into Turkey spread this language.

But starting with the breakdown of settled Kurdish society along the Ottoman-Persian border and beyond in the sixteenth century, Pahlawani was increasingly sidelined. Taking its place was Kurmanji, a language spoken by nomads who emerged from the mountainous region of the Hakkari, west of Lake Urmia. Kurmanji and Pahlawani each have two major related dialects. Pahlawani is now spoken only at opposite ends of Kurdistan: one variant, Gurani, found principally in southern Iranian Kurdistan, is spoken by some 1.5 million Kurds; the other, Zaza, in Turkey, is the language of as many as 4.5 million Kurds and Turks, mainly in and around Tunceli, Bingöl, and Siverek, plus splotches around Malatya, Adiyaman, and Marash. It is also spoken by both Kurdish and Turkish Alevis, a sect with Muslim as well as pre-Islamic elements, and by some Sunni Kurds. Historically, Gurani was the language of literature and polite society throughout Kurdistan.

Kurmanji, too, is divided between a southern branch called Sorani, spoken by most Iranian and Iraqi Kurds, and a northern one, Badinani, used by Kurds in northern Iraq and Iran and most Turkish Kurds. It is reckoned that three-quarters of all Kurds now speak Kurmanji. Speakers of Kurmanji and Pahlawani, whose differences have been likened to those between French and Italian, at best understand about half the others' tongue.

Only fragments of written literature before the sixteenth century have survived the upheavals of the ages. Kurmanji was sufficiently entrenched by the late sixteenth and seventeenth centuries to be used in three epics of early Kurdish significance. The *Sharafnama*, written by Prince Sharaf al-Din of Bitlis, is considered the first pan-Kurdish history. It bemoans the Prophet Mohamed's "curse of disunity" on the Kurds imposed lest their military proficiency "overcome the world." The price of disunity is also a major theme in Ahmed-i-Khani's *Mem o Zin*, a kind of Kurdish Romeo-and-Juliet story embroidering Kurdish aspirations. *Dem Dem* glorifies a Masada-like resistance put up against Shah Abbas I by the Khan with the Golden Arm, a prince of the Baradost tribe, in what is now northeastern Iraq.

In this century Sorani has become the main Kurdish cultural vehicle by default. Whatever Iraq's other shortcomings, first the British mandate, then its Arab-dominated successors practiced, however reluctantly and partially, cultural freedom for the Kurds, and although carefully vetting content, the Baghdad authorities have more or less consistently tolerated the use of Kurdish in newspapers, magazines, books, and radio and television broadcasts, as well as for education from elementary school through university. Consequently, more than 80 percent of Kurdish books published in this century are in Sorani. No other Middle Eastern state has come close to doing as much. In Turkey, until President Turgut Özal had the law changed in 1991, for example, the only Kurdish language publications for nearly seventy years were printed in Europe and smuggled back into the country.

On that score the West has much to answer for. In July 1923, to curry favor with Western governments and end the Allied occupation of Istanbul, Ataturk pledged in article 38 of the Lausanne Treaty that "no restrictions shall be imposed on the free use by any Turkish national of any language in private intercourse, in commerce, religion, in the press, or in publications of any kind or at public meetings." But the Western powers were exhausted by war, and Britain especially was loath to pour more money and diplomatic support into challenging Ataturk after his victory over its Greek protégés the previous year. London was also bent on enlisting his support against the Soviet Union, and determined to find a compromise on the Turkish border with its Iraqi mandate that would safeguard its claims on Mosul's oil. Correctly sensing a lack of Western will to oppose him, Ataturk proclaimed the Turkish Republic that October, then within months abolished the caliphate and banned all Kurdish schools, organizations, and publications along with their powerful religious fraternities and seminaries. So much for the Kurds' entrenched cultural rights in Turkey.

In Syria publication in Kurdish was encouraged under the French mandate but forbidden after Syrian independence in 1946. Iranian rulers, from Reza Shah between the wars to the religious leaders of the Islamic Republic, banned Kurdish for education and publications with two notable, short-lived exceptions: the Mahabad Republic in 1946, and in the first four years following Ayatollah Ruhollah Khomeini's revolution in 1979. Until the Soviet Union collapsed, Kurdish was also used in schools and in publishing for the larger Kurdish communities in Armenia and Azerbaijan, but was of little succor to the many smaller Kurdish communities dispersed by Stalin throughout the other central Asian republics on the eve of World War II.

Were such linguistic variations not sufficient barriers to introducing standardized Kurdish for education, Kurds remain separated by a variety of alphabets. Gurani, in Iran, uses the Persian script. Sorani is written in a modified Arabic-Persian alphabet in Iran and Iraq, as is Badinani in Iraq. But Turkish Kurds abroad are taught Kurmanji in a modified Latin script devised by Prince Kamuran Bedir Khan in Syria during the French mandate. Books, newspapers, and periodicals smuggled into Turkey use that alphabet. Kurds in the former Soviet Union use Cyrillic.

All these factors, plus the natural isolation and fragmentation of an often-mountainous land, have driven to despair those nationalists convinced that Kurdish unity would be better served by a single language and alphabet used and understood by all Kurds. They bitterly note that the Arabs have long since imposed classical Arabic as a lingua franca despite the frequent unintelligibility of spoken Arabic from one country to another. Such is the prestige of the language of the Koran. Ataturk's language reforms in the 1920s and 1930s latinized the Turkish alphabet and rid it of many Arabic and Persian words. Persian classical literature still serves a powerful unifying purpose in Iran.

Even in matters of religion the Kurds are divided. Roughly 75 percent of all Kurds are nominally Sunni Muslims and Kurmanji speakers, but there is a sizable Shia minority of 1–1.5 million at the southern end of Iranian Kurdistan, around Hamadan and Kermanshah, and in the eastern Khorasan enclave. Like Mount Lebanon, Kurdistan's rugged terrain long provided refuge for minority faiths, some of whose adherents have found it prudent to practice dissimulation of their true faith to avoid repeated persecution at the hands of the ruling orthodox religions. Little is new under the Middle Eastern sun, where such practice is known as *taqiyah* in Arabic when practiced by Islamic sects such as the Druze and Alawites suspected of heresy by mainstream Sunni and even Shia Muslims. Accustomed to sudden shifts in often-intolerant political powers, people have learned to change religions, or go through the motions, for protective coloration. In centuries past, Kurds converted in large numbers to Judaism, Christianity, and, of course, Islam. (The majority of Kurdistan's Jews, who lived mostly in Iraq, left soon after the creation of Israel in 1948, although a rump of several hundred departed in the middle 1990s. Christians increasingly have emigrated to the West.)

By far the largest minority of non-Muslim Kurds is made up of devotees of a religion of great antiquity, known generically as the cult of the angels. This cult, a universalist religion far predating Islam, has three still-extant, quite distinct, and otherwise unconnected denominations in Kurdistan—the Alevis, the Ahl-i-Haqq, and the Yazidis. Their numbers are dwindling, but some specialists generously suggest they may account for a quarter—even a third —of all Kurds, although that evaluation, like others in matters Kurdish, may be an exaggeration. All three share a fundamental belief—in some cases contained in holy books, in others passed on orally, but always meant to remain secret to nonbelievers—in seven successive manifestations of divinity that protect the universe from seven balancing dark forces of matter.

Creation is often explained in terms of a cosmic egg, or pearl, in which the Universal Spirit once resided. For example, the *mes'haf*, a Yazidi holy book, holds that "in the beginning God created a White Pearl out of his most precious Essence; and He created a bird named Anfar. After he placed the pearl upon its back, he dwelt thereon forty thousand years." The cult believes in the transmigration of souls through repeated reincarnations of the deity constituting major and minor avatars. They also hold that good and evil are equally important to the creation and continuation of the material world.

All these cult denominations have suffered separate and repeated persecution at the hands of Sunni and sometimes Shia authorities—at times carried out by fellow Kurds. Their persecutors have accused their followers of everything from heresy to wife-swapping orgies under cover of darkness. The cult readily incorporates other religions' doctrine and leaders, typically honoring Jewish, Christian, as well as Islamic, Zoroastrian, and other pre-Islamic figures borrowed via the Shamanism brought by invaders from northern Asia. Such syncretism has not always been innocent and in fact was used to jockey for position with rival religions.

At their most influential, the Alevis, for example, in the fifteenth to seventeenth centuries were credited with strongly influencing —some authorities claim almost swallowing—Shia Islam in Persia. Even the Yazidis, now the smallest of the denominations, during Saladin's time had prosperous communities as far away as the coastal mountains dominating Antioch and the Mediterranean. In the thirteenth and fourteenth centuries they wielded enough influence to convert Christians and Muslims across great swaths of the Middle East, from the Mediterranean to central Turkey, Kirkuk in Iraq, and Lake Urmia in Persia. At the end of the fifteenth century the *Sharafnama* said seven of the thirty Kurdish tribal confederacies had been fully Yazidi.

The Ottomans as both temporal and spiritual rulers of Sunni orthodoxy persecuted these denominations, sometimes on security grounds, sometimes for heresy. The Alevis were first harassed when Sultan Selim the Grim annexed what had been Persian territory in eastern Anatolia after the battle of Chaldiran, when he killed forty thousand men suspected of harboring unprovable pro-Persian sympathies. Four hundred years later, Kemal Ataturk's lay republic followed suit in 1937–38 with "preventive" repression of massive proportions, predictably radicalizing future Alevi generations. The Alevis are credited with counting as many Turkish as Kurdish followers, if not more, and are concentrated in Turkey around Tunceli and Malatya in central Anatolia. Some specialists believe they account for roughly 20 percent of all Kurds.

The Yazidis, the much-persecuted and misnamed "devil worshipers," follow a syncretic faith incorporating elements of Zoroastrianism, Persian dualism, as well as Judaism, Christianity, and Islam. They live in fragmented enclaves primarily in southern Turkey near the borders with Syria and Iraq, in northern Syria in the Jazira and Afrin areas, and in northwestern Iraq around Jebel Sinjar and north of Mosul. Some twenty recorded Ottoman pogroms, starting in the seventeenth century and lasting into the twentieth, aimed at their conversion, eventually driving many north into the Russian Caucasus. In this century many have emigrated to Europe, especially to Germany. Religious taboo forbids them to wear blue, pronounce the letter "sh" (for fear of invoking Shaitan, or Satan), and eat lettuce. In Iraq, where they are thought to number no more than sixty thousand, they have suffered disproportionately under Saddam Hussein. The Ahl-i-Haqq, variously known as the People of Truth or, more accurately, the People of the Spirit, are bunched principally on either side of the Iran-Iraq border in southern Kurdistan.

Such idiosyncrasies, taken together, are part and parcel of many a mountain society. They seem somehow to balance themselves out in the Kurds' case, reinforcing a sense of nationalism here and facilitating state manipulation and control there. Time and again the Kurds' irrepressible predilection for feuding has undermined their cause and facilitated the task of the various states arrayed against them. The Kurds' is not just a Middle Eastern version of the Hatfields and the McCoys, those quintessentially Appalachian feuding hayseeds.

So strong were traditional Kurdish tribal rivalries that one tribal leader's decision to join a nationalist uprising often prompted another to remain aloof or even accept arms and money to fight for the government. Even clans within a given tribe have ended up fighting each other. Mullah Mustafa Barzani, who in this century came closest to rallying Kurdish nationalist sentiment even outside the borders of his native Iraq, often faced at least as many tribesmen fighting for the government as supporting him.

Betrayal is a hoary theme throughout Middle Eastern history. In the four-thousand-year-old Babylonian epic of *Gilgamesh*, Enkidu, an innocent from the Zagros Mountains, falls for the blandishments of a wanton denizen of the temple of love on the plains. She convinces him to clear the cedar forest, thus betraying his old friends the wild animals of the mountains. A somewhat similar tale of treachery recounts the fate of Farhard, a Kurdish sculptor who falls in love with Shirih, the wife of Persian King Chosroes II, in the seventh century B.C. She persuades him to destroy his native mountains but then betrays him, "as is the habit of plains people," and in despair he throws himself off the mountains he had tried to destroy.

But Kurdish history is also replete with Kurds betraying fellow Kurds. This cast of warring stock characters at times starred illiterate tribal leaders arrayed against the urban intelligentsia, as well as villains drawn from both categories and willing to play the government's game for their own short-term tactical purposes. In this century tribal chieftains in the mountains motivated by desire for loot and narrow local concerns, but alone capable of raising and commanding disciplined troops, arrayed themselves against educated, citified elites who championed nationalist aspirations but lacked the muscle to bring them to fruition.

These conflicts mirrored an earlier era's tensions between warrior mountaineers and the "civilized" settled Kurdish farmers of the plains. As this most terrible century for the Kurds unfolded, the conflicts pitting Kurds against governments, and especially Kurds against themselves, degenerated. Isolation, ignorance, government manipulation and barely imaginable repression, bad luck, bad faith, and outright treachery all figured in the reckoning. So did economic migration, political deportation, and underdevelopment, which weakened traditional ties. As the Kurds became educated and urbanized, tribalism declined, only to be resuscitated artificially in the 1980s and 1990s in Iraq and Turkey by governments using discredited and withered traditional landowning networks to arm Kurdish militias against nationalist guerrillas.

The miracle of 1991, when traditionally pro-government Iraqi Kurdish tribes such as the Surchis and the Baradosti threw in their lot with their nationalist brethren, turned out to be the exception that confirmed the rule. In the past it was fashionable in some academic quarters to describe the Barzanis and their Kurdistan Democratic Party as hopelessly rural, combative, and feudal, and Jalal Talabani and the Patriotic Union of Kurdistan as citified, modern, and unwarlike. Saddam Hussein's root-and-branch destruction of so much of Kurdish traditional society emptied such distinctions of much of their validity. The two biggest Iraqi Kurdish nationalist groups cooperated during the fighting in 1991, and the following spring, taking advantage of allied air cover over northern Iraq, they organized genuinely free, if technically imperfect, regional elections. The KDP and PUK agreed to split power when the results proved too close to call. By July 1992 a regional parliament and administration in the old autonomous zone was installed. "Statehood by stealth" seemed a fact of life, although the Kurds were careful to fly the Iraqi flag and outfit police in Iraqi uniforms to deflect foreign criticism about setting up an independent government.

But by early 1994, it was not the tribes but nationalist fighters from both PUK and KDP camps that resumed their feuding, and with disastrous results. To no one's real surprise, three of the most important fault lines in the struggle were geographic, linguistic, and sociological: the PUK controlled the cities Erbil and Sulaimaniyah in Sorani-speaking areas east of the Greater Zab River, while the KDP ruled along the Turkish border in Kurmanji-speaking, largely rural territory to the river's north and west.

Allied policy contributed to the tensions. Kurdish regional authorities lacked revenue to finance their operations and pay civil servants, given the combined repercussions of the United Nations' embargo on Iraq, Saddam Hussein's own boycott of the rebellious Kurds, and Western timidity in helping their economy. It was in no foreign power's interest to foster greater Kurdish assertiveness, even though the United States was pledged to overthrow Saddam Hussein and was financing the Kurdish-based Iraqi National Congress to that end. But Kurds knew they had nobody to blame but themselves for what increasingly disgusted ordinary people called a "suicidal war."

In early 1995, the Central Intelligence Agency first encouraged the INC to enlist the support of the two estranged Iraqi Kurdish mainstream parties in a military drive against the Iraqi army in Kirkuk and Mosul; this was intended to trigger a prearranged plot among Saddam's troops. The United States dropped out at the last minute when Iranian messages were intercepted suggesting that Washington was willing to turn a blind eye on a coordinated Iranian military push in the marsh area of southern Iraq. The INC offensive went ahead, chewed up two Iraqi divisions, but estranged Barzani's party and did not succeed in toppling Saddam. Indeed, that fiasco marked a fateful step in the unraveling of Kurdish nationalism in Iraq. The following year Barzani asked Saddam for help against Talabani, causing major embarrassment to American policy-makers and stunning the Kurds' friends abroad.

3

Suckered

It was Easter morning in 1991. Our small press convoy was caught in bumper-to-bumper traffic on one of the first of many hairpin turns leading down from the Iraqi mountain resort of Salahuddin, the Kurds' command post, to problematic safety. Ahead, hundreds of jam-packed vehicles—private cars, buses, trucks, taxis, tractors hauling trailers—stretched as far as the eye could see. All the way from the valley below, cars and trucks heading up the narrow road toward us were also stuck. Neither lane would give way. Our immediate problem was not just the traffic jam. Iraqi army helicopter gunships were operating just out of sight on the other side of Salahuddin. From the sound of it, they were making methodical rocket and cannon passes on the trapped vehicles that had fled the city of Erbil just an hour or so too late. When would the first gunship appear over the lip of the hill and our turn come?

So here I was, after five years of having exhausted every trick in the book to get into Kurdistan, and trapped desperately trying to get out—along with the colleagues who had joined me. In no particular order I pondered various aspects of the idiocy of my single-minded obstinacy. I saw myself vainly testing my fancy Italian walking shoes a few years earlier along the frozen paths of a Vosges winter, pestering bored editors in Washington about the importance of the Kurds until their eyes glazed over, besieging Kurdish leaders to help me get into Kurdistan when they had better things to do. I now realized that somewhere along the line I had conveniently overlooked Kurdistan's grittier realities.

If you're as unlucky as the Kurds about getting to run a country of your own, it's no wonder that revolt, war, upheaval, and collapse of empire are incantatory virtues looming for you as large as they once did for Poles, whose land was occupied by three empires from the late eighteenth century until the end of World War I. Rapacious neighbors expunged Poland from the map, despite repeated uprisings. The Kurds similarly lost the freedom of running their own affairs, and never enjoyed formal statehood. They hung on to the remnants of autonomy tolerated by the Ottoman and Persian empires as long as they could, sometimes uniting great swaths of territory under a prince before expensive punitive expeditions dispatched from the capitals brought them to heel. But modern nationalism and the hope of creating a Kurdish polity date only from the ruins of those empires in the early twentieth century. World War I delivered Kurds from the Ottoman Empire and promised independence, only to oppress them in the straitjacket of ever more efficient centralized governments of intolerant nation-states. Landlocked, economically underdeveloped despite its oil and water, divided by two forms of Islam, five borders, three Kurdish languages and as many alphabets, Kurdistan exists as much despite as because of the Kurds.

For the Kurds are both stubborn survivors and steady losers, likable for their warmth, humor, courage, and charm and distinguished by a streak of unpredictable violence. The Kurds have been "mentioned in dispatches" by foreign military men from Xenophon in the fourth century B.C. to Prussia's future field marshal Helmuth von Moltke in the 1830s. Young Moltke found that both Arabs and Kurds had a "taste for brigandage," with the "Arab more of a thief and the Kurd more of a warrior."

But even a Prussian military genius can get things wrong, and a century and a half later our group was witnessing a Kurdish comeuppance at the hands of the Arabs in the form of President Saddam Hussein's battered, but still lethal, army. For its sins our group of a dozen journalists knew a rout all too well when it saw one. Vietnam, a generation earlier, was my first war with photographer Don McCullin and Martin Woollacott of *The Guardian*, who were here now. Julie Flint of *The Observer*, Marc Kravetz of *Libération*, Charles Glass and his ABC team were all fellow survivors of Lebanon's interminable "little wars" of the 1970s and 1980s. Gwynne Roberts started covering the Kurds for Reuters two decades earlier and was still at it, producing freelance television documentaries. The younger generation was represented by Geraldine Brooks of *The Wall Street Journal*, Yves Harté of Bordeaux's *Sud-Ouest*, and Scott Peterson of *The Daily Telegraph*.

As we listened to those helicopter gunships, I was so frightened that out of my notoriously faulty memory popped André Malraux's harrowing description of his funk as he waited for zeroed-in German guns to destroy his French tank caught in a deep ditch in 1940. Near us a man comforted a child badly burned by a rocket fired from a helicopter gunship. Four Kurdish *pesh merga*—"those who face death," as the guerrillas called themselves—trotted in front of us with captured Iraqi army maps rolled up under their arms. They were on the lam, to be followed by more than a million Kurds. Once again a Kurdish rebellion was collapsing, and fast. Once again the United States had let the Kurds down.

I had had the first inkling of irreversible catastrophe on Good Friday, March 29, in the city of Sulaimaniyah, as I listened drowsily to the five p.m. news on the BBC World Service, my only connection with the outside world. The announcer quoted the State Department as confirming the Iraqi army's recapture the previous evening of Kirkuk, the country's great northern oil center. I calculated Washington must have known thanks to aerial photos, most likely taken by the U.S. Air Force planes we'd seen loitering over Kirkuk on Tuesday. No doubt they were monitoring the Iraqi army buildup. President George Bush's unambiguous call on February 15 for "the Iraqi military and the Iraqi people to take matters into their own hands" boiled down to documenting America's own inaction. The Central Intelligence Agency's anti-Baghdad radio station in Saudi Arabia kept broadcasting calls for Iraqis to depose Saddam Hussein as late as March 3, three days after the cease-fire effectively ending the allies' "Operation Desert Storm."

How reminiscent were Bush's careless choice of words and the clandestine radio's sloppiness! In 1956 I had been an army private in Europe when Washington was accused of using improvident broadcasts on CIA-financed Radio Free Europe to egg on the Hungarian revolution, then of standing by idly when it was crushed by Soviet tanks. That was not a lesson any American of my generation easily forgot. Yet this time the reckless encouragement was coming not from a radio station during the depths of the Cold War, but from the President of the United States, the world's only super-power, according to his publicists.

To make matters worse, the Kurds' hold on the land they'd liberated was precarious. We had watched the evidence pile up since our arrival barely a week earlier. Even during the ten days the Kurds occupied Kirkuk—for the first time in seven decades of struggle—they never captured all nine defensive lines protecting the strategic Khalid ibn Walid air and army base. On Wednesday night Glass, his ABC team, and McCullin had witnessed fighting not far from the road as they drove back from Kirkuk to Erbil. By the next day Iraqi tanks controlled Altun Kopri, a key town on the Lesser Zab River roughly halfway between the two cities. By all rights Kirkuk was just an hour's easy drive away from Sulaimaniyah straight down a superhighway, and the Iraqis certainly had the wherewithal to crush Kurdish defenses whenever they chose. Barely a month after the American-led coalition forces in a hundred-hour ground war had ended Saddam Hussein's seven-month oc-cupation of Kuwait on February 28, the rump of his humiliated army was now poised to crush the insurrection in Iraqi Kurdistan as it had reasserted control in the Shia south only days earlier.

I pondered the Kurds' predicament—and ours—in bed in Su-laimaniyah's Hotel Salaam with my worst case of dysentery in years, too weak to chase after and warn my colleagues who were off reporting in the city. I was all too well aware of the dangers. Only three days before, we had lost track of three young gung-ho pho-tographers who'd traveled with us from Syria. We feared the worst.* They had insisted on staying in Kirkuk despite our repeated entreaties. When Woollacott returned to the Salaam, I gave him the news about Kirkuk. "So much for riding into Baghdad with the First Kurdish Armored," he said. We alerted our colleagues, then quickly left by car for Salahuddin, a three-hour drive to the north. It was dusk, and we stopped on Sulaimaniyah's outskirts to talk to frightened and exhausted refugees who had just walked the seventy miles from Kirkuk. Helicopter gunships had attacked them, first with white phosphorous in Kirkuk, then with rockets and machine guns farther along the highway. We emptied our pockets of our remaining Iraqi dinars. They were homeless and needed the

---

* Jad Gross, a recent Harvard graduate on his first war assignment, was killed by Iraqi troops reoccupying Kirkuk. His two companions were captured and eventually freed.

money. We needed to get out of Iraq as quickly as possible to tell the story of a people betrayed, and to save our necks.

From the start, the failure of the Kurdish uprising had been a strong possibility, but the speed and circumstances of the collapse were unexpected. And we knew all along that entering northern Iraq at all was a risky enterprise. Ours was the pessimism of accumulated experience in a calling inclined more to systematic doubt than to encouraging daydreams. We had put together our team of survivors with care. Most of us had covered wars for so long that as a matter of course we factored in bad luck, lies, unforeseen reversals, mindless delays, lousy weather, sudden illness, obdurate bureaucracy, abrupt retreats, mercurial official mood swings, wrongheaded military analysis, bad and often maliciously intended advice, ignorant guides, bad faith, shiftless drivers, unsound machinery, especially unreliable cars cursed with faulty brakes, insufficient gasoline, hopeless tires, and bad whiskey.

We were only mildly disappointed when our two satellite telephones, ballyhooed as guaranteeing communications with the outside world despite the allies' destruction of Iraqi telecommunications, refused to function from the outset. Far more disconcerting had been the steady accumulation of evil omens on the ground: the accelerating collapse of Shia resistance in southern Iraq, an Iraqi military buildup south of Kirkuk, the backsliding betrayal of some Kurdish auxiliary army units which had joined the uprising and then returned to Baghdad's orbit, the advance of the heavily armed Mujahedin Khalq, the anti-Islamic Iranian opposition blindly doing Baghdad's bidding in return for bases and matériel. A visit to the monumental modern Kirkuk railway station on the front lines had confirmed all the standard red flags: streets innocent of children or other pedestrians, infrequent, creeping car traffic, silence punctuated by sniper fire, and rocket-propelled grenade rounds.

On and off all week we had been discussing, inconclusively, how to get out of Iraq quickly if the Kurds' uprising started turning sour. Even in the best of times Iraq had an unsavory reputation for mistreating foreigners captured without visas, and of course we had none. Getting back to Syria the way we came in seemed iffy. On our way to Erbil and Kirkuk we'd been bogged down in mud for three rainy days, creeping along deeply rutted, unpaved back lanes through countryside so green and soggy that it might as well have been Vietnam's Mekong delta. Such was the Kurds' lack of control of key paved roads even when they were consolidating their control. Going due north and then cutting west parallel to the Turkish border along the so-called Barzan Road was theoretically possible, but that long-neglected east-west road was said to be virtually impassable except in a four-wheel drive, and we had no such vehicle.

The only official crossing point along the mountainous, heavily mined, two-hundred-and-six-mile frontier with Turkey was an international bridge over the Khabur River in the northwest corner near Zakho, close to where we'd crossed the rain-swollen Tigris River from Syria on inner-tube rafts and come ashore at Peshkhabur. Even then Iraqi troops had been within mortar range of the crossing. In early March, they had blown up the bridge as they retreated, and the Turks routinely shot anyone seeking to enter from Iraq. On paper, Iran seemed the best bet. It was closest, just a few hours down a paved highway. Twice a day flights linked an airport within ninety minutes' drive of the border to Tehran. But none of us had Iranian visas. And Tehran's hostility to Westerners, particularly Americans, was so notorious that we risked being turned back, or worse, by some dyspeptic revolutionary guard at the border.

We were in a pickle, and I felt I was largely to blame. Before the first shot was fired to liberate Kuwait, on January 16, I had been tracking the Kurds, particularly Massoud Barzani, leader of the Kurdistan Democratic Party, the oldest nationalist party in Iraqi Kurdistan. More important, he was co-chairman of the eight-party Iraqi Kurdistan Front, which at long last had overcome debilitating internecine feuds in nationalist ranks. In early February, I had been lucky enough to renew a fluke of an Iranian visa, just long enough, I thought, to travel from Tehran to his mountain headquarters on the Iran-Iraq border near Urmia.

Flying would have made the expedition relatively effortless. But Barzani's people failed to obtain plane tickets. Instead, two young Kurdish drivers and Barzani's favorite interpreter, Siyamand Banna, showed up in a small, locally assembled Peykan car, and a half day late, at that. With time running out on my visa, I could have backed out there and then. God knows I was in a foul mood. From my earlier Iranian days I remembered just how uncomfortable a cramped Peykan could be for anything except city driving. Only when skidding across ice on hilly roads did I realize what I'd boxed myself into: sixteen straight hours' driving on hazardous routes out there, three hours' sleep, three hours to interview Barzani, and sixteen hours back to Tehran.

We kept ourselves awake thanks to constantly replayed tapes of Sivan Perwer's songs in Kurdish, especially his relentlessly haunting dirge for the thousands of Kurdish civilians whom Saddam Hussein had gassed in the city of Halabjah in March 1988. That was the first time in history that a government employed poison gas against its own civilian population on such a massive scale. (Iraq had inaugurated the gassing of Kurdish civilians in a series of smaller operations the previous year, which the international community willfully had almost totally ignored.) Cramped and irritable in the backseat, Banna and I sparred endlessly in what proved to be an invaluable, if argumentative, lesson in Kurdish nationalism. The tension of the long drive was broken by numerous roadblocks inside Iranian Kurdistan. The Kurds were amused by the perplexity of Iranian security officials, torn between a Pavlovian suspicion of my American passport and the overiding authority of my special pass, issued by the all-powerful revolutionary guards.

My interview with Barzani in a snow-covered mountain bomb shelter was all business; he used it chiefly as a signal to calm Turkish worries that the Iraqi Kurds wanted independence rather than their traditional demand for autonomy within a democratic Iraq. While much of the world had gone to war to preserve Kuwait's borders, Barzani said, the Kurds realized no one was willing to accept an independent Kurdistan carved out of Iraq—or Iran or Turkey for that matter. That was a message that Barzani and other Iraqi Kurdish leaders constantly repeated in an unsuccessful effort to convince doubting officials in Iran, Syria, Turkey, and the United States who kept trumpeting the necessity of maintaining Iraq's territorial integrity. Barzani argued that the Kurds were entitled to a country of their own, but the goal must be achieved by political means, not armed struggle, and might take a century to achieve, given the current primitive and often-ruthless politics of the Middle East.

I'd not seen Barzani for several years and had forgotten his small feet and trademark facial warts, though not the horrendous wrongs he believed his people had suffered at the unfeeling hands of the United States in particular and the world community and regional powers in general. A portrait of the late General Mullah Mustafa Barzani, his father, the incarnation of modern Kurdish nationalism for half a century, stared down from the wall. The elder Barzani's hawklike features served to remind Massoud of how the United

States and "especially Henry Kissinger" had hoodwinked the Kurds in 1975 into believing that Washington guaranteed them Iranian aid, then humiliated them by doing nothing when Shah Mohamed Reza Pahlavi sold them out to Iraq.

The Reagan administration was no better, Massoud Barzani said. He ticked off Iraq's success in defeating the economic sanctions the Senate overwhelmingly voted to punish it for gassing the Kurds in August 1988 and the administration's help in providing easy loans and technology for Baghdad's weapons industry. With some four thousand Kurdish villages systematically razed, hundreds of thousands of people herded into so-called "victory cities," and all Kurds scared of further chemical-weapon attacks, he made clear he had no intention of opening a second front against Saddam Hussein during the war for Kuwait.

In any event, since Iraq invaded Kuwait on August 2, 1990, President Bush's administration had shown no interest whatsoever in consulting, much less coordinating, with the Kurds, separately or as part of Iraq's overall anti-Saddam opposition. Jalal Talabani, the other co-chairman of the Front and leader of the rival Patriotic Union of Kurdistan, had rushed to Washington within days of the invasion, convinced that Saddam Hussein had finally signed his own death certificate and the Kurds would be welcomed aboard the international posse. But the State Department cold-shouldered him. So why should the Kurds take chances? Repeating an argument I'd heard Talabani make two weeks earlier that winter in Damascus, Barzani said, "Saddam is weak, but we are weaker." The Kurds took the moral high ground, swearing not to move against Saddam Hussein as long as Iraq faced foreign adversaries in the form of virtually the entire international community.

That sounded reasonable. The Iraqi Kurdistan Front leaders realized they neither should nor could ask Iraqi Kurds to take further chances without formal Western guarantees. Kurdish leaders were known to question their powers of persuasion with their own people in light of their cataclysmic past misjudgments, which had helped turn Kurdistan into a wasteland. What remained of the leadership's tarnished credibility was now at stake. The days of backdoor intelligence ties were over, those of open political ties with foreign powers, much less guarantees, a dangerous dream. Such realism had been dearly paid for. A decade after Mullah Mustafa's fiasco, his son, Massoud, and Talabani had thrown in their lot with the mullahs of the Islamic Republic of Iran, who used and abused the Iraqi Kurds during the 1980–88 Iran-Iraq gulf war. Iraqi retribution knew literally no bounds.

Starting in 1987, and in 1988 at Halabjah and during a six-month search-and-destroy operation code-named al Anfal, repeated use of chemical weapons against civilians and guerrilla soldiers had been Saddam Hussein's indelibly remembered way of dealing with Kurds, whom he denounced as "saboteurs" and "traitors." Without Bush's call to rise up, how many Kurds would have answered any summons to renewed fighting? As if Kurdish memories needed jogging, in the fall of 1990 Izzat Ibrahim Duri, Saddam Hussein's deputy, had traveled to Sulaimaniyah to warn: "If you have forgotten Halabja, I would like to remind you that we are ready to repeat the operation."

My mountain interview with Massoud ended. I rose to leave. But lunch was served and I was asked to stay. The tone of the discussion changed. Over chicken and rice, nuances crept into Barzani's conversation. He made clear he was not as unalterably neutral as he appeared. The public pledge not to stab Iraq in the back during the Kuwait crisis was tactical. It reflected the leadership's prudent fear of retribution, but had also encouraged Baghdad to move troops and matériel out of Kurdistan to Kuwait. Massoud volunteered that he was passing intelligence on to the allies, as best he could, which his agents picked up on bomb damage and other tactical matters. Much of the information dealt with Kurdistan, but some was provided by the many Kurds in the army in Kuwait, who were considered cannon fodder and thus often stationed in the most exposed front-line positions.

Throughout the meeting I'd been intrigued by a mound of small, folded papers on the carpet. Finally I asked what they were. Massoud explained they were handwritten notes from officials of the ruling Arab Ba'ath Socialist Party, ranking Iraqi army officers, and *jash*, or "little donkeys," as the guerrillas derisively called fellow Kurds serving in auxiliary units on the Iraqi army payroll. Those notes showed the *jash* at the very least were hedging their bets: they were concerned lest Saddam Hussein lose and leave them exposed to the wrath of the *pesh merga*. All those notes, Massoud said, pledged allegiance to the *pesh merga* and promised active collaboration at the propitious moment. He gave the impression of finding such fealty normal, if not totally convincing. He argued that the Kurds were just taking prudent precautions and making plans for when and if Saddam Hussein should somehow be overthrown.

In fact, those notes were the payoff for months of meticulous clandestine work. Since the Iraqi invasion of Kuwait, specially trained underground Kurdish cadres had infiltrated Kurdish cities with instructions to soften up anyone in authority. It was those cadres' dogged and dangerous cultivation of the *jash* during the fall and winter that set the stage for the turncoat war, the Kurds' seemingly effortless takeover of army bases, fortresses, towns, and cities that surprised even Barzani and his military staff planners by its unwonted and flawless success. How actually useful that underground effort was remains unclear, given the amazing wild-fire spontaneity of the Kurdish uprising once it started. Also certainly contributing was a call for "national reconciliation," a clever step by Talabani's PUK, which worked wonders with the *jash* by offering them more than a mere amnesty (which, after all, implies formal guilt). Starting on March 5 in the small eastern city of Rania, near the Iranian border, with minimal fighting and casualties the Kurds in little more than ten days occupied more of Kurdistan than ever before in modern times. It was the *jash* who jumped the gun by spontaneously taking over Rania. *Jash* all over Kurdistan followed suit. But in any case the *pesh merga* had penciled in March 10–15 for the uprising, cautiously taking into account seasonal bad weather.

With some notable exceptions, the going had been easier than expected, even in the cities involved in the fighting. Iraqi Kurdistan's cultural capital, Sulaimaniyah, fell to a spontaneous uprising, although the *pesh merga* and the population itself took two days to rout Mujahedin Khalq troops, who doggedly fought for the Iraqi regime. The population then killed in cold blood some four hundred Ba'ath Party members, intelligence officers, and secret-police agents holed up in the notorious Central Security Headquarters.* After all, in early March hundreds of secret police and

---

* A letter from a purported eyewitness in Sulaimaniyah said the population on March 8, 1991, tore their victims' bodies "to shreds" to avenge "what was done in Halabja and other places. The cries of the cowards penetrated to the skies, but there was no mercy shown to these despicable and deviant men." "Seven hundred security and party men" died in the final assault on the Central Security Headquarters building. "Those who had survived the fighting were tried and executed on the spot by the people using iron saws and knives even as they screamed and sobbed."

Ba'ath Party agents unable to run away had been cornered, captured, and killed by outraged Kurds. To be sure, Sulaimaniyah was not the only city where Kurds summarily executed their tormentors. Similar acts of popular vengeance took place in Erbil and Duhok when those cities were liberated.

A visit to Sulaimaniyah's secret-police headquarters helped explain why the Kurds had taken justice into their own hands. Its imposing main entrance, decorated with a giant stylized metal outline of an all-seeing eye, remained a monument to evil—with its windowless cells, dried blood, metal supports, meat hooks, piano wire, and other torture paraphernalia and a special building where Kurdish girls were said to have been raped. Trapdoors led to underground cells where the prison's liberators found recently strangled naked women and children and barely conscious prisoners, some of whom had been detained for more than a decade.

"We'd be calculating how to take Erbil," Barzani recalled later, "and someone would say, 'But Erbil has already fallen.'" Such *Kriegspiel* results were not in the Kurdish military tradition. Only in Kirkuk did the *pesh merga* really have to fight—and fight they did, capturing the long-disputed oil city on March 20 at the cost of some three thousand men. No wonder that at the height of the turncoat war even normally placid Massoud got so carried away that he told a delighted crowd in Koisanjaq, "One second of this day is worth all the wealth of the world." He was still on a high when he told us a few days later that "the result of seventy years of struggle . . . is at hand now. It is the greatest honor for me, what I waited all my life for."

The February lunch in the mountains had given me the opening I'd been hoping for. When the ground war began, I asked, would Massoud help me get in to report on the Kurds? I knew that the Iraqi Kurds, particularly Barzani's KDP, were famous for helping and protecting reporters, often at the sacrifice of their own men's lives. Still, in the middle of the winter that was no small favor I was asking. To my delight, his answer was yes. I never asked why, but suspect it was his way of thanking me for making the arduous trip to see him. Whatever the Kurds' faults, in my experience they have a knack for friendship and a curious soft spot for those willing to take risks for and with them.

Thus when the ground war started on February 24, I flew east across Turkey to Van, where I was met by one of Barzani's men. He seemed to have his people everywhere. So did the Turkish police. We stayed overnight at a cheap hotel and took an early morning bus south through a snowstorm. Police regularly checked my passport and the other passengers' papers. That was routine. We were in a sensitive area close to the Iranian and Iraqi borders, where separatist Turkish Kurd rebels of the Partei Karkaren Kurd, the Kurdistan Workers Party (better known as the PKK), maintained training and rear-echelon bases. I was the only foreigner on the bus, and I feared it was only a question of time before I was questioned more closely and turned back to Ankara, or worse.

My only hope was to stay one step ahead of the police, ever suspicious of foreign journalists traveling in Turkish Kurdistan. In the dead of winter, with no foreign tourists or businessmen around, I had no protective coloration. Three hours later, in Yüksekova, a dreary town renowned as a smuggling center, other Barzani agents took me to a small hotel, fed me, locked me in my room, and told me to rest. We would be leaving at nightfall to cross the mountains to Iraq. I was convinced I had been spotted, and I fretted about the delay. In midafternoon Barzani's men were back with bad news: seven feet of snow had fallen overnight higher up in the Zagros Mountains, so the trip had to be aborted. Sensing complications with the police if I waited for the next bus, I ordered a taxi and left town immediately. I was wise. On my way back to Van, police kept stopping the car every half hour or so, asking if I was "the journalist from *The Times*." Since I wasn't, technically, I played dumb and was allowed to pass. Later, Barzani promised to make it up to me and other colleagues of my choice. True to his word, he made sure we were the first Western reporters to enter Kurdistan from Syria.

He'd kept his word, but with the uprising now collapsing all around us it was a dubious distinction. Until the BBC broadcast I'd heard in Sulaimaniyah, our expedition to Kurdistan had been quite unlike anything any of us had done before, a mixture of danger, messianic deliverance, and joy. I thought I was used to almost everything the Middle East could provide. A generation earlier I'd watched Saudi women flying to the West enter an airliner's toilet in veils and floor-length black cloaks and emerge in miniskirts and see-through blouses. But that was nothing compared to the homecoming delight of Omar Sindi, a modest restaurant employee near Washington, as he doffed his gray flannels, rep tie, and blue blazer for the baggy trousers, black-and-white turban, and cummerbund he had left behind when as a teenager he had fled Kurdistan in the 1975 fiasco. Sindi's pleasure was so infectious that we all but forgot the danger of running the gantlet of Iraqi mortars as, crossing from Syria to Iraq, our overloaded raft drifted in the rapid spring currents of the Tigris; we were guided by two wooden road signs pressed into service in lieu of proper paddles.

What more magical introduction to Kurdistan could there be than awakening early that first morning in Zakho in the home of the local tribal *agha*, or chief, to the sound of approaching drums and songs celebrating Nowruz, the Kurdish New Year. That ancient, pre-Islamic rite of springtime renewal and hope was leavened by a more practical primer of Kurdish survival provided by our host and his sons. The *agha*, a giant who nonchalantly mentioned that he "owned a hundred and twenty-one villages," had placed one son with the Iraqi army, another with the *jash*, and the third with the *pesh merga*. They were all there in the large, carpeted room reserved in the homes of influential Kurds for meals, political discussions, and overnight guests such as ourselves.

The sons' presence also helped to explain why hundreds of Kurds, all armed with Kalashnikovs or revolvers, at the very least, were milling around in good-natured confusion outside the Zakho secondary school that served as *pesh merga* headquarters and cheered us when we first arrived. Many had served in the *jash* but joined the uprising, indeed thus ensuring its otherwise slim chances of success. At stake was a great deal more than just the *intifada*, the Arabic word literally meaning "shaking off" that the Kurds had borrowed to describe their uprising. Indeed a key element of hundreds of years of imperial divide-and-rule had collapsed. Kurds and historians alike long ago identified the curse of the Kurds as their intrinsic divisiveness, coupled with their self-destructive proclivity for alliance with outside enemies.

Every Kurd can quote the passage in *Mem o Zin*, Ahmed-i-Khani's seventeenth-century Kurdish epic poem, lamenting that curse of disunity:

> *These Kurds who have gained glory by their swords,*
> *How is it that they are denied the empire of the world and are subject to others?*
> *The Turks and the Persians are surrounded by Kurdish walls*
> *[But] each time the Arabs and the Turks act, it is the Kurds who bathe in blood.*
> *Ever disunited, ever discordant, they refuse to obey each other.*

If we would only unite, the Turk, the Arab and the Persian [will] be our servants.

Traditionally, Kurdish nationalist uprisings were brought to heel by neighboring governments' success in pitting tribes against each other, thanks to the judicious provision of money, arms, or political favors. In Iraqi Kurdistan so strong were such rivalries that they survived even dynastic marriages designed to end them. Massoud Barzani's much-revered mother, for example, was a Zibari, that is, from a tribe whose other members, with few exceptions, remain resolutely opposed to the Barzanis and are allied with Saddam Hussein, as they were with the Iraqi monarchy, the British League of Nations mandate, and the Ottomans before him.

Barzani and the other members of the Iraqi Kurdistan Front understood the debt they owed the *jash*—and the need to keep them on the straight and narrow. On the very day the Iraqi counterattack to recapture Kirkuk began, Barzani took over the best hotel in the mountain resort of Shaqlawa for a daylong equivalent of a consciousness-raising seminar for some hundred tribal leaders. Surchis, Baradosti, Herkis, and row upon row of Baghdad's other veteran tribal allies were welcomed to the fold, their past sins deliberately overlooked, their recent actions lauded, and future cooperation in defending Kirkuk implored. Henceforth, the "little donkeys" were to be called "armed revolutionaries." Pledging his six thousand "guns," barrel-chested Omar Surchi said, "I'll send my people with my son at their head."

How, we asked, could he have made such a momentous switch? Only recently his men were Saddam Hussein's precious allies, serving as the Iraqi military's efficient eyes and ears, tracking down and eliminating *pesh merga*. He launched into a confused explanation involving the Cold War. He apparently had not grasped that the coalition which had liberated Kuwait had been possible only because the Soviet Union had "lost" the Cold War so decisively—and now so badly needed Western support—that it had dropped their old Iraqi ally. His answer revealed the often-disconcerting ignorance of many rural Kurds—*jash* and *pesh merga* alike—who had spent so much time in the mountains that they had stopped bothering to keep up with changing events in the outside world. Omar Surchi must somehow have sensed my disbelief, for then he invoked another argument: "We know who is behind the Kurds—the West and not the East," he said, "and we

will not make the same mistake again." Sensing that his explanations still lacked clarity, he bellowed out his real message as he
strode away with his impressive bodyguard: "We need help from
the United States." Only minutes before, Massoud had repeated
his call for the entire Iraqi opposition to come to Kurdistan and
had denounced Washington for not shooting down Iraqi helicopter
gunships.

Throughout the Kurdish spring other sometimes similar, sometimes contrasting thoughts kept flashing on and off in the con-
sciousness of leaders and ordinary people alike. For our benefit a
Duhok poet pledged to kiss President Bush "from the roots of my
hair," an image which conveyed its intended fervor even if losing
something in translation. A learned Sulaimaniyah writer explained
that mutual interest between Americans and Kurds constituted a
"marriage made in heaven" because "we have the oil and want
democracy, and you in America have democracy and want the oil."
On Sulaimaniyah streets, long-proscribed photographs of Kurdish
nationalist heroes displayed in glass cases drew large crowds, with
pride of place devoted to Massoud's father, General Barzani. Six
times a day, rapt capacity audiences in an Erbil movie theater
watched a poorly filmed amateur videocassette showing the gassing
of Halabjah. In this century of the image, it is one thing to know,
another to see the forbidden evidence of official repression, visual
proof that unspeakable evil on that scale was not just imagined,
much less exaggerated, in the endlessly repeated retelling.

Such concentration on getting the past right was now shoved
aside by the sheer terror of trying to survive what was shaping up
to be the worst rout in a long history of Kurdish defeats. Indeed
the awakening of the three past weeks of freedom in itself added
to the anger and panic. At least there'd be no more embarrassing
"Hajji Bush!" cries greeting journalists astounded by the Kurds'
infatuation with the President who had called on them to get rid
of Saddam Hussein, then done nothing to help their insurrection
succeed. So much for that *hajji* honorific bestowed on pilgrims to
Mecca. Now the Kurds angrily accused feckless foreigners of again
abandoning them to Baghdad's vengeful whims. Suddenly they all
could, and seemingly did, quote verbatim Bush's incautious February 15 incitement to revolt. The ABC team trying to approach
Kirkuk after its fall recounted understandable but nonetheless nasty
incidents with previously sunny Kurdish guerrillas they had
befriended.

Even if the Kurds had not told us—and one of their most endearing traits was to hide next to nothing from us—you didn't need to be Clausewitz to realize the guerrillas were a formidable fighting force only if they continued to be faced with a demoralized adversary. They lacked modern antitank and antiaircraft weapons. The tanks they captured lacked ammunition, and no one knew where the Iraqis stored the corresponding rounds. Retreating Iraqi artillerymen had removed firing pins from their pieces. The Kurds had to rely on obsolete rocket-propelled grenades to fight armor. They also had a few shoulder-held Soviet SAM-7s, but nothing approaching the Stingers that the Americans so effectively provided the Afghans to shoot down Soviet jets and helicopters.

Their light infantry forces had no idea how to use what little workable heavy equipment they'd captured from the Iraqis. Such was the result of Baghdad's long-standing policy of keeping Kurds away from the armed forces' technical arms. A senior Kurdish military commander had talked vaguely of enlisting those army cadres who'd rallied to the Kurdish cause to instruct guerrillas on the captured matériel. It was not a top priority. The Kurds also lacked command-and-control experience. By their own admission the guerrillas specialized in mountain combat and lacked training in urban street fighting, which might have allowed them to hang on to the plains cities they had often captured so effortlessly—and recklessly.

But the *pesh merga*'s cardinal failing lay elsewhere. Despite their initial prudence, the Kurds had underestimated their foe. Demoralized Iraqi regular army divisions, indeed even some elite Republican Guard units, crumbled during the early stages of the turncoat war. The Kurds claimed they took fifty thousand prisoners, many of them soldiers who simply downed their arms and walked over to the *pesh merga* side. The Kurds interned some officers and other ranks but, as in the past, released the overwhelming majority rather than keep them and give them scarce food. But once that initial euphoria passed, the civilians running Kirkuk appeared better informed than their military counterparts about Iraqi reinforcements heading north—and much more worried. Four days before Kirkuk fell, the civilian authorities estimated that about twenty thousand Iraqi troops, including Republican Guards, were on the way to join some fourteen thousand men still holed up in parts of the Khalid ibn Walid base.

At Kurdish headquarters at Salahuddin, that very night, Newsherwan Mustafa Amin, the Kurdish deputy military commander, played down these civilians' evaluation as excessively pessimistic. He insisted that even if Kirkuk was lost, the *pesh merga* could stop the Iraqis thanks to guerrilla positions on the low hills north of the city, paralleling the road to Erbil. (Later, in London, he told me, "I simply could not imagine that Saddam was capable of sending a corps-sized force" against Kirkuk.) The Americans said they had smashed the Iraqi armed forces. Through their missions abroad, the Kurds had checked as best they could. "The Iranians, the Syrians, the Saudis, the French, the British, the Americans," Newsherwan recalled, "everyone said the allies had destroyed forty-two divisions, including Republican Guards and the Air Force." The guerrillas' own network of informers inside the Iraqi armed forces similarly overestimated the Iraqi army's collapse.

In fact, in Kuwait Saddam Hussein never committed his real power base—the various secret-police organizations and most of the Republican Guards. Three days before Kirkuk was recaptured, American military officials acknowledged that the "number of Iraqi tanks and armored vehicles that survived the war is much greater than . . . initially reported." General H. Norman Schwarzkopf, the American commander of coalition forces, two days later said that had the fighting lasted a further twenty-four hours, "we could have inflicted terrible damage on them." Whether such a desire to cripple Iraq's armed forces ever reflected Pentagon thinking is open to question. The feckless behavior of the administration in March, even giving it the benefit of the doubt, lent credence to those who concluded that Washington implicitly had returned to its pre-August 1990 policy of seeing Saddam Hussein as a source of regional stability.

Just as Massoud Barzani had predicted, Saddam Hussein was weak, but the Kurds were weaker. Even the Shia insurrection that erupted in southern Iraq right after the allies' unilateral February 28 cease-fire played into Saddam Hussein's hands: frightened by the excesses of the Badr Brigade—Iraqi Shia prisoners of war converted to Islamic fundamentalism during their long Iranian captivity during the Iran-Iraq war and infiltrated across the border—just enough of the army rallied to Saddam Hussein in Basra and other southern cities to crush the largely spontaneous uprising there. The sight of Badr Brigade invaders waving Khomeini posters proved particularly sobering for Iraqi officers whose mainly Shia enlisted men initially mutinied, then turned into a rabble.

By no stretch of the imagination did all Iraqi Shia share the revolutionary Islamic fervor of their coreligionists in Iran. Starting in 1980 they had proved it by dying in the tens of thousands for Saddam Hussein in the war against Iran. Now, many Iraqis who were not part of the ruling Sunni Arab minority backed the regime, however reluctantly, because they were terrified by the Shia uprising and the prospect of upheaval it promised. By mid-March Saddam Hussein was free to turn his attention to the Kurds. The rump Iraqi armed forces recaptured most of Kurdistan in even less time than the Kurds took to liberate it.

Iraqi Kurds blamed their defeat—and exodus—solely on a calculated American decision not to shoot down Iraqi helicopter gunships. (Five years later, in what he called "ex post facto criticism," George Bush told a television interviewer that the allied coalition "could have done more" to weaken Saddam. He specifically acknowledged that the United States could have required greater restrictions on flights by Iraqi military helicopters.) Such Kurdish thinking arguably was a military oversimplification, but it became an unshakable political article of faith. General Schwarzkopf himself said he'd been "suckered" by the Iraqis at the initial cease-fire talks into allowing the Iraqis' limited use of helicopters—unarmed ones at that—for liaison purposes only. Why, asked the Kurds, didn't the allied commander get "unsuckered" and shoot down the gunships which were shooting Kurdish civilians and guerrillas alike? God knows the consequences of his oversight, if that's what it was, had been brought to his attention quickly enough: cut off from the outside world, we reporters could only guess at what Washington and the other main coalition capitals were doing—and send our dispatches by messenger to Iran, where, we hoped, they would be forwarded.

What seemed clear to us was that had General Schwarzkopf or anyone in Washington bothered about the Kurds, they would have realized that helicopters were considered the ultimate terror weapon, capable of inflicting heavy civilian casualties, emptying cities, and panicking the population. Counterguerrilla weapons par excellence, helicopters occupied a very special place in Kurdish demonology. For along with fixed-wing aircraft and multiple rocket launchers, helicopters had been used to deliver poison gas against the Kurds time and again during and after the Iran-Iraq war. "You fly, you die"—the American ban on Iraqi fixed-wing aircraft—simply was not enough to erase those terrible memories. Schwarzkopf and the other coalition generals worried constantly about the Iraqis' using chemical weapons against their own forces, which of course had special equipment and gas masks. Yet when it came to the Kurds, an odd amnesia afflicted them, the coalition military and civilian planners conveniently blocking out the ghastly photographs of the gassed dead in Halabjah and the testimony of the more than sixty-five thousand Kurds who fled to Turkey to escape Iraqi chemical attacks in August 1988. Back then, the international community had defeated every effort to stop the carnage of the Kurds or bring Saddam Hussein to book (which had not stopped Bush from brandishing photographs of the Halabjah victims during his 1988 campaign for the presidency). Such Western inaction was, of course, before Bush drew a "line in the sand" in August 1990 because of Kuwait's oil and before he decided to do something about Saddam Hussein.

On the ground in Kurdistan, we didn't require persuading about helicopters. We knew the history. Even if we hadn't, from the first day we set foot in Kurdistan the Kurds kept repeating their fears. We had seen Kurds firing heavy machine guns and rocket-propelled grenades at a helicopter inside Duhok and been told they'd shot one down only hours before we had arrived. We'd also seen four helicopters attacking Kurdish forces in Kirkuk itself. Before the Iraqi counterattack, Newsherwan and other Kurdish military leaders spelled out for us the helicopters' capacity to panic civilians, but they kept insisting that the *pesh merga* could and would stand their ground.

Until the last minute before they were caught up in the modern world's fastest-developing exodus, the Kurds gave every outward sign of thinking they had all the time in the world. At least they sought to give that impression. In those final hours before the collapse, Kurdistan still seemed oddly bathed in unfathomable innocence. Or perhaps the Kurds we kept talking to felt obliged to put on a brave face for the first Westerners in years they'd been able to meet freely. Such are the tribulations of abrupt deliverance from the precautions of living in a police state. Starting with our arrival in Zakho, we were disconcertingly treated by Kurds from all walks of life like so many astronauts, pop stars, or sports heroes. "You can go anywhere, ask anyone anything" became a proudly repeated mantra of what the Kurds called "our Kurdish perestroika."

We had arrived in Sulaimaniyah on March 28, the day before

Good Friday, and half a dozen of us had dined with Western-trained Kurdish engineers and businessmen who barely listened to our fears about the imminent collapse of their uprising. Instead they rounded up the last canned beer in town, prepared a feast, and persuaded their wives and daughters to put on their best finery. We tried timidly to share our concern about the Iraqi juggernaut heading north which we had learned about in Kirkuk. We questioned whether the Kurds had been wise to venture beyond the relative protection of the mountains and occupy the cities in the plains—Duhok, Erbil, Kirkuk, Sulaimaniyah.

Our hosts knew Saddam Hussein was all but done crushing the Shia revolt in the south, but that didn't seem to set off alarm bells with them. They were much too busy getting the city's water, power, and economy working again to show their worry. To be sure, one Kurdish dinner guest said, "If Kirkuk falls, there will be a massacre." Yet his whole manner dismissed that possibility as a statistical absurdity. No, these middle-class Kurds were so competent and confident, they had made no attempt to hide the prominent public roles they were playing. They took no discernible precautions. Why should they? their attitude seemed to be. They had won, after all, and the hated Iraqi occupation of their land was ended. We must have seen, they insisted, the string of treadless tanks, stripped armored-personnel carriers, shot-up trucks, the burned-out Ba'ath Party headquarters, and secret-police headquarters.

Indeed we had. Nor had we missed the giant, now-empty, and fire-blackened stone forts that Saddam Hussein had built at regular intervals along the main roads, interspersed with smaller cement defenses every half mile or so. Although the forts were of Soviet design, these defenses recalled other colonial occupations I'd observed—from Algeria to Vietnam. Unique to Kurdistan were the endlessly repeated piles of methodically flattened rubble that once were villages, the destroyed orchards and vineyards—the rural death Saddam Hussein had so conscientiously wrought in ever-expanding swaths since 1975. The Kurds exorcised past indignities in a special way: from one end of Kurdistan to the other they blasted away with Kalashnikovs at Saddam Hussein's ubiquitous full-length portraits in their concrete frames; bullet after bullet had literally effaced Saddam Hussein's features—as cook with white toque; in uniform as much-decorated commander in chief; as sunny, smiling businessman in riverboat-gambler white suit and panama, and in all his other tricked-out disguises, especially the most insulting of all, Saddam Hussein in Kurdish kit, complete with baggy trousers, cummerbund, and checkered turban.

More touching still, our Kurdish hosts that last evening in Sulaimaniyah were convinced that human rights would now be honored and democratic values would now prevail. They were proud of their leaders' de facto amnesty allowing Baghdad's many agents to walk around scot-free in their midst. Somehow they overlooked the all too likely retribution should Saddam Hussein reoccupy their city.

But just as the Kurds released thousands of Iraqi soldiers they'd captured, they also decided that anyone who wasn't openly against them was with them. Their suspension of disbelief was all the more astounding in light of the terrible punishment that Baghdad had meted out to Kurds for decades. Woolgathering or not, these naive assumptions served to spur the Kurds' mass exodus when the Iraqis' recapture of Kirkuk abruptly forced our hosts and less exalted Kurds to realize the deadly miscalculation of their brief weeks of freedom. It was a terrible awakening, sparing no one and reinforcing the fear and lack of solidarity in Kurdish society that years of Ba'athist rule had ensured.

Key *pesh merga* commanders underestimated the importance of family ties perhaps because they and their cadres in most cases had their immediate families outside Iraq: once the exodus started, no Kurd—*pesh merga, jash,* or civilian—was willing to risk abandoning relatives to Saddam Hussein's vengeance. Middle-class Kurds panicked, belatedly realizing that Ba'ath officials had every opportunity to note their comings and goings in the damning detail Baghdad's agents so gloried in. Also scurrying for safety were the thousands of *jash* who had deserted Saddam Hussein and thrown in their lot with the nationalist uprising. The troops and families of tribal chieftains fled, too, terrified at the prospect of the exemplary punishment likely to be their fate as turncoats. No Kurd needed reminding that "traitor" was a favorite Saddam Hussein term to describe not just nationalist guerrillas but Kurds in general.

The hard core of the smaller but supposedly better-disciplined guerrilla ranks broke and ran, invoking their ostensible duty to accompany their families to safety in Iran and Turkey. Guerrilla leaders who once had commanded tens of thousands of men later confessed they were lucky to count on a few bodyguards. Even the minute Christian minority fled, despite its often-tolerable relations with the regime. The Christians acted partly out of blind fear that Saddam Hussein would punish them as passive "collaborators" dur-ing the uprising, partly out of solidarity with the Kurds or fear that the Kurds would accuse them of siding with Baghdad if they stayed behind.

So ingrained were Kurdish fears of helicopters and poison gas that Saddam Hussein did not have to use chemical weapons this time. In fact, he did not dare do so because he feared provoking retaliation by the allied armies, but Kurds had no way of knowing for sure. The Iraqi armed forces knew exactly what they were doing, as Nizar Hamdoon, former Iraqi ambassador to Washington, confirmed to me in Baghdad only weeks later. Panicking civilians was a deliberate tactic, designed to allow Saddam Hussein to regain control of the north as quickly and cheaply as possible. So much the better if such tactics fulfilled his long-term goal of controlling Kurdish land without the people. With the allies banning the use of fixed-wing aircraft, the Iraqis fell back on helicopters, correctly counting on their previous deployment to panic the Kurds.

When the Kurds lost Kirkuk and the first waves of refugees reached Erbil, Sulaimaniyah, and Zakho, an exodus began that no one in Washington, London, or Paris, much less anyone on Schwarzkopf's staff, had foreseen. That was hardly surprising—but it was shocking. Accumulating evidence suggests that the Bush administration purposely set its mind against grappling with the complexity of Iraqi society before, during, and after the occupation of Kuwait. That is why it refused to have anything meaningful to do with the Iraqi opposition, be it Shia, Sunni, or Kurd. Rarely in the history of human conflict had so great a power mobilized so many allies, moved so many troops and so much matériel, yet remained so purposely incurious about the nature of the enemy's society and its bloodstained history.

From President Bush on down, no one in the administration made any pretense of hiding the fact that its number-one priority after liberating Kuwait was to declare victory and ship the troops home. Once Bush abruptly ended hostilities, General Colin L. Powell, Chairman of the Joint Chiefs of Staff, was clearly determined to keep American troops from being sucked into Iraqi problems in any way, shape, or form. What did or did not happen in Baghdad and the rest of Iraq was left to unfold on its own, although the administration signaled its preference for another Sunni Arab strongman, meaning a general, at the helm if Saddam Hussein was removed without allied agency. From that first cease-fire, the U.S. presence in the Persian Gulf became a domestic American political problem. Even at the zenith of his popularity and prestige, thanks to the liberation of Kuwait, Bush realized that with a worsening economy his reelection chances in 1992 depended on ceasing to be "foreign-policy president." That was fine by the ultracautious Powell, determined at all costs to evade any postwar involvement in Iraq that might replicate, or even recall, the humiliation of American arms in Vietnam in the 1960s and 1970s and in Beirut a decade later.

Encumbered by these political-military imperatives, the administration was genuinely unprepared for the massive exodus in Iraqi Kurdistan. As a result, Bush tarnished his famous victory in Kuwait and, ironically, trapped his own and the next administration in the very open-ended involvement in Iraq that he had sought to avoid. Yet even a cursory examination of random facts on the ground on the eve of hostilities would have spared the administration that embarrassment and exposed the basic fallacy in having no postwar policy on Iraq.

There were obvious signals. In the final days before the Kuwait war began in January 1991, for example, hundreds of thousands of Turkish Kurds had fled their homes in southeastern Turkey. From early morning to well after midnight, panicky families crammed the bus station in Diyarbakir, located four hours' fast driving from the nearest Iraqi territory. Bus companies put on more and more buses but still could not meet the demand for passage to Ankara, Adana, Izmir, Istanbul, and other cities in western Turkey with large Kurdish communities. Late at night in the bus station, I watched desperate men sending wives and children off to other destinations, anywhere as long as it was outside Kurdish areas judged at risk. Even by the region's standards of irrationality, this panicky behavior seemed paranoid.

Meanwhile the Turkish government had moved armor, artillery, and tens of thousands of troops normally stationed opposite the Soviet Union close to the border with Iraq, though Ankara and Baghdad had both signaled a mutual unwillingness to open a new front there. That had not convinced Turkish Kurds, particularly those living close to the frontier. Only the poorest of the poor remained in the border towns. For no Kurd anywhere had forgotten the lessons of 1988. The word Halabjah was now far more than just the name of a town in Iraqi Kurdistan close to Iran. It stood for what was the quintessence of genocide, directed against all Kurds, for it was the place where the Iraqi regime had attacked Kurdish civilians with deadly poisons.

So frightened were Turkish Kurds in the last days before the Kuwait war, indeed, that pharmacists in southeastern Turkey reported a run on atropine, the antidote for an especially lethal poison called sarin. There were nowhere near enough gas masks to go around. As a substitute, Turkish Kurds bought plastic sheeting in profusion. (Indeed, the Kuwait war's first victims were a Kurdish mother and her children in Turkish Kurdistan who were asphyxiated even before the first allied bombs dropped, as a result of her overzealous use of such sheeting.) Western diplomats in Ankara dismissed the panic as the work of Turkey's notoriously irresponsible press. They failed to appreciate the extent of Kurdish fears about chemical weapons, even in Turkey, much less in Iraq itself.

There's nothing quite so unpredictable and potentially so dangerous as the moment when a people comes to think of itself as betrayed. All of a sudden the evil omens skipped over, laughed at, or otherwise nervously suppressed when the going seemed good return with a vengeance. When Woollacott and I got back to Salahuddin that Good Friday night, the ABC team told us they'd had a nasty time extricating themselves from nervous and threatening *pesh merga* over the past two days when they had sought to get close to Kirkuk from the west. Our last forty-eight hours in Iraq turned into a slow-motion study of hostility, as we strained our nerves to organize what amounted to our escape from both furious Kurds and avenging Iraqi troops. Colleagues still in an increasingly panicky Erbil, a half hour's fast drive away, had to be rescued by an official *pesh merga* car and armed guards sent from Salahuddin.

The taxi we had rented all week simply disappeared on the way to pick them up. The ABC team spent much of Saturday painstakingly lining up cars and drivers in Salahuddin for the escape we hoped to make very early on Easter morning. Some reporters had struck out for safety even earlier. The ABC drivers at the last minute tried to back out, insisting they needed the cars to evacuate their own families. Only the authority of Massoud Barzani himself succeeded in changing their minds and obtaining from his own stocks the gasoline we needed for the journey. He also gave us a signed, handwritten pass. He bade us farewell, a lonely figure whose last words were a plea for the Kurds to "stay in Kurdistan and not become refugees, like the Armenians," a people driven from their land, in his view.

No one was listening to Barzani's message, judging by the traffic jam we ran into right after leaving him. Still exhausted from dysentery, I got out of the car and sat with my back against a low retaining wall. What with the helicopter gunships working the other side of the mountain, I suppose I thought I would be safer there than in the car. I began leafing through my notes to relieve my fear, and I found a list of Kurdish words and phrases I had copied out of a guidebook before coming to Kurdistan. I'd scarcely had time to give them much thought. Aside from the cardinal numbers and the words for bread, water, directions, and suchlike, I'd noted *dost* for friend and the phrase *dost-i may* for "You're our friend." I had also boxed, in capital letters, *taqa naka*, for "Don't shoot." The word for "help," according to my hen-scratch notation, was *haricari*. I scrutinized these notes again. Surely that could not be right, I said to myself. Yet that is what it seemed to be. *Haricari* was simply too close to *hara-kiri*. I hadn't seen the humor when I'd written it down. Now I laughed and immediately felt slightly better.

At some point—I was in no condition to gauge when—a half-dozen *pesh merga* military policemen appeared and began ordering about the recalcitrant drivers. Suddenly we were on our way. It was as simple as that. We sped down the Hamilton Road, an essentially military highway built by the British in the 1920s and 1930s to facilitate pacification of the tribes, which stretched east from Erbil all the way to the Iranian border. "I don't know if this is the Kurds' best chance," Barzani had told me in Rayan in February, "but I know definitely it's not our last chance. Who could have imagined the present situation even a few months ago?" I reflected on the irony of Barzani's remark. Given Kurdish history, their present predicament was all too predictable. Yet, as the miles went by I noticed more and more wooden cribs tied to car roofs; then we passed a tanker truck with a defiant message traced by hand in English on its mud-spattered back panel: "Let nobod say the Kurds are dead." The spelling wasn't perfect, but the message was suitably hortatory.

In less than an hour we were in Diyana. Massoud's scribbled message worked wonders with Abdul-Muhaymin, another Barzani relative, who was in charge of the KDP office there. We were still undecided whether to make for Turkey or Iran, about an hour's drive due east. An ABC stringer was supposed to have greased the wheels at the Iranian border, but we didn't much trust him or Iranian officialdom. Abdul-Muhaymin made up our minds for us: we had no choice, he said, because the Iranians had just closed the border. Our rented cars and drivers headed back to Salahuddin to rescue their families. Abdul-Muhaymin gave us a pickup, and we loaded our gear and ourselves aboard and headed almost due north for Kani Rasht, a spot on the map just inside the border with Turkey. It was almost dark when we arrived in the middle of a green field where we would spend the night. The pickup left. We had just enough light left to be able to negotiate with local smugglers for pack animals for early the next morning, to eat, and to lay out our sleeping bags.

Geraldine Brooks of *The Wall Street Journal* suddenly announced that she was frightened, convinced we would all be killed in our sleep. We were all too exhausted to take the warning seriously, especially coming from her: this slight young woman was the bravest of our lot and had proved it by purposefully remaining in Kirkuk overnight to chronicle a Kurdish family's reaction to an intense Iraqi artillery bombardment. In fact, we were lucky. We were relatively safe, we thought. The mountain route across to Turkey was one of the rare unmined passages between the two countries. It did not rain, though we all but froze because of the heavy dew so high up in the mountains.

The moon was full. I woke several times during the night to see a steady stream of refugees following a steep mountain path leading up to an eight-thousand-foot pass and into Turkey. At dawn on the ridgeline a herd of sixteen wild boar stood stock-still watching them. The BBC reported that Erbil, Duhok, and Zakho were back in Iraqi government hands. That proved the wisdom of our decision against trying to escape the way we'd come in. The pack animals did not arrive as advertised. We all fell to repacking our gear, convinced we would have to abandon suitcases and heavy equipment. I walked down to a nearby stream, washed, and shaved. For the first time in a week I did not feel sick, although I had lost a good ten pounds and was still weak.

Three horses and a donkey finally arrived along with their two teenage boy minders. We started walking. Geraldine carried my sleeping bag during the steady climb along a narrow path, which was soon cluttered with city shoes, suitcases, and other impedimenta abandoned by the refugees. From time to time we stopped to rest, to admire the fields of spring flowers and the snow-covered peaks in the near distance and to listen to the refugees' incredulous, outspoken criticism of George Bush and all his works. "Why did you not finish Saddam off?" they asked. "Bush is Saddam's friend." They were the Kurdish elite, who'd been first to realize the defeat and flee—retired civil servants in three-piece business suits, engineers, middle-class mothers with babes in arms.

It was not the first time in a long career that I felt uncomfortable being an American. But rarely had I felt the criticism so justified. Five hours later we reached a concrete marker identifying the border. Forty-five minutes more and we were in a Turkish military outpost at Yesilova, warming ourselves under the omnipresent portrait of Mustafa Kemal Ataturk, founder of modern Turkey and oppressor of the Kurds. A young English-speaking lieutenant was sufficiently impressed by our various American, British, and French newspaper and television employers to alert higher headquarters by radio. Eventually, a Vietnam-era Huey helicopter landed, with regional army and gendarmerie commanders on board.

The army brigadier coldly looked over our bedraggled bunch and ticked off his choices: "I can shoot you as illegal trespassers, I can shove you back across the border, or I can let you in." He let that sink in. Then he laughed a great belly laugh and let us in. He also called for a second helicopter with a doctor, two nurses, and hundreds of loaves of bread. The medical help and food were for the several hundred refugees who had arrived outside the post in the past thirty-six hours, only to be kept in a field, often in drenching rain, without food or shelter. If nothing else, our presence shamed the ever-suspicious and sometimes-brutal Turkish soldiery into treating those refugees with something approaching common humanity. Little did the Turks know that they were but the vanguard of some two million Kurds fleeing Saddam Hussein's feared vengeance.

4

Died and Gone to Heaven

*We know all about the Kurds . . . We used to fight a little war with
them every summer.*

FREYA STARK, British travel writer and civil servant, in *Riding
to the Tigris* (1958)

"No friends but the mountains," runs the hoariest of Kurdish
sayings. But in April 1991 the mountains killed Kurds by
the thousands, and Kurds discovered in their hour of direst
need that they had devoted friends in influential positions in Washington, London, Paris, and elsewhere. The Turkish president, the
French president's wife, a French junior minister, a key senatorial
aide in Washington, an Irish member of the House of Lords, senior
American, British, French, and other diplomats in sensitive jobs,
well-placed newspaper columnists—in their own separate ways
they worked effectively on the Iraqi Kurds' behalf. Even so, the
Kurds owed their salvation first and foremost to television, that
blunt instrument which quickly won over French and British public
opinion to their previously largely unknown cause, forcing the
governments in London and Paris to act.

European diplomats were taken aback by the television-driven
ground swell which, as one American colleague cynically noted,
prompted "the Europeans for once to act altruistically." A
dumbfounded member of President François Mitterrand's staff
with a sense of history was left wondering why the public backed
one cause rather than another. "Why," he wondered, "is there
such enthusiasm for the Kurds, who are neither Jews nor Christians
and to boot were implicated in the World War I massacre of the
Christian Armenians?" Yet even with the British and French gov-

ernments firmly on board and pressing for action—and even with key opposition Democrats in Washington increasingly critical—the Bush administration for more than two weeks dragged its heels in the face of similar U.S. television coverage.

Luckily the Kurds, much to their own surprise, turned out to be made for television, thanks to their compelling telegenic qualities and a Western sense of guilt about causing their plight after so much self-congratulation in the coalition for driving Iraq out of Kuwait. To the embarrassment of the Western political and foreign-policy establishment, the Kurds' suffering brought into public focus the long-submerged history of the West's double-dealing in the Kurdish question over seven decades. Many Britons had what one diplomat termed a "historic guilt complex" about the Kurds, "which runs deep," going back to the unkept promises of nationhood at the end of World War I, then of autonomy within the British-mandated Iraq, when Britain was more interested in safeguarding Kirkuk's oil for itself than in Kurdish nationalist aspirations. In France, a generation of successive governments of the right and left had fawned over Saddam Hussein and the world's second-largest crude-oil reserves he controlled in an arrant pursuit of profit from the lone major French beachhead in Middle Eastern oil. The public now questioned the wisdom—and morality—of a policy which turned almost the entire French non-Communist political elite into sycophantic megaphones for Baghdad's propagandists and resulted in $5 billion in unpaid bills, mostly for armaments (some of which were used against the Kurds).

But above all, in a world of constantly changing images, the Kurds were something new and exotic after decades of African, Arab, and Asian refugees. Long used to seeing suffering in warm climates, television viewers around the globe now watched the Kurds freezing on sleet-whipped mountains, struggling in snow, mud, and excrement, and risking death from mines as they scavenged for firewood and battled with each other for relief aid tossed from trucks. Beatings administered by government troops—Turkish soldiers, in the event—were familiar fare in other climes, as was the survival-of-the-fittest scramble for relief supplies. The men wore turbans like so many Middle Easterners. But their baggy pants and cummerbunds and their wives' gaily colored skirts and petticoats were distinctive, exotic touches for jaded television audiences.

The CBS correspondent Alan Pizzey summed up why he got on the air for twenty-one straight days covering the Kurds in the mountains: "The children are beautiful, the men are fierce and proud, the women unveiled and fine looking." To the outside world's general surprise, some Kurds were blond and blue-eyed. And since the middle class had fled, too, there were enough English-speakers to make the Kurds' case clearly and succinctly in the sound bites television so prizes. The message, Pizzey noted, was television-simple: "The Kurds were victims of American policy calling for an uprising, and to prove it they had the unsigned leaflets in Arabic that American planes dropped urging soldiers to desert."*

After millennia as a virtual non-nation and the quintessential people without a country, the Kurds suddenly were getting the "fifteen minutes of fame" that Andy Warhol observed everyone would have in the television age. Their scattered foreign friends did their best to make that quarter hour last, if only to disprove cynics like the veteran Third World ambassador in Baghdad who predicted that the West's fascination with the Kurds would be no more durable than the Hula-Hoop fad of his youth.

In France, Danielle Mitterrand, the president's wife and a vociferous defender of the Kurds and other downtrodden minorities, needed no encouragement to bring their plight to her husband's attention. She had befriended Kendal Nezan, an influential exiled Kurdish physicist from Turkey, and helped him found the Kurdish Institute in Paris in 1982. When in late March 1991 the Iraqi counteroffensive gathered steam, she alerted specialists inside and outside the government to prepare contingency plans. With the refugee exodus in full swing in the first terrible week of April, she persuaded her husband to watch the television footage of wretched Kurds in the mountains.

Mindful of her own youthful experience in the resistance in Nazi-

---

* Eric Rouleau, the French ambassador, recalled taking Bernard Kouchner, a junior minister for humanitarian action, to the border in early April to talk to some four hundred Kurdish refugees and to encourage them to go back to Iraq gradually. Speaker after speaker mentioned these tracts dropped by American planes as proof of allied betrayal. The tone, Rouleau recalled, was, "Thanks for the nice words, but we don't trust you Westerners after you armed Saddam, then told us to desert and revolt against him and then let us down. You didn't lift a finger for the two weeks we were bombed and massacred. The SPCA treats stray dogs better than you treated us. Give us political asylum in France." When Kouchner said, "Basically, they're right about our helping Saddam," Rouleau told him to pipe down, because "you cannot take in fifty thousand refugees."

occupied France, she badgered Elysée civilian and military officials about the feasibility of parachuting aid to the refugees, only to be told it was impractical. President François Mitterrand was sufficiently moved by the Kurds' plight that France urgently demanded the United Nations Secretary-General to take action, warning that otherwise Paris would act on its own. Approving telephone calls poured into the French embassy and consulates in the United States, embarrassing a Bush administration still determined to do nothing.

Mme Mitterrand's long-standing and deep connection with the Kurds was a classic example of France's enduring, near-monarchical habit of having those close to the throne won over to a seemingly far-fetched and obscurely known cause. She had been sensitized to the Kurds by, among others, Bernard Dorin, a diplomat who abruptly gave up his career to work for the Kurds without knowing much about them. In 1964 he had walked out of the Quai d' Orsay in a huff after a brief spat with his boss, Secretary-General Eric de Carbonnel, who had ordered him to sign a pro forma note from Great Britain informing France of its sale of Hawker Hunter jets to Iraq. Dorin decided to learn something about the people for whom he believed he had sacrificed his diplomatic career. He studied Kurdish and in 1968 decided to see for himself what was happening in Iraqi Kurdistan. At that time Dorin was working on the staff of the minister of scientific research, who indulgently granted him a leave of absence, promising to take him back "if you don't get killed." He did almost die during the six months he spent with Mullah Mustafa Barzani, who once again was fighting for autonomy against the Iraqi army. In 1971 Dorin was allowed to rejoin the French foreign service, and served as ambassador in Haiti, South Africa, Brazil, Japan, and then Britain, and in London he worked in close collaboration with the British government in the critical days of April 1991 when Britain and France, in a rare show of peacetime harmony, cooperated to organize the Kurds' rescue and to goad the United States into assuming its responsibilities.

First off the mark among the Kurds' foreign friends was in fact an American: Peter Galbraith, an energetic staff member of the Senate Foreign Relations Committee, who was in Duhok with Jalal Talabani when the Kurdish uprising collapsed. A relentless defender of the Kurds, Galbraith had been a constant thorn in the side of Saddam Hussein and of the Reagan and Bush administrations since he had chronicled the destruction of rural life in Kurdistan for the Senate during an official visit to northern Iraq in 1987. On Easter Sunday under mortar fire he was one of the last people to cross the Tigris River back to Syria before Iraqi arms closed down that escape route. Once he reached Damascus, Galbraith telephoned the U.S. embassy in Ankara, warning that massive numbers of refugees were headed to the frontier and that American and other foreign journalists were with them. This alert gave the embassy a head start in dealing with the crisis.

Galbraith's videocassette of refugees on the run was among the first footage shown on American television, alerting the world to the extent of the exodus. Back in Washington, Galbraith kept appearing on television on behalf of the Kurds. He helped to orchestrate the unstinting campaign which forced the reluctant Bush administration's hand, tirelessly hounding a reluctant State Department to meet Kurdish representatives. Similarly outraged by the administration's treatment of the Kurds were two Pulitzer Prize–winning newspaper columnists, Jim Hoagland of *The Washington Post* and William Safire of *The New York Times*, who both had long defended the Kurdish cause.

On April 3 Mitterrand dispatched Bernard Kouchner, France's energetic junior minister for humanitarian action, to Ankara, where, with the Turks, he worked out the legal underpinnings for a U.N. Security Council resolution protecting the Kurds inside Iraq. In the early 1970s Kouchner had been a founding member of the nongovernmental medical assistance group called Doctors Without Borders and, later, of a smaller offshoot called Doctors of the World, which provides emergency medical aid in the Third World. Kouchner was that rarity, a politician who knew the Kurdish problem in detail and came across on television with ease and real conviction. For years Doctors of the World had maintained a medical team for Iranian Kurds on the Iran-Iraq border. Horrified by violations of human rights the world over, Kouchner had long advocated the international community's controversial "right to interfere" for humanitarian purposes in the historically sacrosanct internal affairs of sovereign states. In the Kurds' tribulations, at last he saw the chance to put his pet theory into practice.

Given past experience, one would have guessed that Turkey would reject out of hand such groundbreaking interventionism. The prickly, nationalistic Turks never forgave nor forgot the humiliating interference of foreign powers, especially Western missionaries, on behalf of Christian minorities during the slow decline of the Ottoman Empire, nor did they overlook the attempted carve-up of their Anatolian heartland by Britain, France, and Greece at the end of World War I. Moreover, the highly centralized modern state that Kemal Ataturk created on the Ottoman Empire's ruins was rooted in denying the very separate existence of its own Kurds—the largest Kurdish minority in any state and estimated at 20 percent of Turkey's population. More recently, the Turkish government felt much maligned by foreign criticism of its treatment of tens of thousands of Iraqi Kurds gassed by Saddam's troops just south of the international border in August 1988, and allowed into Turkey on humanitarian grounds.

But the French also realized that the last thing President Turgut Özal wanted was half a million Iraqi Kurds in Turkey, an eventuality that, one Western envoy said, "would have been political suicide for the Turkish government." Özal was in the United States on a visit and returned to Ankara only at the end of the fateful Easter weekend. He immediately convoked Turkey's National Security Council, perhaps the most powerful institution in the country and one dominated by the military. The refugee influx could only complicate the problems in southeastern Turkey, where 120,000 troops and police had been bogged down in an increasingly bloody civil war since 1984 against separatists among its own large Kurdish community. Now Ankara was getting a bad press because its troops were visibly preventing the refugees from reaching more hospitable ground in Turkey and in some cases were even forcing them at gunpoint back to the more exposed peaks above the snow line.

The deal Kouchner reached turned on what a French diplomat in Paris later called a "magic phrase" dreamed up by the Turks to solve the unsolvable. Turkey was not on the Security Council and needed the backing of one of its permanent members to sponsor the scheme. France, which almost simultaneously was preparing its own draft resolution, was only too happy to oblige. Their agreement invoked U.N. Charter language about "threats to international peace and security" to justify Turkey's refusal to let Iraqi Kurds across the border and its support for dispatching troops to Iraq to enforce the refugees' return to their homes whether Saddam Hussein liked it or not. U.N. officials sniffily called this *refoulement*, the technical term for turning away asylum seekers. In fact Turkey, in signing after World War II the appropriate international conventions granting political refuge to asylum seekers, had specifically excluded asylum seekers from its eastern and southern neighbors. (This had not stopped Turkey from accepting a million or so Iranians after the Islamic revolution ended the Pahlavi dynasty in February 1979, or, for that matter, from taking in Iraqi Kurds in 1988, of whom more than twenty-eight thousand remained—in miserable conditions in camps in southeastern Turkey—until 1991, when the vast majority returned to Iraq.)

Now, thanks to Kouchner's visit, France and Turkey jointly proposed a revolutionary draft resolution which the Security Council approved on April 5, to many professional diplomats' surprise and eventual concern. (They had expected China's and/or the Soviet Union's vetoes.) For the first time in seven decades Kurds were specifically mentioned in an international document—U.N. Security Council resolution 688. That in itself constituted a major concession, which Turkey granted only grudgingly. In fact, it had little choice. Nor did the Bush administration, despite its initial surprise and displeasure with a scheme that involved deploying troops to northern Iraq and thwarted its overriding priority of sending American troops home from the Persian Gulf as quickly as possible.

But George Bush was anxious to help a desperate Özal. In the first frantic days after Iraq's invasion of Kuwait, Özal's prompt closure of Iraq's trans-Turkey oil pipeline made him a key ally in putting together the coalition against Saddam Hussein. Moreover, Bush's much-vaunted New World Order was evaporating, thanks to the television coverage of Iraq's repression of the failed Kurdish and Shia uprisings. As one dogged proponent of the "right to interfere" described the adoption of resolution 688, "In voting to send humanitarian aid to the Kurds and other Iraqi citizens despite the Baghdad government's opposition, the Security Council certainly did not ensure that henceforth governments will not mistreat or even massacre their citizens, but never again will sovereign states enjoy the same juridical ease in refusing outside humanitarian aid."

In Ankara the Iraqi Kurds had another influential old friend in the French ambassador, Eric Rouleau, for decades the Middle East specialist on the authoritative newspaper *Le Monde* before he embraced diplomacy. In the months leading up to the war, Rouleau tutored the American ambassador, Morton I. Abramowitz, about the subtleties of Middle Eastern politics, especially the nature of

Iraqi society, which he demonstrated was considerably more varied and complex than the Bush administration allowed. Those were crucial lessons.

Abramowitz had never before served in the Middle East, but he was a dab hand at refugees. While ambassador in Thailand in the late 1970s, he had been amazingly successful in dealing with the outpouring of "boat people" from Vietnam, combining unswerving moral fortitude with extraordinary bureaucratic and political skills. Normally, the Turkish government was jittery about the presence of foreign diplomats in sensitive areas, especially along its borders. But seizing on the pretext of concern for the welfare of a relative handful of American journalists escaping from Iraq, Abramowitz now deployed his large embassy staff to obtain firsthand information about the Kurdish refugees piling up against the Turkish border in the hundreds of thousands.

He also lobbied tirelessly for action in a slumbering official Washington, sending telegram after telegram to the State Department, working the telephones with a network of powerful friends in and out of the government, even sending messages to the White House marked for Bush's attention. Convinced by his boat-people experience that to be successful "you had to move quickly and energize people," Abramowitz said, "In situations like this my attitude is to assume and emphasize the worst." Brent Scowcroft, the President's national security adviser, "knew of the ambassador's refugee work during the 'boat people' saga and recognized that his warning of impending disaster was serious in the extreme both for Turkey and for the U.S.," according to an American diplomat conversant with the cable traffic. Abramowitz "kept beating the drum in Ankara" while the insistent Özal "did a lot on the telephone with" Bush.

The ambassador also advocated parachuting relief supplies in the mountains, which the U.S. Air Force initiated on April 7, soon followed by similar British and French flights, all of them made possible by Turkey's agreement to allow the planes to use Incirlik air base, at Adana. The U.S.A.F. mobilized its worldwide pool of cargo riggers at Incirlik, but despite the effort, senior military officers in Washington dismissed the airdrops, long considered to have only limited effectiveness, as "throwing popcorn at pigeons." Worse still, wayward pallets landed directly on some refugees and crushed them to death; other Kurds died detonating land mines as they scrambled to reach the parachuted relief aid. But airdrops were filmable, looked good, and at least demonstrated that the allies were doing something. And Bush needed to be seen as taking decisive action after his initial indifference.

The payoff for Ambassador Abramowitz was persuading Secretary of State James A. Baker III to visit Cukurca, one of the biggest and most desperate refugee camps along the mountainous border. At the time of the visit, on April 7, the press made light of the cowboy-booted Baker, who left within less than a quarter hour of having been helicoptered in to witness the distress of these tens of thousands of wretched people, dismissing his appearance as yet another self-serving photo opportunity by a man known for the importance he attached to promoting his image in the media. Yet, if the tough politician in Baker had entertained initial doubts about the crisis, he left Cukurca genuinely moved and worried by what he had seen. "Perhaps the best-invested twelve minutes in the history of refugee relief work" was Abramowitz's satisfied summation.

Baker now realized that major international action was required to solve this crisis, which had catapulted the Kurds onto the world's agenda for the first time in recent history. No sooner was he back in Diyarbakir and aboard his official plane heading for Israel than he telephoned Bush, Secretary of Defense Richard Cheney, and U.N. Secretary-General Javier Pérez de Cuéllar. Ever so slowly, President Bush was being forced to consider abandoning his stubborn, heartless refusal to deal with the Kurds, to whose dire predicament he had contributed so much. For if Bush trusted anyone, it was Baker.

Bush's increasingly exasperated allies were in no mood to wait. In Luxembourg, British Prime Minister John Major on April 8 won full support from European Community members for the pioneering idea of using coalition troops to protect "safe havens," areas on the plains of northern Iraq that would encourage the refugees to leave the mountains. Public opinion was outraged about what was happening to the Kurds, and his predecessor, Margaret Thatcher, was hectoring: Major was determined to prove he was his own man, and doing the right thing by the Kurds became a matter of extreme political importance. He needed to show he could handle this, his first major foreign-policy crisis since moving into number 10 Downing Street four months before.

Even the French, more often rivals than allies of the English in recent years, were impressed by his determination. In an edifying display of cross-channel goodwill, their diplomats played down their own claims of paternity for the safe-haven concept and emphasized Major's unusual willingness to take such an important decision without prior consultation with Washington. For the French government, too, doing right by the Kurds helped to stake out a distinct postwar identity, after months of following the American lead, which was always uncomfortable for the nationalist French political elite. It also helped to correct, if not efface, France's image as Saddam Hussein's principal Western arms supplier.

Yet for all their eagerness to help the Kurds, Britain, France, and other concerned European nations were stymied. They could do nothing on the ground by themselves. Early on they realized that only a military operation could deal with such a vast refugee problem in such inaccessible terrain, and only the United States could marshal the logistics. Moreover, resolution 688 and the safe-haven idea meant nothing in isolation. As a first practical step to coax the refugees home, the British and French governments persuaded Washington to approve a ban on Iraqi air activity north of the 36th parallel, ostensibly to protect the lumbering C-130 Hercules transport planes being used for the relief airdrops.

The C-130s' airdrops were of no real succor to the Kurdish refugees. For days and days, local Turkish Kurds provided far more effective aid to them than the Turkish Red Crescent, international relief organizations, or the airdrops. Nonetheless, the C-130s fulfilled an essential function: with them came fighter and helicopter gunships, escort aircraft based at Incirlik. And A-10 ground-support aircraft were used to subject Iraqi troops to their characteristic screech directly overhead—an unmistakable message to pull back when coalition soldiers entered northern Iraq to encourage the refugees' return from the mountains. Over the months, then years, these allied overflights were meant to reassure the Kurds and to warn the Iraqis not to stampede another exodus to the Iranian and Turkish frontiers.

These flights, which were regularly renewed (with reluctant Turkish approval) every six, then every three, months were the only meaningful deterrent to Iraqi temptations to recapture the large area in the north of the country under de facto Kurdish administration. The arbitrary line at the 36th parallel left more than 60 percent of the Kurdish population unprotected—especially many of the 1.4 million who fled to Iran—though it covered most of the homes of the 400,000 to 500,000 refugees on the Turkish frontier. (It also excluded the Kirkuk oil fields, to allay latent fears among Iraq's neighbors that the allies favored an independent Kurdish state in northern Iraq.)

The allied coalition still had to flesh out the French idea of so-called humanitarian corridors—roads equipped with way stations, complete with food, water, gasoline, and medical care, that would funnel the refugees down from the mountains to camps set up in the more clement plains that were now safe havens. Worked out with the U.N. in Geneva, the corridors were yet another piece of the puzzle designed to ensure U.N. involvement and defuse charges of interference in Iraq's internal affairs. So determined was the Bush administration to extricate American troops that it insisted on involving a reluctant United Nations in any humanitarian action in Iraq. And still it resisted. Even the much-vaunted special trans-atlantic relationship—and Britain's unstinting cooperation with the United States during the war to liberate Kuwait—were of no immediate avail. As members of parliament, the press, and ordinary Britons registered their growing consternation day after day in early April, during those "terrible weeks when there was no one at the end of the telephone in Washington," a senior Foreign Office official later recalled, if he ever did get through "my calls were not returned."

Among the Kurds, exhaustion, exposure, not to mention lack of food, clean water, and sanitation, produced epidemics of diarrhea, dysentery, and other communicable diseases. The death toll rapidly mounted, although probably never reaching the sustained rate that American officials and a U.N. spokesman in Iran in late April estimated at 1,000 to 2,000 a day. Most of the victims were under five or elderly. U.S. health authorities estimated that 6,700 Iraqi Kurds along the Turkish border died during the three weeks of exodus—which was 6,200 more than would have been considered normal in northern Iraq. The U.N. High Commissioner for Refugees estimated that 12,600 of the Kurds who sought refuge in Iran also succumbed. God only knows how many Kurds died inside Iraq on the roads and mountain paths leading to the borders, but there are a great number of simple jagged rock-splinter burial markers and of more formal tombstones.

This Kurdish death toll—and relentless allied and domestic critics branding President Bush as a moral leper and a wimp—finally registered with the administration and its senior military and civilian officials. On April 16, more than two weeks after the exodus began, Bush reversed himself: less than two hours before, David Mack at the State Department was telling an Iraqi opposition delegation that the United States would give "neither a single dollar nor a single American soldier" to save the Kurds. Now Bush committed U.S. troops to what was called Operation Provide Comfort, which also included British, French, Dutch, Italian, and Spanish soldiers—more than 21,700 all told. Within ten days of the first contingents' deployment, Kurds began returning to their homes, in many cases bypassing the temporary shelter in camps that the allied soldiers built for them on the plains outside the border town of Zakho. Much of the credit was due to the initiative of the American Special Forces teams, dispatched to the mountains complete with their own communication and medical capabilities. They rapidly organized the dispirited refugees by city, town, and village, and marked out landing zones for giant helicopters, which efficiently delivered food, tents, and blankets without causing the deaths usually inevitable in the air-dropping of pallets.

The very speed of the operation's success underlined the seeming perversity of the previous foot-dragging. White House spin doctors insisted that Bush's New World Order did remain untarnished. Yet President Bush had delayed his crucial decision so long that when he finally announced it, people thought of it as a graceless and reluctant change of heart. By waiting so long, Bush let himself in for scathing criticism, and was taken to task for "never losing an opportunity to rise above principle" or deciding to "cut his winnings and go home."

———

For those outside the administration's inner circle it seemed all but incomprehensible that Bush had taken so long to change course in the face of so much suffering, embarrassingly and relentlessly served up on television around the clock. The reasons were tangled and had everything to do with long-held tenets of U.S. foreign policy, unhealed Pentagon wounds from previous wars, domestic American politics' impinging on foreign policy, and the Bush administration's bizarre organizational arrangements in its foreign-policy sector. But all these elements had one thing in common: a consistent refusal to deal with the opposition within Iraq, and especially its most important single component, the Kurdish nationalists. Whatever its weaknesses, and they were many, the opposition was eager to help the coalition. It ranged from experienced Kurdish guerrilla leaders and disaffected Sunni veterans of the Ba'ath Party to Shia clerics and lay politicians. One would have thought that any knowledge of these diverse elements was better than none, any contact with their people more instructive than simply rehashing dry theories.

The administration's refusal to meet the Iraqi opposition to discuss political problems—before, during, and even for seven weeks after the Kuwait war ended—expressed a spectrum of fears and presumptions. American planners argued that the opposition were out-of-touch has-beens, too long removed from the Iraqi political arena to have useful insights, much less practical help on the ground. The Pentagon didn't trust Iraqis of any persuasion and feared that any information shared with the opposition might end up in Baghdad. By nature military planners tend to be incurious when it comes to the internal workings of foreign societies.

Neither the United States nor its coalition partners had intelligence or other sources of any civilian or military importance inside Saddam Hussein's preternaturally closed country. That did not faze the Pentagon, which turned the argument inside out, saying that since the war to free Kuwait in large part was waged from the air, there was no need to learn about Iraqi society and its complicated, violent history, as would have been the case were infantry units involved to take and hold ground. An air war also meant a "clean" war with minimal casualties, at least for the coalition.

The Pentagon was no exception to the hoary military truism that soldiers tend to fight the previous war and inevitably overstate the enemy's strength. Haunted by the humiliation of American arms in Vietnam and Beirut, General Colin Powell demanded—and got—maximum troops and equipment for minimal objectives. Kuwait was freed without any of the "one arm tied behind our backs" restrictions that had rankled the Pentagon ever since the Korean War. Iraq's armed forces, overgenerously described in coalition propaganda as the "world's fourth largest" in large part to justify the American-led military buildup, were to be deprived of nuclear, biological, and chemical capabilities, it was said.

When the war began, Powell said of the Iraqi army, "First we are going to cut it off, then we are going to kill it." But such was American haste to end hostilities, for basically political reasons, that Powell backed Bush's neat "hundred-hour ground war" formulation and left the promised killing undone. The noose around Iraqi forces in southern Iraq was never closed. Saddam Hussein's armed forces were only cut down to size; its elite military and secret-police units, vital to the regime's control of the Iraqi people, remained largely intact, thus also strong enough to keep Iran at bay, although no longer threatening to the West's friends in the gulf.* The tactical presence of allied troops inside Iraq was limited, for once Kuwait was liberated, Powell wanted American forces out of the gulf as quickly as possible, an objective easier to achieve if Iraqi society's delicate inner workings—and its opposition—were obscured.

From the time of the occupation of Kuwait, the administration found a way of dodging the awkward question of how it was dealing with the Iraqi opposition: responsibility for this subject was palmed off on Great Britain, Iraq's onetime colonial master, which, it was thought, at least liked dealing with Iraqis. Official Washington conveniently convinced itself that the British were better equipped to do this, since in any case the opposition had congregated in London. British officials diligently contacting the Iraqi opposition did not have the impression that the Bush administration was very interested in the information they passed on. In this circumstance, the Washington planners were sincere in professing ignorance about the Kurds' uprising, its initial widespread success, its sudden collapse, the exodus and its extent. But ignorance was not bliss. The wretched refugees and the jagged roadside grave markers were proof of that.

This was predictable mismanagement. The American planning was a hodgepodge of naïveté and realpolitik, more tactics than strategy, seemingly consistent only if its peculiar assumptions were correct. Inflexibility is an odd quality to value when one is trying to understand, much less deal with, what passes for normal times in the Middle East, a region renowned for its eternal devotion to abrupt change. No one should have been surprised by anything that happened from August 2, 1990, when Iraq invaded and occupied Kuwait, to the end of the following March, when Saddam Hussein crushed the Shia and Kurdish uprisings.

Yet American policy remained one-dimensional, static, and un-

---

* That proved illusory as well. During the next few years Saddam Hussein on several occasions moved troops to the Kuwaiti border, or seemed poised to do so, which required the expensive dispatch of American air, naval, and ground forces to the region.

inquisitive as to the likely repercussions that the war would have on Saddam Hussein's regime. Long before the first shot was fired, this approach seemed mindlessly naive. For example, the United States and Britain made no secret of their intention to have their forces enter Iraq as part of the Kuwait campaign: a glance at a map demonstrated that such a maneuver was a simple matter of military tactics; and common sense dictated that even without marching on Baghdad the thirty thousand U.S. troops who ended up deep within Iraq were bound to provoke unforeseeable and quite possibly profound repercussions on Iraq's body politic.

Just before Christmas 1990, during a fleeting visit to Washington, my sense of foreboding increased when I met with one of the American administration's few genuine Middle East specialists involved in decision-making. By then it was clear that the administration wanted simply a humiliating military defeat for Saddam Hussein and ardently hoped that he would not withdraw from Kuwait on his own. So after a few preliminary remarks, I asked what kind of postwar Iraq the administration had in mind.

To my annoyance, and possibly that of my interlocutor, we were not alone: another official was taking notes, and the proceedings, because of his presence, became flat and without substance. There was a longish silence after I asked the question. I was about to rephrase it, fearing I had not been clear. Then, without saying a word, the official I'd come to see answered in his own way: he began ever so slowly raising his eyes up along the wall of his high-ceilinged quarters in the Old Executive Office Building, next to the White House. So it was to be not just the fog of war but the fog of postwar as well.

Even nearly a year after the war, key American officials were defensive about all this. Richard Haass, in charge of the Middle East on the National Security Council and a key player despite his lack of field experience, could manage no more than the old bureaucratic truism "It is not easy for governments to change policy." When Haass agreed to meet me in the same building in December 1991, he was unrepentant to the point of cockiness. The Bush administration was justified in its wariness about helping the Kurdish refugees, he argued. Forced first into airdrops to keep the Kurds from starving and freezing to death, then to safe havens to entice them back home, the administration, he said, all the time feared the Iraqi "tar baby"—by which he meant Iraq's potential for involving the United States beyond the narrowest war aims.

Other coalition planners in Washington and abroad were determined to avoid what they called a "second Gaza strip"—diplomatic shorthand for getting bogged down in an insoluble problem. Too many people had a "romantic view of the Kurds, who would have been only too happy to get the United States involved," Haass said. He was not alone in blaming the victim. A middle-level State Department bureaucrat, conveniently overlooking President Bush's February 15 appeal and the desertion leaflets, argued that "the Kurds did not ask our advice in advance about starting their insurrection—only in retrospect did they really make claims that Bush triggered the uprising."

Phebe Marr, a political scientist and senior fellow at the National Defense University, where her advice contributed to administration policy-making, said that planning was driven by fear of exposing American troops to "a hostile population," especially in the Sunni Arab heartland. Hers was a curious (though widely shared) argument for an advocate of the administration's military solution, for it borrowed from the arsenal of those who *opposed* fighting to free Kuwait. This school argued that economic sanctions alone could bring Saddam Hussein to his senses, that waging war risked setting off an anti-Western chain reaction that would threaten moderate regimes throughout the Arab world.* Using force to march on Baghdad or the heartland of the ruling Sunni Arab minority would only stiffen the regime's resistance. And if one dumped the Baghdad government outright, any successor regime would be branded as pro-American, which would complicate withdrawal and drag Washington into needless difficulties. Above all, Marr also said, was the determination that "we did not want an independent Kurdistan." Neither she nor apparently anyone else in the administration paid much heed to the Iraqi Kurds' repeated denials—before, during, and after the war—that independence was their goal. The Kurds were liars or inconsequential or both, it seemed.

When the uprising in Iraq did take place, with Iraqis joyfully demonstrating their pro-coalition sentiments and their yearning to get rid of Saddam Hussein, the administration was unprepared, ungracious. It wanted nothing to do with them. Unfortunately for

---

* The feared chain reaction never took place. In fact, the farther a country was physically removed from the Persian Gulf—in North Africa, for example—the greater was support for the Baghdad government and the more the local governments felt obliged to bow to public opinion.

the Bush people, there was the trail of evidence of their incitement—Bush's appeal, the leaflets exhorting desertion, and a CIA-financed radio station beamed into Iraq from Saudi Arabia. Given American government treatment of the Kurds in the 1970s, when Henry Kissinger was in office, and the legacy of that betrayal (a history to which I shall return in chapter 6), the suggestions made that the Kurds had craftily sought to bamboozle savvy Washington policy-makers show only ignorance, bad faith, or an odd manifestation of guilt. A clinical sense of guilt alone seems to explain the administration's regularly repeated protestations, from Bush on down, that the "U.S. has misled no one."

A fear of "getting sucked in," another theme often enunciated at the White House in March and April, suggested the bitter lesson that American policy-makers had learned in Vietnam and Beirut.* The political danger of going to war without genuine public support had become the Pentagon's Eleventh Commandment. Similarly, the White House feared casualties, and to save the Kurds would be to risk the lives of coalition troops. But Bush's appreciation was skewed: the more he refused to help the Kurds, the greater became the groundswell in favor of protecting them, as opinion polls showed. The American public had a clearer view of the moral stakes, realizing that innocent Iraqis were losing their lives because Washington's policy misguidedly supposed Americans would not stomach more fighting on any terms.†

Marr's specific fears of encountering a "hostile population" suggested a view about the often-xenophobic politics of Arab nationalism in general and Iraq's Ba'ath Socialist Party in particular. She

---

* U.S. policy-makers had been traumatized by the deaths of 243 U.S. Marines in Beirut in 1983 at the hands of Iranian-backed Shia terrorists. But those deaths stemmed directly from the lack of definition of the Marines' mission in Lebanon, which did indeed suck them into first Lebanese, then regional, politics, During Israel's invasion of Lebanon the previous year, the Marines—and allied troops—had been dispatched to oversee the withdrawal of the Palestine Liberation Organization from Beirut. The Marines left when that limited mission was accomplished. After Israel violated promises not to occupy West Beirut and encouraged its allies, the Lebanese Christian militiamen, to massacre hundreds of Palestinian civilians in the Sabra and Shatila refugee camps, the Marines were sent back. The plight of the Kurdish refugees was, in contrast, directly the result of American-led military action, and the American people recognized the difference.

† According to a Gallup poll reported in *The International Herald Tribune*, April 11, 1991, 59 percent of those queried thought the coalition should have kept on fighting until Saddam Hussein was overthrown, and 57 percent favored shooting down the Iraqi gunships harassing the Kurds.

was fixated on the chaotic decade of violent, revolving-door governments in Baghdad that had ensued after the overthrow of the monarchy in 1958. She could not easily entertain the thought that Iraqis would welcome outside assistance in ending seventeen years of Ba'athist rule, marked by disastrous foreign wars and internal repression, and she seemed to have a lingering sympathy for Ba'athist propaganda claims of turning Iraq into a modern, strong, assertive, and secular nation.

If somehow the Iraqis themselves did uproot Ba'athist rule, however, and one had to deal with all the turmoil and uncertainty likely to attend the end of its long ascendancy, she was not alone in instinctively shying away from a radical rethinking of Iraqi society. State Department hands spoke of their fears of a "revolutionary resistance" to any coalition troop presence in Iraq. Yet throughout the Middle East Sunni Arab nationalism and its central theme of Arab unity had started to decline with Israel's victory in the Six-Day War in 1967, though they still exercised considerable influence among Western policy-makers, shaken by the rise of Islamic fundamentalism and the difficulties inherent in encouraging democratic institutions. During the 1960s and 1970s, in Arab nationalist eyes nothing symbolized "imperialist and Zionist" attacks on their values more than Kurdish nationalism, the struggle for a non-Arab minority's place in the sun, a minority then aided and abetted by Iran, Israel, and, finally, the United States. In the 1980s such was the Iraqi Kurds' attachment to secular Western-style democratic institutions that they steadfastly opposed Ayatollah Ruhollah Khomeini's repeated efforts to win them over to Iran's brand of Islamic fundamentalism, not just because they were Sunnis opposed to the ayatollah's militant Shiism.

Kept somehow out of focus were the excesses of Saddam Hussein's megalomaniacal rule, based to an extraordinary degree on his own minority within the ruling Sunni Arab minority. Increasingly over the years it was the members of Saddam Hussein's extended family and clan from his hometown of Tikrit who really ran the show, not the Sunni Arab community as a whole, accounting for perhaps 20 percent of Iraq's population.

Thus were the military and political factors of American policy locked into place long before the shooting war started in mid-January 1991. To the limited extent that Washington planners thought of postwar Iraq at all, they thought in terms of a neat military takeover or, in practical terms, of another Sunni Arab strongman, quite likely from Saddam Hussein's own extended family. A natural disinclination to bring imagination into play in reordering postwar Iraq was magnified because of the eclipse of the State Department, especially its Middle East specialists who normally would have guided policy, in the planning councils.

Emblematic of the State Department's problems was Secretary Baker's singular lack of interest in the Middle East. Preoccupied by Germany's reunification, by the death throes of Communism in Eastern Europe and the Soviet Union, and by negotiations for nuclear-weapons reduction, he had given the Middle East a wide berth until August 2, 1990, and he remained on the sidelines for the first few weeks thereafter. His well-advertised impatience with Israel's truculent Prime Minister Yitzhak Shamir helped to explain this lack of interest in the region, but in any case, Baker, the consummate deal-maker, had little interest in foreign-policy questions except how anything he did about them would "play" in Washington and affect his close friend George Bush. "If you talked to Baker about long-term consequences of German reunification or the ramifications of the breakup of the Soviet Union until the end of the millennium," a senior aide remarked, "his eyes would turn blank. If you dealt with Baker very long, you didn't use that kind of phrase." He reorganized the State Department to express his bent and from the beginning relied heavily on his own small staff, not the specialized bureaus of the State Department.

In another administration the State Department's Bureau of Near Eastern and South Asian Affairs (NEA) would have been at the very center of wartime Washington's policy-making regarding the complex relations between Iraq's Kurds and Shia and the Sunni Arab ascendancy. Under Baker, the bureau scarcely came into play. When Iraq invaded Kuwait, Baker's reaction was one of irritation. He felt that somehow the bureau had let him down, got it wrong, was a loser. April Glaspie, the American ambassador in Iraq, was thrown to the wolves—with the connivance of Baker, his staff, and her immediate boss in the bureau, Assistant Secretary of State John H. Kelly. She was made the scapegoat for a failed policy whose roots long predated her arrival in Baghdad in mid-1988. For Baker's inner circle, the entire bureau became suspect, if not guilty by association. As the senior aide explained, "When you thought of expertise on the Middle East and Iraq, Baker and his staff thought of April Glaspie, and she didn't fit into the category of people who make you look good."

In fact, the American establishment in general and Baker and his inner circle in particular were paying the price for an accumulated lack of intellectual curiosity. Ever since Iran's Islamic revolution overran the American embassy in Tehran in November 1979 and kept its diplomats hostage for 444 days, NEA, successive presidents, and the country at large had been viscerally anti-Iranian. The Bush administration feared the negative political repercussions of anything that might seem to be dealing with the Shia fundamentalist regime in Tehran, and for many Americans fear and loathing of Iran extended to Shia of any description. Never mind that Iraq's Shia under the old monarchy had been so secular that they provided a goodly portion of the Communist Party's rank and file. Khomeini had now made Iran in particular and the Shia in general anathema to ordinary Americans. In American domestic politics there was no such thing as good Shia.

Had not the Iranians hoodwinked Ronald Reagan in the arms-for-hostages scam during their war with Iraq in the mid-1980s? Only Reagan's enormous popularity had saved his presidency from the embarrassment caused by what came to be known as the Iran-contra affair. That hare-brained scheme, revealed in 1986, was organized by the National Security Council, the CIA, and Israel to exchange the American hostages held by Iran's acolytes in Lebanon for U.S. arms and spare parts which Iran needed for its war, and to divert profits (in defiance of a law against this) to finance the contras fighting Nicaragua's Marxist government.

Such tomfoolery could only help Iraq. In Washington veteran foreign-policy specialists were put back in charge of damage control at the National Security Council after the eviction of Vice Admiral John Poindexter and Lieutenant Colonel Oliver North. The administration thought it had something to be forgiven for in Baghdad. Reflagging Kuwait's oil tankers with the Stars and Stripes in 1987 was a clear gesture against Iran, a pro-Iraqi act of expiation. Washington thus resumed its step-by-step slide toward Saddam Hussein. Two years after he invaded Iran in 1980, the United States had abandoned its previous neutrality and given Iraq soft loan credits to buy American farm produce; then in 1983 it began to campaign for an arms embargo against Iran; diplomatic relations with Baghdad were restored in 1984 and the Reagan administration proclaimed its preference for Iraq the following year. Now, in the final stages of the Iran-Iraq war, in common with its major European allies, the Reagan administration tilted still more sharply toward

Baghdad, all in the name of preventing any victory of the Islamic revolution bent on overthrowing moderate, pro-U.S. regimes and attacking Israel. Washington began regularly to supply Iraq with U.S. spy-satellite photographs of Iranian military positions, information used with devastating effectiveness to pinpoint targets in the "war of the cities," a Scud missile onslaught that finally helped to break Iran in the spring of 1988. Even after the end of the Iran-Iraq war in August 1988, the United States singlemindedly backed Iraq as the strongest military force in the Persian Gulf region.

Washington policy-makers convinced themselves that Saddam Hussein would be a bulwark against Iran, which Kuwait, Saudi Arabia, and the other weak Arab oil states needed. The problem was that Saddam Hussein, broke but spending billions on re-equipping his armed forces, did not consider the postwar support he was getting from the United States as encouragement to sweet reason. Instead, he construed it to mean he could get away with seizing Kuwait, if necessary, staring down an America that was unwilling, in his own words, to sacrifice "10,000 lives in one battle" to stop him.

Such bullying was a tried-and-true Saddam Hussein tactic and should not have come as a surprise. Yet no one in the Bush administration apparently thought Saddam Hussein would possibly go back to what he had done with such relish in the 1970s—threatening and shaking down the very same Arab oil states he was now supposed to be shielding with Washington's approval. In fact, he had never really ceased that tactic, for during the war with Iran that he had started without their advice or knowledge, he squeezed them, and once the conflict was over he indignantly refused to reimburse them for these forced loans on the grounds that he had saved them from destruction at Iranian hands.

Still, no one in Washington had any illusions about the totalitarian nature of the Ba'athist regime in Iraq. At issue was using this thuggish regime in Baghdad against another thuggish regime in Tehran. The Iraqi government's horrendous record of human-rights violations and of coercion of other Arab regimes neatly balanced Tehran's equally sorry human-rights record and its proclaimed determination to disgrace the United States and export its militant brand of fundamentalist Islam everywhere. This policy, however justified during the Iran-Iraq conflict, was never revised, even after Khomeini announced he was forced to "drink the cup of poison" and leave Saddam Hussein in power, though this colorful phrase for accepting the August 20, 1988, cease-fire effectively ended his dream of exporting Islamic fundamentalism, the price he had to pay for preserving the Islamic Republic inside Iran.

The end of the Iran-Iraq war did not prompt American policy-makers to give serious consideration to revising U.S. policy on Iraq. God knows Saddam Hussein provided an opening: five days after the cease-fire took effect, in a minutely planned operation Iraqi aircraft and troops used chemical weapons extensively against Iraqi Kurds, sending tens of thousands fleeing across the border into Turkey and killing countless others. The gassing eventually drew a pointed but fleeting rebuke from Secretary of State George P. Shultz. A State Department spokesman denounced this renewed use of chemical weapons as "unjustifiable and abhorrent" and "unacceptable to the civilized world." I was covering the arrival of those terrified refugees in Turkish Kurdistan, and I remember dropping dozens of coins into a miraculously located mountaintop pay telephone to urge a colleague in Washington to tackle the State Department: was not the Kurds' plight a perfect opportunity for the administration to take its distance and adopt a more evenhanded policy on Iraq? (Some years later, when the Middle East equation had changed again, the Clinton administration adopted a "dual containment" policy of keeping both pariah regimes in Baghdad and Tehran at arm's length. Had it been in force in 1988, it might have obviated the Kuwait war, but by the middle 1990s it made little sense and served to complicate further U.S. policy.)

For all the practical good it did I might have saved my breath, although I am glad I said and wrote what I did then. If anything, the end of the war spurred Western governments into a frenzy of sucking up to Saddam Hussein, all in hopes of landing succulent postwar reconstruction contracts. This simpleminded greed skipped over the untidy truth that Iraq owed in excess of $40 billion (some sources said $80 billion), principally to Arab, Soviet, and Western creditors. U.S. exports to Iraq spurted, and in 1989 the Bush administration formally favored giving further assistance to Iraq. Whatever export restraints existed during the war were loosened, as a string of scandals involving sub-rosa arms deliveries by U.S., French, British, and German firms was later to demonstrate.

Within days of the gassing, the U.S. Senate voted overwhelmingly to impose stringent economic sanctions on Iraq for violating

the 1925 Geneva accord banning the use of chemical weapons.*
Human-rights activists began taking up the Kurds' long-ignored
claims that they were indeed victims of genocide. But the Senate's
sanctions bill collapsed because of a jurisdictional fight in Congress:
wheat, rice, and other powerful lobbies doing business with Saddam Hussein had intervened. The administration was only too
happy to find such a lucrative market for American food exports
and showed no outward concern about the wisdom or folly of allowing domestic lobbies to dictate policy toward such a controversial country.

No one in the Republican administration worried that Saddam
Hussein might misinterpret such largesse until years later, when
Iraq's corrupting role in the Atlanta branch of the Banca Nazionale
del Lavoro came to light. And no American official seemed puzzled
as to why billions of dollars of food imports were necessary in what
traditionally was the Arab world's only agriculturally self-sufficient
country. The answer was simple: Iraq's oil revenues—and easy
American credit terms—allowed the Baghdad regime to do without
Kurdistan's rich farming land, now shut down and depopulated to
punish Kurdish civilians and guerrillas alike. The regime was so
genuinely upset at the prospect of losing cheap American financing
that a giant, "spontaneous" protest demonstration was staged outside the U.S. embassy in Baghdad. At the time an Iraqi central
bank source confided that Iraq's foreign-exchange reserves were
so depleted that Baghdad was extremely vulnerable to even short-
term sanctions.

The defeat of the proposed sanctions greatly relieved NEA. It
had never hidden its opposition, fearing, as an old State Department friend put it to me in late 1991, that "the Europeans would
sell more and we would end up with no influence." Sanctions then
would have "only driven Saddam Hussein into doing sooner what
he did" two years later in invading Kuwait, my friend said. "We
thought we had to retain a relationship with Iraq, the dominant
regional military power, bestriding the Gulf like a colossus, to
restrain Saddam Hussein from further military adventures and
avoid accentuating his worst instincts." All in all, it had been "a
very close-run thing"—which had come to grief because "we did
not count on Saddam Hussein's absolute insanity." But hadn't gas-

* The official name is the 1925 Geneva Protocol for the Prohibition of the Use in War
of Asphyxiating, Poisonous or Other Gases.

sing those Kurds—fellow Iraqis and mostly civilians at that—qual-ified as absolute madness? It had happened after the cease-fire and was an unambiguous act of reprisal that could not be written off as a decision taken in the heat of battle.

With the exception of a brief and rapidly repudiated fit of doubt-ing by civilian planners in the spring of 1990, the only official American to judge Saddam Hussein for the bully he was after the 1988 cease-fire was General Schwarzkopf, who in 1991 was to com-mand the coalition armies that liberated Kuwait. In the summer of 1988 this politically savvy general had inherited the U.S. Army's Central Command, set up in 1983 to counter a Soviet threat to the Persian Gulf. He immediately junked as a logistical nightmare the plans dating back to 1947 for having an expeditionary force in northern Iraq. The Cold War was ending anyhow. But Schwarzkopf extracted more assets for his command, accurately assessing that the Iran-Iraq cease-fire had "left Iraq with a million-man army and an economy too weak to absorb the soldiers back into civilian life."

Admittedly, the State Department had condemned the use of poison gas periodically during Iraq's long war with Iran. And alone of Western foreign ministries, it had denounced the August 1988 gassing of Kurds in no uncertain terms, extracting the Iraqi gov-ernment's promise not to use chemical weapons again. But Ba'athist rule in Iraq was strewn with notoriously unkept promises, and in any case the Geneva Convention did not cover the use of chemical weapons *against one's own countrymen.* When Iraq finally agreed to attend a conference organized by Western powers the following January in Paris, which restated the ban on using chemical weap-ons, Baghdad accepted only after France promised that the Kurds could not attend, even as observers.

Saddled with a policy that so thoroughly failed in its aim of restraining Saddam Hussein, by the fall of 1990 NEA was also suffering from the most debilitating organizational crisis in its his-tory. Of the handful of trusted aides with whom Baker ran the State Department, none was more important than Dennis Ross, a Reagan administration political appointee now in charge of the Policy Planning Staff, the State Department's in-house think tank, traditionally considered less prestigious or powerful than the line bureaus. But under Baker formal titles meant little. Ross exercised particular clout because of his easy access to Bush, whose foreign-policy adviser he had been during the 1988 election campaign. A neoconservative who did not hide his pro-Israel bent, Ross was determined to clip the wings of NEA, traditionally one of the State Department's star performers.

By the time Baker and company got through with it, NEA resembled a Rube Goldberg contraption. The contentious Arab-Israeli question was handled by Daniel Kurtzer, an able diplomat with past postings in Cairo and Tel Aviv. But as a deputy assistant secretary of the bureau, Kurtzer oddly answered not to its own chief but directly to the director of Policy Planning. Relations among the twenty nations of the Arab world were left to the bureau. But, adding insult to injury, Baker put John Kelly in charge of it, by common agreement the most divisive and ineffective boss ever to head NEA. In the past the post had gone to Arabists with long field experience such as his immediate predecessor, Richard Murphy, to area specialists such as Alfred Leroy Atherton, or to master practitioners of Washington bureaucratic turf fights such as Joseph Sisco. But Kelly's only Middle East experience had been as ambassador to Lebanon, or rather to Marounistan, the truncated Christian enclave that alone was deemed safe for American diplomats during his tour in the mid-1980s. Abrasive, arrogant, and thoroughly detested by his peers in the field as well as by his Washington staff, Kelly managed to demoralize what had long been the State Department's most close-knit and bureaucratically effective bureau. Never before in its often-contested history had Near Eastern Affairs—and its Arabists, relentlessly denounced by the Israeli lobby—been so emasculated. It was a Zionist lobbyist's dream, and it ended up as a prescription for disaster.

With the invasion of Kuwait, a discredited and dispirited NEA hunkered down, showing little disposition to conduct the kind of detailed self-examination calculated to generate new ideas from the ruins of its disgraced policy. "NEA was simply too bruised to speak out," recalled an American diplomat then in the thick of the planning, "and no one asked" for its advice. Outside their purely military aspects, administration policy decisions, the diplomat added, were made entirely by the White House and the National Security Council, which with Haass was devoid of seasoned or senior Middle East expertise.

All these factors and failings cut little ice with critics of the State Department and other Western foreign ministries, or with Kurds. They were convinced that these Arabists were solely concerned with preserving influence and lucrative contracts in an oil-rich region and had long favored authoritarian Arab regimes, even those with the most reprehensible human-rights records. Who, after all, provided the ingredients and technical know-how, often even the engineers and technicians, for Iraq's chemical war factories, whose products had killed so many Kurds? Kurds read European newspapers and could and did quote chapter and verse about the European firms caught red-handed in this dubious trade, long tolerated by their governments. At the heart of the embittered criticism was a belief that the West's Arabists were willfully ignorant and/or morally myopic, and not just because the totalitarian nature of much of Middle East governance complicated their quintessential diplomatic task: getting to know people in and out of public office. Western officials, the critics argued, tended to suck up to the rulers, quite apart from the admitted difficulty of keeping in touch with the ruled.

In their defense, American diplomats were latecomers to Ba'athist Iraq.* Diplomatic relations between Iraq and the United States had been severed in 1967–84, with only a small American interests section represented in Baghdad. Indeed long before Saddam Hussein invaded Kuwait his police state was so well entrenched, foreign diplomats so isolated, and the population so intimidated that the American embassy, and any other diplomatic mission for that matter, lacked real knowledge of either the rulers or the ruled. Former ambassador David Newton said, "We worked on intuition, with very few sources. We never really knew what was going on. There were only the rumors, what we called the soul-telegraph." It was as if the nightmare of the fall of the Persian monarchy, which had exposed the administration's ignorance of the opposition in Iran, was being played out again. In both cases Western specialists were taxed with accepting at face value the "modernist" image and "reformist" intellectual rationales churned out by the propaganda machines of the likes of Saddam Hussein or the Shah of Iran.

In that they differed little from their predecessors of an earlier generation, who had wholeheartedly backed Ataturk in Turkey and Reza Shah in Iran between the two world wars, two autocratic military men who justified their seizure of power in the name of "modernizing" ancient lands along the highly centralized lines of

---

* However, the United States and Great Britain were long suspected of having favored the original Ba'ath coup d'état in 1963 and the putsch in 1968, for the ostensible reason that Ba'athists in both periods opposed the Communists and pro-Nasserites contending for power.

a European nationalism marked by the intolerant Jacobin tradition of the French Revolution. Both regimes gave their numerous minorities short shrift. Before the invasion of Kuwait, the Kurds and other parts of the Iraqi opposition thought that Western Arabists did not take them seriously. After the invasion, the American Arabists were in disgrace and not at the vital center of U.S. policymaking.

Academic members of the "modernist" schools, such as Marr and Christine Moss Helms, who in the past had praised Baghdad's Ba'athists, were among those the administration—and Bush himself—consulted about what should be done in Iraq after Kuwait's liberation. Predictably, they favored keeping the regime in place, albeit without Saddam Hussein, for fear that the entire country would implode if any redistribution of power were attempted —a tidy outcome, designed to maintain the Sunni Arab ascendancy under a malleable general of similar lineage, possibly one of Saddam Hussein's Tikriti relatives. But after so much horror and so many years of totalitarian rule, only on paper did this failed formula look like a durable solution. It paid no mind to the ever-increasing violence underpinning the very entity of Iraq, itself an artificial state that the British had cobbled together after World War I from three distinct Ottoman vilayets, or governorates—predominantly Kurdish Mosul, with its oil; Basra, the fief of the new country's Shia majority; and Baghdad, the capital and center of the ruling Sunni Arab minority. And not only the dismantling of the Ba'athist state was off limits: in January 1991 the American diplomat in the London embassy entrusted with keeping tabs on the Middle East had her knuckles rapped for even trying to see a visiting Kurdish nationalist leader.

Even if NEA had been in better order and odor, could it have questioned its ability to influence events? As early as September 1990, Bush was ill disposed to anything that swerved away from his increasing determination to go to war. Such was Bush's own "wimp problem," his driving need to assert himself in what one insider called "the White House locker-room style." Equally unwelcome were suggestions that the liberation of Kuwait might help to make Iraq a less terrorized society, might encourage a more equitable distribution of power among its constituent peoples. In Washington the watchword seemed to be "Better ignorance than a surfeit of confusing detail." Bush locked himself into a narrow military solution, pretty much on Powell's terms predicated on

force. (Ironically, the overwhelming size and firepower of the coalition force that Powell assembled only increased the astounded
world's questions about the administration's foot-dragging reaction
to the uprisings in Iraq.) Diplomacy's job was to get as many countries as possible allied as quickly as possible. Baker astounded his
own staff—and a doubting world. He used the relationship he had
developed with Soviet Foreign Minister Eduard Shevardnadze on
European security questions to deprive Saddam Hussein of the
Russian support he had assumed would be automatic. That mas-
terstroke helped Baker stitch together a coalition with U.N. blessing, supplementing his own extraordinary deal-making skill with
Bush's subtler and deeper understanding of international politics.

But in the hallowed tradition of coalitions, this one too functioned
on the basis of the lowest common denominator. For example, the
United States needed Egypt and France on the team, the former
because the participation of the most populous Arab country demonstrated that the coalition was not just another Western crusade
against a Muslim state, the latter because Saddam Hussein was
trying to win over a key Western country that worried about the
repercussions of the war on its emotionally pro-Baghdad former
colonies just across the Mediterranean in Muslim North Africa.
For fear of exacerbating the already vocal Arab nationalists, neither
Cairo nor Paris wanted the coalition army to push all the way to
Baghdad and remove an Arab head of state, no matter how de-
testable. That, in turn, also suited Washington.

For all Bush's talk comparing Saddam Hussein to Hitler and
endorsing democracy in the Middle East, he was wary of tinkering
with established Sunni Arab minority rule. Without the sidelined
NEA's active participation, his administration lacked the know-
how to establish a new government framework in Baghdad even if
it had been tempted to do so. But doing nothing could—and indeed
did—produce predictable disaster. It was left to a retired Kurdish
specialist, William Eagleton, to keep impressing on former colleagues in NEA the dangers of leaving the military job half done
with Saddam Hussein and the Ba'ath regime still in place. Long
before Bush abruptly stopped the ground fighting after a hundred
hours, Eagleton had seen the catastrophe coming. He realized that
Saddam Hussein had not committed to battle all his elite Republican Guard units, two dozen regular divisions, or the multifarious
secret-police apparatus, the very forces he had always used to
remain in power. Eagleton had the courage to keep reminding his

NEA colleagues of this. After Washington's decision to end the ground fighting on February 28 predictably led to disaster for the Kurds and the Shia, a senior Pentagon official summed up the price for leaving Saddam Hussein in place: "He did not pose a threat to us. We didn't factor in the threat to his own people."

Part of the Republican administration's reasoning showed the usual Washington interpretation of Middle Eastern geopolitics, especially of its principal gulf ally, Saudi Arabia. It was convinced that the rigidly Sunni monarchy in Saudi Arabia loathed the very concept of one-man one-vote democracy, and feared that Iraq's Shia majority automatically would produce a carbon copy of Iran's Islamic Republic, the world's only predominantly Shia state. Such arithmetical political calculations ignored the Iraqi Arab Shia's historical tradition of independence from Iran and their unflinching loyalty to Baghdad during the 1980–88 war. But the Saudi royal family, sitting on the world's largest oil reserves in what had been Shia tribal land in the Eastern Province, was against taking chances. It had been not to liberate Kuwait but to protect Saudi oil that Bush had originally dispatched American forces to the Persian Gulf in August 1990. (For that matter Iran, Kuwait, Saudi Arabia, and indeed most other governments in the region shared a repugnance for democratic government.) Such was the conventional thinking.

In the months before the liberation of Kuwait, Britain, France, and the United States separately conducted studies. Curiously, none supposed that Saddam Hussein would survive a war and go back to oppressing the Shia majority and the Kurds. The conclusions were an exercise in wish fulfillment, since no one wanted to do the dirty work in any case. The prevailing hope, and not just in Washington, was, in Marr's words, "If we got lucky the Iraqi army would go to Baghdad and kill Saddam Hussein." Yet all three Western governments also calculated that if Saddam Hussein survived the liberation of Kuwait, he would represent a diminished rampart against Iran, but a useful rampart nonetheless.

Such fuzzy thinking implicitly assumed two seemingly diametrically opposed outcomes: that Saddam Hussein would be cut down to size yet survive; or that he would be overthrown during turmoil involving the Shia and Kurds, but that Sunni Arabs commanding the military would triumph over both him and the rebels. The only point in common in such *Kriegspiel* was a belief in the need to maintain minority Arab Sunni power. The unspoken predicate of all this was an unsubstantiated conviction that Iraq was such an artificial construct and had suffered so much from the Sunni Arabs that it would fall apart if the majority Shia or Sunni Kurds got a fair shake in governing. But this was not necessarily foreordained, and the unknown had not been tested. In light of Iraq's miserable record as a state over seventy years, a determination to keep it in one piece suggested a slavish devotion to unrealistic but recognized international borders, a perceived need for a military counterweight to Iran, even when it was badly war-weakened, and a knee-jerk desire to please Iraq's neighbors.

Iran, Syria, and Turkey kept proclaiming their devotion to Iraq's sovereignty and territorial integrity, but these were diplomatic code words for their opposition to anything suggesting sympathy for Kurdish independence—and that included the genuine autonomy Saddam Hussein had promised the Kurds in 1970. There was nothing new here: the proclamations were replays of the Saadabad Pact, concluded at a Tehran palace of that name in 1937, which pledged Afghanistan, Iran, Iraq, and Turkey to cooperate in putting down subversion. Except for Afghanistan, the other contracting parties' abiding concern was Kurdish nationalism, a disease that was considered highly contagious and thus especially suspect to the highly centralized states they were then forging in the West's modernizing image. A generation later the same concerns were addressed, this time with overt Western backing, in the Baghdad Pact in the 1950s, renamed the Central Treaty Organization (or CENTO) after Iraq dropped out in 1958.

The Bush administration's civilian policy-makers decreed it as an article of faith that the Iraqi opposition represented no more than aging marionettes manipulated by Iran and Syria. True, Syria's ties with the Iraqi opposition were long-standing, and so, too, were Iran's, albeit with rival groups. (Saudi Arabian officials were so out of touch that at one point in the fall of 1990 they bandied about the names of Iraqi opposition figures long since dead.) Iran was of course not to be trusted, and Syria was not in good odor in Washington, despite its participation in the coalition, for the stiff-necked Syrian president, Hafiz al-Assad, had opposed American-blessed policies ranging from the Israeli-Lebanese separate peace in the mid-1980s to Washington's condemnation of his country as a state supporting terrorism. The Bush administration also constantly worried that Iraq's neighbors would misinterpret American contacts with the opposition as a pretext to leave the coalition.

What really counted for Bush was Turkey, Washington's only NATO ally in the Middle East. During many regimes and administrations in Ankara and Washington over four decades, humoring Turkey was an often-delicate enterprise, and the United States now did its utmost to avoid giving the impression of favoring Kurdish aspirations of any kind anywhere. With the end of its Cold War function as protector of NATO's southern flank against the Soviet Union, Turkey had worried about its future usefulness to its Western partners. The occupation of Kuwait was a new, godsent mission but, unhappily for Ankara, the conflict focused attention on its own Kurdish problem, for so long a taboo. For nearly forty years its NATO partners had closed their eyes to human-rights abuses and other shortcomings in Turkish democratic practices, especially in Turkish Kurdistan. And starting with the foundation of the Turkish Republic in 1923, Ankara had purposely avoided meaningful contacts with the Iraqi Kurds for fear of encouraging Turkey's own large Kurdish minority. Turkey had had a burgeoning civil war on its hands against its own Kurds since 1984; it now awkwardly found itself without contacts with the Iraqi Kurds or the rest of the Iraqi opposition and at a decided disadvantage compared with Iran and Syria.

But President Özal in his own way was just as iconoclastic as Ataturk himself. Despite Ataturk's carefully nurtured distaste for close contacts with non-European powers, Özal entered into lucrative economic relations with both Iran and Iraq during their war. Starting in 1982 Saddam Hussein, his own troops tied down facing Iran, allowed Turkish forces to carry out hot pursuit against rebel Turkish Kurds who were using the border area of northern Iraq as a sanctuary in their own war against Ankara. Yet Turkey was notoriously suspicious of the slightest foreign interest in its Kurds. Their very identity was denied, to the point that for decades they were known officially as "mountain Turks," much to general amusement in the Middle East.*

Indeed, so sensitive was it about foreigners' contacts with Kurds

---

* When in the 1960s Turkey complained to Egypt's president, Gamal Abdel Nasser, about Kurdish-language broadcasts on Cairo's Voice of the Arabs radio, then listened to avidly all over the Middle East, Nasser cut short the diplomatic demarche by asking the diplomat, "But are there any Kurds in your country?" Assured there were none officially, Nasser replied, "Then what are you complaining about?"

of any provenance that the government complained when a middle-level State Department official in June 1988 received Talabani to hear his complaints about Saddam Hussein's gassing of Halabjah. The meeting was designed to send Iraq a message of strong U.S. displeasure about the use of chemical weapons, and a vituperative denunciation was expected. But the official was both unwise and unlucky: Talabani, a well-known and self-admitted blabbermouth, lost no time in talking to the press. (His volubility was understandable, in light of the State Department's deliberate policy of stringently restricting visas for Kurdish leaders.*) Worse still, the official had not realized that Turkish president Kenan Evren was also in Washington. Evren as a matter of course took umbrage.

So, too, did then–Secretary of State Shultz. He hated to be blindsided, especially over an issue involving a NATO ally. In his anger he disavowed the State Department official and the meeting with Talabani. What was meant as a carefully calibrated diplomatic signal to Iraq backfired, and, to boot, Baghdad in August again used massive amounts of poison gas against Kurdish guerrillas and civilians. Some State Department hands were convinced that this incident helped to persuade Saddam Hussein that he could get away with most anything—including, just fourteen months later, his invasion and occupation of Kuwait.

The Turkish grousing certainly was noted at the State Department. "It was always controversial to have official contacts with Kurds," as an American diplomat later said, "and now no one was tempted to do so, even when circumstances changed radically." During the Kuwait crisis key Kurdish and other intelligence sources in London were so confused by the State Department's behavior that they accredited rumors of a supposed 1988 presidential executive order empowering intelligence agents as the only American officials allowed to talk to the Iraqi opposition.

In August 1990, once Saudi Arabia accepted the presence of U.S. troops on its soil, at President Özal's instigation Turkey became the first regional country to join the American-led coalition

---

* Kurdish leaders were so unwelcome that some of the United States' most diplomatically sensitive embassies, such as Damascus, a city where Iraqi Kurds and other opposition forces kept offices, refused to deal with them. NEA officials kept insisting that this "no contact" policy did not exist, but in fact their claims to study each request for a meeting on a "case-by-case basis" amounted to the same thing. Kurdish leaders passing through Paris were reduced to calling on the likes of the author even to get a foot in the U.S. embassy door, much less to obtain visas to the U.S. to explain their case in Washington.

against Saddam Hussein. And—a crucial decision—he promptly shut down the giant pipeline carrying Iraqi crude oil across Turkey to the Mediterranean. Although Turkey eventually would have been obliged to go along with U.N. economic sanctions against Iraq in any case, his timing helped Washington mightily in its coalition-building efforts. Özal insisted on the dispatch of token NATO air-defense units to Turkey, moved Turkey's army units facing the Soviet Union to the Iraqi border, and allowed U.S. Air Force planes to use Incirlik for bombing raids against Iraq. He even favored sending Turkish units to Saudi Arabia to take part in the land war, and was only stopped by the all-powerful Turkish General Staff. Thus did he deliberately run roughshod over the Turkish civilian and military establishment's sacrosanct refusal to get involved in the former Arab provinces of the former Ottoman Empire. Into the garbage can of history as well went Ataturk's injunction of neutrality in the Middle East: "Peace at home, peace with the world." That was a sentiment many Turks rendered in an earthy phrase—"Arab hair"—contemptuously dismissing their southern neighbors' allegedly complicated ways.

Yet while Washington was bending over backward to avoid any contact with Iraqi Kurds for fear of angering Turkey, Özal was pondering the establishment of links with them himself. At no point did any Western government consider that the same Özal who had violated Ataturk's sacred rules for the coalition's benefit might also be capable of breaking the taboo of dealing with Kurds. But that was exactly what he did.

Özal was nothing if not logical. From the very beginning of the Kuwait crisis, he said publicly that Saddam Hussein had to be overthrown. As Iraq's only neighbor without ties with Iraqi opposition groups, Turkey could ill afford to copy Washington's aloof disdain and remain uninformed about Iraqi politics: an Iraq without Saddam Hussein opened up too many possibilities. An obvious corollary was that Turkey was best served by being on good terms with whoever controlled the 206-mile border: that would likely mean the Iraqi Kurds, more especially Massoud Barzani and his Kurdistan Democratic Party. That meant meeting the Iraqi Kurdish leadership.

At the end of January 1991, I became quite inadvertently involved in Özal's iconoclastic decision. Özal was infamous for granting quarter-hour interviews to one journalist after another, an assembly-line technique guaranteeing that he did all the talking and suited less for eliciting solid information than for producing the presidential one-liners that so delighted the Turkish press. During one such frustrating quickie interview, I nonetheless managed to get in a question: I asked Özal why he kept saying that Turkey would not abide an independent Kurdish state in northern Iraq. I'd just returned from Damascus, where Talabani and other Iraqi Kurds angrily denied they had any such intention, insisting they knew that autonomy within a democratic Iraq was the best they could hope for. If the Iraqi Kurds had their autonomy accepted by a post-Saddam central government in Baghdad, managed a tight ship, and effectively sealed the border, I asked Özal, why should he oppose such an outcome? Özal answered me with a vague remark about a federation with the Iraqi Kurds, but my allotted time was soon up and I went away disappointed.

The next day Kaya Toperi, Özal's spokesman and the Turkish Foreign Ministry's former press chief, sought me out and paid me the nicest compliment a reporter could ask for: "Your questions were more interesting than the President's answers," he said. "Do you think we should talk to the Iraqi Kurds?" I protested that I was a reporter, not a diplomat. I was all too aware that even a rational old friend like Toperi was not totally immune to entrenched Middle East suspicions about foreign correspondents' "real employers" among the hooded fraternity. Noncommittally I suggested such a meeting might not do much harm and indeed might do some good. Back in Europe just long enough to change planes for Tehran, I left a message outlining Toperi's remarks on the answering machine of an Iraqi Kurdish representative in London. The main reason Barzani received me in the mountains at Rayan a week later was to reiterate his party's record of having kept the Iraqi-Turkish border trouble-free all the way back to his father's uprising in 1961.

Whether Özal acted after reading Barzani's truncated remarks published in *The Washington Post* is debatable. (Even so, in the wake of Özal's own disclosure on March 11 of a meeting with the Kurds, Turkish newspapers, notoriously loose with the facts, suggested that an American journalist with links to the CIA had played a major role in the affair. Luckily for me, my name was not mentioned.) But a fortnight later, with the ground war still more than a week off, he set in motion a train of events with two other journalists which led to an invitation to Iraqi Kurdish leaders that they secretly visit Ankara. Özal was well prepared for the meeting. Long before the Iraqi Kurds arrived in Ankara he had ordered the Foreign Ministry and Toperi to dig out relevant material from the state archives. He later confided: "I read three hundred to four hundred pages, material from novels, Ottoman archives, League of Nations debates, the Lausanne Treaty." This last, as I have said, at Ataturk's dictation made no mention of the Kurds, casting them into their long official limbo.

One of the reporters was Genciz Çandar, a Turk well versed in the Arab world from his days in Beirut during the 1970s. Soon after the occupation of Kuwait, Özal and Çandar, who had not known each other previously, started meeting frequently. The president confided to Çandar that he seemed to have an uncanny gift for writing "things I have not yet been thinking about." Specifically, they saw eye to eye about the need to shuck off the sacrosanct but ossified weight of Ataturk's heritage, solve Turkey's own Kurdish problem, and revamp its stagnant relations with its Arab neighbors.

Çandar also had an eye for a scoop built around Saddam Hussein's likely successors in Baghdad, and that meant talking to the Iraqi Kurds. Largely because President Özal did not trust the Foreign Ministry's purist devotion to Ataturk dogma, Çandar got his blessing to sound out Iraqi Kurds in London about coming to Ankara to discuss the future. And this oldest of tricks in the reporting game worked. Çandar knew no one in London, but on February 16 he talked his way into a meeting with the Iraqi opposition leader Ahmad Chalabi, an exiled Shia banker and tried-and-true friend of the Kurds since his youth in the 1970s, when he had helped General Barzani buy arms.

When Çandar mentioned Özal to Chalabi, Chalabi telephoned Talabani, who happened to be in London. The next day Çandar met Talabani and Barzani's London representative, Mohsin Dizai. Since Talabani's disappointing visit to Washington the previous August, the Kurdish leaders were so sure of Turkish opposition to them that they had disregarded suggestions that they should approach Özal. But with the ground war about to start, Talabani and Dizai now signaled an interest in visiting Turkey.

This change did not come as a surprise. Only the night before Talabani had been telephoned from Istanbul by Kamran Karadaghi, an Iraqi Kurd and foreign editor of *Al Hayat*, a Saudi-owned newspaper in London, who had just emerged from an extraordinary ninety-minute interview with President Özal. To his amazement

Özal had asked a barrage of questions, listened patiently, and talked little, taking advantage of Karadaghi's firsthand knowledge to inquire in great detail about the Iraqi Kurds, their leaders, and who was where on a map of Iraqi Kurdistan that he produced for the occasion. Özal expressed astonishment that Iraqi Kurds were allowed to use their language, publish in Kurdish, and have a university of their own.

"Please, please, please, tell the Iraqi Kurds that they must trust me," Özal told Karadaghi, arguing that Turkey could become the Iraqi Kurds' protector. Özal also let slip that his grandmother was Kurdish, and volunteered that he planned soon to junk Turkey's "very bad laws" banning the use of the Kurdish language, which he had inherited from the military regime of 1980–83. When Özal asked about the Iraqi Kurds' relationship with the Turkish Kurd insurgents of the Kurdistan Workers Party (the PKK), Karadaghi, acting on his own initiative, replied, "Mr. President, why don't you meet with the *pesh merga* leaders? I'm sure they would like to meet you directly."

Özal said nothing, but with Çandar's initiative doubtless in mind, he looked knowingly at Toperi, who was taking notes. All but the most pedestrian parts of the interview dealing with the Kurds had been off the record. Karadaghi had interviewed Özal once before, in October, and had recommended then that the Kurdish leaders approach the Turks, but they had done nothing, convinced that Turkey was a hopelessly implacable adversary. When this second interview ended, Karadaghi went straight back to his hotel and telephoned Talabani in London. "I've asked Özal to establish contact with you. Do you approve?" Talabani did indeed. He told Karadaghi to tell Özal officially that he and Barzani (or, as it turned out, Barzani's trusted Mohsin Dizai) wanted to meet the government. Early the next morning Karadaghi telephoned Toperi to pass on this message before he flew back to London, but Toperi was out, and what amounted to the first official Kurdish written communication with a Turkish government in seven decades was simply a short note in English that Karadaghi left for Toperi in an envelope marked "private and confidential."

Within a week, Toperi confirmed with Karadaghi that the Turkish government wanted to meet the Iraqi Kurds, possibly in London or Stockholm but in any case before March 11, when Özal was to visit Moscow. Both sides finally settled on a March 8 and 9 meeting in Ankara. The Iraqi Kurds arguably should have pressed for an immediate meeting, to enlist Özal's help in gaining access in Washington, since the American imprimatur was essential for the international community's acceptance. Had they moved faster, they might have met before the uprising started on March 5, and much subsequent misunderstanding and suffering would have been avoided. Instead Talabani went first to Washington, where he hoped to persuade the Americans to lift the ban and thus open communications with Ankara. Predictably, he was snubbed once again.

Predictably, too, the Kurds once again had picked up the wrong end of the stick. The Kurdish leaders never considered starting their uprising in Kurdistan while the late February ground fighting was still going on, though such a daring approach, a veteran American diplomat speculated, might have worked to their advantage. "Iraqi troops would have been on the move against the Kurds in the open and thus considered fair game by Schwarzkopf," he conjectured. "He would have needed no higher headquarters' approval; the U.S. Air Force was gung ho and would have been delighted to do the job." It all might have clicked, he said, "if the Kurds had only known how we worked." American refusal to deal with the Kurds had precluded such an outcome, of course. Thus was forfeited the potential for bringing about dramatic change in Iraq.

Absent such dramatic events, the Bush administration remained wedded to its outdated certainties, and this despite a last-minute alarm. Sensing what was in the Ankara air, Ambassador Abramowitz cabled the State Department to suggest the time had come to talk to the Iraqi Kurds, especially if they were part of an overall opposition delegation, and, of course, only after first so informing Turkey. His State Department interlocutors "laughed and asked what had gotten into me," he later recalled, noting that in the past he had vehemently opposed such contacts for fear of angering Turkey. This lack of responsiveness was one more contributing factor in Washington's dilatory response to the unfolding crisis.

Neither Turks nor Iraqi Kurds had an inkling that the uprising was about to collapse when on March 9 and 10 in Ankara Talabani and Dizai were received by Tungay Uzçeri, the Foreign Ministry's undersecretary, at a guest house belonging to the MIT, Turkey's intelligence organization. Uzçeri realized the "sense of the occasion" as he listened to the Kurdish leaders jubilantly recount the latest *pesh merga* gains in Iraq, outline how future cooperation with Turkey could work, and plead for humanitarian aid and arms. They also wanted Turkey's help in the international community, most especially in persuading the United States to reverse its ban and deal with them. Breaking Ataturk's ancient taboo seemed to make sense, now that the Cold War was at an end and the Turks were talking to their other ancient foes in Armenia. Uzçeri agreed with Özal's advice to his largely unconvinced fellow diplomats at the hidebound Foreign Ministry: "You should come out of your cocoon at a time when everyone is talking to everyone."

After Uzçeri's first encounter with the Kurds, Özal convened a meeting of his inner cabinet and the chief of the Turkish General Staff to report on the noncontroversial substance. He made the others speak first, helping to ensure their approval of the initiative, and he disarmed ultranationalist critics, arguing that Turkey had just as legitimate an interest in protecting its own Kurds' threatened kin in Iraq as it did in protecting Turkish minorities in Bulgaria and Cyprus. Nonetheless, when Özal publicly revealed what he had done, the Turkish establishment and press expressed horror. Yet within weeks Özal was openly receiving Iraqi Kurdish leaders, and so indeed were other Turkish government and opposition politicians. Özal was also true to his word in promptly recommending that the Bush administration talk to the Kurds.

For all his prescience, not even Abramowitz detected the exact steps of Özal's fast footwork. Somewhat peeved that Özal had not filled him in beforehand, he learned of the meeting with Dizai and Talabani from a Turkish newspaper. To all intents and purposes the State Department could not have cared less. Its reaction paralleled the Pentagon's own lack of interest in the tactical military intelligence the Kurds had provided during the war. As a result, the Kurds first sent this new information to a Kurdish-American dentist in Michigan, who relayed it to Peter Galbraith at the Senate, who in turn informed the Pentagon.

———

On February 28, the day the war in Kuwait abruptly ended, American officials refused to receive a delegation of Kurdish leaders who were in Washington. Invited by Senator Claiborne Pell, the Rhode Island Democrat and then chairman of the Senate Committee on Foreign Relations, the opposition leaders in formal and informal discussions spelled out the imminent likelihood of a mass uprising, emphasizing the depth of anti-Saddam and pro-American sentiment in Iraq. No ranking administration official wanted to listen. Even Richard Schifter, Assistant Secretary of State for Humanitarian Affairs, at the last minute backed out of a previously arranged meeting. When three Kurdish delegates showed up in the State Department lobby for their date, they were met by an underling who, in the standard American diplomatic show of disrespect to which the Kurds were accustomed, offered to meet them for coffee, but only outside the building. In the past, NEA officials had at least allowed that Baghdad's human-rights record warranted consultation with them and palmed them off on someone from Schifter's shop. The new message of contempt could not have been clearer.

In the executive branch, only Zalway Khaledzeh, a policy-planning official at the Pentagon, challenged the status quo. During the dissidents' Washington visit one of his staffers met the Kurds at the Brookings Institution and tentatively arranged to meet with them. Reminded that NEA's approval was required, he asked for the authorization, only to have his request turned down. "Whatever the justifications were for such a policy before Kuwait was liberated, I couldn't believe the restrictions should continue to apply after the war," he said. "I was in total shock."

When the uprisings began only days later in Kurdistan and the south, the consequences of such political myopia became evident. A member of the National Security Council said on March 1, "Our policy is to get rid of Saddam Hussein, not his regime." That apparently was the sum total of Washington's endgame in Iraq. In the event, this policy ensured that Iraqis and the international community were saddled with Saddam Hussein *and* his regime for the foreseeable future. And the State Department's public snub helped to discourage the formation of the very military regime the NSC seemed to favor. Iraqi military leaders who might have been tempted to move against Saddam Hussein had no real knowledge of what Washington wanted. Such is the hermetic nature of totalitarian regimes: potential military opponents needed a clear signal of support from the leader of the anti-Iraq coalition in Washington. As the uprising began spreading, the Iraqi military figures who had put out feelers to the opposition soon thought better of it when Washington's manifest lack of interest became apparent.

This refusal to deal with the Iraqi opposition soon produced a cascade of practical problems, all the more daunting in that the Americans had deliberately not wanted to foresee them. For a month they watched from afar, as if events in Iraq somehow did not and would not concern them. Only in April, when Kurds by the hundreds were expiring in the mountains, did the alarm sound. Then the fastest-growing refugee crisis in contemporary history caught them off guard. In the early days of April, "Washington was in total confusion," said Frederick Cuny. "No one at the State Department knew what to do and everyone thought somebody else was tagged with responsibility."

Cuny was not surprised. A maverick free-lance disaster specialist from Texas whose brash and innovative ways had frightened gray bureaucrats for decades, he had laid out for the State Department's Bureau of Refugee Affairs in December the likely scenario: a massive, spontaneous Kurdish uprising, a massive Kurdish defeat, and a massive Kurdish exodus. He was then advising the Kuwaiti government-in-exile about what to do—and especially what not to do—after Kuwait's liberation. The State Department bureaucrats listened to his prognosis but took no action: contingency planning for an ethnic group like the Kurds could be construed as favoring a revolt on their part and the breakup of Iraq. Long before he took on his Kuwait assignment, Cuny was belittled behind his back, and he kept on making a good living while waiting for his disaster scenarios, systematically disdained by the establishment, to come true.

Nonetheless the bureaucrats were genuinely taken aback by the speed and scope of the uprising in Kurdistan and in Iraq's Shia south (where U.S. troops actually stood by as Iraqi army units moved to put down the rebellion). The State Department had expected no more than 50,000 to 100,000 Iraqi refugees, and by its own admission it had not anticipated widespread strife, much less a gigantic exodus. Unsurprisingly, given their ban on talking to the opposition, administration planners kept referring in later discussions to how hazy the information had been on which they based their erroneous assumptions.

"We were surprised that city dwellers joined the exodus," said one academic, remembering that in 1975 few urban Kurds had joined the general exodus to Iran and evidently forgetting Saddam Hussein's subsequent systematic destruction of traditional Kurdish rural society. For all intents and purposes, all Kurds were urban, either living in cities or forced to inhabit jerry-built housing complexes located on main roads for easy surveillance. And all Kurds feared Saddam Hussein would wreak vengeance with chemical weapons. After all, he had done just that in 1988. One State Department official frankly acknowledged, "We didn't know diddly."

As so often during the 1980s, it was desperation that forced a hard-pressed administration to overcome its qualms and ever so reluctantly hire Cuny to deal with the Kurdish mess. Landing in Kurdistan in mid-April, even Cuny was astounded by the "crass ignorance" of American civilian and military officials. "No one had the foggiest idea of whom to talk to and no one even knew who the Kurds were," Cuny recalled. When Major General Jay M. Garner arrived to assume command of coalition forces within Iraq and asked for a briefing, no one could answer his questions about the Kurdish nationalist movement, its leaders, organization, and aspirations. "The briefing book was a joke, with party leaders and their affiliations mixed up," Cuny recalled, "and it was still inaccurate two months later." In a way, the Republicans had only themselves to blame: the Reagan administration had weeded out the specialists on such out-of-the-way places as Kurdistan. Thanks to the British government's links to the Iraqi opposition, the Royal Marines sent along Arabic-speaking officers and a high-level official with intimate knowledge of the *pesh merga* and Kurdish tribal structure and mores. The Dutch Marines were accompanied by young Kurds who had been granted asylum in the Netherlands over the years and now served in Dutch uniform as guides and interpreters.

Politically the administration's easy assumptions about the Middle East were skewed partly because of ambiguous, confused signals in Washington. For example, in public at least, the Saudi kingdom went through the formal motion of playing down its traditional fears of democracy and of Shia subversion. Key Shia religious elements in the Iraqi opposition, notably the Dawa, had assured them that they had no troublemaking designs on the Eastern Province oil fields. During the uprising itself, "Saudi officials proposed that the U.S. and Saudi Arabia together militarily assist both the Shia and Kurdish rebels," a Senate report noted, a proposal related to a presidential intelligence "finding," just before the fighting started in January, that pledged aid to the Iraqi opposition.

The administration hedged its bets. "This time the Saudis and the Kuwaitis were the paymasters and in the end they came to fear" that regional instability could be the fate of not just Iraq but Iran, Syria, and Turkey as well, one knowledgeable intelligence officer said. "And so they chose not to continue." The Saudis must have asked themselves what Washington's intentions were, since by late March the administration had failed to answer about the proposed military aid. Yet in the third week of March the Saudis summoned Hoshyar Zibari, a key Barzani aide, to Riyadh, and were making suggestions about full-blown cooperation. Then Brent Scowcroft and Richard Haass, his Middle East specialist, unexpectedly flew in from Washington on what was meant to be a secret mission. The Saudis got the point, and so did the Kurds. After Scowcroft and Haass left, Zibari was abruptly handed an airline ticket back to London and told there was no reason for him to stay longer.

The Scowcroft mission, dispatched to the Middle East right after Bush met with seven senior advisers on March 26, sealed the doom of the Kurdish uprising. Everyone acknowledged the Iraqis' defiance of the warnings not to use helicopter gunships to fight the Kurdish rebels, and it was decided to do nothing to stop them. The insurrection in the south was already crushed, in part because of coalition inaction. With Republican Guards, helicopters, regular army troops, and armor of Saddam Hussein's Iranian vassals in the anti-Tehran Mujahedin Khalq all bearing down on Kirkuk, this slow-motion decision-making finally jelled: the Kurds had few effective antitank and antiaircraft weapons and no adequate command and control (military jargon for effective mastery of their forces). In such circumstances, administration spokesmen argued, satisfying the ever more shrill Kurdish requests to shoot down gunships would be "empty symbolism" and might suck the United States and its partners into an endless commitment. "We never made any promises to these people," said one official after the crucial meeting, again deliberately overlooking Bush's own appeal and its clear implications. "There is no interest in the coalition in further military operations." Of course, the longer the coalition did nothing, the truer rang the claims that the Kurds were doomed in any case and that intervention would merely postpone the inevitable.

Over days and weeks the administration left a trail of public statements clearly establishing its calculated decision to allow the remnants of Iraq's army to smash the southern and northern rebellions. By his own admission, the first tactical mistake was General Schwarzkopf's, at a meeting on March 3 at Safwan, where the terms for a cease-fire were set forth to the defeated Iraqi army: he granted Iraqi Lieutenant General Sultan Hashem Ahmad's request—which "should have given me pause," he later allowed —exempting helicopters (and gunships at that), from the coalition's "You fly, you die" ban on fixed-wing aircraft. Soon enough he realized the "son of a bitch" Ahmad had "snookered" him. Instead of ferrying officials around the war-devastated country, as Ahmad had said, the helicopters were being used to "suppress rebellions." Although Baker exactly two weeks later remarked that Iraq's armed forces were in such shambles that "I dare say we could have gone to Baghdad," neither he, Schwarzkopf, nor anyone else ordered the Iraqi government to ground the helicopters forthwith. In fact Schwarzkopf passed the buck, noting, "By that time"—meaning by the time he realized the helicopters' misuse—"it was up to the White House to decide how much the U.S. wanted to intervene in the internal affairs of Iraq."

Almost every day in Washington brought a new hint of treacherous ambiguity, sometimes corrected under pressure from irate public opinion, but followed only by more slippage. On March 9 Baker warned the Iraqi government against using chemical weapons against the insurgents; the next day a Pentagon general speculated that the coalition would place no restrictions on Baghdad's use of more than 130 of its planes, which to escape destruction had been flown to safety in Iran, in the unlikely event Tehran returned them. A ranking American official quoted that old chestnut beloved of all bureaucracies throughout history: "It is far easier to deal with a tame Saddam Hussein than with an unknown quantity."

But such was the growing public outcry that in a March 13 news conference in Ottawa Bush said, "Helicopters should not be used for combat inside Iraq" and that deploying them against the rebels violated the coalition's understandings with Baghdad. Meeting Iraqi counterparts again in Safwan on March 17, the coalition brass warned that continuing use of gunships was considered a "threat to coalition forces." Despite these reiterated warnings, the allies, who shot down two Iraqi jets to underline their ban on fixed-wing aircraft, never destroyed a single Iraqi helicopter.

In the next few days the last pockets of Shia resistance in southern Iraq were crushed. But the Kurds captured Kirkuk on March 20, a precarious victory that apparently helped to tip the balance in Washington against them. By March 26 the new line was that Iraqi helicopters "would be shot down only if they posed a threat to coalition forces." White House spokesman Marlin Fitzwater sought to justify this moral disengagement, arguing that Schwarzkopf's original arrangement at Safwan involved "just an oral discussion" with "nothing in writing." An anonymous U.S. official remarked that Washington decision-makers "don't approve of what Saddam Hussein is doing, but they are not unhappy to see him have to do the dirty work."

Christine Moss Helms so feared that the coalition would be accused of encouraging a civil war in Iraq that she warned of "opening Pandora's box" if allied troops intervened. Speaking with the cynical lucidity provided by anonymity, another American official said: "Frankly, we wanted to wait for the civil war to be over so that our involvement would not be seen as a decision to help the rebels, but as a decision to provide humanitarian aid." In a pathetic appeal for help the day after Kirkuk was recaptured and with the exodus already under way, Barzani and Talabani told President Bush, "You personally asked the Iraqi people to rise up against Saddam Hussein's brutal dictatorship," then abandoned them to the "night of Saddam Hussein's tyranny."

———

In that dark night the *pesh merga* collapsed, deserting their leaders in a historic rout. Barzani and Talabani separately stood their ground, determined to die fighting rather than run away. At one point Talabani, his wife, Hero, and a small band of followers, defended by only five guards, defiantly set up a diminished headquarters a few miles east of Sulaimaniyah, stubbornly disregarding pleas that they seek safety farther afield. His example rallied a small force which successfully fought back Iraqi attacks at a critical mountain pass.

Farther north, similarly deserted by his troops, Barzani half cajoled, half insulted what was left of his personal bodyguard, some of them veterans of his father's legendary retreat from Mahabad in 1947 and of the subsequent eleven-year Soviet exile. (For several years the wrecks of an Iraqi armored column on a stretch of mountain road between Salahuddin and Shaqlawa bore witness to Massoud's courage in leading an attack that ended Iraq's efforts to press forward there; in another culture, the smashed armor would have been protected, regularly repainted, permanently commemorating the feat of arms. But every time I drove past the wrecks at Derbend

Khoré, there was less to see, for the vehicles had been picked clean or had simply disappeared. Such acts of valor, in any case, were few and far between.)

During the uprising, a young *pesh merga* doctor named Sabra-khan Gring had taken over the Kirkuk hospital. *Pesh merga* dead were stacked like cordwood in its entrance, and Iraqi artillery intermittently shelled the building when I interviewed him. He was still there on the morning of March 28 when he looked out the window and to his horror saw that with no warning four tanks had surrounded the hospital. As round after round smashed into the hospital, he and the *pesh merga* guard realized they were about to be overrun. They ran for it. The *pesh merga* wounded pleaded with Gring not to abandon them. One badly wounded man with an amputated leg dragged himself out of bed and grabbed Gring's trousers in a gesture to stop him.

"Help me," the man said.

Gring pushed him aside. "I cannot help myself. How can I help you?"

He slapped a hysterical Kurdish doctor to bring him to his senses, and together they fled as the Arab nurses ululated in rejoicing at the prospect of restoration of Baghdad's control. As Gring ran to safety a shell fragment glanced off the hospital gate and zinged by his head.

Gring told me this story in Rania. By chance I met him again roughly a month later when I smuggled myself back into Iraqi Kurdistan. I'd been reporting on the Kurds' plight from the Iranian side of the border, where hundreds of thousands of refugees were still waiting to join some one million already in Iran, but my editor asked me to go back to Iraq to find out why, to general stupefaction, the Kurds had just begun negotiating with Baghdad and why, especially, Talabani had seen fit to embrace Saddam Hussein on television.

In Washington that may have sounded like a reasonable—and easy enough—request. But I wasn't so sure I could get back in. I needed to be in touch with the Kurds' representatives in Europe, who maddeningly were in Washington and difficult to pin down, to alert the *pesh merga* leaders in Iraq that I was trying to come. In any case, I knew better than to think that the Iranian border guards would let a foreigner, much less an American reporter, cross into Iraq, and I wasn't about to risk crossing that frontier illegally. I needed to be stamped out of Iran, if only not to create future problems with Iranian bureaucrats. Iranian visas were hard enough to come by and I dared not risk getting my newspaper blacklisted.

The immediate problem was that Iranian authorities were suspicious of anyone wanting to enter or leave Iran by land. Like my other colleagues, I was told to fly out of Tehran airport just as we had flown in. But I wanted permission to cross the Iranian-Turkish border. That way I could double back to the rugged mountains where Turkey met Iraq and where, I hoped, I could bluff my way across to see Barzani, Talabani, and the other leaders. I counted on the goodwill generated by the coalition's humanitarian aid to ease my way through the suspicious Turks guarding the normally closed border.

Above all, I wanted to avoid flying out of Tehran to Europe and then having to fly back across the length of Turkey to Van, where, I reasoned, my second presence there in two months would set off alarm bells about my intentions in even the dullest Turkish policeman's mind. In Tehran, days of repeated groveling finally paid off: the Iranians granted me permission to leave via the land border with Turkey. So I flew west to Urmia, went to Barzani's local office, and waited. After a maddening amount of time I was given a note with the names of his people in Yüksekova, the notorious Turkish smuggling town, instructing them to help me. Yüksekova was where, in late February, I had aborted my first attempt to join the *pesh merga*.

This time Barzani's people in Yüksekova seemed to work for the Turkish police. They were certainly not helpful. They showed up, read the letter, and simply disappeared, never to reappear or answer their telephones. The next day I drove to Hakkari, a muddy mountain town under Turkish military occupation. Such was the threat there from rebel Turkish Kurds that even in the best of times, which these were not, police, army commandos, special forces, gendarmes, and plainclothesmen patrolled night and day.

Thanks to friendly Kurds I stumbled on there, two mornings later I was drinking tea with an official in the city hall, arranging for an overseas call with a Barzani lieutenant in Washington. Barzani's man was supposed to call the official back at a specified time at a private number outside the city hall to vouch for me. I was pessimistic, convinced I was being let down easily, but I told myself that even explaining my odd request to a Turkish official bordered on the surreal. In any case, I had no choice.

Late that afternoon I was back in the city hall. Over more tea, I was told I would be helped. Before the official could change his mind, that very evening I drove back to Yüksekova, then to Semdinli, even closer to the border, where I spent the night with other Barzani admirers who somehow seemed to know all about me. Early the next morning I was driven down potholed and rutted dirt roads at breakneck speed, past suspicious Turkish army posts and their snarling, chained Alsatians.

At a tent camp for refugees near the border I picked up an English-speaking guide. The Turkish guards at the border doubtless suspected I was a journalist, but I played dumb and was lucky. Along with humanitarian aid workers, tough British Special Air Service operatives, and the usual international flotsam and jetsam thrown up in these crises, I was not the only odd foreigner crossing that normally forbidden border without asking for a stamp in my passport. (That still left the problem of how to get back into Turkey without being stamped in, since I had not been stamped out.)

At the last village in Turkey, I arranged for a horse to carry my gear. When my guide said I was on my way to see Barzani, my money was refused. The guide, puffy and out of shape, soon lagged badly behind and at my bidding rode the horse. For the next four hours I trekked alongside jagged peaks superimposed one upon the other, some still snow-capped, and past lower mountainsides dotted with scarlet tulips, clumps of tiger lilies, and blue gentians. Still lower down in the valleys grew red poppylike ranunculus, blue irises, yellow marigolds, and red and white anemones. It was a perfect day for walking, overcast but mercifully neither rainy nor too warm. When I left the dirt path and emerged in late afternoon on what remained of a badly eroded but still vestigially paved road on the Iraqi side, Barzani, by pure coincidence, was waiting.

The next day Barzani sent me down to Rania by car to see Talabani. He was on the defensive because of his televised embrace with Saddam Hussein. Even his wife had taken him to task, he conceded. How could he have sent such a confusing signal to the outside world, which only so recently, even providentially, had discovered the Kurds and taken up their cudgels? If negotiations with Iraq were required, why in Baghdad of all places rather than on neutral turf, and why, in any event, without international observers or under U.N. auspices? What was now left of the Iraqi opposition's joint action committee, so laboriously stitched together the previous December?

In one ill-considered gesture shown round the world, Talabani had reinforced the image of Kurds as politically immature politicians who ruined the few openings that history provided them. Even a normally pro-Iraqi statesman like President Mitterrand had ticked off the Kurdish Institute's Kendal Nezan for being so timid as to limit Kurdish horizons to mere autonomy. "Your role is to plead the Kurds' right to a state," he scolded. Now the Iraqi Kurds themselves had thrown away their best chance for statehood since the collapse of the Ottoman Empire.

Whatever critics in Kurdistan or abroad said, Talabani insisted that the negotiations had accomplished the essential: getting crucial time and encouraging the skittish *pesh merga* to return to the ranks by the thousands. Now the families would come back as well, he said, and in droves. Our discussion zigzagged between bitterness and hope. Despite the optimistic public talk of a general agreement with Baghdad, he privately predicted (accurately, it turned out) that Saddam Hussein, playing for time, would not agree to Kurdish demands for sharing Kirkuk's oil, the size of the proposed autonomous Kurdish zone, or the right to maintain their emerging relations with the West. Saddam Hussein had never accepted such conditions in the many past negotiations with Kurds, so why should he now?

In any event, Talabani said, the Kurds had been set up by the Bush administration. First, Washington encouraged them to revolt, then by not shooting down the helicopter gunships gave Iraq the green light to attack Kurdistan.

If that was the case, had the uprising proved worthwhile, with its humiliating exodus and countless dead? Especially for a leadership already blamed for disastrous involvement in the Iran-Iraq war?

"Yes," Talabani said. "You can say all the deaths and suffering were worth it. World public opinion put pressure on Western governments. For the first time the Kurdish national problem was on the international agenda. Security Council resolution 688 mentioned the Kurds by name—the first time in seventy years they figured in an international document. Even the State Department has just said the Kurdish problem is not just strictly a humanitarian one, but a question of political rights within the framework of Iraq. For the first time Turkey received Kurdish delegates and promised us support. For the first time the European Community . . ."

Uncharacteristically, Talabani stopped talking. I looked up from the laptop computer on which I was taking notes. "Now off the record," he said, closing the computer lid so I could not type, "We are alone. We have no money, no ammunition, no antitank weapons, no antiaircraft weapons. No one is supporting us. How can I even feed my men without foreign support? The Iranians are siphoning off aid that was sent for us, stealing our cars, seizing our weapons at the border."

This argument was both self-serving and embarrassingly accurate. It also had vast implications for Washington and the European partners involved in Operation Provide Comfort. The Bush administration wanted to do the absolute minimum for refugees on the Turkish border, then withdraw quickly, leaving the Kurds to their fate. The operation was designed exclusively as damage control to return refugees, and it was carefully, some critics even felt obsessively, micromanaged from Washington. The relatively small allied security zone did not even include Duhok, the southern apex of the triangle within which the overwhelming majority of those refugees had lived, as Cuny knew, thanks to the Special Forces who had conducted an impromptu census of the Kurds on the border with Turkey.

Many Kurdish refugees refused to leave the mountains until coalition troops entered the provincial capital of Duhok, whose regional secret-police headquarters and prisons were for them a symbol of Ba'athist oppression. To the despair of the British and French, General Powell opposed the presence of coalition troops in Duhok, fearing that it would provoke renewed fighting. Threatened by the A-10s and their overhead sonic booms, the Iraqi troops in Duhok cleared out, but then they returned.

In the end, American soldiers and civilian advisers on the ground were forced to trick their way into Duhok with a token—and temporary—force, over the handwringing opposition from the cautious micromanagers. "Back in Washington they kept wanting us to play by Marquess of Queensberry rules," one of them remarked, "but Saddam was no gent and we had to think up ways of faking out both Baghdad and Washington."

Colonel Richard Naab, the American liaison officer who'd picked up a few tricks from serving with the U.S. Army liaison mission to Soviet forces in East Germany, first blustered his Iraqi counterpart into agreeing to invite a small, virtually unarmed American force into Duhok, an exercise he likened to "negotiating with Hitler." The Americans then turned around and told Washington they were confident they could get Americans invited into the strategic provincial capital, which sounded so outlandish in Washington that Pentagon colleagues suggested, "If you can get the Iraqis to let you into Duhok, why not go to Baghdad while you're at it?" That clinched the deal. Without further communication with Washington, American civic-action troops and private humanitarian-aid workers entered Duhok, and Iraqi forces withdrew. Washington was furious—until congratulatory messages from allied governments arrived at the White House and Pentagon.

By May 30, when Powell himself flew to Zakho to announce that coalition forces would "leave sooner than we thought," only eight thousand refugees remained on the Turkish border. But his remarks upset the Kurds, and the British and French as well. If Saddam Hussein ever meant to negotiate in earnest, Powell was giving him ample reason to procrastinate. London and Paris had hoped that the presence of European troops might encourage conclusion of the negotiations, followed by an honorable Iraqi withdrawal. But they could do no better than extract a face-saving two-week respite from Washington. On July 15, the last 3,170 troops crossed back into Turkey with General Garner, the force commander, assuring doubting Kurds, "We are just a telephone call away." In a way he was telling the truth. Turkish-based American, British, and French war planes maintained air patrols north of the 36th parallel, protecting Kurds outside the security zone.

The allies had warned the Kurds that they would be on their own if they pushed the Iraqis around and ended up in trouble. Within days, Kurdish guerrillas became involved in a series of clashes with demoralized Iraqi troops; there was more serious fighting in October. The Kurds easily captured Erbil and Sulaimaniyah, while thousands of listless Iraqi soldiers surrendered rather than fight to the death. Saddam Hussein was stymied. In retaliation he stopped paying civil servants in late October, drastically reduced food and fuel deliveries, and instituted an effective embargo on the Kurds on top of the U.N. economic sanctions punishing the entire country. Fearing that Baghdad would use any lifting of these secondary sanctions as an argument to end the U.N. embargo, Washington repeatedly refused Kurdish pleas to allow the import of spare parts for its few factories, to generate income and even foreign exchange. Instead, the United States and its allies now had to spend hundreds of millions of dollars in aid to keep the Kurds just barely alive. They were also obliged to close their eyes to the

Turkish tanker trucks' lively blockade-busting trade in Iraqi diesel fuel across Kurdish-held territory. The diesel sold at bargain-basement prices, but in hard currency which Baghdad desperately needed; it gave the Kurds a lifeline of disguised customs revenue; and it pumped money into the local Turkish economy, depressed by the interruption of the once-flourishing cross-border traffic. Middle Eastern meandering had muddled through.

The regional powers and the West were so intent on keeping the Iraqi Kurds on a tight leash that they misread their reaction to the Iraqi boycott, and so did Saddam Hussein. Instead of destroying Kurdish morale, the boycott backfired. Even Massoud Barzani, who kept doggedly negotiating with Baghdad well into November, concluded that talking had become useless and called for elections in the old autonomous zone for a regional assembly. The following May, much to the fury of Baghdad, Ankara, Damascus, and Tehran, all of whom feared and loathed Kurdish nationalism in any form, Iraqi Kurds conducted their first free elections and chose a parliament for their zone.

Like it or not, Washington was hooked, and now it was obliged to work out a new policy, which under the Clinton administration called for carefully dosed but unmistakable minimal aid to the Iraqi opposition to keep Iraqi troops at bay. Kurds and other Iraqi opposition leaders were now in good odor. That did not mean that Washington thought through a consistent policy beyond opposing lifting economic sanctions against Iraq as long as Saddam Hussein remained in power. As one of its practitioners noted years later, Washington was stuck with a frequently irrational "policy requiring constant management," of expensively "keeping things broke instead of fixing them." The Iraqi Kurds railed against its costly inconsistencies, which kept them cash-short, stopped them from achieving economic self-sufficiency, and encouraged the exodus of the educated middle class. Yet compared to the neglect, contempt, and manipulation which had been their fate for decades, the Kurds of Iraq did exist on the international chess board, if only just.

Trying to pin down what had gone so wrong in 1991, an NEA hand ran through a litany of factors, from the draining fourteen-hour days preparing for the war to its limited goals, misread signals, and especially the lack of warning from within the foreign-policy establishment or from journalists or academics. "For the last forty years of U.S. history," he said by way of explanation, "from the Korean War to the Gulf War—and especially in the last twenty years since Vietnam—the overwhelming theme of journalists and specialists was 'Know your limits.' "

Yet it had not all been a total disaster. With the passage of time the manic part of Talabani's schizoid remarks no longer sounded so much like whistling in the dark. To be sure, Barzani and Talabani started fighting each other, at the cost of thousands of lives* and much disgust among Kurds at home and friends abroad. Yet the Kurds now controlled more territory and people than ever before in their modern history. In June 1991, a foreigner wise in the ways of the region came away from an afternoon listening to local Kurdish leaders in Duhok. Were they worried about the withdrawal of coalition troops? I asked. Would they head back to the mountains at the first sign of trouble?

"No," he said, "not at all."

I expressed surprise.

"Don't you see, they never thought they would survive after the disaster. It's as if they had died and gone to heaven."

For the first time in Kurdish history in this century, outside powers had intervened in Kurdistan on behalf of Kurds.

---

* As many as four thousand, one British diplomat estimated in a discussion with me on February 12, 1996. There are no reliable statistics. Amnesty International, which collected data in Iraqi Kurdistan through October 1994, estimated the toll at between six hundred and two thousand civilian and military deaths, but serious fighting and casualties resumed thereafter. Even within a single organization the numbers varied widely. Hoshyar Zibari of the KDP estimated the toll at three thousand; Sami Abderrahman, also of the KDP, estimated "about two thousand" dead, "mostly *pesh merga.*"

5

Alchemy: Gold Coins
into Horseshoes

In 1993 the portraits of half a dozen Kurds prominent in a century's nationalist struggle faced out onto Sulaimaniyah's main traffic circle from their proud display high up on a building wall. They included locally revered "martyrs" who had sacrificed their lives fighting in Kurdistan's cause and men once in the political forefront of ill-starred Kurdish nationalism. All had paid the price for rebellion in Iran, Iraq, or Turkey. Most had died with their boots on. Such homage was not an uninspired copycat enterprise to match the thousands of billboard likenesses of Saddam Hussein in his various stylized guises plastered on walls throughout Iraq lo these many years. Those inescapably ubiquitous portraits were mass-produced commercial art in all its nondescript slickness. But the Kurds' often crudely rendered likenesses were part of an older tradition of Third World pictorial political propaganda, pre-dating four-color double-truck spreads and television.

The artlessness of this genuflection to the past unintentionally underscores the Kurds' enduring lack of mastery in other, more crucial endeavors. What mattered was that for the first time in living memory Kurds could freely contemplate in one place their luckless leaders and comprehend that Kurdish nationalism ex-tended across artificial political borders imposed by regional states. The more illustrious had exercised influence beyond their country of birth, sometimes even coming to the fleeting attention of the great powers, which were only too happy to overlook all things

Kurdish when given half a chance. Now, ironically, these portraits were on public exhibit thanks to the West's de facto protectorate in northern Iraq.

Among the honored Kurds were Sheikh Said, a man of religion whose leadership of a short-lived revolt in 1925 ended in his being hanged in Turkey; Qazi Mohamed, another religious leader executed by Shah Mohamed Reza Pahlavi of Iran in 1947 for founding the ephemeral so-called Mahabad Republic; and Abdul Rahman Qassemlou, a fellow Iranian assassinated in Vienna by the Islamic Republic's secret police in 1989. All three were overshadowed by Mullah Mustafa Barzani, whose life was intertwined with the vicissitudes of Kurdish nationalism for half a century. His pride of place was only fitting, though his faults were many.

Of all the martyred heroes Barzani's likeness alone is to be found everywhere—from the homes of modest Kurds in Turkey or Azerbaijan to the offices of prominent journalists in Washington. Barzani's long life was the stuff of legend. His battlefield exploits, told and retold hundreds of times wherever Kurds live, are a rare cause for pride and kept the very notion of Kurdish nationalism alive for decades. He possessed that essential ingredient of leadership, the gift of commanding emotional loyalty, which moved men and women to drop everything and follow him despite impossible odds.

At the height of his powers he united illiterate fighting men from the tribes and thousands of doctors, engineers, teachers, and policemen who abandoned the comforts of urban life for the rigors of mountain warfare. Yet he always had to contend with rival tribes and political forces, the *jash*, ever willing to settle recent quarrels or ancient grudges by taking up arms in return for government money. At his least inspired he was an unbending autocrat of limited schooling unwilling to share power with better-educated Kurds, capable of delivering Iranian Kurds to their enemy, and bringing disaster upon his cause by naively trusting foreign powers. These contrasts showed the rough edges of a man caught in transition between the relatively unpoliced world of his youth and the increasingly destructive powers of a highly centralized police state which he dealt with as a mature leader.

Early on, Barzani was influenced more by tribal and feudal devotion to the goal of throwing off the resented constraints of central government—a mountaineer's pastime in many a clime—than by the need for patient organizational work, which any successful national liberation movement requires. But when the going was good,

Barzani was simply Mr. Kurdistan, the first modern military commander who even remotely resembled that most illustrious of all
Kurds, Saladin, who defeated the Crusaders at the head of a Muslim
army. When things turned sour, even one of Barzani's sons came
to question whether his father was truly interested in achieving his
self-proclaimed nationalist goals if success meant he would have to
sacrifice the powers of tribal chiefs, beginning with his own. With
Barzani largely in mind, Kurdish and foreign scholars have noted
a central inconsistency in Kurdish nationalism: "The Kurdish nationalist struggle during the 20th century has been one not only
between Kurds and non-Kurdish rulers, but also between the concept of tribal rule and modern government, the lands of insolence
against the lands of docility [the inaccessible mountaineers against
the malleable people of the plains], a struggle which has split and
weakened the Kurdish movement," one authority has written. And
Kurdish nationalism is still split, albeit in more varied ways.

Born in 1904, Mullah Mustafa Barzani drew his initial inspiration
from his family's combined function as temporal landowning *aghas*
and spiritual sheikhs, which together constituted most power in
rural Kurdistan. By the time he died in bitter American exile in
1979, he had plumbed the strengths and pushed the limits of a
nationalist movement trying to survive in a neighborhood dominated by governments never shy to shed blood. When he was
growing up, the Barzanis were considered the toughest of the
tough. A poor, small, 750-family clan spread out in hardscrabble
country in the mountainous northernmost territory of what was to
become Iraq, they were known for punching above their weight.
In Ottoman times they were "famous for their fighting qualities"
and for the influence they exerted through hereditary religious
leadership among the mystic Naqshabandi dervish orders of Sufi
Islam.

Those were still largely nomadic times, and Barzan, their center,
a small town in the Badinan, an untamed corner of the Ottoman
Empire close to the Hakkari mountains that demarcate the line
between present-day Iraq and Turkey, had a reputation as a kind
of oddball utopian society, gathering in nontribal peasants and
taking in refugees, Christian or Muslim. The Ottomans hanged
Mullah Mustafa's grandfather, his father, and a brother for various
acts of rebelliousness. Mullah Mustafa boasted he was suckled in
prison. Indeed he was only nine months old when he, his mother,
and other family members were jailed in Mosul. Yet, as a younger

brother in a feudal society ruled by male primogeniture, nothing predisposed him for preeminence.

Mullah Mustafa (a given name unconnected with the Islamic religious title of mullah) was brought up and greatly influenced by his authentically clerical brother, Sheikh Ahmed, thirteen years his senior. In the mid-nineteenth century their grandfather's participation in the Naqshabandi order had put the Barzani confederation on the map, filling the vacuum in temporal power left by the Ottomans' destruction of the Kurdish principalities. Sheikh Ahmed was a respected if unorthodox religious leader who was also a fervent environmentalist. He forbade Barzanis to hunt partridge, mountain gazelles, or deer and, in a possible throwback to pre-Islamic belief, ordered that no trees be cut down. His enemies claimed he had Friday prayers said in his own name, with the faithful facing in the direction of Barzan rather than Mecca, ordered his followers to eat pork and drink wine, and tolerated free love. True or not, these stories contributed to his reputation for eccentricity. Later, when his own fame outshone the rest of the family's, out of respect Mullah Mustafa always stood in Sheikh Ahmed's presence and insisted he be served first at meals.

The sheikh's family considered itself half holy, and many Kurds believed that an unseen hand helped the Barzanis in times of crisis. Perhaps because they owned little land, and not very rich land at that, the Barzanis had little to lose by fighting. An old Kurdish proverb has it that *chaktira la bekariya*—"fighting is better than idleness." Another holds that "the male is born to be slaughtered." In combat Barzanis were famous for their unquestioning discipline; their combination of religious and temporal authority made for an effective natural command structure. So blind was obedience to their sheikhs that foreign visitors were told that Barzani tribesmen would unquestionably "even jump off the edge of a precipice" if so instructed.

Small, stocky, craggy-featured, possessed of great physical strength and stamina, Mullah Mustafa had thick, bushy eyebrows, and his piercing black eyes naturally commanded respect. Such was his strength of character that Kurds claimed they felt his influence from far away. "Everyone in the Barzani family considers himself a prince," a veteran lieutenant recalled. Musing about Mullah Mustafa's career, he speculated about the early years in Barzan. "In those mountains, under those oak trees, you can imagine anything. You can be very unrealistic. But his daydreams turned into reality." The transition took time. Mullah Mustafa once confided that he was already twenty-six "when I knew I had to lead." That was on the eve of his first major rebellion.

Mullah Mustafa possessed a quick intelligence and a gift of judgment reliant more on instinct than analysis, the unsurprising result of a rudimentary education—six years of private tutoring plus a further four years' study in a backwoods village Islamic school. (Paradoxically, both the Kurdish feudal order into which Barzani was born and its governmental foes long shared a common suspicion of education and its liberating consequences on the lower orders.) In addition to his native northern Kurmanji dialect, he also spoke fairly fluent Arabic, Persian, and Russian. He peppered his speech with Kurdish and Persian fables involving animals. In his later years he kept up with outside events by listening regularly to shortwave Arab-language news on a German-made Braun radio that was one of his most prized possessions.

Mullah Mustafa was suspicious of praise and flattery and saw through deceit. Like many a Third World leader of his times, he did not appreciate being challenged and was no democrat. In his world the leader held court—if such a phrase can be said to apply to his simple habits. With a long, curved dagger thrust into his cummerbund over his baggy trousers, he smoked hand-rolled cigarettes of local tobacco in a long cherry-wood holder and whittled as he sat cross-legged receiving visitors. He kept a rough lump of sugar in his teeth, Iranian-style, when gulping his tea. He often relaxed by playing chess. No matter how pressing the events, he always made time to receive foreigners as well as all sorts of Kurds, from simple *pesh merga* guerrillas to senior commanders.

In the field he traveled light. Experience had taught him to change camp every night, moving from village to village with his escort, to thwart spies he automatically assumed kept close track of his movements. Such is the well-established legacy of treachery in Kurdish society. His stripped-down logistics had little place for record keeping, but tea, sugar, and rice were kept stashed in the myriad caves the Kurds used as protection against air attacks. He shared the lives of his men and slept rough under the stars. Although a Turkish proverb claims that "only compared to the unbeliever is a Kurd a Muslim," Mullah Mustafa regularly found time to pray morning and evening, if not always the prescribed five times a day. He was physically courageous, renowned for not showing emotion during intense bombardments. He left tactical military decisions to his commanders, men often chosen from his own tribe, of whom he liked to say, "I can keep [the rest of] my country at bay with fifteen hundred Barzanis." At times he left other nationalist Kurds with the galling impression that for him to be a Barzani was more important than to be a Kurd.

He also had a ruthless side, as Margaret George, a much bal-lyhooed young Christian woman *pesh merga*, discovered when she fell from favor. In the early 1960s she distinguished herself in combat at the head of an otherwise all-male unit. Soon Kurdish propagandists transformed her into a Kurdish version of Joan of Arc, and Kurdish fighters carried her portrait into battle as a kind of talisman. But success went to her head, and she demanded a say in senior political councils. That was her undoing, even had it not been for hitherto barely tolerated tales of her voracious sexual appetites indulged with Barzani's eldest son, Obaidullah, among many others. When foreign correspondents visiting Kurdistan thereafter asked to interview her, they were told she was suffering from contagious leprosy and had returned to her village. In fact, Mullah Mustafa, who as a rule was extremely careful about risking the lives of his *pesh merga*, had her killed.

He could also be a stickler for tribal tradition. An Israeli officer recounted Mullah Mustafa's treatment of a *pesh merga* who had disobeyed the *sulha*, or blood payment, settlement of a crime of honor, and exacted his own justice by killing a man. Pulling out what he called his "office"—a prized gold Parker pen, a writing pad, and gold-rimmed eye-glasses in a case—from under his blanket, Barzani wrote out orders for the offender to be arrested, tried, found guilty, sentenced to death, and executed, all before dawn. When the Israeli asked him why he went to all the trouble of making out the paperwork, Barzani impishly replied, "And what about justice?"

The gallows-humor sophistication hints at the distance Barzani had traveled from mountain notable to national leader. The very notion of Kurdish nationalism had barely existed when he was born. Indeed, for many Kurdish historians modern nationalism took form only with the growth of an educated urban intelligentsia, and Kurdistan was one of the last Ottoman possessions so endowed. The Sublime Porte was well practiced in dealing with Kurdish tribal chieftains and others who challenged it; they were assassinated, imprisoned, or bought off with honors.

Starting early in the nineteenth century, the Kurds had made repeated efforts to resist direct Ottoman rule and to unify parts of Kurdistan. The Ottoman powers had largely brought these revolts on themselves. Intent on reversing their steady decline since their failure to take Vienna in 1683 and, more recently, to put down various revolts in the Balkans, and fearful of Russian encroachment, they cared most to assert centralized control, so they set about taming the autonomous principalities and *sanjaks* dotted through their vast Kurdish dominions.

The Ottomans' *tanzimat* reforms of 1839 were designed to end three centuries of increasingly loose governance inherited from Sultan Selim the Grim's victory over Shah Ismail of Persia at the Battle of Chaldiran in 1514, when the Sublime Porte had enlisted most of the Kurdish tribes on their side. But only in 1639 did the Ottoman and Persian empires durably delineate borders that sliced through and divided northern Kurdistan and that largely remain the borders of the modern states of Iran, Iraq, and Turkey. As a reward for their formal allegiance to the Ottomans, sixteen Kurdish vassal states were given wide powers of autonomy, in return providing tax revenue and troops when required and maintaining a modicum of law and order.

In an unraveling process that lasted forty years, much of Kurdistan was laid low by successive Ottoman punitive expeditions dispatched to bring to heel the Kurdish principalities set on perpetuating their privileges. Sometimes Ottoman and Persian Kurds cooperated against their distant overlords in Constantinople and Tehran, but more often most Kurds fought for the Ottomans in a series of three wars against Russia while others selectively decided to remain neutral. Sometimes Christian tribes joined rebellions and sometimes remained loyal. The Ottomans could always count on enlisting some Kurdish tribes against the rebels, which sometimes sought and sometimes got aid from Russia or Britain. Such were the Ottomans' gifts for bribery and tribal intrigue that even when Kurdish leaders triumphed on the battlefield they were invariably tricked in the subsequent negotiations and ended up deported, imprisoned, or assassinated.

Kurdish gullibility was matched by their opponents' cunning. In 1885 Emir Nizar, a Persian military commander, lured a Kurdish chief named Hamze Agha to his tent, assuring him that "as long as you are on earth no evil will befall you." No sooner had the Kurd set foot in the tent than the Persian gave an order and hidden soldiers shot his guest dead. He claimed he had respected his word:

he had slyly ordered the ground underneath the tent excavated and laid a rug over the hole so that his victim was not on terra firma when he was struck. Kurds could be equally cruel and insidious: Ismail Simko Agha, a chief of the Shihak tribe in the first three decades of this century, obtained the surrender of rebellious lieutenants by promising to spare their lives and guarantee their freedom. His retainers then smashed the lieutenants' right wrists to pulp and cut their neck tendons, leaving them free, with their heads lolling helplessly on their shoulders.

Intimations of nascent nationalism flickered occasionally. Two years before he led an initially successful revolt near the Ottoman-Persian border in 1880, Sheikh Obaidullah of Shemdinan insisted, "The Kurdish nation is a people apart. Their religion is different and their laws and customs are distinct." In a letter to the local British vice-consul, he added, "The chiefs and rulers of Kurdistan, whether Turkish or Persian subjects, and the inhabitants of Kurdistan one and all are agreed that matters cannot be carried on in this way with the two governments."

Obaidullah's revolt was put down by the combined Ottoman and Persian armies, in an early illustration of regional powers' abiding willingness to work together to crush any sign of Kurdish nationalism deemed a serious threat to their own integrity. In the twentieth century such collusion did not stop governments from manipulating Kurdish rebelliousness to influence a neighboring regime's policies. The governments of the region were past masters at interfering in carefully graduated doses—ranging from toleration of rebels' transit through their territory to active economic and military support. Kurdish rebels in one country learned not to take on more than one regional power at a time. The corollary was that active support from a rival regional government was often needed, or at least benevolent neutrality.

With enforcement of the *tanzimat* reforms, Kurdistan's traditional equilibrium was thrown out of kilter. In its place came warring clans and tribes whose fortunes waxed and waned at the expense of law and order, which by the early twentieth century was "merely nominal outside the larger towns." The disorder was somewhat tempered by the expanding authority of the Naqshabandi and Qaderi dervish brotherhoods, which linked tribes otherwise often estranged by traditional enmities. But overall, Kurdish society was at an ebb, its leaders driven into exile or co-opted by the government in Constantinople. Emerging Kurdish nationalists began to flourish alongside similar-minded groups in the Ottomans' Arab and Balkan dominions, then were repressed by the Young Turks, who seized power in 1908.

This descent into chaos could not have come at a less auspicious time. World War I swept away the Ottoman, Austro-Hungarian, and Russian empires and raised the hopes of suppressed peoples across a huge swath of territory. The Kurds, who had participated in the massacre of their Armenian neighbors in 1915, had also paid a terrible price for Ottoman rule. Like the Armenians, they had been deported from the war zone in northeastern Turkey for fear they might join the Russian enemy, and tens of thousands died from exposure in the winter of 1916–17 in their trek westward.

Thus, unsurprisingly, the Kurds were ill-prepared for their best chance for nationhood. The twelfth of President Woodrow Wilson's Fourteen Points specifically assured the Ottomans' non-Turkish minorities "of an absolute unmolested opportunity of autonomous self-development." But the British, French, and tsarist Russian signatories of the Sykes-Picot agreement of 1916 had agreed to divvy up the Ottoman Empire among the wartime allies.

At this point various Kurdish groups favored complete independence, while others campaigned to remain within Turkey, which was reduced principally to Anatolia—such was the pull of religion and traditional ties to the caliphate. The *agha-sheikh* governors also feared that reform-minded urban intellectuals favoring independence would diminish their powers. Lord Curzon, in charge of the British delegation to the peace negotiations, despaired of finding out "what the Kurds want . . . After enquiries in Constantinople, Baghdad and elsewhere, I have found it impossible to find any representative Kurd . . . No Kurd," he said, "appears to represent anything more than his clan."

Yet the negotiations carving up the Ottoman Empire among the victorious allies (minus Soviet Russia, which had renounced the tsarist claims in 1917) were an important marker for the Kurds. For the first time Kurdish political rights were being formally recognized. Inscribed in the Treaty of Sèvres, a Paris suburb renowned for its delicate porcelain, the document providing for a Kurdish state turned out to be just as fragile. Signed on August 10, 1920, the treaty was a dead letter less than three years later. But for generations of Kurds articles 62, 63, and 64 of Section III were proof both of their rights in international law and of their betrayal at the hands of the great powers.

Article 62 appointed a commission to oversee the establishment of Kurdish autonomy under the League of Nations, but only in the mountainous part of geographical Kurdistan that today is in southern Turkey, east of the Euphrates River. Considerable Kurdish areas west of that river were excluded. France and Britain were unwilling to give up their League of Nations mandates over Kurdish areas in their territories (which became Syria and Iraq, respectively). Independent Kurdistan's northern boundary was to be demarcated by an Armenian state. Despite Wilson's high-minded devotion to self-determination, the United States toyed with the idea of assuming a mandate over these future Armenian and Kurdish states in present-day eastern Turkey, but the schemes collapsed when the Senate blocked American participation in the League of Nations.

Article 63 committed the Ottoman regime to approve the commission's findings. Article 64 was a masterpiece of diplomatic hedging: if, a year after Sèvres went into force, the Kurds could prove that "a majority of the population in these areas wishes to become independent of Turkey, and if the council then estimates that the population in question is capable of such independence and recommends that it be granted," the article stipulated, "then Turkey agrees, as of now, to comply with this recommendation and to renounce all rights and titles to the area." But the article also provided that "no objection shall be raised by the main allied powers should the Kurds living in that part of Kurdistan at present included in the vilayet of Mosul seek to become citizens of the newly independent Kurdish state." The ifs all but negated the likelihood of a Kurdish state.

The potential independence of "useful Kurdistan"—the oil-rich vilayet of Mosul and its oil fields near Kirkuk—was made dependent on the existence of the future state in Turkey. The meaning was clear enough: the British, who had occupied Mosul four days after the official end of hostilities in October 1918, intended to keep practical control of the vilayet and its unexploited oil deposits. (The entire vilayet had been originally assigned to France, but Paris dropped its claims in exchange for 23.5 percent of Kirkuk's oil.) The language of article 64 virtually ensured that the League Council would ask Britain to exercise its mandate over Mosul and the oil.

In subsequent years, Britain found it politically expedient to share the vilayet's oil with Dutch, French, and American companies. In the succinct tongue-in-cheek words of a CIA document dated 1979—and publicized by Islamic revolutionaries in Iran when they seized the American embassy that year—"the discovery of oil in 1927 near Kirkuk in a concession held by U.S. and European oil interests acted to limit Western sympathy for the Kurdish independence movement." Those oil fields near Kirkuk—in 1920 a racially mixed city with a Turkoman plurality and large Kurdish and small Arab communities—and other deposits on land the Kurds considered rightfully theirs accounted for some 75 percent of Iraq's oil production by the mid-1970s.

The Treaty of Sèvres was never ratified. The upshot was that the Kurds, virtually alone of the Ottoman Empire's subjects, could not establish their own state but were instead divided up among Iraq, Syria, and Turkey. And so they remain today. The Kurds' fate in Turkey was determined by Mustafa Kemal Ataturk, who tricked them into cooperating in their own undoing. He first enlisted them "as brothers and as equals" to get rid of his enemies, French and Greek occupation troops in the west and surviving Armenian forces in the northeast. With those objectives achieved by 1922, he then turned on his Kurdish allies and their nationalist aspirations. Britain and France were too exhausted by war to take on Ataturk and expend men and money fighting for a Kurdish nation in Turkey. They were content to keep the Ottomans' former Arab provinces and shore up Turkey as a bulwark against possible Soviet encroachment.

"Sèvres had been humiliating for the Turkish people and deeply unjust to the Kurdish people," says the Kurdish historian Kendal Nezan. The Treaty of Lausanne, signed on July 24, 1923, recognized the new Turkish state at the expense of the Kurds, who were condemned to a "new phase of servitude," he added. Lausanne made no mention of the Kurds nor of their national rights, though it accorded guarantees to non-Muslim minorities such as Jews and Greek Orthodox. Within months Ataturk abolished the Ottoman Empire in favor of a republic. The following year he ended the caliphate linking the Sultan's Muslim subjects spiritually and politically. And as we have seen, he banned the use of the Kurdish language along with Kurdish dress, schools, associations, publications, and religious fraternities. The very notion of being a Kurd disappeared. Kurds were henceforth "mountain Turks." Carved into hillsides in giant capital letters and painted on walls was the defining Kemalist slogan: "Happy is he who can call himself a Turk."

The shock Turkish Kurds felt as a result of these mores, taken together, was explosive. In early 1925, in the name of Kurdish nationalism and to protest the end of the caliphate, Sheikh Said of Piran led a short-lived revolt in Turkish Kurdistan, which at one point covered a third of the region, but Ataturk put it down handily.

The fledgling Turkish republic readily acknowledged what its Ottoman predecessors had never quite brought themselves to admit in public through centuries of revolt: the Kurds longed for a separate state. The Diyarbakir military prosecutor in a harsh, specially instituted Independence Tribunal told Sheikh Said and four dozen lieutenants, "You are all united on one point: that is to say, the constitution of an independent Kurdistan which inspired you. For that, on the gallows, you will have to pay." And so they did. Before the Independence Tribunal was disbanded two years later, 7,440 Kurds were arrested and 660 executed. Hundreds of Kurdish villages were burned, and between 40,000 and 250,000 peasants died in an ensuing "pacification." Over the next dozen years or so, perhaps a million Kurdish men, women, and children were uprooted and shipped to western Anatolia. Sixteen more Kurdish revolts in Turkey ensued at irregular intervals over the next decade and a half, and all of them were brutally repressed. The Kurds were not the only victims in the Sheikh Said rebellion: Ataturk seized on the occasion to snuff out experimental political opposition and a free press for the Turks themselves, notions that came back again only a generation later.

Britain and Turkey fenced over Mosul's oil: each posed as the vilayet Kurds' protector, ignoring the Iraqi Kurds' own clear desire for an independent state. In 1921, the British rigged the election as King of Iraq of Emir Faisal, Lawrence of Arabia's comrade-in-arms during the Arab Revolt and briefly King of Syria before the French deposed him in 1920. But so strong were Kurdish feelings against inclusion in an Arab Iraq that the Sulaimaniyah Kurds boycotted the referendum, the Kirkuk Kurds voted to delay consideration, and only Mosul and Erbil approved the choice of Faisal.

Politically, like the Ottomans before them, the British favored the Sunni Arab minority at the expense of the Shia majority, estimated at 55 percent of Iraq's population, and of the Sunni Kurds, accounting for another 23 percent. Yet, of all the Kurdish com-

munities in the Middle East, the Iraqi Kurds—with their appre-
ciable numbers and fighting qualities and the remoteness of their
mountains—had the best chance of achieving their political goals,
on paper at least. A British military intelligence report in 1945
helped explain why: "A long history shows that the Iraqis have
never been satisfied for long with their governments and overlords
and there are no indications to suggest that this national characteristic has changed. There are few countries which at the best of
times present more security problems than Iraq. It has tribal and
minority problems. The maintenance of security with so many
political causes would tax the ingenuity of a sophisticated country,
how much more so of Iraq."

The British had learned the hard way. Nonetheless, they felt
occasional pangs of guilt about attaching the Kurds to their artificially created League of Nations mandate called Iraq. Whenever
the British got in trouble, they went through the motions of acced-
ing to Kurdish wishes, at least those about using Kurdish in schools
and administration, which did not threaten their rule. In fact they
had little choice, because they were determined to police Iraq on
the cheap, using principally the Royal Air Force rather than costly
ground troops. In those early years a few bombs launched in the
general direction of a target were enough to sow panic in Kurdish
rebel ranks and end a revolt.

In 1922, faced with Ataturk's pressing claims to the Mosul vilayet
and the uninvited and unwelcome presence of a Turkish garrison
in Rawanduz, in northeastern Iraq, the British recalled from exile
Sheikh Mahmoud Barzinji, in hopes of buttressing their argument
that the Kurds wanted no part of Turkish rule. Only three years
earlier they had named him governor of Sulaimaniyah only to regret
their decision, for in April 1919 he had raised a Kurdish flag—a
red crescent on a green background—and declared independence;
army units sent to bring him to heel had been routed and only
RAF bombers had forced his surrender; he had been condemned
to death, but his sentence was commuted and he was banished to
India. Now brought back to Sulaimaniyah, he immediately ex-
ceeded British instructions: he declared himself Mahmoud the
First, King of Kurdistan. He formed a Kurdish government complete with eight ministers, postage and excise stamps, and a newspaper, *Rhozh-i-Kurdistan*, or the Kurdistan Sun, which proclaimed
"the right to life of a great independent people with a country of
its own."

In a statement to the League of Nations Council on December 22, 1922, the British and Iraqi governments said they would "recognize the rights of the Kurds living within the boundaries of Iraq to set up a Kurdish government within those boundaries and hope the different Kurdish elements will, as soon as possible, arrive at an agreement between themselves as to the form which they wish that government should take and the boundaries within which they wish it to extend and will send responsible delegates to Baghdad to discuss their economic and political relations with His Britannic Majesty's government and the government of Iraq." That calmed the crisis. By the spring of 1923, the Turks were forced out of Rawanduz. The British then played off Sheikh Mahmoud against rival Kurdish leaders in Mosul and Kirkuk who chafed under his claims to leadership. When Mahmoud refused government orders to go to Baghdad, British infantry units were dispatched and the RAF once again bombed his forces. On March 3, 1923, he sought refuge in Iranian Kurdistan, but before long he was back in Iraq, where periodic RAF raids and a newly deployed Iraqi army garrison kept him from threatening Sulaimaniyah.

By then Ataturk was negotiating what became the Lausanne Treaty, which of course denied Turkish Kurds any rights whatsoever and reneged on the Sèvres clause obliging Britain as mandatory power to keep open the possibility of allowing Kurds in the Mosul vilayet to join a future Kurdish state in Turkey. With the Turkish option and Sheikh Mahmoud out of the way, the government statement and its far-reaching promises of local autonomy were conveniently forgotten, much to Britain's relief. The British High Commissioner said, "Given the limited publicity which was given this publication, I doubt it will ever be mentioned again." Should it be invoked, he suggested that the Kurds be told the offer had "lapsed."

Not until December 16, 1925, did the League Council rule in favor of Britain and grant it a twenty-five-year mandate. The Mosul vilayet was formally attached to Baghdad's domains. Seven months later, in a treaty with Britain, Ataturk formally dropped Turkey's claims in exchange for a 10 percent stake in the renamed Iraqi Petroleum Company and a British promise to refrain from agitation on behalf of the Kurds and Armenians.

A League of Nations investigating commission earlier had favored independence for the vilayet Kurds on the grounds that they represented at least five-eighths of the population—seven-eighths, if like-minded Turkomans and Yazidis were included—and had virtually no empathy for the Iraqi state. Nevertheless, the council accepted the British argument that Mosul should be included in Iraq for economic reasons alone, and asked only that Kurdish be permitted in schools and the local administration. That undertaking was carried out halfheartedly—instruction in Kurdish, for example, limited to primary schools and only in Sulaimaniyah and part of Erbil provinces. Honored in the breach was the warning that Iraqi Prime Minister Abdul Mohsin al-Sadun delivered before resigning in 1926: aware of the full-scale Kurdish revolt in Turkey in 1925, he said, "The fate of Turkey should be a lesson for us . . . we should give the Kurds their rights." That remained unheeded advice, which an increasingly frustrated Britain, mindful that its precarious grip on power depended on a few old war planes, some armored cars, and locally trained troops, kept repeating to the Arab-dominated governments in Baghdad. They never learned from the scattered and spasmodic Kurdish risings over the years. By the end of the decade British officials lamented, "Iraq is still scarcely more than a geographical expression."

In June 1930 in a treaty signed in Portsmouth, Britain abruptly ended its mandate and granted Iraq nominal independence, to take effect within two years. As in the Lausanne Treaty, not a word mentioned the Kurds or their rights. The British and Iraqi governments brushed aside increasingly outspoken Kurdish petitioners, convinced, as a British report put it, that the Kurds were "entirely lacking in the characteristics of political cohesion which are essential to successful self-government." These petitioners "should be informed that there can be no question of establishing Iraqi Kurdistan as a separate state under the auspices of the League of Nations."

For the third time since 1919, Sheikh Mahmoud led a revolt in Sulaimaniyah. In a bitter letter to the League of Nations, he argued that ending Britain's mandate "logically" should mean freedom for the vilayet's Kurds, and demanded that "every link of every kind" be severed with Baghdad. "We cannot tolerate that the right of self-determination recognized even to some primitive peoples of Africa—such as Liberia—be refused our nation . . . If the forces of the Arab government of Iraq were not backed by the planes and troops of the English government, to which your honorable League gave a mandate to manage this country in its name, repeating history and marching on Baghdad and occupying it would only be a question of days," he said.

As Sheikh Mahmoud so accurately divined, RAF planes helped Iraqi troops put down this insurrection as they had past ones—but not before a precedent-setting strike in Sulaimaniyah, with workers, merchants, and ordinary city dwellers publicly demonstrating nationalist feelings for the first time. Yet, even as the six-month revolt expired in April 1931, another broke out in November, this time in wild and woolly Badinan, where the Kurds protested Iraq's acceptance into the League of Nations. They also had more concrete and traditional grievances: they opposed government plans to settle on their lands displaced Nestorian Christians originally from the Hakkari, just across the border in Turkey, who had served as British army auxiliaries in Iraq, frequently in operations against the Kurds. Nor did they welcome the prospect of government police posts and tax collectors.

By the spring of 1932, that rebellion, too, was repressed with RAF help. But the rising marked the emergence of Sheikh Ahmed Barzani and his younger brother, Mullah Mustafa, who were following the footsteps of earlier Barzanis who had rebelled against Ottoman central government. The brothers fled to Turkey, where they were arrested and handed back to Iraqi authorities. Once again, regional governments found it expedient to cooperate on Kurdish matters: the Barzanis were subjected to the standard punishment—banishment in the Arab south. Eventually they were transferred to Sulaimaniyah under modified house arrest and there, in Iraqi Kurdistan's cultural capital, began Mullah Mustafa's metamorphosis from backwoods rebel to leader of Kurdish national liberation. While he was in Sulaimaniyah, in virtually every odd-numbered year sporadic revolts of varying magnitude erupted in Iraqi Kurdistan and were predictably put down.

Kurdish nationalists who knew him in Sulaimaniyah said Mullah Mustafa's conversion was slow and difficult. They were urban leftists—Kurds were prominent in the Communist Party and other clandestine nationalist political groups and parties—and at first found him too conservative. But he always respected learning and came to be won over to their wider view of politics and patriotism. But theirs was always an uneasy relationship. When it came to practical politics, the poorly educated authoritarian felt uncomfortable with these city elites formed in the schools and universities of the British mandate, with which they were so vociferously at odds. "That the primitive Barzanis, pressed into this feudal mode, should have become a vanguard for leftist Kurdish nationalism, was indeed ironic," one specialist has noted, "since the urban nationalists detested tribal life, feared tribal power and sought the collapse of the feudal system." But these urban Kurds realized they had no troops, and only the Barzanis and their hold on rural tribes had the muscle needed to realize their dreams of an autonomous, much less independent, Kurdistan. Time and again the Kurdish nationalist movement in Iraq has been weakened by power struggles between variants of the same basic ingredients in Kurdish society. Ironically, Mullah Mustafa's personal authority was never stronger than during repeated bouts of fighting with the government, when thousands of educated Kurds from as far away as Baghdad escaped to the mountains to avoid repression and military service and join the nationalist cause.

After a decade's confinement, Mullah Mustafa escaped in 1943, taking advantage of lessened British surveillance because of the exigencies of World War II. One possibly apocryphal story has it that he decided to take to his native hills because the government-provided pittance, eroded by wartime inflation, no longer sufficed to feed his family; he realized his financial plight one day, it is said, when he put his hand in his wife's hair and discovered a horseshoe in place of the gold coins the family stored there. She had been reduced to selling the coins. Furious, he crossed into Iran before doubling back into Iraq and heading for Barzan. Once there, he reformed the coalition of northern tribes—the Dola Mari, Shirwani, Mizuri, Barushi—known collectively as the Barzanis. Then he led a revolt, settling scores with rival tribes in government pay who had betrayed the Barzanis years earlier and humiliating the still-inexperienced Iraqi troops sent to subdue them.

Exasperated British officials complained almost immediately about the "evasive and petulant" behavior of this "turbulent tribal chieftain," also described as "vain, predatory and dictatorial." "He pretends to represent Kurdish nationalism," an intelligence report said, "but in fact aims at achieving freedom to raid and loot in the old-fashioned tribal manner." The British High Commissioner, Sir Kinahan Cornwallis, fretted that the Baghdad government had brought the problem upon itself, reneging on "repeated promises" and postponing "tackling legitimate grievances." Bringing Mullah Mustafa to heel, he noted, "can only increase his prestige and eventually make him a martyr." With no British troops or war planes readily available to help him, Iraqi Prime Minister Nuri Said, himself a wily Kurd formed in the Ottoman army, opted for accommodation. Mullah Mustafa and other Kurdish offenders were pardoned in April 1945. It was a gesture he chose to take for weakness.

A more evenhanded American critic did not share British doubts about Barzani's nationalism. But he noted that if "endurance and audacity were stamped on his mind and body," Mullah Mustafa also displayed "less commendable characteristics—egotism, opportunism, short sightedness and intractability." Few Kurds saw those failings, at least then. On the contrary, Mullah Mustafa electrified them. Mohsin Dizai, who served the Barzanis all his adult life, remembered the tremendous excitement he felt as an elementary-school student in Erbil in 1943 when he heard that Mullah Mustafa had escaped from Sulaimaniyah. "Kurdish nationalist feeling was running very high, even among us schoolboys," he recalled. A year or so later, Barzani walked into Erbil protected by a dozen bodyguards fitted out with cartridge belts, old long-barreled Brno rifles from Czechoslovakia, and distinctive Barzani red-and-white checkered turbans. "We all ran out of school to see him," Dizai said. "He was physically small, but in Kurdish dress to me he looked like a giant." A generation later, another future lieutenant recalled that his heart pounded on the fine spring day when for the first time he caught sight of Mullah Mustafa emerging from fields of wildflowers on a white horse at the head of a "magnificent procession of bodyguards."

In August 1945, just as World War II ended, Mullah Mustafa rose again, declaring a general revolt. But after his considerable initial success against green government troops, the Iraqi Interior Minister judiciously handed out money to rival tribes, who were delighted to take up arms against an old foe and be paid handsomely for their efforts. Soon the Barzanis were on the run. They crossed into Iran in mid-October with some ten thousand followers, a third of them fighters, albeit not all from the Barzani tribe. It was a soft landing: the border was wide open and Barzani and his men were a welcome surprise for Iran's Kurdish nationalists and their embryonic administration in Mahabad. No Iranian troops opposed their arrival, for the good reason that much of Kurdistan was a no-man's-land between British and Soviet occupation forces. The nearby presence of the Red Army—and the absence of the Iranian government—dated from 1941, when the Soviets and British intervened in Iran and deposed and exiled Reza Shah, fearing his pro-German sentiments. They had prudently left a buffer zone between their troops, who were busy shipping Allied military aid from the Persian Gulf through Kurdistan to the Soviet border for the hard-pressed Kremlin.

Iranian Kurds—and the Soviets—had taken advantage of the power vacuum. The former were in the most advantageous position yet since Tehran had snuffed out the last Kurdish principality, the Ardalans, in 1878. A Soviet general encountered near the border placed Barzani's destitute force at the disposition of Qazi Mohamed in Mahabad. Qazi Mohamed, fifty, an erudite and much-respected hereditary religious leader and Koranic judge whom the Russians were helping to install as president of the so-called Mahabad Republic, was a popular member of Mahabad's leading family and de facto ruler of the area. The arrival of Barzani's forces was a godsend for him, for he lacked an army and hitherto commanded the undivided loyalty only of Mahabad's townspeople and of a few Iranian Kurdish tribesmen. Masters of mountain warfare, the Barzanis provided an effective mobile strike force.

Mahabad was a pale carbon copy of the autonomous Democratic Republic of Azerbaijan, which Soviet allies with Red Army help set up after seizing Tabriz in December 1944. In the name of the Kurdistan Democratic Party of Iran, founded on August 16, 1945, at Soviet suggestion, Qazi Mohamed followed the Azerbaijanis' lead, though reluctantly, and formally proclaimed his Kurdish People's Government on January 22, 1946, at the Chwar Chira square, where the town's only two paved streets crossed. In attendance as he raised the Kurdish flag were Iranian tribal chiefs, KDP officials, three Soviet officers in a jeep with machine guns, and Barzani, soon to be seen decked out in a Soviet general's uniform with high boots and stiff shoulder straps.

Both the founding of the KDPI and the government proclamation had been prompted by a surprise visit that the Soviet Union had organized for Qazi Mohamed and a group of Kurdish tribal chiefs to Baku in Soviet Azerbaijan in September 1945. Stalin was toying with annexing northwestern Iran, and the Kurds were part of his plan. In Baku the Kurds were promised money, a printing press, heavy weapons, and slots at Soviet military academies. Technically, the KDPI wanted "autonomy within the limits of the Iranian state" rather than formal independence, and to this day its supporters—

and some historians—question whether the republic really embarked on complete independence. The flag was red, white, and green, a turned-over version of the Iranian emblem, as if the Kurds could not quite bring themselves to divorce themselves from Tehran. For the Iranian monarchy's weak government, and for its American and British friends, such subtleties were at the time a distinction without a difference. Young, untested Shah Mohamed Reza Pahlavi, who had replaced his father on the Peacock Throne, was mindful that the Kurds together with Baluchis, Azerbaijanis, Turkomans, and Arabs accounted for more than half of his country's population and that even the mildest autonomy represented a challenge to his precarious hold on centralized power. The Allies were increasingly worried by the Kurds' participation in Soviet designs: it was rapidly developing into the first skirmish of the Cold War.

Right from the start the Soviets preferred dealing with conservative Kurdish tribal chiefs such as Qazi Mohamed to working with the KDPI's constituent organizations, comprising better-established nationalists, the Komala-i-Zhian-i-Kurd (Kurdish Resurrection Group), a few Communists, and local representatives of an underground Iraqi Kurdish party called Hewa (Hope). The clandestine Komala, founded in 1942, soon set up branches in Erbil, Kirkuk, Rawanduz, Shaqlawa, and Sulaimaniyah, as well as in Syria and Turkey. The Soviets' suspicions of its democratic practices motivated an insistence that Qazi Mohamed, known for his authoritarian if soft-spoken ways, be admitted to its ranks in April 1945.

The republic's writ never held sway over more than a third of Iran's Kurds and extended no more than sixty miles around Mahabad, itself in the Soviet-influenced no-man's-land. But it was a magnet to Kurds everywhere, especially young dissidents who were disappointed with the failures of older parties. Kurdish delegations from Syria, Turkey, and Iraq were warmly welcomed. Despite obvious Soviet support—and unlike the repressive Azerbaijan regime to its north—the regime was remarkably free and open: no Marxist indoctrination, no social revolution, no secret police, no serious land redistribution. School textbooks, a newspaper, a political monthly, and two literary magazines were produced, thanks to the promised printing press delivered by the Red Army. During its brief existence the Mahabad Republic had hopes of rivaling Damascus and Sulaimaniyah as the "center of Kurdish culture and the Kurdish nationalist movement."

Yet the Mahabad Republic was soon doomed—abandoned by its fair-weather Soviet friends. Relentless British and, especially, American pressure forced Stalin to honor a wartime pledge and end the Soviet military presence in Azerbaijan in May 1946. The Red Army's departure was sweetened, for the Soviets, by an Iranian promise of an oil concession, which was an important-enough incentive to drop the Azerbaijani and Kurdish protégés. (Iran promptly discovered a loophole to queer the deal once Soviet troops had left its soil.) It was simply a matter of time before the Kurds and Iranians realized the Red Army would not return. When they did, the Mahabad Republic fell like ripe fruit. The Kurds, traditionally suspicious of any government, failed to appreciate that this time they were being ruled by fellow Kurds who were worth defending, and instead took their distance from Qazi Mohamed, whose links to the Soviet Union constantly reminded them of the depradations of tsarist Russian troops in Kurdistan during World War I.

Faced with a continually reinforced Iranian army force nearby, Qazi Mohamed desperately sought help from Kurdish tribal chiefs. Most of them were capricious, feckless, and quarrelsome; aside from Barzani's force, only Mahabad's small home tribe and part of another minor tribe remained loyal. The Barzanis were variously used to quell open tribal opposition to Qazi Mohamed and to fight the Azerbaijanis and the Iranian army. Tanks, artillery, machine guns, and other matériel promised by the Soviet Union never materialized. Qazi downgraded his administration, himself reverting to the title of KDPI leader and his ministers becoming mere chiefs of department. He insisted anew to visitors that autonomy was his only goal.

He tried to persuade the Iranian authorities to appoint him governor of a new, much-enlarged province—running from the Soviet border to south of Kermanshah—with some local autonomy. The scheme came to nothing. Desultory fighting ensued in May just as Soviet troops were heading back across the border. On the home front, trade with the rest of Iran was cut, the region's cash crop, tobacco, went unsold, and the mood soured. Food was short, all the more so since Barzani's forces (who had outworn their welcome) also had to be fed. Barzani himself was no great admirer of his host: for years thereafter he called Qazi Mohamed a "bad man" out to "line his pockets," guilty of unspecified acts of "treason" and "making *tujaret*," or commerce, "with Kurdistan," although he acknowledged that his forces got 1,250 rifles and 30 machine guns from him.

On December 10, 1946, Iranian troops attacked a key pass held by the Azerbaijan Democrats and less than twenty-four hours later resistance collapsed and the Azerbaijan Republic with it. Qazi Mohamed promptly agreed to surrender, too. Unlike the Azerbaijan leaders, who fled to safety in the Soviet Union, Qazi Mohamed stayed to face the music. He did not fight, in keeping with Kurdish traditions of dignified total submission, a decision younger Kurdish nationalists were to criticize. He even welcomed the Iranian soldiers who entered Mahabad without a shot fired on December 17. He was arrested two days later. He, a brother, and a cousin were hanged in public at three a.m. on March 31, 1947, in Chwar Chira square. Other executions were carried out in other Iranian Kurdish towns. Thus succumbed the only independent Kurdish state of the twentieth century.

Barzani earned the much-prized general's title that Qazi Mohamed had bestowed on him; with every passing month the republic relied on his force for defense all the more, as support waned from Iran's own fickle Kurdish tribesmen. Qazi Mohamed's problem was a classic example of an urban political elite at odds with an uncomprehending tribal military force contemptuous of its leaders and its policies. Most of the Iranian Kurdish tribes that had been loyal to the republic rapidly returned to their bad old ways, shaking down travelers and taxing the peasantry.

Barzani never hid his disdain, and it embittered his relations with Iranian Kurds for decades to come. At no point, apparently, did he ponder the danger for the Kurds of relying on a foreign power. That clear lesson of the Mahabad Republic remained unheeded. Rather, the Mahabad experience comforted him in his righteousness as he demanded that other Kurds blindly follow his lead. The deals he later cut with the Shah of Iran were at the expense of Iranian Kurds. The Kurdish struggle in Iraq came first, he made clear time and again. He never wavered in his conviction that the Iranian Kurds—as well as those of Syria and Turkey—should sacrifice their own political aspirations to his own.

Furious when in 1968 young Iranian Kurds staged a revolt despite his stern injunctions to the contrary, Barzani executed an Iranian Kurdish leader named Sulaiman Muini, who had sought refuge in Iraq. He delivered the body to the Shah's men, who paraded it through towns in Iranian Kurdistan. At least forty-three

KDPI men who sought refuge in Iraq between 1961 and 1975 were either killed or detained on Barzani's instructions and handed over to the Iranian government. When Barzani needed help, the Iranian Kurds were too weakened—and embittered—to be of use. And the tensions among Iraqi, Iranian, and Turkish Kurds were enduring. A generation further along, the Iraqi Kurds, totally dependent on Turkey for access to the outside world, ended up fighting against Turkish Kurds, who believed that their war against Turkey deserved top priority.

To Barzani's credit he remained loyal to the Mahabad Republic even after the Iranian tribes deserted Qazi Mohamed. But he had little choice: he had nowhere to go. "The Kurds have not been defeated by the Iranian army," he said at the time. "Rather it was the Soviet Union that was defeated by the United States and Great Britain." Within days of the fall of Mahabad, he obtained an Iranian safe-conduct pass and spent more than a month in Tehran unsuccessfully trying to enlist British guarantees to return to Barzan and sounding out the Americans about asylum in the United States. The Shah offered to settle the Barzanis near Hamadan, in northwestern Iran. That was too far from his base for Mullah Mustafa, who rightly suspected that the Shah wanted to assimilate his followers.

But Mullah Mustafa went through the motions of accepting the offer before finally rejecting it. In fact, he was stalling. During the deep winter snows, the Barzanis were playing for time in Naqadeh, just north of Mahabad. They now had outfitted themselves with the best of the republic's weaponry—3,000 rifles, 120 machine guns, two field pieces, and grenades. Finally, the Iranian army lost patience and pursued them, after first enlisting Mullah Mustafa's ertswhile tribal allies against the Barzanis with the promise of a pardon. In an epic fighting retreat starting on March 11, the Barzanis "proved a resourceful and elusive foe" who "fought in familiar conditions, on their kind of terrain and usually at a time of their choosing." In almost daily clashes the Kurds inflicted far higher casualties than they themselves sustained. But constant bombardment from a dozen obsolescent Iranian fighter planes and unrelenting pressure on the ground began gradually to tell on the morale of the men, women, and children. The Barzanis split their forces. In early April Sheikh Ahmed, four renegade Iraqi army officers, and most of the men and families decided to face the music and go home to Iraq. They surrendered to an Iraqi force at the border.

Sheikh Ahmed was jailed for eleven years and many of the Kurds with him were exiled to southern Iraq as punishment. As Mullah Mustafa in vain had warned would be their fate if they surrendered, the four officers were hanged.

On April 13 Mullah Mustafa and a fighting force of 493 men took a less exposed route back into Iraq at night, just ahead of the pursuing Iranians. He headed for the remote mountains north of Barzan, but two weeks later he was on the move again, having failed to obtain an amnesty from Baghdad: he could expect no quarter from the Iranians or the Turks. Barzani called a meeting to harangue his men and explain that their only option was to head for the Soviet border. "You'll get tired. You'll go hungry. You'll be barefoot. I've talked to the Russians," he claimed, without offering to explain how, when, or where. "They've said they might receive you." In keeping with the best of myths, Mullah Mustafa forced destiny because he had no alternative. On this three-week leg of his retreat Barzani briefly crossed from Iraq into Turkey on May 27, then two days later appeared in Iran heading north. At one point he crossed back into Turkey briefly, then to Iran with two battalions of government troops in hot pursuit. The Kurds had only enough pack animals for their meager supplies and their wounded, so Barzani and his able-bodied men walked all two hundred twenty miles across the Zagros Mountains, still covered with snow, twelve feet deep in places.

Anarada Dola Mari, a bodyguard still in the Barzani service in 1991, survived the retreat. He recalled Mullah Mustafa as a "very simple man" who "refused to let anyone carry his bags." He "always joked with everyone" and insisted on being "in the center of the action. I did all my fighting for Mullah Mustafa," the veteran said proudly, "not for Kurdistan." To avoid detection, Barzani's force moved through the mountains at night and devised shoes from old car tires, which were "very effective and made no noise." The men threw away their automatic weapons because they were too heavy and relied on the hand-me-down Brno rifles which the Shah had supplied in happier days. Each man was given five hundred rounds. Local Kurds they encountered were "too frightened" to offer bread, and the *pesh merga* rarely slept in villages for the same reason, instead bedding down on rocks or snow. Their main problems were lack of water—"we itched all the time"; their clothes fell apart "because we were often walking on all fours to avoid being seen." At times the terrain was so difficult that "even our mules could not pass" and "we had to abandon our wounded." During the retreat Barzani lost twenty-eight men in combat and twenty more of wounds or exhaustion. He fought three major and a half-dozen minor engagements, but the Iranian forces sent to crush him never succeeded.

Forty-four years later I understood why. In my own flight from Iraqi troops I was shown the exact spot near the Iraqi-Turkish border where Barzani and his men had forded a mountain stream dangerously swollen by snow melt. Nothing outwardly distinguished that stretch of water, but I was told that during the spring it was the only safe crossing in miles. Barzani was also an expert on Kurdish flora and fauna and boasted he knew the exact paths that Alexander the Great had taken during his passage to India: a lifetime spent acquiring this intimate knowledge of the terrain helped him shake off his pursuers.

In a manner of speaking the Iranians caught up with the Barzanis on June 18, on the banks of the Aras River, which forms the border with Armenia; awaiting them were the cadavers of two men who'd drowned crossing the river, some ammunition, and a few unserviceable rifles. Barzani and his force had arrived twenty-five miles southeast of snow-capped Mount Ararat and within sight of the river eight days earlier, and dispatched two scouts to talk the Soviets into taking them in. They crossed the river on June 15. Their exile lasted more than eleven years.

The Soviet Union split the Kurds up in small groups, scattering them around their immense country. That was Stalin's classic tactic for dealing with minorities. In the winter of 1949–50 Barzani vexed his hosts by refusing to head a projected government-in-exile as a prelude for resuming the Kurdish revolution, his position being not ideological but personal. Such was his abiding dislike of Qazi Mohamed that he took umbrage at the Soviets' insistence that the executed leader's cousin, Rahim, be his foreign minister. Mullah Mustafa's attitude did not sit well with the Soviets: he was arrested and exiled. At one point he worked on a state farm weighing fruit. He was shunted around from Baku to Tashkent to Moscow on Stalin's orders. Even locating him was a daunting task. Jalal Talabani, then a young admirer determined to meet his idol, recalls that he inveigled an invitation to a Communist youth festival in Moscow in 1957; he succeeded in slipping his Soviet minders and, after much effort, located Barzani in a small Moscow apartment, where he gave him news and photos of his family. They spent all of Talabani's free time talking about Kurdistan's future. Talabani then was a convinced Marxist, but soon realized that Barzani was not. (His own interest, he confessed, was so limited that he left a Communist Party school after an examination in which he forgot to mention Lenin as the founder of the Soviet state.)

That did not stop the Western powers, especially the United States, from cataloguing Barzani as a Soviet cat's-paw. In 1951 a report prepared by the President's national security adviser, for example, insisted that "in exchange for promised autonomy" the Soviets "have paid special attention to the Kurds through their agent, Mullah Mustafa Barzani, who is at present in Russia. The Kurds have been promised autonomy for their cooperation." That appreciation was wrong on two counts: Barzani was too much a nationalist to be taken in by the Soviet system; and the Kremlin was not in the habit of making binding promises to the exiles it harbored. Barzani was particularly irked by the Western press's later habit of labeling him "the red mullah," a nickname that was twice wrong. "I am not a Communist," he insistently kept telling Western visitors. "When I sought asylum in Russia I had no choice."

To listeners in later years, Barzani made a convincing case that his Soviet exile held few charms. Cynics would argue that he had every reason to say so after he had thrown in his lot with Iran and Israel in the 1960s and the United States after 1972. In fact, he telegraphed his preference years before, telling often-dumbfounded Western visitors, in a decade when American prestige was eroding fast because of the Vietnam war, that he wanted Kurdistan to become "the fifty-first" American state. In fact, his willingness to swing from one Cold War superpower to the other was typical of leaders of Third World national liberation movements. Barzani was also following the feudal tradition of telling his foreign visitors what he thought would please them. Talabani recalled working as an interpreter for Barzani in the early 1960s when the general granted separate and successive interviews one day to various foreign correspondents visiting Kurdistan. An American was told of Barzani's desire for Iraqi Kurdistan to become "the fifty-first state," a Russian that he was ready to have Kurdistan be "the sixteenth Soviet republic." Apparently, Barzani hoped that Cold War tensions would keep the journalists from comparing notes.

Those who knew him nonetheless credited him with instinctive suspicion of the kind of flattery that he so liberally could dish out when furthering the Kurdish cause.

John Foster Dulles, Secretary of State in 1952–60, was suspicious of any world leader not totally in the Western camp. But, as Egypt's Gamal Abdel Nasser proved in spades, Third World leaders thought they were at such a disadvantage in the game of nations that they had no qualms in allying themselves with the devil to achieve their aims. Barzani was no exception. But even for a man so firmly—and inexplicably—pro-American, he could occasionally conjure up a pro-Soviet scenario. His only unchanging loyalty was to Kurdistan, even if his critics argued that his Kurdistan was narrowly identified with his own tribe. Holding out Kurdistan's wares, including Kirkuk's oil, was one of the few arrows in his barren quiver.

It seems that in Russia he did little else but learn Russian, a language he spoke with his comrades in exile and with Russian-speaking visitors, especially when he did not want his other staff or family to understand. He also ate bread and butter before drinking, an anti-hangover trick he'd picked up in Russia. And he maintained working relations with Soviet officials until 1972, when the Soviet Union succeeded in signing a fifteen-year Treaty of Friendship and Cooperation with Iraq's Ba'athist regime. That treaty was the Kremlin's greatest coup in the Middle East to date. It placed the U.S.S.R. all but inside the corridors of power in a major oil exporter, and it opened up vast markets for Soviet weaponry and for military and civilian advisers. Shoved into the background was Russia's earlier flirt with the Iraqi Kurds. (In 1963, for example, the U.S.S.R. had openly denounced in the United Nations what they termed Iraqi "genocide" against the Kurds and had used the Kurds to pressure a succession of Baghdad regimes.) To the Soviets' credit, they made a genuine, if unavailing, effort to avoid the outbreak of fighting between the Kurds and Iraq in 1974.

Still, the Soviets certainly intended to introduce a major irritant in Iraq when they encouraged Mullah Mustafa's return from exile in October 1958 following the overthrow of the British-backed monarchy. His return was a decision as fateful in its own way as Germany's sending Lenin back to Russia in a sealed train during World War I was for the Russian Revolution.

During his absence, modern Iraq and Kurdistan had enjoyed a "halcyon period" of calm and informal understated development under Nuri Said, who applied the lessons he'd learned from the Ottomans. Two successive chiefs of staff as well as the air-force commander were Kurds. One of Iraq's two infantry divisions was predominantly Kurdish. Many Kurdish tribal chiefs were happy to cooperate with the government, whatever their private preference for autonomy and their realization that education and administration were eroding their power base. Foreign diplomats traveled to the remotest mountains of Iraq without escort. But Barzani's return helped to unleash a real revolution in one of the world's most violent lands. Five wars against the Kurds and unparalleled casualties and destruction ensued over the next seventeen years.

In the first flush of victory, Abdel Karim Qassem, the new leader of Iraq, whose mother was Kurdish, recognized the Kurds' "national rights" as "partners" "within the Iraqi state." During his rule the Iraqi flag featured a stylized yellow Kurdish sun disk with seven red rays to symbolize this partnership. Sheikh Ahmed, released from prison where he had languished since 1947, had been instrumental in persuading Qassem to invite Mullah Mustafa back, and Moscow arranged for Mullah Mustafa to travel first to Prague and then to Cairo to play down his long sojourn in the Soviet Union. To this day, Kurds who flocked to Baghdad airport to greet Barzani speak of his tumultuous welcome with unfeigned emotion. Soon a Soviet ship docked in Basra bringing Barzani's veterans home from Odessa.

Once the initial euphoria faded, Qassem realized that he lacked a solid power base, and he tried to remain in office by playing off rival political parties against each other. Power literally was in the street. A turbulent decade of bewildering chaos in Baghdad involved the Kurds from the start. Until Qassem was gunned down in his office in a bloody Ba'athist coup in February 1963, he tried to keep his opposition off guard in a dizzying series of violent operations. For the first fifteen months Barzani was his most effective ally and enforcer.

In 1959 Barzani's tribesmen were a strike force against big Kurdish tribal landowners opposed to Qassem's agrarian reforms (many of them were the leaders he'd fought during the monarchy), and again that year they put down an Arab nationalist-monarchist mutiny in Mosul, and, with the Communists, one in Kirkuk to punish the Turkomans. At Qassem's bidding, Barzani's Kurds then turned on the Communists and the Ba'athists, who never forgot or forgave him. As a reward Qassem in January 1960 legalized the KDP, a decade after the monarchy banned it. That was the high-water mark of their relations. Settling old tribal scores, Barzani killed the leader of the long-rival Zibari tribe. Realizing Barzani commanded the last legal political organization capable of threatening him, Qassem then welcomed back from Iran the very Kurdish tribal leaders he had earlier incited Mullah Mustafa to chase out of Iraq.

More challenging for Barzani than reestablishing his authority in the north was the task of sorting out the tangled political loyalties of educated urban Kurdish nationalists, whose numbers had multiplied during his exile. During his absence many urban Kurds had become attracted to the Communist Party, which had opened a special Kurdish section and was far more popular than the KDP, although self-described as "Marxist-Leninist minded" in its original manifesto. Within the KDP itself, seeds were sown for lasting future discord.

Secretary-General Ibrahim Ahmad had kept the clandestine party alive while Barzani in his Soviet exile was virtually forgotten by all but the hard-core faithful. A lawyer by training, Ibrahim Ahmad now resisted knuckling under to Mullah Mustafa's every whim and relinquishing any power for the urban elite. Barzani responded by replacing him with Hamza Abdullah, a former Communist whom Ahmad had forced out during Mullah Mustafa's exile. But soon he changed his mind and sent his tribesmen to storm party headquarters and evict Hamza Abdullah and his supporters. Politics as well as personalities were involved.

Hamza Abdullah had been willing to cut deals with the conservative tribes, which he knew had the muscle Kurdish nationalism needed; Ibrahim Ahmad wanted a bigger say for urban Kurds; and Barzani suspected Hamza Abdullah's alliance with the Communists. To reread KDP fulminations against "imperialism," "feudalists," and "the bourgeoisie" of those years is to recall the ideological baggage of the 1950s and realize that these broadsides flew over the heads of many a Kurd, especially the untutored mountain ones.

Relations were so strained that Ahmad's urban KDP initially tried to remain neutral when fighting started in earnest in September 1961 between the government and Barzani's forces in the north. The Kurds and the government remained at war until 1975, though with periods of extended cease-fires. The KDP was sucked in willy-nilly when Qassem banned the party in December 1961. Then Ibrahim Ahmad and Jalal Talabani, his talented and ambitious son-in-law, set up a separate KDP force in the south and east, around

Sulaimaniyah and all the way to the Iranian border. This was a harbinger of enduring splits in Kurdish ranks. For Barzani and Ibrahim Ahmad each saw himself as the legitimate leader of the Kurdish movement.

As complicated as all these events were, the central—and simple—problem for the Kurds and their adversaries was unchanged: from the founding of the Iraqi branch of the KDP in August 1946, Barzani's official political goals never varied; Kurds wanted not independence, he said, but "democracy for Iraq and autonomy for the Kurds." That sounded reasonable enough on paper, but Barzani's changing adversaries in Baghdad—royalists, Arab nationalists, Ba'athists, Communists—did not believe him. It was as simple as that.

To those political rivals, it seemed that the Kurds wanted a chunk of Iraq, the chunk they considered rightfully theirs (and no doubt Kurdish chunks of Iran and Turkey if they could get them). And if the Kurds succeeded, that would mean in their adversaries' eyes the dislocation of the always fragile Iraqi body politic. This was not entirely wrong: after the fighting started in 1961 many Iraqi Kurds genuinely thought they were poised to achieve a special status for themselves—and why not independence? "We knew even then that Barzani was trying for a Kurdish state," one of his principal lieutenants recalled.

In the Middle East, especially in what the Greeks were the first to call Mesopotamia, power is always a zero-sum game. You either have power or you don't. And if you don't have power, someone else does, someone who thinks the same way you do, at least about power. Thus power is not to be shared. Nowhere was this truer than in modern Iraq itself, an artificial British Tinkertoy construction in lands whose entire history since antiquity is one of despotism leavened by occasional merely authoritarian rule. Any illusions about this can be dispelled by a mere glance at the massive, unsmiling, fear-inspiring statues of Assyrian kings in the Louvre, the British Museum, or the Metropolitan Museum of Art in New York. In any case, no twentieth-century power was about to back Kurdish independence—or even make gestures about autonomy for that matter—and within the Middle East Iraq was considered somewhat suspect for having gone further than its neighbors in tolerating the Kurds, permitting them Kurdish dress, the use of Kurdish for schools, administration, newspapers, and books.

That constant bedrock distrust was formally enshrined in the

1937 Treaty of Saadabad, which committed Iran, Iraq, and Turkey to joint punitive action against the Kurds, then in the new Baghdad Pact, which the United States and Great Britain foisted on the Middle East in 1955 supposedly to fight Communism. In hindsight, it is easy enough to claim that Barzani's openly proclaimed tactics of trying to escape from the logic of the zero-sum game were doomed from the start. Kurds from Barzani on down would argue, accurately enough, that they could not single-handedly overthrow a government any more than the government could eradicate Kurdish nationalism. Yet successive regimes in Baghdad, which Barzani kept helping to undermine, grew progressively crueler and better organized thanks in large part to what Kurds believed were their purloined oil revenues from Kirkuk. Much of what Barzani accomplished, even when he was at his most impressive, when Kurds everywhere listened to scratchy clandestine shortwave radio broadcasts in Kurdish to follow his exploits, was due to fickle foreign support. That infuriated Baghdad.

It was easy enough to blame Barzani for sacrificing at the negotiating table what he had won on the battlefield in the Kurdish wars. That tactic had long been a Kurdish failing. He sometimes seemed more taken with boasting about toppling the Iraqi governments than with examining why he rejected terms for limited autonomy as a first step toward greater concessions. Yet when he returned from exile, no reasonable person could have dreamed that the Kurds' enemies would eventually resort to the horrors they finally visited upon them. Before 1961 was out, Qassem's Air Force destroyed 1,270 Kurdish villages, punishment regarded as within acceptable limits.

In Barzani's universe, the phrase "the great powers" meant that certain restraints obtained in political governance. He was a man of honor who lived up to his word and believed in the word of others. In the terms of his world, Barzani thought he had a decent chance of keeping alive that basic Kurdish conviction that Kurds were different—not Arabs, Iranians, or Turks—and deserved a better shake. But the world had changed its values and was applying Gresham's law, constantly devaluing morality at the expense of the Kurds, among many others.

The first Kurdish war stopped only when the Ba'athists assassinated Qassem in February 1963. They immediately demonstrated their propensity for violence by killing some seven thousand Communists at the instigation of the United States, all too glad to weaken the Middle East's strongest Communist Party. Desultory negotiations began. As so many subsequent negotiations did, they broke down over conflicting claims to Kirkuk. Successive governments refused the Kurds' claims to the city and its oil, conveniently invoking the argument that early in the century, before the fields were developed, Kirkuk was basically a Turkoman town with large Kurdish and Arab communities. In June the Ba'athists started fighting again. Defense Minister Salah Mahdi Ammash boasted that this time the army was ready and the campaign would be a mere "military promenade, a simple mountain picnic." But the army once more suffered heavy losses. The Ba'athists themselves were ousted the following November 18, and Marshal Abdel Salam Aref took over. More negotiations led to a cease-fire on February 10, 1964.

The second Kurdistan war ended after causing an open—and recurring—split in Kurdish nationalist ranks. The Ahmad-Talabani group charged that Barzani's acceptance of the cease-fire had been a sellout, all the more so since the KDP political bureau, on which they sat, had not even been consulted. Barzani riposted in July by forcing them and some four thousand followers across the Iranian border. The Iraqi government coaxed them back again and recruited them to fight Barzani. This rivalry sapped Barzani's energies, and the very mention of Talabani—a much younger rival of equal military and political leadership gifts—visibly angered him.

More fighting in Kurdistan ensued in March 1965. Aref was killed in a mysterious helicopter accident, and his brother, General Abdel Rahman, took over. In May 1966 the Iraqis launched a major offensive designed to cut the Kurdish front in two and deprive Barzani of his vital logistical access to Iran. Despite help from Talabani's *jash*, they failed ignominiously. On Mount Hendrin, overlooking Rawanduz, Barzani won his most important victory, and the next month civilian Prime Minister Abdel Rahman Bazzaz acknowledged a major Kurdish demand, publicly avowing the "binational character of the Iraqi state." But the Iraqi army scuttled peace talks with Barzani after first opening negotiations with Talabani as well. Barzani bristled, warning that "Jalal Talabani is a traitor and I refuse to negotiate if he participates in any way whatsoever in peace talks." He also charged that Talabani was "an agent for everybody." To this day Barzani loyalists call Talabani and his group Sixty-sixers. In lieu of peace, yet another cease-fire was agreed upon.

The Ba'ath Party again seized power in July 1968, and Saddam Hussein soon emerged as the real power, outshining President Ahmed Hassan al-Bakr. At first the Ba'athists bided their time with the Kurds. They were too busy purging officer ranks to use the army against Barzani. Instead the Sixty-sixers fought the Ba'aths' war against him. And when the fighting resumed in earnest in April 1969, the Iraqi army suffered such heavy losses that the following January Saddam Hussein traveled to Kurdistan to negotiate with Barzani. On March 11, 1970, President al-Bakr read over Baghdad radio the public part of their agreement: it recognized "the existence of the Kurdish nation," transformed the *pesh merga* into border guards, and provided for Kurdish rights for education and administration, the establishment of a Kurdish autonomous zone with its seat in Erbil, and the participation of a Kurdish vice president and ministers in the central government. To this day Kurds remember the next four years as a golden age of peace, prosperity, and cultural invention.

But once again, the Kurds appeared to have been outsmarted. Barzani failed to extract Iraqi agreement on the essentials—Kirkuk, the size of the autonomous zone, and the terms and exact timing of a census needed to establish Kurdish claims—and settled for a vague secret protocol, which called for a census to help delineate the frontiers of the autonomous zone within a year. This was meant to last until complete autonomy was proclaimed within four years. Iraqi Kurds insist that government skullduggery ensured that the census was never carried out. Arabization of Kurdish land meanwhile proceeded apace around Kirkuk and other oil areas. All Kurdish workers were dismissed from the Kirkuk oil fields. Kurdish scholars figure that only 7 to 12 percent of Iraq's development budget was earmarked for the autonomous zone during the transitional period, and indeed only four industrial projects were built. Scholarships for Kurdish university students and slots in Iraq's military academy were even rarer.

With desultory negotiations still under way, Baghdad announced it would start unilaterally applying its version of autonomy in 1974 on the fourth anniversary of the March 11 deal. Given the climate of mistrust—heightened by isolated armed skirmishes—this brusque tactic bespoke the Ba'athists' impatience and a willingness to go back to war if the Kurds predictably refused what was on offer. But some Kurds later questioned whether Barzani ever took the agreement seriously. (He contributed to this "time out" interpretation by describing the agreement as "a ruse. I even knew it before signing it.")

One of the doubters was Barzani's oldest son, Obaidullah. He defected to Baghdad, proclaiming that his father "does not want self-rule to be implemented even if he was given Kirkuk and all its oil. His acceptance of the [autonomy] law will take everything from him, and he wants to remain the absolute ruler." Be that as it may, just three days before the anniversary-deadline, Saddam Hussein proposed sharing Kirkuk fifty-fifty. Barzani turned down the offer, understandably enough, at first glance. After so much violence—including Ba'athist attempts on Barzani's life—neither side trusted the other, and in retrospect the March 11 agreement can be seen as little more than allowing another breathing space before fighting inevitably resumed.

Abdul Rahman Qassemlou, leader of Iran's Kurds, who had good reason to question Barzani's stewardship on many scores over the years, was especially exercised by his refusal to compromise on Kirkuk. Speaking more than a decade later, Qassemlou regretted that the option had not been taken and that the manifold gains for the pan-Kurdish cause, which he felt Barzani thus compromised, had been lost. Barzani's decision was an emblematic error of appreciation, Qassemlou believed—and not just because he was aided and financed by Baghdad. "The Iraqi Kurds have nothing so far, because they applied more sentiment than reason in politics," he said. "They asked for all or nothing, everything had to be black or white. That's why they got nothing. You cannot be black or white in politics. What's possible today is not possible tomorrow. I think Barzani should have accepted the Kirkuk deal, consolidated autonomy and fought in the future for the rest. Imagine if he'd had autonomy and his troops intact when the Iranian Revolution happened in 1979. Just imagine what an opportunity for Iranian Kurds that would have been."

In any event, on March 11, 1974, Baghdad proclaimed an autonomous area covering little more than half the 29,000 square miles the Kurds claimed and excluding Kirkuk. To no one's surprise the fifth Kurdistan war erupted almost immediately. Barzani's camp was supremely confident: the Kurds fielded 40,000 front-line troops backed by 60,000 militiamen. Joining their ranks from as far afield as Baghdad itself were 60 doctors, 4,500 teachers, 5,000 policemen, 160 engineers, and 100 defecting army officers. The fighting was by far the most devastating and demoralizing yet, prompting an agonizing reappraisal in Kurdish nationalist ranks. Barzani's *pesh merga* from the start gave up ground, abandoning more territory in six months than the government had controlled since 1961. Long before the snow flew, the nationalist Kurds had been mostly reduced to a slender sliver of land abutting northwestern Iran, where they were protected by Iranian long-range artillery and ground-to-air missiles. In fact, they were so totally dependent on the Shah, whose government even provided food and American cigarettes, that they no longer grew their own food supplies. Then on March 6, 1975, the Shah abruptly cut off his aid; Barzani never recovered from the shock. Such was his disarray that he ordered his men to end their resistance—a decision that shook Kurdish nationalism to its foundations—arguing that to continue fighting Iran and Iraq would lead to the wholesale massacre of his people.

As it was, the KDP acknowledged losing two thousand *pesh merga* in the fighting; the toll was probably considerably heavier, even without counting the doubtlessly higher civilian casualties. A nationalist then barely twenty years old has recalled his bitter tears and anger at Barzani's decision. "Barzani was like a God to us—he put us on the map," he said, and if Barzani had continued he would have "been like Lenin for the Soviets and George Washington for the Americans."

The image of Kurds from all walks of life united against their oppressors did not survive the shock. Many of Barzani's Kurdish detractors—especially the younger ones—were convinced that he had deliberately scuttled the struggle rather than have leadership pass into other hands. Once again Iraqi Kurdish nationalists began fighting each other. More than a decade passed before they closed ranks and again fought together against Saddam Hussein.

As for General Barzani, he ignominiously lived out his final years in exile in Iran and the United States, the two countries that had betrayed him. He had plenty of time to ruminate not just on the wisdom of turning down Saddam Hussein's offer to share Kirkuk, but also on the folly of trusting the foreigners who had influenced that decision. Such reliance was an old habit, a long process which he had initiated after his return from Soviet exile, warily at first, then with such abandon that critics questioned his judgment and even his national credentials.

6

Kissinger: Missionary Work

Among a Hill Tribe

For President Richard M. Nixon, flying into Tehran from Moscow on May 30, 1972, was welcome relief. "Getting out of the bush leagues" was how Dr. Henry Kissinger, his national security adviser, put it. They had just spent eight days in what Nixon called "absolute purgatory" in the Kremlin, painstakingly negotiating the SALT I treaty with the Soviet Union limiting strategic weapons of mass destruction. It had been a wearing but finally triumphant spring, dominated by the North Vietnamese Easter offensive against South Vietnam, which had been stopped only by massive U.S. bombing and the mining of North Vietnam's ports. So controversial were Nixon's decisions about Vietnam—and so apparently humiliating for the Soviet Union, North Vietnam's principal backer—that the Moscow trip had hung in the balance until the last moment.

By comparison, the twenty-two-hour Tehran stopover, with its prospect of resuming the stimulating periodic overall strategic review that Kissinger so enjoyed conducting with Shah Mohamed Reza Pahlavi, looked to be relatively carefree for the Americans. That was not the case for the Shah. He had prepared for the visit with an attention to detail worthy of a major military campaign. Two sets of talks—plus a formal white-tie dinner and a small lunch—went well. Both Nixon and the Shah knew what they wanted, and their desires coincided: Nixon was determined to extract the United States from the war in Indochina and wanted to support and strengthen friendly regional powers in Asia that were capable of defending their own—and Washington's—interests against Communism without a U.S. troop presence.

What became known as the "Nixon doctrine" was judged especially applicable to the Shah. By now a retrenching Great Britain had abandoned its long historic presence east of Suez. Iran saw itself as the logical entity to fill the power vacuum and maintain stability in the Persian Gulf, through whose waters passed two-thirds of the world's oil exports. In practice, assigning Iran such a function was sure to upset Saudi Arabia, the gulf's premier oil producer, and Iraq, a bumptious, radical state with the world's second-biggest oil reserves and regional leadership pretensions to match. "Giving the Shah Everything He Wants," as a prescient article in *Harper's* defined Nixon's policy, meant giving the Shah what more prudent American administrations had denied him—a free hand to buy the most sophisticated U.S. military hardware and training. Long-depressed crude-oil prices were now rising and the Shah had the money to indulge his military fantasies.

When Amir Aslan Afshar, Iran's ambassador to Washington, asked the Shah if President Nixon had given him what he wanted during the Tehran visit, the answer was "Yes, more than I wanted, more than I expected." In fact, the visit turned out to be a cautionary tale illustrating the danger of answered prayers for both the Shah and Mullah Mustafa Barzani. Nixon unwittingly contributed to the Shah's downfall and to epic instability in the Middle East by encouraging the monarch's naturally autocratic ways and his insatiable appetite for U.S. military hardware, a combination that helped burn out Iran's economy and undermine confidence in the Shah, thereby paving the way for Ayatollah Ruhollah Khomeini's Islamic revolution a half-dozen years later.

Without mature reflection on the likely consequences, the President also decided to please the Shah further. Nixon agreed to finance a small share of the overall costs of underwriting Barzani's continued rebellious defiance of the Iraqi government. This decision, which represented a stunning abandonment of long-standing, stubbornly defended American policy, condemned the Kurds to one of the most decisive defeats in their history and effectively ended Barzani's decades of ascendancy in the Kurdish nationalist movement.

The mechanism for the two linked disasters was diagnosed by George W. Ball, a former Undersecretary of State whom the White

House later called on in a doomed eleventh-hour effort to save the Shah from his own folly in 1978. "Once we anointed [the Shah] as protector of our interests in the Persian Gulf we became dependent on him," Ball wrote in a secret report. "We have behaved as though Iran was a power equal to America." Indeed, "the extent of our ally's leverage over U.S. policy was such that he [the Shah] made no effort to notify his junior American partner that the program's end was near." That was the phrase used by the Congressional Select Committee on Intelligence chaired by New York Democrat Otis G. Pike which in 1975 picked through classified documents dealing with the Nixon and Ford administrations' sub-rosa under-cover operations, an investigation set up after the Watergate scandal drove Nixon to resign the presidency in August 1974.

Pike's secret report gave a detailed rundown of American undercover operations from Angola to Kurdistan. Leaked in early 1976, it revealed how the Shah, with American connivance, first inveigled Barzani to resume hostilities against Iraq, while purposely depriving the Kurds of the wherewithal to win, then (without a peep out of Washington) abruptly abandoned them to Baghdad's tender mercies when he got what he wanted in March 1975. The report concluded that for Tehran and Washington the Kurds were never more than a "card to play," a "uniquely useful tool for weakening" Iraq's "potential for international adventurism." For all the shock caused by its disclosures, the report did not delve into the separate and often-contradictory motivations, misunderstandings, and miscalculations which made the Kurdish connection a textbook case of betrayal and skullduggery.

Nixon's radical decisions in Tehran flew in the face of the earlier U.S. policy, consistently reiterated, of discouraging the Shah's military and geopolitical ambitions. The Shah was equally successful in reversing U.S. opposition to aiding Barzani's rebellious Kurds against the Iraqi government. Nowhere in the State Department's exhaustive forty-three-page briefing book for Nixon's visit was there any suggestion of helping Barzani (although Kissinger in any case would probably not have informed Secretary of State William P. Rogers of anything, for he constantly undermined him and eventually replaced him the following year). True to his abiding cult of secrecy, Kissinger has never said exactly when he began thinking that the United States should back the Kurds. David Kimche, a key intelligence officer in Israel, has noted vaguely that Kissinger had been "kept informed" about well-established Israeli and Iranian efforts to "encourage and strengthen" Barzani before being "persuaded to join us" over State Department objections. All the official public record shows is that the Shah asked Nixon and Kissinger to initiate contact with Barzani and that they ordered it done: it was as simple as that. So total was the policy shift that Kissinger enveloped the operation in deepest secrecy to shut out even the State Department. Three times in as many years State Department and CIA officials had recommended against giving clandestine aid to the Kurds as the Shah and Israel had suggested. (Indeed less than three months before the Tehran meeting, Kissinger himself had concurred with a State Department decision disapproving such a program.) Starting in November 1971, Barzani had succeeded in establishing contact with Thomas Carolan, the chief political officer at the U.S. embassy in Beirut, but Washington insisted that Carolan limit himself to listening to what the Kurds had to say and not give advice, much less promise help. The Beirut contact was maintained but effectively became insignificant after the Tehran agreement. Nixon's about-face was so hush-hush that in August 1972 Richard Helms, the director of the CIA, instructed his Tehran station chief, Arthur Callahan, not to tell Ambassador Joseph Farland about it. Helms was only being logical: Secretary Rogers had not been informed.

Underpinning Washington's new policy was acceptance of Iraq the artificial state, where British interest in Kirkuk's oil after World War I had prompted attaching the predominantly Kurdish inhabitants of the old Ottoman vilayet of Mosul to the more populous Arab south. Initially the United States had refused to recognize the new state the British had created and acquiesced only when London agreed to cut American oil companies in on the Kirkuk fields a decade later. Thereafter unbending respect for international borders was at the center of standard U.S. dogma sworn to uphold national independence, sovereignty, and territorial integrity. For Kurds everywhere, that meant that anything smacking of autonomy was automatically suspect in Washington. Successive administrations unquestioningly backed the governments of Iran, Iraq, and Turkey about the Kurds and turned a blind eye to their unstinting efforts to repress or assimilate them. (Bureaucratic pigeonholing also helped: the State Department, for example, never developed a policy embracing all Kurds or considering them as an ethnic grouping of major demographic proportions. At it and other Western foreign ministries, Turkey was considered part of Europe, Iran and Iraq came under the Middle East, and their respective Kurds were viewed as nothing more than downtrodden, occasionally troublesome minorities.)

How much Nixon and Kissinger thought about all this before departing from the orthodoxy remains murky even now. Only Kimche's tantalizing remark confirms that they had been actively thinking about such an outcome before the May 1972 meeting in Tehran. No written record of the President's conversations with the Shah has ever been released. What, if anything, Nixon and Kissinger knew about the Kurds, or, more to the point, cared, was open to question. Two decades later, in what passed for remorse and an admission of carelessness, Kissinger conceded that "we did not know much about the Kurds—we thought they were some kind of hill tribe." In fact, that evaluation was economical with the truth, according to Helms, who served as ambassador in Tehran after Nixon removed him from the CIA in early 1973 and who insisted that "we knew plenty about the Kurds at the agency, thanks to the station chief [Callahan], who was a Middle East specialist." Presidential failure to exploit intelligence data is a traditional bane of the profession, but still, Helms believed that the real point was that "the President and Kissinger were pleasing the Shah and they did not think much more about it." For Morris Draper, the State Department official who followed Iraqi affairs then, "the Kurds were just part of the arms deal for Henry."

Three events provide clues to the U.S. policy change. The first was the March 11, 1970, agreement between Barzani and Saddam Hussein, which for the first time in contemporary history granted the Kurds an autonomous zone and ended nine years of sporadic fighting. That was what continued to anger the Shah. He had long armed and financed Barzani deliberately to weaken Iraq, but had withheld aid in favor of a harebrained coup that ended in disaster.*

---

* The Soviet Union had brokered the deal. In October 1969 it dispatched a leftist Kurd named Dara Tawfik from Prague with a message to Barzani asking him to open negotiations with the Ba'ath Party. Barzani immediately informed General Nematollah Nassiri, the head of the Iranian secret service, SAVAK, who came to see him; Barzani told him he would forgo the proposed negotiations in exchange for modest Iranian aid. Iran promised to deliver this aid but did not. Meanwhile, unbeknownst to the Kurds, the Shah supported an ill-conceived attempted to topple the government in Baghdad, a plot that was penetrated by the Ba'athists with disastrous results: some seventy Iraqi army-officer plotters were rounded up and executed on January 20, 1970. Only thereafter did the autonomy negotiations get started in earnest.

Technically, the Shah was not consulted formally about the autonomy decision that ended the fighting, but it could not have come as a complete surprise. Even before the deal was concluded formally, the Shah confided to his court minister, Asadollah Alam, his fears that Iraq would "concentrate her forces on the border with Iran."

Of course, by encouraging Barzani to renew fighting to achieve viable autonomy for Iraq's Kurds, the Shah risked spurring similar dangerous ambitions in Iranian and Turkish Kurdistan. He glossed over this inconsistency, arguing that aiding Barzani pleased his own Kurds and helped to keep them quiet. In fact, he simply wanted to keep his arch rival, Iraq, off balance, and Iraqi Kurds were expendable pawns to that end. Specifically, the Shah wanted the Kurds to weaken Baghdad, and so they did, in March 1974, thanks in large part to Kissinger and Nixon.

The Shah's desires were shared by Israel, which was, as always, interested in distracting the Iraqis from the Arab-Israeli dispute. But the Shah also knew that Barzani, an old acquaintance, did not trust him. After all, Iranian troops had ended the short-lived Mahabad Republic in Iranian Kurdistan in 1946, which Barzani had defended, and had harassed Barzani's force during its epic retreat that led from Iran to Iraq to Turkey, then back to Iran, and on to eleven years of unhappy exile in the Soviet Union. Aware of Barzani's blind faith in the United States, the Shah hoped to overcome his suspicions about Iranian intentions by winning American support for the Kurdish rebellion. But Barzani baited his own trap, pestering the Shah and the Israelis to open up a direct channel for the Kurds to American officials. The Shah never gave up despite reiterated American rejections.

Back in 1946, American backing for the Shah had stopped a threatened Soviet expansion in Central Asia and helped to restore his authority in Iranian Azerbaijan and Kurdistan. Now, once again, the Cold War came to the Shah's rescue. The second fateful event shaping Washington's change of heart was the signature on April 9, 1972, in Baghdad of a fifteen-year Iraqi-Soviet Treaty of Friendship and Cooperation. Suddenly, the Shah could play the superpower rivalry card, all the more easily because the Soviet Union had previously concluded similar treaties with Egypt and Syria. Washington worried that Moscow might put pressure on weak, underpopulated Saudi Arabia and the smaller, defenseless gulf oil emirates; Kissinger found it expedient to go along with the Shah's Cold War reasoning.

The day after Nixon flew home, the Shah confided to Alam that Kissinger "greatly appreciates the stability of Iran and the responsibilities we've assumed in the Persian Gulf." Kissinger, he said, believed that "the Russians have gone too far in their relations with Iraq, adding that something would have to be done to stop the rot." As Kissinger himself put it years later, "Our perfectly clear strategy was to weaken any country tied up with the Soviet Union. Since the Soviets had just made a military tie with Iraq, we were very receptive about helping the Kurds."

That was exactly what the Shah hoped. For a decade his sub-rosa aid to Barzani via Israel's intelligence service, Mossad, had contributed to the increasing desperation that colored Baghdad's treaty with the Soviet Union. (All but coincidentally Israeli Prime Minister Golda Meir, who strongly favored aiding Barzani for Israel's own reasons, made one of her periodic incognito visits to Tehran and met with the Shah at this juncture. Israel's influence with the United States and Iran had grown immeasurably in just a few years. Perversely, Moscow shut down its once-outspoken support for Kurdish autonomy, from which the Shah had benefited indirectly.) But now the Shah worried about the Baghdad treaty's implications. He recognized all too clearly the similarity between the United States' influence (and thousands of military advisers and technicians) in Iran and the now-certain arrival of massive numbers of Soviet advisers and influence-peddlers next door.

During the Cold War Israel was never happier than when its American protector and the Kremlin were at loggerheads. For Nixon and Kissinger, going along with the Shah meant that the Nixon doctrine could become a reality in the highly volatile gulf region, opening up billions of dollars' worth of U.S. arms sales in Iran to boot. The entire U.S. outlay to the Kurds in 1972–75 was only $16 million, earmarked mainly to pay for Soviet weapons Israel had captured in the Six-Day War in 1967. Monthly payments were funneled through SAVAK, which controlled the aid to Barzani so carefully that *pesh merga* salaries were even paid in Iranian rials.

Iraqi Kurdish leaders have charged that SAVAK director General Nematollah Nassiri and grasping senior Iranian officers pocketed a percentage of the aid earmarked for them.* But, in any case, the American contribution was scarcely a crushing financial investment in the Kurdish rebellion. Indeed, it was dwarfed by the Shah's own commitments—in cash, food, hardware, and troops. But it was just important enough to comfort Barzani in his most persistent and dangerous illusion, that of a genuine American guarantee for the Kurds.

The third clinching event took place the day after Nixon and Kissinger left Tehran for Washington, when Iraq nationalized the Iraq Petroleum Company, long the property of British, Dutch, French, and U.S. oil interests. This was a major event, a milepost in the Middle East's shucking off of Western oil tutelage during the decade when the acronym for the Organization of Petroleum Exporting Countries, a cartel, became a household word worldwide. The IPC nationalization was yet another reason for Iran, Barzani, and the United States to justify their deal, for each had reason to fear the repercussions of this first Soviet penetration of a major oil producer in the Middle East.

Still, the new policy was so controversial that administration naysayers, probably in the State Department, soon leaked details to the press about the American financial contribution. (That did not stop the State Department from denying to its own confused diplomats any connection with the Kurds. For example, Washington stonewalled a mystified—and finally furious and disgusted— Thomas Carolan, the Beirut embassy's political officer, whose well-informed sources kept giving him detailed evidence of CIA involvement with the Kurds in Tehran.) Nixon's fixation with secrecy was such that he dispatched Treasury Secretary John B. Connally from Washington to Tehran incognito to assure the Shah the program was under way. That meeting between the monarch and the Texas politician in June involved "one oilman to another," in the words of the Pike report. Only after Connally returned home was the Forty Committee, a group overseeing covert intelligence operations, advised and then only perfunctorily, even by its often-undemanding standards. There was no real discussion, much less a vote. Its members were not even given the traditional two- or

---

* The charges about Iranian sticky fingers are a constant Kurdish complaint. They were renewed in the spring of 1991, when *pesh merga* leaders charged Iranian officials with keeping for themselves first-rate food, blankets, clothing, and other items donated to the Kurds by the international community, and of substituting miserly amounts of second-rate equivalents.

three-page rundown. Instead, as the Pike report noted, they "were directed to acknowledge receipt of a sparse, one-paragraph description of the operation." Only four years later did congressional investigators digging into clandestine intelligence operations come across the relevant documents, including a key secret memo signed by Kissinger.

From the very start Barzani wanted to go to Washington to settle details. He had a near-blind belief in the United States but was worldly enough to want to judge his interlocutors in person. Kissinger turned him down, the first of many times Barzani was denied a visa and palmed off with the argument that the operation would be compromised if his presence in Washington were known. Long used to clandestine arrangements, Barzani swallowed his pride and agreed. In July he dispatched his son Idris and Dr. Mahmoud Othman, his virtual "foreign minister" and closest collaborator outside the family, to Washington. They were received at CIA headquarters in Langley, Virginia, by Helms, General Alexander M. Haig, Jr., the White House Chief of Staff, and Colonel Richard Kennedy, Kissinger's top deputy at the National Security Council.

Helms didn't gild the lily. "He told us very clearly that he was receiving us because the Shah wanted the American government to help us," Othman recalled. "That was the only reason Washington was helping us. As long as the Shah continued that policy, the U.S. would, too. Personally, I did not feel very comfortable. I went to Washington because Barzani told me to. I did my duty, but I didn't think it was a very serious relationship for us, because I knew the key for the Americans was the Shah. The Americans were not in it completely. There was no guarantee. I was not very optimistic."

But Barzani was, at least at the beginning. At long last he had achieved formal working relations with American officials, after more than a decade of having to make do with telling himself that individual Americans he met, even journalists, were officials in disguise.* No matter how tenuous, a link of sorts existed. The Western journalists and other visitors he received thought Barzani was not at all upset about the United States being bogged down in a debilitating ideological war in Vietnam, the bane of many Third

---

* Barzani's suspicions were not unreasonable. The Israelis used a journalist to initiate ties with Barzani in the 1960s. Moreover, the CIA also used journalists, both American and foreign, in dealing with Iranian Kurds.

World nationalists as well as many Americans. Dr. Sami Abderrahman, one of General Barzani's principal aides, said, "In his heart of hearts Barzani loved Americans." It was a relationship spanning three decades, starting with his encounter in Tehran on New Year's day of 1947 with Archie Roosevelt, then the assistant U.S. military attaché there. Even today Kurds wrestle with a question that has bothered them ever since: why was Barzani so completely taken, even dazzled, by the United States—to the point of persuading himself and his people that Americans were serious guarantors of the Shah's scheme despite ever-mounting evidence to the contrary?

Obviously Barzani was a victim of his own limitations. He was a barely educated man without wide horizons, pitting his own intimate conviction and knowledge of his people against the unsuspected fecklessness of a superpower doing a client state a favor at his expense—and pretty much as an afterthought at that. Whatever their faults, the Turks, British, Arabs, and Iranians with whom Barzani had learned to deal over the decades were not as offhand as the Americans he had idealized over the years. Seen in that light, Barzani is guilty of the unforgivable political sins of immaturity and lack of sophistication. After all, Kissinger had been peddling his brand of latter-day Metternichian realpolitik since 1968. Caveat emptor.

Yet Barzani's infatuation was a widely recognized run-of-the-mill hazard in the sorts of sub-rosa intelligence operations that brought small and great powers together. In Barzani's case, it was his very experience that was confusing, since people assumed he could not possibly have left American motives unquestioned. How could a veteran leader who had survived what he had survived, including exile in the Soviet Union, so trusted the other superpower, so unaware that it might ruthlessly pursue its own interests? Foreign visitors who got to know Barzani could not believe he was as naive as he portrayed himself. They supposed his stance was tactical when, for example, he proposed that Iraqi Kurdistan become the fifty-first state or suggested that American companies take a half-interest in Kirkuk's oil fields. To be sure, he had never traveled abroad, except in the Soviet Union, Romania, Iran, and Israel. He was untutored in geopolitics. But foreigners came away from meeting Barzani convinced he was one of the toughest national leaders they had ever encountered, in the same class as Mrs. Meir, having survived, like her, for more than a half century in difficult and hostile circumstances.

Even if Barzani knew better, he may have had no choice by 1972 but to go along. The euphoria surrounding the signature of the 1970 autonomy agreement had been short-lived. By the spring of 1972 relations with the Iraqi government had rapidly deteriorated, with two Iraqi attempts on Barzani's life and his certainty that the Ba'ath Party had no intention of honoring the autonomy accord on terms acceptable to him. Instead of carrying out the census stipulated by that accord, Baghdad deported Kurds from Kirkuk and other oil centers and replaced them with Arabs, both in the oil fields and in rich Kurdish farmlands.

Nonetheless, Barzani's understandings with the Shah and the Americans doubtless influenced his response to Iraq's renewed offer in 1973 to share Kirkuk and its oil revenues. Barzani did not reject the offer out of hand. Other Kurds argued with him in favor of taking a chance on it—and later they claimed that for all its faults, acceptance would have spared the Kurds defeat in March 1975 and allowed them to sit out the Iran-Iraq war. And Barzani also came under constant pressure from the Shah to reject Iraq's acceptance of revised Kurdish demands. Right up to the last minute he hesitated, but the die was cast when, in March 1974, Iraq further reduced the scope of the 1970 autonomy agreement and said that the diminished version would be implemented in two weeks willy-nilly. Both sides by then knew further fighting was inevitable.

Barzani shared none of his decision-making with fellow Kurds before, during, or immediately after the collapse of his rebellion in 1975. Only after President Jimmy Carter's inauguration in January 1977 did Barzani overcome his inhibitions and begin to argue his case in public, in hopes of enlisting the support of the incoming American administration. Disgraced, living in exile near Washington, and suffering from advanced lung cancer, Barzani that February maintained, in letters to congressmen and senators, that had they known of the skullduggery involved in the original 1972 understanding, "they would either have opposed it and thus left us —without any damage done—free to exercise other options then at our disposal; or they would have supported it and then prevented the betrayal of the Kurds." In a letter to Carter that same month, Barzani argued that only American promises in 1972 had dissuaded him from striking a deal with Iraq "contrary to American interests and causing trouble for Iraq's neighbors . . . I could have prevented this calamity which befell my people, had I not fully believed in the promise of America." Assurances of the highest American officials, he went on, had convinced him that cooperation with Iran and the United States would help achieve the goal of Kurdish autonomy and democracy for Iraq. Justified or not, totally or in part, Barzani's arguments over the years have for most Iraqi Kurds taken on the luster of truth.

It seems likely that the Iraqi-Soviet friendship treaty in 1972 was the critical, defining act. For the first time Iraq had the crucial military heft it had lacked, and Barzani was driven into the trap laid by the Shah and Washington. Once the treaty was signed, Moscow cut off its remaining aid to the Kurds and started supplying Iraq with vast quantities of jet fighter-bombers, long-range artillery, and helicopters and other modern weapons. In 1963 the Soviet Union had threatened to bring to U.N. attention the "genocide" of the Iraqi Kurds, but now it preferred good relations with the Arabs, especially those in an oil-rich secular state like Iraq. The Iraqi Communists, whose ranks included many Kurds, backed the government, which further isolated Barzani. And, with the coming of the militarily reliable helicopter, the great days of guerrilla warfare were drawing to a close.

American participation may, under these circumstances, have seemed better than total reliance on the Shah. It was thanks largely to Iranian help, after all, that Barzani had come to rule over large parts of northern Iraq on and off since 1961—surviving, in his words, "five regimes and nine governments" in Baghdad. Some Kurds are convinced that the gambler in Barzani instinctively knew in 1972 that this was the last roll of the dice even for a man who at sixty-eight remained physically vigorous and mentally alert. If so, then Barzani may have calculated that the original, admittedly imperfect American policy that Othman detected in Washington in July 1972 might somehow be upgraded to the Kurds' advantage at some later point. "We do not trust the Shah," Barzani told *The Washington Post*'s Jim Hoagland in 1973. "I trust America. America is too great a power to betray a small people like the Kurds."

In March 1975, with his entire career turning to ashes, Barzani seemed to acknowledge the extent of his miscalculation. "The U.S. government did not give us any formal assurances, but we thought they would never abandon us," he told Hoagland, who had traveled to Kurdistan to report on the collapse. "Now we see we were wrong." But Barzani's faith in the United States was also a reaction to his disappointment with all things Russian, after suffering so many privations and tribulations during his Soviet exile. Also, his older brother, Sheikh Ahmed, who had long exercised a great influence on him, had advised him to pursue the American connection. Mohsin Dizai, one of his senior lieutenants, said Barzani "believed nothing was done in the Middle East, or most of the world, without the support of the U.S." Dr. Othman recalled, "General Barzani just thought the U.S. was the key superpower, and it eventually turned out he was not wrong in that."

In the Kurdish camp the exact details of the American commitment's limits, until the very end, remained a tightly held secret known only to Barzani's immediate family and a very few senior aides. Yet, an American connection of some sort was generally taken for granted. "Indeed, it was inconceivable to any politically minded person in the Middle East," noted a Kurdish historian, "that the Shah would embark on such a major financial and military venture in Kurdistan without some form of prior consultation with the U.S. administration." On the eve of renewed fighting between the Kurds and the Iraqis in March 1974, wary senior cadres questioned Barzani and the witting inner circle about assurances of outside aid until the wee hours of the morning. Without giving details, Barzani, Idris, and Dr. Othman insisted that sufficient assurances existed. No one bothered to listen to the muted urgings of caution. Until it was too late, Barzani remained convinced that the United States "as a great power would not let the Kurds down once it had agreed to entertain relations with us." But in his letter to Carter in 1977, Barzani would indirectly acknowledge that there had been no written guarantee, writing that the Kurds were "honor-bound by verbal commitment, both to the U.S. and Iran," that the Kurds had put their "hearts and faith . . . in the belief that the American commitment, whether verbal or written, is iron-clad."

Yet verbal agreement is not the same as a formal guarantee, as Barzani well knew. In a lawyer-minded society such as the United States, a written commitment might have prompted the administration to keep to the straight and narrow if only to avoid the embarrassing disclosure of any reneging. And in all fairness, since in this century we have witnessed many a strongman tearing up the most lawyerly of treaties, would even a formal treaty have prevented the Shah from dumping the Kurds? The apparent lack of a binding document points up both Kissinger's penchant for covering his tracks and Barzani's wishful hope at its most tragic. Barzani was wrong and lived to acknowledge the most serious miscalculation of his career, a humiliation all the more galling in that he lived out his final years in Iranian and U.S. exile, effectively gagged from denouncing the very men who had betrayed him. At the end of his life he was reduced to half-jokingly expressing the "hope I end up in Peking and then I can say all I want about the Americans and the Soviets." After all, he had his place in a kind of Third World Guinness Book of Records as the only leader who had spent more than a decade in the Soviet Union *and* figured on the CIA payroll *and* was used and abandoned by Stalin and the Shah of Iran.

But the puzzle of Barzani's character—and of how he was judged by the governments that manipulated him—lies at the very center of this splendid exemplar of great-power manipulation of an isolated and desperate minority. His inveterate naïveté about the United States struck Americans as suspect or beside the point. Twenty years later a defensive Kissinger told me, "I don't know what difference it would have made" if he'd understood Barzani's pro–U.S. bent, which he clearly had not. Helms, perhaps because from the very beginning he felt he had been straight with the Kurds in spelling out the nature and limitation of the U.S. role, said that everyone concerned with the Kurds considered Barzani a "big boy" after a lifetime of intrigue and rebellion. In turn, Kurdish nationalists (except for those in the inner circle around Barzani who knew better) assumed that without formal American guarantees their leader would not have gotten involved in renewed fighting in March 1974. But even had the U.S. guarantees been copper-bottomed, plenty of troubling inconsistencies began to crop up.

There simply was no way of deterring Barzani. Sensing potential disaster in fresh fighting between the Ba'athist government and the Kurds, General Andrei Grechko, the Soviet Defense Minister, who had known Barzani during his Soviet exile, flew to Iraq to help the government find a compromise with the Kurds. At the prompting of Tehran and Washington, Barzani refused. On the virtual eve of renewed hostilities, in a meeting in Baghdad Saddam Hussein again offered to share Kirkuk and its oil, but Barzani's son Idris turned him down. "We're stronger than you believe," he said, "and will oblige you to accept all our demands." Never a man to accept a threat without countering with one of his own, Saddam Hussein warned: "If there is war, we will win." Not only did he now have sophisticated Soviet weaponry, but he knew Barzani was relying on the Shah's determination to wrest away at least partial control of the Shatt al Arab, the estuary connecting the Persian Gulf to the Iranian oil port of Abadan and the Iraqi port of Basra.

In 1937, the British, who had controlled the entire estuary as the successors to the Ottoman powers, had persuaded Iraq to give Iran limited rights at Khorramshahr and Abadan, where ships at anchor would henceforth fly the Iranian flag; they had feared that any revision might hamper the passage of their own warships to the British-owned oil refinery at Abadan or to Basra. Until 1969 all ships entering Iranian ports on the Shatt had to be piloted by Iraqi pilots, an arrangement which the Shah construed as a humiliation forced on his father, since Iran was still obliged to accept the international border on the Iranian bank of the estuary and to agree that shipping on the Shatt had to fly courtesy Iraqi flags. "If we were to find ourselves in a corner faced with the choice of either giving up half the Shatt al Arab or the whole of Iraq," Saddam warned, "we would give up the Shatt al Arab in order to keep the whole of Iraq in the shape we want."

Within months Saddam was again toying with the very terms he had outlined (as, indeed, the CIA discovered he had been doing as early as October 1972). The Shatt al Arab was at the center of a meeting in August between the Iranian and Iraqi foreign ministers in Istanbul, a meeting requested by Iran and arranged by Algeria, which was determined to end the conflict and strengthen OPEC. Those talks soon became the focus of Barzani's attention. He discussed the possibility of an Iran-Iraq deal "more than once" with his inner circle, but he "failed to see the full implications"—that the Shah would cut off all aid and even collaborate with Iraq to enforce the Kurds' surrender. Whenever Barzani brought up this worry, Iranians told him to forget it, but Kurdish suspicions should have become more concrete later that summer when Eric Rouleau, Le Monde's Middle East editor, told them that the Shah had boasted in a recent interview that their very existence was a tap he could turn on or off at will. Rouleau was struck that the Kurds attached little importance to the Shah's crude warning and seemed to dismiss its implications out of hand. He formulated serious doubts about their powers of analysis. "When my information failed to open their eyes," he recalled, "I put it down to their rather limited experience on the world scene." Indeed, most of the leaders of the Kurdistan Democratic Party, especially the group around Barzani, convinced themselves, until it was too late, that Iran would

not cut a deal with Iraq. But logically how could Washington prevent the Shah from striking such a deal if he wanted to? That
remained a never-solved conundrum.

There was something touching and despairing about the Kurds'
simply refusing to accept the accumulation of evil omens. Instead
they persuaded themselves that autonomy, indeed independence,
was just a few years, perhaps even months, off. Cooler heads could
have moderated such enthusiasm by invoking a half-dozen cautionary reasons. But the Kurds believed as an article of faith that
they knew everything there was to know about Iranians, as if suspicion of Tehran was a Kurdish genetic characteristic. Perhaps this
blanket suspicion lulled them into sloppy thinking, kept them from
piecing together the plentiful fragmentary evidence. Until it was
too late, Barzani never fathomed the Shah's fine grasp of timing,
his attraction to cold-blooded brutality, and his taste for cruelty.
From the very beginning it was the Shah's game and no one else's.

Militarily, the Kurds were paradoxically ill prepared for Iraq's
motivated and beefed-up onslaught. On paper the Kurds had never
been so strong: they'd been trained by American, Israeli, and Iranian advisers; and unlike their preparedness in the 1960s, when
they had only light infantry weapons, this time the Kurds had some
artillery power of their own as well as modern infantry weapons.
Almost all their matériel was Soviet (captured by Americans in
Vietnam or by Israelis in their wars with the Arabs), a provenance
that gave the donors the perfect cover of "plausible deniability."
Eventually the Kurds within Iraq were backed up by two and a
half Iranian artillery battalions—more than a hundred pieces—and
British-made Rapier ground-to-air missiles stationed at the border
and manned by retired British servicemen. Still, they steadily fell
back to the mountains and even in their traditional strongholds
held out in great part thanks only to Iranian artillery protection.
The Kurds' problem was that their foreign backers had talked them
into forsaking hit-and-run guerrilla tactics, at which they excelled,
for conventional warfare, for which the *pesh merga* were neither
trained nor talented.

Worse, the change of tactics made the Kurds ever more dependent on these foreign backers, especially the Shah. Barzani complained in his letter to Carter that "belatedly, we realized—as we
faced eight Iraqi army divisions, hundreds of tanks and more than
a hundred sophisticated airplanes—some of which were piloted by
Russians and Indians—that assistance from our friends was both

inferior in quality and quantity." Iran repeatedly squeezed off supplies when the Kurds were advancing, only to restore normal logistics when they were thrown back on the defensive and as a rule made sure that the Kurds never accumulated more than three days' worth of artillery rounds. Eventually the Kurds comprehended that the job their allies intended for them was to tie down, not to conquer, the Iraqi army.

In retrospect the Kurds seem to have been either dim-witted or fatalistic to a fault. But in Barzani's defense it must be said that Iraqi Kurds did not find such a spoiler's business totally unreasonable or out of character with past strategy. Unwaveringly, they argued that they could destabilize Iraqi governments, but never march on Baghdad and take over themselves. From 1961 on, with varying degrees of success, they had held their own, tactics that had produced the 1970 autonomy agreement which, whatever its failings, had produced what Kurds even today consider a golden age.

By September 1974 the Iraqis had already gained considerable ground. So grave were the Kurdish setbacks that Iran gave Barzani more long-range artillery and antitank missiles; still, by the new year the Kurds' military situation was dangerously exposed. In his posthumously published secret diary, Alam, the Shah's court minister, noted on January 3 that the Shah was delighted with reports that Iranian troops "fighting like lions" had saved the day, stiffening the resistance of Kurds about to buckle and flee. Despite the Shah's pride in the "terrible beating" inflicted on the Iraqis, Barzani clearly was worried: for weeks on end he was kept waiting, cooling his heels in Tehran for a constantly put-off audience with the Shah. Rumors proliferated about rival initiatives brokered by Algerians and Jordanians to settle differences between Iran and Iraq at the Kurds' expense. In his letter to Carter in 1977, Barzani was to say that Iraq had sent "indirect signals" to Washington that it would curtail its ties with the Soviet Union and settle with Iran *if* the Shah dropped the Kurds. Whether he knew that at the time is questionable. But Barzani was concerned enough to offer Iraq an eleventh-hour deal of his own, which Saddam Hussein turned down, for his own negotiations with the Shah were by then too far advanced.

The Shah was nothing if not devious, encouraging the Kurds on a fool's errand to consult King Hussein of Jordan about forming a government-in-exile with other opposition groups; in January, when the emissaries arrived in Amman, they were kept waiting for a week, and in the end the King refused to see them. Then, in February, President Anwar Sadat asked Barzani to dispatch Sami Abderrahman to Cairo. At their meeting he inveigled Abderrahman into agreeing to have Egypt transmit a compromise offer to Saddam Hussein on the Kurds' behalf, but unbeknownst to the Kurd, Sadat had the conversation taped and sent to the Shah, who was furious.

No wonder that Barzani wanted once again to go to Washington to get the Americans to redress the increasingly bleak military and diplomatic situation. It was a long shot. Hoping to ingratiate himself, he had three rugs sent to Kissinger, then a gold and pearl necklace on the occasion of his marriage to Nancy Maginnes, but the gestures were to no avail. Kissinger, by now Secretary of State, had been scaling back U.S. aid to the Kurds since 1973. Nonetheless, in a letter of January 22, 1975, Barzani again broached a Washington visit. Kissinger had long since "known everything, in detail, about the whole process," as Othman later put it. It took Kissinger one crucial month to reply to "my dear general," assuring him of "our admiration for you and your people and the valiant efforts you are making" and, amid other flowery compliments, turning down his request. "The difficulties you have faced are formidable," his letter read.

I very much appreciated reading your assessment of the military and political situation. You can be assured that your messages receive the most serious attention at the highest levels of the United States Government because of the importance we attach to them.

If you would like to send a trusted emissary to Washington to give the U.S. government further information about the situation, we would be honored and pleased to receive him. I am convinced that secrecy has been of paramount importance in maintaining our ability to do what we have done; it is only for this reason—plus our concern for your personal safety—that I hesitate to suggest a personal meeting here with you. I look forward to hearing from you.

Please accept my sincerest good wishes and high esteem.

In fact, as that brush-off indicated, Kissinger did not look forward to hearing from Barzani at all. But many anguished messages kept coming, via Callahan, the worried CIA station chief in Tehran; the first was dated barely two weeks later, dispatched in the wake of the deal the Shah struck in Algiers with Saddam Hussein at two-thirty a.m., on March 6, at a private encounter on the sidelines of a scheduled OPEC summit meeting. The Shah abruptly dropped the Kurds, in exchange for which he gained sovereignty over half the Shatt al Arab, Iraq's abandonment of its irredentist claims on Khuzistan, Iran's richest oil province, and an end to Iraq's subversion of Iranian Baluchistan along the border with Pakistan. (For years Baghdad had underwritten subversion in "Arabistan," as the Ba'athists called Khuzistan, which they claimed was unjustly torn from the Arab nation.)

Kissinger, Helms, CIA director William E. Colby, and every other U.S. official involved claimed to be genuinely surprised at least by the timing, if not by the substance, of this agreement in Algiers. As Colby put it, the CIA considered this outcome "always an option for the Shah." Still, the administration did nothing and said nothing, despite the Kurds' increasingly desperate appeals. "It was a tragic story, not a pretty story," Colby remarked later, "but that spring we had several other tragic tales in Southeast Asia of considerably greater moment"—by which he meant the collapse of Cambodia and South Vietnam.

With the United States still a superpower, albeit a wounded one, Kissinger that spring was rebuffed in his Egypt-Israel disengagement talks and confronted with impending humiliation in Indochina. The administration did not have the excuse (as Israel did) of being too small to raise its voice in defense of a traduced ally. No document that has yet come to light suggests that the Ford administration even considered such an excuse. As Helms said many years later about his reaction to the Algiers deal, "I thought Washington would be pleased"—after all, America's ally, Iran, had got the best of the Soviets' Iraqi friends. And, as Kissinger wrote in his memoirs, the Shah "was for us that rarest of leaders, an unconditional ally, and one whose understanding of the world situation enhanced our own."

Still, Washington understood that the Shah had clearly violated the essence of the 1972 agreement he had struck with Kissinger. A March 22, 1974, CIA cable, disclosed in 1976 in the Pike report, summed up the stakes: "Iran, like ourselves, has seen the benefit in a stalemate situation . . . in which neither Iran nor ourselves wish to see the matter resolved one way or the other." But now the Shah on his own had ended the stalemate and resolved the conflict without warning the Kurds, or, apparently, even the Israelis or Americans, if their officials were to be believed. Kissinger later recalled being "stunned" when informed about the Algiers agreement and said he detoured to Zurich to meet the Shah on the monarch's way home. "He did not ask our opinion," Kissinger said defensively. But his memory was playing tricks on him: in fact his meeting with the Shah in Zurich *preceded* Algiers, and Kissinger must then have figured out what was about to happen even if the Shah did not spell it out in so many words.*

In terms of realpolitik, the Shah acted as he did not because he was threatened by imminent military defeat, although his forces were bogged down and Kurdish resistance had virtually ended during the normally slow winter months, when for the first time the Iraqis had stayed in the mountains rather than retire to winter quarters. The traditional spring fighting season was approaching with its unforeseeable expenses and risks, and the Shah and others believed he might well settle or face having a real war with Iraq on his hands. But in fact, the Shah acted as he did because it was to his advantage and because his foreign partners either could not or would not stop him. What struck hardheaded diplomats and politicians at the time was how much Saddam Hussein ceded, especially the readjusted Shatt al Arab border, now drawn along the *thalweq*, or deep-water median channel—just what the Shah wanted most, for tactical and family reasons.

Until 1991 Kissinger limited his explanation of all this to a brief paragraph and footnote in his voluminous official memoirs, oddly innocent of any mention of the Shatt al Arab, and promised to return to "the Kurdish affair and its tragic outcome" in a later volume, which he never did. The footnote, apparently motivated by a desire to justify the Shah, says that the monarch's "decision in 1975 to settle the Kurdish problem with Iraq was based on the judgment, almost certainly correct, that the Kurds were about to be overwhelmed; they could not have been saved without the intervention of two Iranian divisions and $300 million in assistance from us." How close Barzani's forces really were to collapse remains

---

* Ahmad Chalabi, then a young Beirut-based Iraqi Shia exile friend of the Kurds, had "smelled a rat" just before Algiers and flown to Tehran to warn Barzani. The tipoff for Chalabi was not just the Zurich meeting but the Shah's flying detour to brief key officials before Algiers. Also, Sadat and King Hussein both knew of the impending deal. Nassiri ordered Chalabi to leave for Beirut immediately, "if you know what is good for you." But Chalabi managed to see Barzani, nonetheless, at the SAVAK safe house where the Kurdish leader was staying. (The premises were bugged, so they talked in the garden.) Barzani sighed, cursed the Iranian officials who had prevented him from seeing the Shah.

open to conjecture even today: just before the Algiers meeting, when Chalabi warned Barzani, he found him "sad, weary and complaining that only 3 percent of the *pesh merga* were fighting." Yet Iraqi Kurds remained convinced that at the very least the Shah might have obtained more honorable conditions for them in Algiers. In his memoirs Kissinger does not explain how he decided that the Shah was "almost certainly correct," how the $300-million figure was arrived at, or why the United States should have been expected to foot such a bill after years as a token contributor. Without a suggestion of criticism of the unilateral move, Kissinger merely noted that dumping the Kurds was the Shah's "sovereign decision to make." From beginning to end it was basically the Shah's war, not Washington's.

Still, Kurds found Kissinger's footnote suspiciously self-serving. Under pressure, and only in 1992, Kissinger revealed in an interview that the Shah had approached him about the $300 million "four to six weeks" before Algiers, and acknowledged that in broaching that sum the Shah may have been laying the groundwork for the unilateral deal, giving himself a pretext for acting on his own. If Kissinger, too, smelled a rat at the time, he did not let on. But bandying about this considerable figure was an obvious tipoff, a clear signal of the Shah's growing impatience with supporting the Kurds, and of a desire to have a pretext to drop them and blame it on others, to wit, Americans.

A sum like $300 million was, after all, an obvious nonstarter. The Shah, of all people, who kept close tabs on Washington, realized that by 1975 Kissinger's Superman image was tarnished and that the undercover operations he supported on so many continents were catching up with him: the situation in Vietnam was on the point of collapse, and the Israelis were about to derail their negotiations with Egypt about their withdrawal from the Sinai. Along with everyone else, the Shah could see that Kissinger was unable even to persuade Congress to allocate funds to save Saigon from collapse, much less win approval of $300 million for the Kurds. In contrast, the Shah, fat with the quadrupled oil revenues he had helped to mastermind for OPEC after the 1973 Arab-Israeli war, operated under no such institutional or financial constraints. For the Shah, money was not the determining factor.

In his first message to Kissinger after the Algiers accord, Barzani on March 10 went to the nub of the matter:

. . . our hearts bleed to see that an immediate byproduct of their agreement [in Algiers] is the destruction of our defenseless people in an unprecedented manner as Iran closed its border to us completely and while [the Iraqis] began the biggest offensive they have ever launched and which is now being continued. Our movement and people are being destroyed in an unbelievable way with silence from everyone. We feel, your Excellency, that the United States has a moral and political responsibility toward our people, who have committed themselves to your country's policy . . . Mr. Secretary, we are anxiously awaiting your quick response.

Twelve days later Callahan, in Tehran, cabled CIA director Colby, noting that Kissinger had not replied and warning that if Washington "intends to take steps to avert a massacre it must intercede with Iran promptly." Nothing was said or done. But Barzani's words were to haunt Kissinger for years. That spring Kissinger set his face against the repeated Kurdish requests for humanitarian aid for their tens of thousands of refugees and instead issued a cynical defense that he later gave every sign of regretting: "Covert action should not be confused with missionary work," he said (he is the anonymous "high U.S. official" quoted in the Pike report).

Barzani had not claimed that the Kurds had ever had a formal American guarantee, nor had he threatened to publicize his outrage. The weakness of his position was all too clear, and any detailed accusation would surely prompt the Shah to close Iran's borders even more tightly. But Callahan was worried that the Kurds might not confine their complaints to the back channel but instead broadcast them to the world. Callahan asked:

Is headquarters in touch with Kissinger's office on this? If the U.S. government does not handle this situation deftly in a way which will avoid giving the Kurds the impression that we are abandoning them they are likely to go public. Iran's action has not only shattered their political hopes, it endangers thousands of lives.

The series of messages Barzani addressed to the CIA, President Gerald Ford, and Kissinger that spring remained unanswered. Of all the Pike report's revelations, this silence after the Algiers agreement perhaps rankled most. First leaked by Daniel Schorr, a veteran CBS reporter, then in toto in a special issue of *The Village*

Voice, the liberal New York weekly, in February 1976, the report moved William Safire, the conservative *New York Times* columnist, to enduring outrage. Safire, who was never to deviate from a spirited defense of Iraq's Kurds, denounced the "unconscionable sellout" of Barzani and demanded that Ford fire Kissinger for foisting this "dishonorable act" on the administration.

Safire was exercised by the administration's failure not only to pressure the Shah to "make a decent deal for Kurdish autonomy in Iraq" but to provide "even a dime for humanitarian aid." The Pike report succinctly concluded that from the beginning

the president, Dr. Kissinger, and the Shah hoped that our clients [as it termed Barzani's Kurds] would not prevail. They preferred instead that the insurgents simply continue a level of hostilities sufficient to sap the resources of our ally's neighboring country [Iraq]. This policy was not imparted to our clients, who were encouraged to continue fighting. Even in the context of covert operations, ours was a cynical enterprise.

The Pike report further said that documents "made available to the committee" chronicled how the administration, acting as the Shah's "junior American partners," had gone along with his plan, serving "in effect as a guarantor that the insurgent group [of Kurds] would not be summarily dropped." Notwithstanding these implicit assurances, the Shah had abruptly cut off the Kurds three years, thousands of deaths, and $16 million later. "It appears that had the U.S. not reinforced the Shah's prodding," the report added, in its most hedged conclusion, "the Kurds may have reached an accommodation with [Iraq's] central government, thus gaining at least a measure of autonomy while avoiding further bloodshed. Instead the Kurds fought on, sustaining thousands of casualties and 200,000 refugees."

The report may have exaggerated the likelihood of a possible accommodation, but the resumed fighting in 1972 certainly laid waste to large swaths of Iraqi Kurdistan and gravely damaged the cause of Kurdish nationalism. What was certain was the Shah's delight in 1975. Upon his return from Algiers, his cynical self-satisfaction with his Machiavellian double-dealing at Barzani's expense was boundless. His court minister, Alam, recorded the Shah's pleasure when told that his Algiers trip had been his "most successful" ever. The Shah felt he had righted "two infuriating problems inherited from my father"—the shame of a humiliating obligation to accept dictation at the hands of a British-controlled oil company and Iraq's control of the Shatt al Arab. Asked about the Iraqi Kurds' fate, he coldly replied that their autonomy had been "moonshine from the word go." But the tough-talking Shah had not yet received Barzani, and he struck Alam as "apprehensive" and "naturally . . . a little embarrassed to meet the man face to face." Defensively, the Shah insisted to his confidant that the Kurds had gone from defeat to defeat and "without our support they wouldn't last ten days against the Iraqis." He quoted Saddam Hussein in Algiers as admitting that "several times the presence of our troops and artillery had been the only factor to stand between the Iraqis and total victory." Alam recalled that in 1971 only the Shah's intervention had prompted Barzani to reject Iraq's acceptance of Kurdish demands: "Both sides knew that Iraq had no serious intention of honoring her promise," his diary quoted the Shah as saying. "It was more a cheap gimmick than a promise."

Gimmick or not, the Kurds first heard about the Algiers deal without prior formal warning on the evening of March 6, when, at the guest house where SAVAK put up Barzani in Tehran, they listened to the BBC Arabic and Farsi broadcasts (regularly and anxiously monitored by Barzani, Mohsin Dizai, and Dr. Othman). "This is the end for us," Dizai said, but Othman dismissed the reports as "diplomatic games." A somber Barzani said nothing. Later that evening Iranian television showed a tired but triumphant Shah landing at Tehran airport and talking to no one but the army chief of staff. "We couldn't hear what he was saying, but we could just see," Dizai recalled. "I said I had the impression that conversation was about us." Again Othman disagreed. Again Barzani said nothing.

At breakfast the next day, the Kurds' Tehran representative arrived with depressing reports of the overnight radio traffic from Idris Barzani, in Iraqi Kurdistan. Without warning during the night Iranian army units—complete with artillery, ammunition, even food—had moved back across the border into Iran and coincidentally Iraqi troops began a big offensive. Dizai told Dr. Othman, "I told you last night the Shah was talking about us." General Abdul Ali Mansourpour, an Iranian Kurd on the staff of SAVAK director Nassiri, indignantly denied that there had been any sellout, insisting, "The Shah will never betray you." Then he left, only to return a half hour later, crestfallen, to confirm the Kurds' fears. He took Barzani aside, and when he departed a few minutes later he was weeping. He telephoned the Kurds later, entreating them not to mention his tears.

It was left to Nassiri himself to soften up the Kurds for the Shah. Any argument was good if it masked the Shah's own rapaciousness. Nassiri told them that the tape recording which the duplicitous Sadat had forwarded to Tehran had so angered the Shah that he rushed into the Algiers agreement. Nassiri also said the Shah was under pressure from Sadat, the Americans, and others, who wanted him to drop the Kurds in exchange for Saddam Hussein's offer to alter Iraq's foreign policy, become very anti-Soviet, and have good relations with Iran. Iranian support for the Kurds was the sole obstacle to Iraq's ending its reliance on Moscow, went the argument.

Barzani was "so very angry that he was shaking inside," Dizai remembered. He asked the SAVAK commander, "Why did you not warn us? How can you trust Saddam, who once he gets rid of the Kurdish revolution will be stronger and then change his mind? You will regret this." Nassiri said the Kurds were free to fight on, but without Iranian support, and would be welcome in Iran as refugees. Dizai was dispatched immediately to Iraqi Kurdistan to size up the situation. He later reported back to Barzani that the KDP leadership and fighters, although extremely upset and disappointed, wanted to keep on fighting. Unbeknownst to Barzani, the Shah had made other secret undertakings to Saddam Hussein in Algiers, but apparently found it expedient to let the Kurds down gradually.

The Shah delayed his audience with Barzani until March 11 (deliberately, some Kurds argued, to coincide with the fifth anniversary of the signature of the Kurdish autonomy agreement and thus rub in the price he had exacted for their disregarding his repeated opposition to it). The meeting at the Niavaran Palace provided a classic illustration of the Shah's casuistry, mixed with what Barzani considered his thinly disguised satisfaction in dispensing such humiliation. The Shah said the Kurds had only themselves to blame; a year after resuming the fighting, they not only had not succeeded in overthrowing Saddam Hussein but had lost so much ground that to save the situation Iran would have had to commit many more troops, tantamount to formal war with Iraq. Embroidering on Nassiri's arguments, he remarked that Iran's allies now blamed him for tilting Iraq toward Moscow.

Shifting the discussion back to the moral high ground, Barzani told the Shah, "We put our hands in yours. We did not expect ours to be chopped off." Dr. Othman asked: "What are we going to tell our people, we, who relied on Iran?" The Shah became angry and nervous. He blamed the Kurds for talking too much. Dizai pointed out that the Kurds had lots of experience with Saddam Hussein, "who did not keep his promises and who will betray you when he becomes stronger." Drawing on his days as an Iraqi ambassador, he added, "I know, because I have seen official Iraqi documents about the Gulf and Khuzistan" that encouraged irredentism among its original, if outnumbered, Arab inhabitants.

The Shah reiterated that the Kurds could keep fighting, but without his support, and that Iran would welcome Kurdish refugees even then fleeing to take advantage of the formal two-week cease-fire ending April 1 (which Iraq soon broke). But as Alam's diary revealed, the Shah was uneasy about criticism of his handling of the Kurds: "The international community [was] accusing us of betrayal," but "in any case an independent Kurdistan was never likely to do us much good." On March 20 Alam was sufficiently moved by the plight of tens of thousands of Kurdish refugees to note Barzani's pleas for more time to get the guerrillas' families across the border. The Shah adamantly stuck to the letter of the Algiers agreement, which limited asylum to the fighters alone and trusted Iraq not to harm the Kurdish guerrillas' women and children. "I replied that whilst this may be true," Alam noted, "we can hardly expect the Kurds to believe it or to abandon their families." The Shah's only reaction was to suggest that the International Committee of the Red Cross protect the abandoned Kurdish families. That appeared to be Washington's main effort to respond to Barzani's entreaties.

Back in Hajj Omran on March 12, just inside Iraqi Kurdistan, the *pesh merga* leadership debated what to do far into the night and again the next day. Barzani talked only in general terms, buoying the diehards who were determined to keep fighting albeit with reduced forces. Then General Mansourpour appeared, dispatched by the Shah, with more bad news. The Shah now recollected that he had promised in Algiers not to condone any further fighting by the Kurds, and Iraqi troops were authorized to cross into Iranian territory to enforce this promise. Nor was there to be an extension of the formal, if increasingly notional, cease-fire to allow Kurds in the furthest reaches of the Badinan in northwestern Iraq to make the long journey on foot to Iran. "You can surrender to Iraq or you can surrender to us," Mansourpour said. "You have no other choice."

Cornered and dispirited, Barzani sent Iraq a telegram proposing new negotiations; Baghdad cabled back an outright rejection. That evening as a group of judges and lawyers gathered to hear him, Barzani, recalling his truly heroic history of struggle and betraying an "unmistakable note of farewell," suddenly ordered the Kurds to stop fighting. There had been no meaningful consultation outside his family and immediate inner circle, certainly none involving the KDP central committee or politburo. Stopping fighting was the lesser of two evils, Barzani said. Anyone wanting to go to Tehran could do so. Kurds pleaded, professed understanding for his opposition to further fighting given his great age, implored him to "leave one of your sons to rally the resistance." The next day stunned cadres at headquarters kept repeating, "The revolution is over."

Barzani's seemingly abrupt decision generates anger to this day, skews Kurdish politics, and tarnishes his image. At first it struck the majority of Kurds ignorant of the background as having been plucked out of thin air. Further efforts were made to try to change his mind, but "to no avail," Sami Abderrahman recalled. "Remember, Barzani in those days was still a demigod. I think if he'd been younger and the family poorer Barzani would have fought on. But he was old and the Iranians had given him millions."* American protection, which Barzani's inner circle hinted at to doubters, of course proved to be nonexistent. With every passing day a growing shock and sense of betrayal among rank-and-file Kurds showed their dawning disbelief at their leadership's naïveté. Within two weeks, Barzani's *pesh merga* army of some fifty thousand men followed his order and ceased to exist. Even as devoted a Barzani loyalist as Dizai thought at the time, "This is going to hurt Barzani a lot." Others were less well disposed. "Had Barzani stayed on to lead the fight in Kurdistan or committed suicide," one veteran cadre said, "he would have been a hero forever. No one would have dared criticize him."

Pent-up frustration with his leadership burst into the open even before he left Iraqi Kurdistan for the last time and crossed the border into Iran, a bitter, broken, and ill old man. The backbiting concerned everything from favoritism toward his clan and family

---

* Kurdish critics of Barzani's stewardship said he left Kurdistan with about $70 million.

to his penchant for secrecy, his authoritarian rule, and his unjustified faith in foreign allies. Suddenly, ordinary Kurds realized how rash and smug their leader had been in trusting a national liberation movement's fate to the Shah's proven skullduggery, on the will-o'-the-wisp notion of getting support from a superpower with a proven record of hostility to Kurdish aspirations. The comeuppance was all the more galling in an era still heavily freighted with leftist ideology. American prestige was at a low because of the debacle in Vietnam, and the Kurds blamed themselves for failing to woo Third World opinion and allowing their oppressors to bask in the support of the "socialist camp" and "progressive forces." Some suggested that Barzani was deterred not just by his conservative foreign backers but by the "red mullah" nickname which the British press had given him after his long sojourn in the Soviet Union.

With horror the Kurds now understood that they lacked sufficient arms and ammunition to fight a long guerrilla war alone. More damaging still, perhaps, to a mountain people proud of their warlike reputation, was their military collapse. The Kurds had grown dependent on Iran's now abruptly withdrawn heavy artillery, and Barzani to please the Shah even handed over Iranian Kurdish leaders who had sought refuge with him. Within two weeks the Kurdish rebellion simply dissolved. The retreat to Iran prompted a Kurdish historian to lament, "I can think of no other example of a people's war ending so lamentably, following a leadership decision at a time when the people were still willing to fight and had the means to do so." Foolishly, the Kurds had even relied on food trucked in from Iran rather than their own crops. Such were the major themes contributing to debilitating divisions and disputes within the Iraqi Kurdish nationalist movement. In one form or another they have lasted ever since. As usual, the neighboring powers were delighted.

At the time, most Iraqi Kurds accepted Barzani's orders, if only because in their anguish they saw no alternative. Like it or not, the Shah was right in that: Iran was the Kurds' only window on the world and the Shah was slamming it shut. Some *pesh merga* refused to obey and did fight on, some committed suicide, still other Kurds broke and burned their few belongings in bonfires of despair before trudging through muddy roads and freezing mountain passes across the border into Iran to join the more than a quarter-million Kurds who had already sought refuge there from the fighting. It was an orderly retreat by tens of thousands, often barefoot and clad in only cotton and nylon clothes, but a retreat nonetheless. Turkey refused to open its borders to the Iraqi Kurds, invoking its standard exclusion of all but European refugees.

To no avail Barzani repeatedly sought American and Iranian help in extending the cease-fire so that more distantly based *pesh merga* and their families could escape Saddam's inevitable wrath. He did what he could: he sent a car to evacuate Issa Swar, the veteran *pesh merga* commander in Badinan, and his family. Infuriated *pesh merga* fighters, realizing that he was effectively abandoning the rank-and-file, assassinated Issa Swar in revenge. The killers knew full well what fate awaited them at Saddam Hussein's avenging hands. Indeed thousands of Kurds, mostly civilians, were killed, and tens of thousands were driven into exile in Iran.

Convinced of the uselessness of armed struggle, the vast majority soon took advantage of Iraq's offer of the general amnesty and, within months, returned; Iranians forced others back across the border. Then Baghdad began mass expulsions as part of a policy that branded Kurds as incorrigible enemies of the state. Between 120,000 and 300,000 Kurds who had returned from Iran under the amnesty were shipped to the center and south of Iraq and kept there for around a year; militants, especially students and teachers, were singled out for vengeful measures that ranged from imprisonment to torture and execution.

Soon Iraq began to create a strip of no-man's-land between five and fifteen miles deep and running some six hundred miles along the borders with Iran, Syria, and Turkey, so as to deny Iraqi Kurds easy contact with their fellow Kurds abroad. Some fifteen hundred rural villages within this so-called security zone were dynamited and bulldozed, their orchards cut down and wells cemented over. Their 750,000 inhabitants were deported to hastily built new mass housing, dubbed "victory villages," often located next to military and police camps for easy surveillance. Arabs were encouraged to take over Kurdish land in the name of the Ba'ath Party's "strategic security" concept, which displaced Kurds from the borders, from fertile farm country as well as from Kirkuk and other contested oil centers. Thus were the seeds sown for what became known as "cultural genocide," the gradual but increasingly efficient uprooting of the Kurds' traditional rural life that lay at the heart of their society. By the late fall of 1975, in the first of many summaries of the human-rights abuses visited upon the Kurds, Amnesty International reported that 389 Kurdish women and children were under arrest not for anything they had done but because of their menfolk's guerrilla activities.

Yet the CIA's Callahan, who had pleaded that cushioning the Kurds' suffering "would be the decent thing for the U.S.G[overnment] to do," turned out to have been overwrought at least on one major point. On April 10 he had warned that "if senior Americans like Kissinger . . . do nothing to help the Kurds in their present extremity we may be sure that they will not lie down quietly to be buried without telling their story to the world." In fact it was years before Barzani ever talked about this in public. Why he remained silent so long astounded Kurds and foreigners alike. Yet, for an old revolutionary who over the decades of more downs than ups had learned not to insult the future with emotional outbursts that could weaken an already weak hand, his discretion made sense. He knew he could expect little from the Shah, but had still counted on Washington. Only weeks after the Algiers agreement, at a news conference in Hajj Omran in March, he took aside the journalist Jim Hoagland, whom he had known earlier, and who he insisted on assuming was an American official, despite Hoagland's elaborate disclaimers both times they met. Now Barzani asked him to communicate to the U.S. government a personal request for political asylum and for protection of the Kurds.

Barzani, a lifetime heavy smoker, was suffering from pains behind his collarbone—soon to be diagnosed as lung cancer—and he adopted a low profile. He wanted to go to the United States both for medical reasons and for his own physical safety. In light of proven Iraqi proclivities for brutality and revenge, he had good reason to fear assassination, and he realized that as long as he stayed in Tehran SAVAK would bottle him up, silencing and isolating him as the price for their minimum aid to his refugees. So in talking to Hoagland and other reporters, Barzani prudently spoke of "betrayal" in only the most general terms. The United States had "let us down," he confided, "to face a war of genocide. We were given definite encouragement by Iran and many promises were made which were not kept. We were offered full support in all aspects." More to the point was his plaintive question: "Have the Kurdish people committed such crimes that every nation in the world should be against them?"

So serious was his pain that in June 1975 Barzani was allowed to fly to the United States for treatment. To his fury he was accompanied by a SAVAK agent. His mood did not improve when at New York's Kennedy Airport a CIA operative and Morris Draper, head of the State Department's Iraq desk, joined him for the flight to the Mayo Clinic in Rochester, Minnesota. There Barzani's cancer was judged incurable, and he was given no more than six months to live. He wanted to go straight to Washington where Mohamed Dosky, a former Iraqi diplomat who had become his representative in the United States, had won over to the Kurdish cause Senators Henry M. Jackson and Richard Stone as well as George Meany, the head of the AFL-CIO. Barzani hoped they could bring quiet, behind-the-scenes influence to bear. At one point he toyed with asking Meany to hire a small plane to "kidnap" him and fly him to Washington. But his guardian angels had other plans. While Dosky anxiously wondered why Barzani and his small party had not arrived as planned, they were being trundled around the American West, visiting Lake Tahoe and California for a month to keep them out of sight.

Eventually, a Barzani aide furtively telephoned Dosky to arrange a meeting, inventing an excuse to escape from the CIA safe house in McLean, Virginia, where Barzani was being held incommunicado. There was desultory talk of leaving for Switzerland, which Barzani's son Massoud described as "better than house arrest" in America. Dosky was so upset that he disobeyed Barzani's standing order about avoiding the press. Determined to extract better treatment from the administration, he got in touch with Daniel Schorr at CBS. Schorr wanted to put Barzani on the air to relate the American betrayal of the Kurds, but Barzani refused: he wanted to stay in the United States and thought he was in no position to endanger his precarious guest status.

Barzani also correctly sensed that with the presidential election campaign about to start, the Ford administration wanted to force him to return to Iran. In November 1975, armed with six months' supply of medicine and the assurance that Iran's doctors were just as competent as the Mayo Clinic's, he was sent back. Draper, who like so many others was fascinated and touched by Barzani, was proven right: when he'd first been assigned to keep in touch with Barzani, he'd been instructed to assess the chances of Barzani's embarrassing the administration publicly but had quickly predicted that Barzani would not be a troublemaker.

Soon Congress did the muckraking for Barzani. While he was in Iran, the Pike report was leaked in America. Yet he still remained

silent. Had he been tempted to speak out earlier, as Colby remarked, "we certainly would have made some effort to dissuade
him from spilling the beans," and doubtless, the CIA's surveillance
of Barzani while he was in the United States came under that
heading. But by the spring of 1976 "we were up to our ears in
congressional investigations," Colby said years later, a wry allusion
to the probes into the agency's undercover activities in Angola and
to the Indochina collapse. "We would have liked to avoid" Barzani's
denunciations, he added, "but we would not have been that upset."

The Ford administration nonetheless was taking no chances in
an election year. Barzani, in increasing pain, tired by repeated
chemotherapy and his medicine exhausted, ran into a brick wall
when he wanted to return to the United States for a checkup.
Dosky asked the office of Joseph Sisco, Undersecretary for Political
Affairs, for a visa on medical grounds, but he was brushed off.
After further delay an assistant to Sisco received him; nothing could
be done, he was told, since Barzani traveled on an Iranian passport
and Tehran had turned down his request. Angrily Dosky accused
Washington of washing its hands of responsibility: "You murdered
Barzani politically, now you intend to murder him physically."

Eventually Dosky succeeded in getting the State Department
to give Barzani a visa, though it would do him little good since the
Iranians would not let him leave. Infuriated by the State Department's efforts to hide behind the Shah's skirts, he now threatened
that Barzani might publicly tell his story. That further concentrated
the administration's mind. Dosky was invited to the State Department to discuss the conditions under which Barzani could be
in the United States. He was not to talk to the press, given the
election campaign, and, unlike the first time, when the CIA had
picked up the tab, he would have to pay his own way, although
the U.S. government would give him bodyguards. In turn, Dosky
insisted that Barzani was to be free to travel and meet anyone he
chose, without surveillance.

But when Barzani arrived at Kennedy Airport in June 1976, a
SAVAK tail, Draper, and a CIA man accompanied the Kurdish
party back to the Mayo Clinic. After the checkup, Barzani took up
residence in Washington, moving from a hotel to an apartment,
then to a house in the city itself, before settling in a five-bedroom
colonial house in McLean. He was in and out of remission, chart-
ering planes to fly to Minnesota to see his doctors, often in great

pain but stoic. In public, only his hawklike features betrayed his suffering.

Foreigners who had known Barzani in Kurdistan were horrified by his plight. Hoagland, who has kept a photograph of Barzani in his office since their first meeting, declined several approaches from the Kurdish entourage suggesting a visit. "I just couldn't steel myself to seeing the eagle in a cage," he recalled. "Emotionally I just couldn't do it." Haim Levakov, the old Mossad agent in Kurdistan, had wanted to visit Barzani in his "virtual house arrest, but the Americans caused problems. If he had seen me," the Israeli said, "he would have said, 'Let's die together.'" Barzani went on putting a good face on his Washington stay.

Refusing to admit to himself that he was in exile, determined to bring the Americans around somehow, Barzani entertained as a way of keeping in touch with anyone from Washington officialdom. But he was handicapped by language barriers; his English, despite valiant efforts with a bilingual dictionary, never progressed beyond "It's delicious" and "Thank you." At dinners with Senators Jackson and Stone, Draper, and journalists like Jack Anderson and Smith Hempstone, Barzani talked freely but never on the record, despite friends' repeated efforts and an offer to help him write his memoirs by taping his stories; Draper thought that Barzani superstitiously believed recording his life story would only hasten his death.

Barzani's caution was perhaps justified, for yet another effort was made to force him back to Iran. In the early fall, the Shah sent a telegram, quite possibly at American suggestion, asking Barzani to return to Tehran, in order to spare the Ford administration the anguish of a last-minute outburst during the final months of the election campaign. This time Barzani refused, knowing he could count on his friends in the Senate and in the labor movement. To the Americans he invited to his Kurdish meals, Barzani recounted his scarcely believable life, with its repeated betrayals by Iran, Iraq, Turkey, the Soviet Union, Israel, and now the United States, always faced by hopeless situations, always fighting. "It was like having the Chinese describe the Long March," Draper recalled. Barzani readily acknowledged his own miscalculations and errors. Still, he could not understand the priorities of American policy in the Middle East, with its fixation on the Arab-Israeli dispute. Barzani struck Draper as a generally pretty cautious person after bouncing around all these years. He was absolutely consistent and insistent—and I had many talks with him—that he would never have joined in in 1972 if the Americans had not given their O.K. For him the Iranians were worse than the Iraqis, and he didn't trust the Turks, either.

Barzani kept reiterating that his goal was "limited autonomy" for the Kurds, which he defined as preservation of the Kurdish language and culture and a fair cut of the oil revenues. "I took it all down and faithfully passed it on," Draper recalled. "But it was quite clear with Henry" Kissinger "up there on the seventh floor" of the State Department that "it was just an embarrassment." Indeed Kissinger was so determined to maintain good relations with Iran that he and the Shah had belittled the Pike report at a news conference held at the imperial summer palace on the Caspian Sea that August.

U.S. weapons sales were accelerating, and the Shah arrogantly remarked, "Do you have any choice?" In a remark which Kissinger himself liked to repeat, he also said, "If the U.S. does not help its friends, the only alternative is nuclear holocaust and more Vietnams." As was now abundantly clear, Kissinger did not consider the Kurds as friends. In turn, Kurds took a grim satisfaction in hearing that the very mention of them sent Kissinger into something approaching a tizzy. The word around the State Department was that anyone mentioning Kurds to Kissinger risked being cut off.

Barzani was delighted when Jimmy Carter defeated Ford in the presidential race that November and Kissinger was sent packing. Given Carter's high priority for human rights in the formulation of foreign policy, Barzani's hopes for a more favorable policy toward Iraqi Kurds briefly soared, only to be dashed. Received at the State Department for a pro forma "tea and sympathy session," he learned from Carter's Mideast hands that there would be no change in policy, much less a meeting with the new president. Such was the Shah's importance for successive administrations. Barzani reluctantly accepted his fate. He "had his friends in the Senate and the press, but never succeeded in establishing high-level executive contacts," Draper said. "I was very frank in telling the Kurds it would not happen." Polite, dignified, and proud, Barzani kept his disappointment and anger under tight control when receiving foreigners. In mid-January 1979, when he had had the satisfaction of watching a cancerous Shah forced out of Iran and into exile by revolutionary forces, he exulted: "Look at what happened to the guy who did me in!"

By then Barzani himself was fading fast. Unable to bear the sight of his diminishment, Draper, by his own admission, "chickened out." In his stead he sent Mary Ann Casey, the Iraqi desk officer, to see this vanquished leader whom he so respected. When she arrived, Barzani was very short of breath, but sensing this was his last chance to get what he really wanted to say off his chest to an American official, he launched into a long and eloquent denunciation of the U.S. government. In telling detail and with great emotion, he went over everything he had previously refused to say, leaving nothing out—the injustices he felt, the betrayals, the American untrustworthiness. "His breathing got stronger as he went along," Dosky recalled, "as if he knew he was going out." To this day Casey has refused to talk about their meeting.

By the last days of February 1979, Barzani lay unconscious in Georgetown University Hospital. Members of his household spelled one another around the clock at his bedside. He wanted to be buried in his village of Barzan, long since thoroughly destroyed by avenging Iraqi troops intent on leaving no two stones standing, and in any case Iraq was in no mood to cooperate. His next choice was Ushnavieh, in Iranian Kurdistan, where he had fought in defense of the Mahabad Republic three decades earlier. But above all he wanted to die in Kurdistan, in the bosom of his family. He was far too ill to fly by commercial airliner, so a chartered plane was laid on, complete with an oxygen cylinder, to fly him to Tehran on March 2. On March 1, Barzani said he wanted to sit up. Dosky rose to get a pillow, and Barzani said no, he wanted to sit up in a chair. "His head went forward," Dosky said, "and he was dead."

———

Thirty-two years earlier Barzani had met Archie Roosevelt in Tehran, whither he had been brought to face punishment for helping to defend the recently crushed Mahabad Republic. "I am not afraid of death," Barzani had told this first American official he met. "I care about only two things—my honor, and keeping my word." Even that was now denied him. Barzani did get his wish to be buried in Kurdistan—but not without a subsequent bitter irony. Barzani's casket was flown by plane from Tehran to Urmia (thanks to the cooperation of Iran's new revolutionary government). The original plan called for the funeral cortege to drive to Ushnavieh; instead, at the last moment the casket was taken by helicopter, a change that Iran's revolutionary authorities imposed as a precaution, fearing trouble between Barzani's supporters and the many Iranian Kurds who had never forgiven him for arresting and executing their leaders to please the Shah in the past.

In Ushnavieh, where ten thousand Kurds gathered from as far away as Sanandaj, in southern Iranian Kurdistan, and the Badinan, in northwestern Iraq, Barzani was laid to rest without incident. But in early 1980 radical Iranian Marxist Kurds desecrated his simple grave. The Barzanis recovered the corpse and reburied Mullah Mustafa in their mountain stronghold at Rayan, just inside Iran on the border with Iraq. In the fall of 1993 his body was taken by helicopter to the border itself, whence it was escorted by road—first by his old disciple-turned-adversary, Jalal Talabani, then by his son, Massoud—to the village of Barzan, where at last he was buried as he wished. Two American helicopters circled overhead and two American F-16 fighter-bombers made two ceremonial fly-pasts. The United States was finally making amends for the betrayal of 1975.

Americans were among many foreigners who helped tarnish both Barzani's honor and his word. The United States was implicated a quarter century before Kissinger's decision in 1972 to go along with the Shah. Back in 1947 Archie Roosevelt had been canny enough to discern the legitimate Kurdish nationalist aspirations in the Mahabad Republic. Most observers saw only the opening chapter of the Cold War, with Moscow backing the Kurds and Azerbaijanis against the triumphant Shah, supported by Britain and the United States. Upon hearing of the death sentences handed down that January 23 against the Mahabad Republic's three top leaders, Roosevelt prevailed on Ambassador George Allen to intercede with the Shah. "If they are executed," he argued, "we shall be considered a party to an act viewed with horror by Kurdish nationalists everywhere." The Shah, receiving Allen promptly, asked with a smile, "Are you afraid I'm going to have them shot? If so, you can set your mind at ease. I am not." The Shah kept his word in a peculiarly Iranian way. The leaders were not shot but hanged.

Thus did Roosevelt's prophecy about Kurdish distrust of the United States start to take form. In his Washington exile Barzani embroidered on the theme in the time-honored oral tradition of the Middle East, gradually changing emphasis to play down his own errors of appreciation and shifting the already heavy burden of guilt squarely onto wily outsiders. In his letter to President Carter in 1977, a summation of his frustrations and grievances, Barzani wrote, "We were not militarily defeated by our enemy. We were destroyed by our friends," and asked, "Can so great a nation as the U.S., whose declared fundamental principles of honor, integrity, freedom and democracy for all peoples, hold [up] its head after their role in the Kurdish downfall?"

For the next fourteen years, successive American governments seemed outwardly unbothered by what had happened, aside from a handful of often genuinely conscience-stricken State Department and CIA employees who had had direct involvement with the Kurds. In the closing period of the Iran-Iraq war, Washington took no punitive action against Saddam Hussein's use of poison gas, which killed thousands of Kurdish civilians at Halabjah in March 1988; thousands more succumbed to chemical weapons in the final months of the war; and still further thousands died even after the August 20 cease-fire ending that conflict. In February 1991, President George Bush encouraged the Kurds to rise against Saddam Hussein, then tried to turn a blind eye to their massive exodus when their revolt collapsed in part because of his own government's refusal to shoot down Iraqi helicopters spreading terror in northern Iraq. Only exhaustive television coverage of the plight of Kurds freezing on mountaintops forced his hand.

It was that spectacle that finally prompted Kissinger to come to terms, in his own way, with his responsibility for some of the Kurdish distrust of the United States. In a syndicated column of May 5, 1991, he wrote, "No one can view the heart-rending scenes of suffering along the frontiers of Turkey and Iran without welcoming any move that promises to avert disaster among the Kurdish refugees." He had not been moved by similar scenes in 1975, which were equally compelling, although virtually absent from television; as the Pike report noted, he did nothing then to provide American humanitarian aid to Kurdish refugees. Now, for the first time, Kissinger said, "For us in government at the time, the decision was painful, even heartbreaking." Ever true to his realpolitik, he added, "The lesson to be learned concerns the original commitment, not the final outcome. The United States should have determined from the start how far it could reasonably go in helping the Kurds, and should have made these limits unequivocally clear before offering assistance."

In August 1991, a Kurdish delegation visiting the United States took the initiative for arranging a meeting with Kissinger. Theirs was a gesture all but formally absolving him of guilt, if not responsibility, for 1975. "We need all the friends we can get," a Kurdish participant explained. A year later when at long last Kissinger agreed to meet me to discuss the Kurds, the ordinarily outwardly composed foreign-policy specialist was visibly nervous. He kept juggling the exact time of our appointment, finally scheduling it in such a way as to limit its duration to barely twenty minutes before his departure for the airport; throughout our meeting he kept consulting his wristwatch. Nonetheless, his answers were studded with remarks such as "If I have to blame myself," "In retrospect I should have been more careful," and "I did not analyze the situation carefully enough." What had he thought about the Shah's behavior toward the Kurds? "I thought he was playing a rough game, that he had been terribly rough on them," Kissinger answered. But "the Shah did not ask our opinion" before signing the Algiers accord, he said defensively.

Did he remember the letter he had written (now in Dosky's possession) putting off a meeting with an anxious Barzani, who wanted to confer in Washington in January 1975? He could not recall but hypothesized that it would have been "incautious" to have put such thoughts in writing. What about that remark in the Pike report about undercover operations not being missionary work? Was that his phrase? "I could have said that," he allowed, but "did I?" What was most important in meeting the Kurds after all these years? "I wanted to be clear," he replied, "that I did what I thought was my duty."

7

The Blind Beggar:
Ecumenical Arbaeen

Even in the annals of arcane Middle East intelligence games, this was a very strange evening at the servicemen's club in Tel Aviv, an event in April 1979 to which several hundred Israelis were bidden by written invitation, including former prime minister Yitzhak Rabin, the past and present heads of the Israeli intelligence agency, Mossad, and army and Mossad personnel who served in what Israel stubbornly called an undercover operation, although long since the worst-kept secret in the Middle East.* During a forty-five-minute ceremony, the speeches were short, heartfelt, sometimes sentimental. Buglers from an army band sounded taps, and the Star of David was raised and lowered in homage to a comrade in arms. What made the commemoration ceremony singular was that it was taking place forty days after the demise of the man eulogized, and it was an *arbaeen* (derived from the Arabic word for forty), an Islamic rite commemorating the dead. Israelis are not given to Muslim memorials in honor of Muslims.

But the honored man was Mullah Mustafa Barzani, and for a critical decade he had been Israel's ally in its efforts to weaken successive Iraqi governments. He had died in Washington's

* On September 29, 1980, Prime Minister Menachem Begin became the first Israeli official to disclose that Israel had provided money, arms, instructors, and training to the Kurds—and he infuriated Mossad staffers in so doing. Israeli newspapers the next day revealed that General Barzani had made several secret visits to Israel in the 1960s and early 1970s.

Georgetown University hospital, his bitter American exile alleviated only by the comeuppance of those all-powerful statesmen who had engineered his humiliating betrayal in Algiers in March 1975. U.S. President Richard Nixon had resigned over the Watergate scandal in 1974. His tarnished Secretary of State, Henry Kissinger, had been turned out of office when President Gerald Ford lost his reelection bid in 1976. Houari Boumediène, the Algerian leader who had helped arrange the sellout of the Kurds in 1975, had died a painful, lingering death in December 1978. And, only six weeks earlier, the Islamic revolution had driven Shah Mohamed Reza Pahlavi into exile.

As the *arbaeen* itself suggested, the Israeli participants felt no overt guilt for Barzani's undoing. Their unfeigned veneration of Barzani and his cause notwithstanding, a senior Mossad officer later recalled, they were haunted by "not simple or easy memories." But for these men at least, the ambiguities of Israel's relationship with Iraq's Kurds generally stopped well short of soul-searching about its advisability. With the passage of time, Israelis involved with the Kurds convinced themselves that Israel had had no part in Barzani's betrayal at the hands of Iran and the United States. Like so many other intelligence field hands involved in similar undercover exercises throughout the world, they preferred to dwell on the glory parts, on what they had accomplished, and on the friends they had made far away.

For two crucial years in the mid-1960s Israel's help in a little-known war had arguably saved Barzani's movement from destruction, and for a decade it contributed to maintaining the semblance of independence he presided over in much of northern Iraq. The total cost for its helping lightly armed Kurdish guerrillas pin down tens of thousands of Iraqi troops, Mossad calculated—troops that might otherwise have participated in both the 1967 and 1973 Arab wars against Israel—was less than that of a Mirage fighter-bomber. Never mind the final disaster, and never mind that the aid failed in its proclaimed goal of immobilizing entire Iraqi divisions. Israeli veterans of the Kurdish adventure, interviewed more than a decade later, found it difficult to keep a misty-eyed nostalgia from obscuring the starker real world. They proudly brought out photographs showing themselves with Kurdish leaders, refought past battles on coffee tables, criticized recent Kurdish tactics, inquired after old Kurdish friends and wished they could see them again. A British ambassador to Iraq in the 1940s not known for sympathizing with the Kurds once scathingly remarked, "The Anglo-Saxons are always falling in love with strange people," and so, in turn, did these Israelis, admiring the Kurds for their mountaineers' openness, courage in combat, and stoic acceptance of suffering. "Put a Kurd atop a mountain with a rifle, pita bread, and onions," enthused a Mossad veteran, "and he'll stop a whole of column of troops for you." The Israelis also professed to see parallels with a persecuted minority in distress, albeit one without the overseas ties, educated and powerful diaspora, international political backing, or even an outlet to the sea that Israel enjoyed. Occasional hardheaded dissenters cautioned that Israeli aid was exploiting the Kurds for Israel's own ends.

As it turned out, the Kurdistan experience was also to bear bitter fruit for Israel, which developed a dangerous penchant for questionable sub-rosa operations. For it emerged that Israel's Kurdistan veterans later became involved in undercover operations from south Sudan and Ethiopia to Lebanon and Latin America that brought Israel into disrepute for two decades. Some of the same Israelis who served in Kurdistan were enmeshed in corrupting relationships with the Maronites of Lebanon, with the Medellín drug cartel, and with Central American dictators from Anastasio Somoza Debayle of Nicaragua to Manuel Antonio Noriega of Panama.

These far-flung rogue activities were unimaginable in the wake of the 1956 Arab-Israeli war over Suez, when Israel cautiously put into practice what became known as the "periphery policy" to break out of its regional isolation. Brainchild of Reuven Shiloah, who was Mossad's first director, the policy was rooted in his youthful espionage activities in Iraq for the Jewish Agency, the Zionists' proto-state administration in British-mandated Palestine. For three years in the early 1930s, he posed as a schoolteacher and part-time journalist, wandering around Iraq making contacts with the Kurds and other non-Arab minorities under cover of collecting material for never-published articles.

Clandestine ties with non-Arab minorities inside nominally Arab countries and with neighboring non-Arab Muslim states became a tenet of Israeli intelligence operations. It all boiled down to institutionalizing that ancient dictum: "The enemy of my enemy is my friend." Designed to create problems for Arab regimes and give Israel breathing space, the policy was rooted in formal but sub-rosa intelligence-sharing arrangements in the Middle East with non-Arab Muslims in Iran and Turkey and, later, in the Horn of Africa with Christian-run Ethiopia. To this end Mossad set up a foreign-relations department in 1958 focused on containing the growing influence of Egyptian President Gamal Abdel Nasser, whom it considered in all but formal league with international Communism.

The so-called Trident Organization, which brought together Israel, Iran, and Turkey, organized regular intelligence meetings starting in 1958 and was based on shared links with the United States and a mutual fear of strident Arab nationalism and Communism. Until the Shah of Iran was overthrown two decades later, Iran remained the jewel in the crown of this system, giving Israel everything from oil to forward defenses in the form of massive amounts of modern Western arms that Iran purchased ostensibly as protection against the Soviet Union but in reality to outgun and cow Iraq. Helping the Iraqi Kurds was a neat fit for both Israel and the Shia Aryans of Iran, with their age-old tradition of hostility to Arabs.

Both governments "feared a too powerful and homogenous Sunni Arab Middle East," Mossad veteran David Kimche has noted. "Israel did not want an Iraqi army reinforcing Syria and Jordan in a future war." Iran, meanwhile, wanted to distract the Iraqi army from the disputed southern frontier along the Shatt al Arab and from oil-rich Khuzistan. After the 1948 war, Iraq had remained the only Arab combatant state that refused to sign a formal armistice with Israel. Tying down Iraqi divisions—indeed at times most of the Iraqi armed forces—became the central geostrategic factor underpinning the aid-the-Kurds policy, for the Jewish state was determined to offset its numerical weakness by creating maximum mischief in the Arab camp.

Israel justified this policy by pointing to the seemingly ever shriller anti-Zionist propaganda pouring out of successive regimes in Baghdad. Of course, Iraq's vituperation was partially an expression of frustration that it could not end the Kurds' Israeli connection. These considerations did not prevent Iraqi expeditionary forces from bolstering Arab armies in the 1967 and 1973 wars with Israel, but the long-term irritant on the Kurdish front did dilute Baghdad's ability to be of greater help to the Palestinian cause.

The point of departure for Israel's Kurdish policy came with the overthrow in July 1958 of the Hashemite monarchy in Iraq and the end of Great Britain's virtual regency, in place since creation of the state after World War I. With General Abdel Karim Qassem's revolution, a decade of near-constant political instability began— and with it the chance for Israel to intervene. Destabilizing Iraq was a constant goal shared equally by Israel, Iran, and the Iraqi Kurds, but the three players were far from being equally important. Iran formally recognized Israel in 1950, authorized regular El Al flights to land in Tehran, but never officially allowed Israel's diplomatic mission in Tehran to fly the Star of David or even display a brass plate identifying itself. So crucial was this relation with Iran that the Israelis could ill afford to thwart the Shah on matters great or small. Given the imbalance, the Kurds were never Israel's main priority in the relationship, despite some Israelis' romantic disposition to see the two forces as oppressed minorities helping one another. As for Barzani—poor, underarmed, isolated, and in rebellion against Baghdad since 1961—he was uncomfortably and totally dependent on Iran as his only lifeline to the outside world.

Throughout the decade, Iran provided the lion's share of the aid to the Iraqi Kurds, aid that ebbed and flowed in relation to the Shah's perception of Iraq's political mood—spurting, for example, when pro-Nasser Abdel Salam Aref seized power in Baghdad in 1964. For the Shah it was all for the better that Israel was a small power, and untainted by a long history of treachery toward the Kurds like his own. Using Israel to help the Kurds also gave the Shah that most desirable of intelligence payoffs—"plausible deniability."

Thus, it was with Iranian approval that Israel and Barzani were allowed to stumble into each other's arms in the 1960s. Who made the first step remains unclear. A key initial player was Kamuran Ali Bedir Khan, a fervent Kurdish nationalist and descendant of a princely Turkish Kurd family with revolutionary credentials going back to the mid-nineteenth century. Then in his seventies, Bedir Khan was Barzani's spokesman in Europe, eking out a pittance in Paris teaching Kurdish at the Ecole Nationale des Langues Orientales Vivantes (better known as Langues O.). He was no stranger to intelligence work. Right after the Ottoman defeat in World War I, he had acted as guide and interpreter for Major Edward W. C. Noel, Britain's legendary Kurdish specialist, whose expedition into Turkish Kurdistan in April 1919 so enraged the Turkish authorities that he was recalled. The Turks condemned Bedir Khan to death in absentia for his part in subsequent uprisings. Thereafter he lived between Beirut and Damascus, where France exercised a League of Nations mandate, publishing Kurdish magazines and working as a lawyer. In 1947 he went to Paris at the bidding of Roger Lescot and other French orientalists who also dabbled in Middle East intelligence work. Soon Lescot went to work full-time for French intelligence and bequeathed Bedir Khan his Kurdish language teaching post at Langues O. Bedir Khan set up a Kurdish study center, but was so poor that he could often not afford to print his publications and had to make do with a mimeograph machine.

Bedir Khan also had long-standing Zionist undercover connections. Within months of the creation of the state of Israel in May 1948, he was moving around the Middle East—Egypt, Syria, Lebanon, and Transjordan—and at one point that summer he brought back King Abdullah's conditions for settling Transjordan's outstanding problems with Israel. He also sought in vain Israeli support for plots to overthrow the Lebanese and Syrian governments by recruiting Druze, Circassians, and Maronite Christians, all of whom had occupied senior posts in the governments and armed forces trained by the only recently departed French during their League of Nations mandate. Bedir Khan argued that such operations could knock Lebanon and Syria out of the war with Israel—and encourage, by example, Kurdish nationalist aspirations throughout the region. In itself the idea was not new. Zionists from David Ben-Gurion on down had long toyed with similar notions of taming the Arab world by creating so-called "mosaic states" favoring various minorities at the expense of the national boundaries created from the ruins of the Ottoman Empire. Israel finally succumbed to temptation, entering into full-blown undercover alliance with Lebanon's Maronites in the 1970s and 1980s—with disastrous consequences. Many of Mossad's old Kurdistan hands became involved.

Bedir Khan's penchant for intelligence work stemmed, according to his French friends, from his rueful conclusion about the impossibility of armed uprising after the rapid collapse of a well-planned Armenian and Kurdish revolt against Turkey in 1930, in which he had been a leading player. His views did not change in the aftermath of World War II, with a Middle East polarized by the Cold War, traumatized by the creation of Israel, electrified by radical Third World ideologies, and enamored of Arab nationalism. In such a world the Kurdish cause—with its implicit irredentist claims on Iraq, Iran, Turkey, and even Syria likely to upset the artificial political boundaries—found no serious backers among the world's established political parties or governments. Bedir Khan thought that the best the Kurds could expect was discreet backdoor crumbs provided by the shadowy intelligence world. This was a country-cousin heritage that Kurds, especially Iraqi Kurds, found difficult to shake off, and it brought them much grief.

In the spring of 1963 Mossad, in a variation of Shiloah's own experience three decades earlier, dispatched a foreign journalist based in Paris to Kurdistan, where he interviewed Barzani and Ibrahim Ahmad, secretary-general of the Kurdistan Democratic Party; he suggested sending an emissary to talk to the Israelis at a Right Bank hotel in Paris, near the Israeli embassy, then located in old Rothschild palace on Avenue de Wagram. Hard-pressed by Iraqi troops, Barzani agreed, although less enthusiastically than might be supposed, since he would have far preferred a deal with the United States or the Arabs, had they but shown serious interest. However deep a nationalist Kurd's distaste runs for his Arab, Iranian, or Turkish tormentors, it is generally leavened by a healthy respect for the power of their modern centralized states and a desire—rarely translated into fact—to negotiate gains rather than risk outright warfare.

Barzani, as we have seen, never entertained the thought of seizing power in Baghdad; at best he hoped to use outside help to preserve what he could of the Kurdish north, free of direct Iraqi rule. To that end "the Israelis were small potatoes and Barzani would have dropped them in a flash," a Kurdish historian maintained, "if the Arabs gave him a nibble." But they didn't. Like the Palestinians, Barzani believed he had little choice but to back every horse in the race. He once told a Palestinian women's delegation reproaching him for collaborating with Israel that he was like "the blind beggar outside the main Sulaimaniyah mosque," incapable of seeing who put a coin in his outstretched hand.

Thus, in the fall of 1963 Ahmad traveled to Paris, took a room at the recommended hotel, and telephoned the journalist, who notified the Israelis, who were surprised and delighted. They had not been sure Barzani would follow up on the suggestion, much less dispatch someone of Ahmad's importance. Menachem "Nahik" Navot, Mossad's man in Paris (later its deputy director), was the first Israeli to meet Ahmad, who was then forty-nine but "looked older like so many people who suffer." Ahmad later met Ambassador Walter Eytan, who listened at length to his tale of woe and pleas for help. Ahmad pushed all the right buttons. He compared the Kurds' fate to that of the Jews, explained that the Kurdish fighters were so poor they could not even afford tea or sugar, appealed to Foreign Minister Golda Meir's maternal instincts. Although the Israeli establishment was scarcely known for being sentimental, Navot years later recalled that he and Eytan were moved. Mrs. Meir, once filled in, rapidly sent back instructions to initiate the fateful relationship. Ahmed, shrewdly assessing Israel's interests, was not surprised.

Nor was he astonished when Bedir Khan, whom he had purposely not informed about his meeting with the Israelis, took him to the Lido nightclub on the Champs-Elysées and struck up a seemingly spontaneous conversation with the man at the next table, who turned out to be an Israeli Communist parliamentarian. The Israelis sent Ahmed back to Kurdistan with twenty thousand dollars and a promise of aid to come.* The first weapons arrived within a month. When Ahmed returned to Kurdistan, Barzani was pleased about the weapons but disappointed that he had raised so little money. Ahmed complained about Barzani's accepting a cease-fire with Baghdad on terms he and the KDP found wanting, but Barzani replied that he did not have enough money to go on fighting.

Almost everything else, weapons, ammunition, military advisers, training, an enterprising cabinet minister, agricultural experts, doctors, dentists, a field hospital—and resumed warfare—followed in due course. A visiting foreign journalist reported mysterious airdrops of weapons as early as 1963. (Other sources said military cooperation was full-fledged by 1965.) Yaakov Nimrodi, the Israeli military attaché in Tehran, was instrumental in getting weapons from Israel to Iran for the Kurds; later he made a fortune in arms dealing and eventually played a key role in the arms-for-American-hostages scandal in the 1980s. Weapons deliveries increased sharply after the 1967 and 1973 wars, especially of ever more sophisticated Soviet arms which the Israelis had captured from Arab armies.

In one of its first moves, Mossad also dispatched a dentist with an old pedal-operated apparatus to pull out all of Barzani's teeth and replace them with dentures made in Tehran. In what some Kurds insist was Israel's most significant involvement, Mossad in

---

* By way of comparison, another Barzani lieutenant, Sami Abderrahman, only a few years later persuaded Franz Josef Strauss, the Christian Socialist politician in Bavaria, to pony up $2 million for the Kurds.

1966 helped set up Parastin (meaning "protection" in Kurdish), the Kurds' intelligence organization, which was commanded by Barzani's son Massoud, who was trained intensively by Mossad in Kurdistan and Israel. Parastin ramified among Kurdish communities everywhere, and Mossad advised it "on anything they wanted advice on," in the words of an Israeli academic with excellent intelligence links. Inside Kurdistan Mossad dressed its men either in Iranian kit or in Kurdish uniforms complete with cummerbunds and checkered turbans, at times designating their quarters as "the press tent" to throw the inquisitive off the scent.

At no one time were there more than a handful of Israelis inside Iraqi Kurdistan, and most never strayed from the relative safety of the area near the border with Iran. Oddly, Mossad did not draw on the tens of thousands of Israelis actually born in Kurdistan, preferring to use Arabic speakers or have Arabic-speaking interpreters with their advisers.* Despite constant Iraqi accusations about Iran's and Israel's aid to Barzani, foreign journalists and other visitors never discovered the Mossad teams. When Eric Rouleau, then *Le Monde*'s Middle East specialist, inadvertently happened upon Israelis giving Kurds some weapons training, one Mossad instructor suggested killing him and then claiming an accident. The Kurds demurred, gambling—correctly, as it turned out—that Rouleau had not cottoned on to the Israeli presence.

In any case, only a few senior Kurds were privy to Mossad's secret work in Kurdistan (although an Israeli officer included in a Kurdish delegation negotiating with Iraqi officials deliberately revealed his identity, apparently with Barzani's blessing). Military training took place in Iraqi Kurdistan, Iran, and Israel—Kurds were flown to Haifa in an operation code-named Omenet Tova

---

* Before their mass exodus to Israel in 1950, as many as 30,000 to 40,000 Jews called Kurdistan home; they were centered in Zakho, Akra, Amadiya, Duhok, Erbil, and Sulaimaniyah. Like the Christians of Kurdistan, they spoke Aramaic as well as Kurdish, and claimed descent from the Jews of the Babylonian captivity under Nebuchadnezzar in 605–562 B.C. Although 90 percent illiterate, they included merchants, shopkeepers, boatmen on the Khabur River, and, most unusual for Jews, landowners and farmers. Most of the rural Jews lived in mixed villages with Kurdish Muslims or Christians. Sundur, a village of four hundred farming families located between Amadiya and Zakho, was the only entirely Jewish community in Iraqi Kurdistan. Many Kurdish Jews in Israel even two generations later continued to be deeply interested in all things Kurdish, and militantly backed government efforts to help Iraq's Kurds. Until recent years bus trips of Israelis of Kurdish extraction have ventured close to the Turkish border in atavistic tourism to renew acquaintance with their roots.

("good nanny" in Hebrew)—at first concentrating on simple infantry tactics, including handling mortars and recoilless rifles, and, later, operating Soviet-built antitank and shoulder-held antiaircraft missiles.

The Israelis never tried to change basic Kurdish fighting traditions. There was no need, remarked Haim Levakov, a tough Israeli Arabist who shuttled back and forth between Israel and Kurdistan from 1966 to 1973, because "the Kurds knew the terrain and how to fight." He compared his work with the Kurds to his own youthful experience in the late 1930s with Jewish units being trained in guerrilla warfare by Orde Wingate, the maverick pro-Zionist British officer who later distinguished himself with similar tactics against the Japanese in Burma during World War II. Mossad instructors introduced the Kurds to the fast-firing Soviet Kalashnikov and Swedish Carl Gustaf assault rifles, and they admired the ammunition-efficient Kurdish marksmen's uncanny ability to hit targets at more than five hundred yards with old Czechoslovak long-barreled Brno Mauser rifles, which were the Shah's hand-me-downs. "Every man a sharpshooter," marveled a former Israeli instructor, "best shots I'd ever seen." The Israelis and other foreigners were also impressed by the Kurds' fearless retrieval of their own wounded no matter what the odds. The Kurds returned the compliment, telling the Israelis they were "built for battle."

Israeli advice contributed to the Kurds' most famous victory in the 1960s, the destruction of an entire Iraqi brigade on Mount Hendrin, near Rawanduz, on May 12, 1966. Basically Hendrin was a Kurdish show commanded by Barzani's son Idris, seconded by *pesh merga* veteran Fakher Mergasuri in the field and crucially aided by Communists and left-wing Arab officers who had deserted.* So many people have claimed credit for this victory that it has become almost impossible to separate fact from fiction. Indeed, even among Mossad veterans there is a lively controversy about the importance of Israel's contribution, especially that of Colonel Tsuri Saguy. Acting as the Kurds' unofficial chief of staff, Saguy concluded from listening to Iraqi army radio traffic that Iraqi artillery officers had lied about their batteries' forward positions to please higher-ups. He studied the terrain and trained Kurdish commanders in Tehran and in Israel in consequence, his advice

---

* Parastin later executed Mergasuri, as well as his family, without trial on ill-elucidated charges of treason.

reinforcing what the lightly armed Kurdish guerrillas already knew: don't expose yourself to Iraqi aircraft and armor by getting out in the open; don't build fortifications, because they're easy to spot from the air; and do use natural tree and rock cover.

As the overwhelmingly large Iraqi force occupied one mountain after another around Rawanduz, Barzani and the Israelis understandably fretted. Barzani knew his forces lacked the weaponry and command and control vital for conventional warfare. At one critical point he had to order a proud local Kurd commander, convinced that his men could handle any Iraqi onslaught, to fall back and bait the trap for what turned out to be an epic ambush. Organized in clumps of company-sized sharpshooters with a small, two-battalion force hidden in reserve, the Kurds with only rifles and a few light mortars held their fire as the Iraqis climbed higher up the mountain slopes. When the Iraqis reached about 6,000 feet, the Kurds opened up from two sides, and cut the Iraqi Second Division's 1,800-man Fourth Brigade to pieces in three hours. The Kurds were past masters at what the Vietnamese called "hanging on their belt"—getting in so close that the better-armed enemy dared not risk using air force or artillery for fear of killing his own troops. Fewer than twenty Kurds died. The Iraqi dead—twelve hundred in one division alone, according to its commander's after-battle report—were buried in the nearby town of Diyana with empty 7UP bottles serving as gravestones. In ten days' fighting around Rawanduz, the Iraqis lost at least two thousand men killed, not counting *jash* casualties.

Before the battle Barzani was so worried about potential casualties in his amateur army that he had to be persuaded to approve a scheme which combined guerrilla and set-piece tactics. He was downright angry when he heard about the outcome. "Thirty or forty Iraqi dead," he told a surprised Saguy, "that's possible. But three thousand dead—now I can never speak to the Iraqi army." In vain Saguy protested that the Iraqis had got what they deserved for having initiated the attack. When Iraqi emissaries appeared in two jeeps flying white flags and asked to see Barzani, Saguy suggested their terms might well become even more interesting if the Kurds chewed up their five remaining brigades. Barzani overruled him: "Sorry, but I've waited a lifetime for them even to deign to speak to me." Israeli brass back in Tel Aviv were incredulous when they learned of the Iraqi casualties. "That's impossible," General Aharon Yariv, head of military intelligence, said. "It's a guerrilla war. What are you talking about?" The Hendrin victory prompted the Iraqi government on June 6 to proclaim a cease-fire that was to last for two years.

The Israelis got a massive return on their Kurdish investment. On August 15, 1966, the Kurds helped Mossad in a painstakingly organized defection of an Iraqi Christian pilot named Munir Redfa, who flew his state-of-the-art Iraqi Air Force MiG-21 to Israel. Mossad agents picked up Redfa's family, ostensibly out on a picnic, and conveyed them from Baghdad to the Kurds, who smuggled them to safety across the Iranian border. Israel offered Redfa $1 million and asylum in Israel for himself and his family, considered the money well spent, and invited the delighted Americans to study the Soviet-built plane. Mossad basked in the glory, which added to its reputation in Washington.

The Kurds were also extremely adept at an operation that was dear to Israeli hearts—smuggling out of Iraq the rump of what before the legal emigration of 1950 had been a more than 100,000-member Jewish community. The Kurds put the summers of 1970 and 1971 to good use, taking advantage of yet another cease-fire; Kurdish cars carried Baghdad Jews northward (to diminish government suspicion, the exodus was timed to coincide with the traditional summer exodus of Iraqi city dwellers fleeing to the mountains to escape the summer heat), thence to Iran and eventually to Israel. At no point did the authorities intervene to stop the departures. So many Jews were involved—some three thousand—that Mossad decided the Iraqi government was closing its eyes for reasons of its own. The exodus operation alone, Mossad veterans insisted, made the entire relationship with the Kurds worthwhile.

With the Shah's blessing Israelis also helped to plan the Kurds' March 1969 attack on Kirkuk's oil fields, at that point producing at least 65 percent of Iraq's oil. This was designed to show the outside world that Barzani's men were capable of crippling the Iraqi economy. Levakov's old black-and-white photographs show one of two masked platoons setting off on foot with four pack animals carrying mortars and recoilless rifles; the mission was led by Sami Abderrahman, a British-trained engineer and then-rising star in the Kurdish firmament. The attack, which hit natural-gas tanks and some other installations, created the desired sense of danger, but it was not as successful as the Israelis hoped. "Would've been better," sniffed Levakov, "if the Kurds had not kept the explosives for themselves."

Even if the Israeli-Kurdish relationship was not letter-perfect, it had other, less obvious uses, especially for extending Mossad's perceived clout. Mossad was flattered that an embarrassed Iraq kept overestimating its numbers, ascribing their own military setbacks to the presence of "thousands" of Mossad agents. Mossad's Kurdistan destabilization operation also displeased the United States. Washington, which wanted to shore up Iraq's various regimes during the decade of revolving-door government that followed the monarchy's downfall, and, in the early years of the Israeli-Kurdish relationship, considered Barzani the "red mullah," dangerously pro-Moscow because of his long Soviet exile and because he received Soviet diplomats when Baghdad occasionally allowed them to travel north.* (Never mind that Barzani had developed an enduring distrust of Communism and Communists during his Soviet exile and, as a tribal leader, was opposed to the leftist ideology dear to the educated urban Kurds influential in the KDP.) But Mossad was delighted that the Americans took its operation seriously enough to bring pressure on Israel to stop helping the Kurds. "We are a problem for them," one Mossad official remembered thinking. "That means at least we exist as nuisance value." Creating and maintaining problems between the U.S. and Arab governments was Mossad's bread and butter. Such were Israel's small pleasures in the years before Tel Aviv became more expert in manipulating American policy.

Israel had real trouble gaining access in Washington for Barzani, for whom entrée with movers and shakers there was a constant priority. With no introductions Ibrahim Ahmad applied for a visa in 1963 and was turned down cold. He was told that Washington hoped to patch up Iran-Iraq relations; receiving an emissary from Barzani could be interpreted as inimical to that end. But Barzani counted on Israel's opening the right doors. The Israelis tried, with only partial success. Ismet Sharif Vanly, a Syrian-born Kurd who worked for Barzani in Europe, visited Israel in 1964 after a serious split developed between Barzani and Ibrahim Ahmad, Jalal Talabani, and other members of the KDP. He saw Yaakov Herzog, director general of the Foreign Ministry, then Shimon Peres, seem-

* Among the visitors was Yevgeni Primakov, then an intelligence agent masquerading as a Baghdad-based newspaper correspondent. Much to the Bush administration's fury, he later made an eleventh-hour effort to persuade Saddam Hussein to evacuate Kuwait in 1991. That same year he became top man at Moscow's post-Soviet foreign-intelligence operations and in 1996 Russia's Foreign Minister.

ingly permanent deputy Defense Minister, and Prime Minister Levi Eshkol, and came away starry-eyed. "All the officials I met in Israel said Iraqi Kurdistan was heading for independence. I was sure that Israel was sympathetic toward the Kurds."

Barzani was reassured, Vanly recalled, and convinced "that now collaboration with the United States was in the bag. Such was his belief in Israel's wisdom and power." The next year Vanly contacted the Israeli embassy in the United States, which put him in touch with a friendly Madison Avenue public relations firm. In Washington he spoke at the National Press Club and met senators, but "I soon saw the Israelis had not convinced the Americans and the Americans did not want to get involved." Justice William O. Douglas, who had written favorably about the Kurds in the past, refused to meet him. "I got the cold shoulder everywhere," he recalled, "nothing happened." State Department officials refused to receive him but were instrumental in setting him up to give a lecture, which its specialists attended. (That particular stratagem was a State Department favorite, repeated time and again over the next three decades.)

When Vanly reported back, "Barzani was surprised and disappointed." But until the final betrayal in 1975, Barzani never gave up believing in the Israelis' ability to influence the United States. "Just whisper in the American President's ear" was a persistent Barzani request of his Mossad advisers. During the last of his several visits to Israel, where he was received by ministers and generals, he suggested to Shimon Peres that the Kurds would overthrow the Iraqi government if Israel did likewise with Syria. When the Israelis protested that Soviet treaties of friendship with both Arab countries ruled out such adventures, Barzani replied, "You got rid of de Gaulle and Nixon. You cannot fool me." Nothing would dissuade him.

In 1972 Barzani's ship came in—or so he thought. Prime Minister Meir was in Tehran pleading for more help for the Kurds; this was a month before the Shah met Nixon and Kissinger and talked them into dropping the U.S. policy of determined opposition to involvement with the Kurds. And Mossad's Kimche also claimed credit for Israel in bringing about the change. But Washington changed policies to please the Shah, increasingly worried by Moscow's arms deliveries under the recent Iraqi-Soviet Friendship Treaty (itself a reflection of the effectiveness of the military aid that Israel and Iran were giving Barzani). Ironically, despite a substantial increase in Israeli aid to the Kurds that summer, Israel's overall influence in Kurdistan suffered with this new American and now overt Iranian support for the Kurds.

But Israel's civic-action programs continued, and Barzani frequently consulted Israeli military officers in Tehran. During the 1973 Arab-Israeli war, there was desultory talk of the Kurds' opening a second front to keep Iraq from transferring troops to help the Syrians on the Golan Heights. To this day it remains unclear if this idea was Israel's, as seems likely, or the Kurds'. A key Barzani lieutenant has insisted that Israel asked the Kurds to "create trouble for Iraq" by establishing such a front, but that Barzani "was not much for it," especially after Americans advised against involvement in the Arab-Israeli dispute.

Barzani counted on the United States more than on Israel. The Pike Committee report said the advice was personally issued by Kissinger, then secretary of state; in his memoirs, Kissinger has it both ways, boasting both that he discouraged the second-front operation and that the value of the Kurdish connection was proved when "only one Iraqi division was available to participate" in the war. Fifteen years later he confirmed that he had opposed the Israeli plan because he feared the lightly armed Kurds would get "chewed to pieces if they left the mountains," and in any case he did not want to increase aid to Barzani, as an all-out offensive would have required, for fear of the consequences once the Yom Kippur war ended. For reasons of their own, Israeli intelligence sources equally adamantly asserted that the initiative was Kurdish and that the Israelis opposed it because they could not protect the Kurds from Iraq's likely retribution.

A possible explanation of the seeming contradiction can be found in Kissinger's "impression that Israelis in Tel Aviv understood my point of view but that Israelis on the scene" in Kurdistan favored the scheme. In the event, no action was taken, and Iraqi forces— 30,000 troops, 60 aircraft, and 400 tanks—were transferred to the Golan Heights. Saddam Hussein was worried enough first to obtain the Shah's promise not to take advantage of the situation. In fact, the Shah was then saying, "I've no desire to have the Kurds branded as mere henchmen of Israel and the USA," but nonetheless he extracted resumption of diplomatic relations as his price for tolerating Iraq's expeditionary force (which lost 125 men, 21 planes, and 80 tanks in the Golan fighting).

After that conflict Israel sent the Kurds masses of captured Soviet arms—artillery, Strella shoulder-held antiaircraft missiles (which proved unreliable), and Sagger antitank weapons.

But when hostilities between Iraq and the Kurds resumed in March 1974, an uneasy Mossad found itself playing second fiddle to the Shah and the Americans. To protect the hard-pressed Kurds, Iran moved inside Iraq one battery of Soviet-made 120-mm guns and a second of 130-mm guns; more artillery was to follow; British-built Rapier antiaircraft missiles were stationed on the border. But the Soviet Union had provided Iraq with even more and varied modern arms, from helicopters to aircraft and tanks. Very quickly, massive Iraqi armored drives methodically pushed back the Kurds from the plains around Erbil to their mountain strongholds. Iraqi engineers, undeterred when a key bridge was blown up, blocking the hitherto impregnable mountain called Gali Ali Beg, bulldozed a road across the mountains; a reinforced tank company moved along the slopes of Mount Kurrek and onto the plains around Diyana beyond.* Mossad chief Zvi Zamir, who knew Kurdistan first-hand, again dispatched Saguy, who was taken aback upon his arrival to learn that Barzani and his sons could not produce the Iraqi order of battle. "They'd lost control," he recalled.

A subsequent meeting with Kurdish military commanders in a cave near Zozik Mountain, outside Rawanduz, confirmed that the tactical situation was perilous. Nonetheless, Saguy organized massive ambushes for the Kurds armed with Saggers and 106-mm recoilless rifles. Noting that Iraqi armor never left the roads or got out ahead of artillery protection, the Israelis devised an ambush which destroyed a hundred Iraqi tanks in a half hour. Other ambushes inflicted heavier casualties, but this time the Iraqis kept coming. They fought their way up Zozik, which changed hands repeatedly in desperate fighting that slowed down but did not end with the first snows. For the first time in their long conflict with the Kurds, Iraqi troops were managing to fight a winter campaign in the mountains. A worried Saguy returned to Israel to ponder a riposte.

He was still puzzling over plans when an agreement between

---

* In *pesh merga* ranks, there were suggestions of treachery. The Iraqi armored column moved down from the mountains to the plains at night "at exactly the right time and exactly the right place," just after a *pesh merga* unit had withdrawn from the line under questionable circumstances. The unit fell to quarreling, real or simulated, and pulled back to headquarters for the leaders to arbitrate their differences.

Iraq and Iran in Algiers was announced on March 6. Two and a half battalions of Iranian artillery and antiaircraft guns and their troops, stationed in Iraq, were abruptly ordered back across the frontier and, under the incredulous eyes of the Kurds and Israelis, they "packed up and walked away." Too embarrassed to tell the truth, Iranian officers described the withdrawal as a routine troop rotation. Acting on sudden orders from SAVAK, the Mossad team still in Kurdistan put its gear in jeeps and left immediately. It was a bitter end to the adventure.

In Tehran, Uri Lubrani, Israel's urbane unofficial ambassador and a longtime Mossad periphery-policy practitioner from Ethiopia to Lebanon, was taken aback by the Shah's "cruelty and callousness." A senior Iranian official brushed aside the Israelis' protests, taking them to task for allowing "sentiment to interfere with politics. Helping minorities should not be considered as an end in itself but as a means to obtain useful concessions from the majority," he argued. "Good politics" involved cutting off aid at the right moment to obtain maximum concessions, and that was what the Shah had done. Lubrani realized Israel's error in presuming that the historical Persian-Arab enmity was immutable and allowing that presumption to govern Israeli encouragement of the Kurds. He was chillingly mindful that a similar fate could befall Israel's own relationship with Iran whenever the Shah found it expedient.

But, he recalled, "I never received any instructions to argue" with the Shah on the Kurds' behalf, not even concerning humanitarian help for the refugees now flooding into Iran. "Of course, as Israelis directly involved in the field, we felt guilty," he said, knowing that hundreds of Iraqi Kurds were massacred and thousands driven into exile either in Iran or in arid southern Iraq. "If Israel had been a country not of 4.5 million but, say, of 25 million," he mused many years later, "we would have talked differently, thumped the table." But this was basically self-serving reasoning. Whatever its pretensions to possessing the "world's fourth most powerful armed force," Israel was never more than a smallish regional state unable to project durable power so far from its Mediterranean base, and from the beginning the Shah had encouraged Israeli involvement with the Kurds for that very reason, cognizant that the Israelis were totally beholden to him and could not mount a challenge.

The next year, when Lubrani was alone with the Shah on his

Kish Island retreat in the Persian Gulf and could let his hair down, he asked the Shah what the de facto alliance with Israel meant to him. The Shah cited Israel's usefulness as a magnet attracting Arab energies and hatreds; this gave Iran time to prepare for an inevitable showdown with the Arabs as well as drawing Tel Aviv close to Washington, which was helpful in explaining Iranian positions to the Americans and in understanding theirs. At no point did he mention the Kurds, but doubtless they, too, had bought time for him to prepare.

Key Kurds have acknowledged that the inner circle around Barzani knew about secret meetings between Iraqi and Iranian foreign ministers that helped clear away obstacles to an agreement in mid-1974, but they insist they had no inkling of its imminence. Nonetheless, the Kurds maintain, they were particularly angry with the Israelis for not having warned them of Algiers, since Mossad for sure must have known about it in advance—such was the aura of Israeli omniscience among them. But Israeli historians disagree, protesting that Israelis could be as stupid as anyone else. Had not the Israeli government failed to read the handwriting on the wall in 1973 and been totally surprised by Egypt and Syria's coordinated offensive initiating war?

Kimche has denied that Iran gave Israel any "forewarning" of the betrayal in Algiers, but an Israeli historian who has studied the Kurdish alliance confesses to uncertainty about Israeli government innocence on this score. Given its long-term interest in weakening Iraq, Israel certainly had lots to lose—and nothing obvious to gain—if the fighting ended, for then Iraq was free to move its army westward against Israel. At the time Joseph Kraft, a syndicated American columnist who was close to Kissinger, reflected this thinking when he described the Algiers agreement as a "hard blow to the United States," Israel's major protector.

Uri Lubrani later remarked that he was "not so sure the Kurds were to be believed when they blamed the Algiers agreement on" their inconstant allies. He had a point: the fighting was going badly and Iraq was offering the Shah a diplomatic victory without risk of further military involvement in what looked more and more like a quagmire. But the Barzanis never forgave Israel. To his dying days, Mullah Mustafa would change the subject when asked about his connections with Israel.

His son Massoud was more pointed. When in October 1991,

during a visit to Kurdistan, I told him I was going to Israel in hopes of talking to Mossad veterans, that most self-contained and gentlemanly of Kurds turned nasty, and said he never wanted to talk to me about them; he was all but hissing. He made clear that he believed, as a Barzani, that the Israeli connection had led his father, his tribe, his family, his party, and the Iraqi Kurds in their entirety down a disastrous path. The souring of once-confident relations with outside powers left durable anger.* Justifiably or not, the Kurds talked themselves into believing that were it not for the Barzanis' initial Israeli connection, they would not have been so naive about the later full-fledged collaboration with the Shah and Washington.

Yet in Israel, undiminished genuine public support for the Kurdish cause persisted. In the spring of 1991, when Iraqi Kurds rose against Saddam Hussein, Israeli Kurds demonstrated outside government buildings to enlist Prime Minister Yitzhak Shamir's help; humanitarian aid was dispatched, though realpolitik won out. Even William Safire, the *New York Times*' normally unconditionally pro-Israeli columnist, condemned Israel's indifference to the Kurds' plight, "based on the selfish concern that Kurdish independence might lead indirectly to Palestinian statehood."

Unshakable beliefs, exaggerated expectations, and bitter recriminations, any veteran intelligence agent knows, are the unpleasant but often unavoidable price of conducting undercover business in the Third World. That is a given whenever a major power talks to poor and downtrodden peoples such as the Kurds. "The closer you get to one of those operations," William Colby, director of the CIA at the time of the Kurds' betrayal, remarked to me years later, "the more the emotional involvement, especially among your own people on the ground."† Colby, an old Asia hand, knew what he was talking about. For Israel there was an additional special hurt:

---

* However, in talking to the journalist Kamran Karadaghi of *Al Hayat* in 1992, he indicated that his refusal to deal anew with Israel was based less on lessons of the past than on his knowledge that Arab members of the Iraqi National Congress, the anti-Saddam Hussein opposition, would not countenance such contacts.

† The CIA's relations with Iraqi Kurds was to haunt U.S. relations with Iran for years. Immediately after the Shah's overthrow, Ray Cave, a former CIA station chief in Tehran, was called back to have secret talks with Iran's new government, which was especially worried about Israel's possible links with Iran's Kurds. Cave said there were none—as far as the CIA knew.

after March 1975, Lubrani said, "simple people in the region, Kurds and Iranians and many others, just thought Jews would do anything for financial gain," which seemed to him a throwback to the stereotypical "Jews depicted in the *Protocols of the Elders of Zion*," that classic anti-Semitic tract forged by the tsarist secret police at the turn of the century.

8

Ali Chemical

*All that is needed for the triumph of evil is that good men do
nothing.*
—EDMUND BURKE

In the summer of 1994 Simon Wiesenthal listened to me
with the same amiable forbearance that I recalled from our
only other meeting more than a quarter of a century earlier.
Back in 1968, when I first came to the Vienna office of the tireless
tracker of Nazis responsible for Hitler's "final solution to the Jewish
question," I was the *New York Times'* correspondent in Warsaw.
I was new to Eastern Europe's demons, and I needed his enlight-
enment to understand what struck me as the surrealistic dynamics
of anti-Semitism in a country virtually without Jews after Hitler's
extermination program. Such was the odd hallmark of the "anti-
Zionist" campaign taking place that year inside Communist Poland's feuding *nomenklatura*. He patiently provided chapter and
verse.

This time I was back in Vienna seeking his guidance in deciphering the horrendous punishment that Saddam Hussein had
meted out to Iraq's Kurds. Their travail was immeasurably worse
than that suffered by the Old Testament's Shadrach, Meshach, and
Abednego, who were cast into Nebuchadnezzar's fiery furnace (said
to have been the tar pits of modern Kirkuk's oil fields in Kurdistan).
Those biblical worthies, after all, were saved—not so the Kurds,
who were subjected to chemical weapons, deportation, and wholesale destruction of their villages. Many tens of thousands were
massacred in an inventive display of extrajudicial executions and
other excesses which Saddam Hussein was accused of having raised

to a "fine art."* I hoped Wiesenthal might have some special insight into what prompted modern dictators, German or Middle Eastern, to plan and carry out such terrible suffering, to keep such thorough records, and to devise their methodologies of mass murder, and insight into the larger indifference to these horrors—in fact, any clues to what had been allowed to happen and why. I had no idea whether Wiesenthal had any interest in the Kurds or knowledge of their fate, but he had a well-known soft spot for journalists, so I didn't mind asking what must have struck him as ignorant questions. There was so much I knew I didn't comprehend that I felt little compunction about bothering him: I figured a man who specialized in chronicling the century's most industrialized machinery of mass murder would likely have some answers, even if at face value the sheer scale and efficiency of the Holocaust discouraged comparisons.

Still, I was wary of approaching him. Decades spent covering African, Asian, and Middle Eastern wars and human-rights violations made me leery of overheated accusations that terrible excesses, even mass murders, constituted cases of genocide, much less a new Holocaust. These easy analogies overlooked the incontrovertible essential difference. The Jews of Europe had committed no overt acts of aggression; they had never taken up arms against their adversaries; they certainly were responsible for nothing remotely comparable to the recurring armed rebellions that studded Kurdish history or even the Armenians' anti-Ottoman nationalist temptations, which had helped trigger our century's first genocide during World War I. Nor were Kurds without sin in the deaths of more than a million Armenians: clouding the Kurds' own record was their undisputed participation in the Armenian massacre in Turkey, variously as individuals, tribal bands, or members of the Ottomans' Hamidiyah cavalry (modeled on tsarist Russia's Cossacks). Yet exhaustive if largely ignored research by the U.S. Sen-

---

* "In Iraq the perpetration of extrajudicial executions has been developed into a fine art. The methods used included the use of chemical weapons against civilians; mass executions by firing squad; burying people alive or tying heavy weights to their feet and pushing them into rivers while alive; poisoning them through the use of thallium (a substance used in rat poison) and other poisons; bleeding prisoners and detainees to death; assassinations by shooting; and 'accidental deaths' supposedly occurring in car accidents or helicopter crashes. In addition, thousands of people have died in custody in unknown circumstances, or as a result of torture." From " 'Disappearances' and Political Killings: Human Rights Crisis of the 1990s, A Manual for Action," Amnesty International, 1994.

ate's Foreign Relations Committee, Amnesty International, Human Rights Watch, other organizations, and the Kurds themselves showed that Saddam Hussein's Iraq was guilty of genocide, defined in the words of a 1948 United Nations convention as the "intent to destroy in whole or in part national, ethnical, racial or religious groups, as such."

In the event, my qualms were unjustified. Wiesenthal was not in the least surprised by my questions. It turned out that Kurdish students had beaten me to his door years before. They, too, counted on his help in understanding what place the Kurds' suffering occupied in this terrible century's annals of evil. For the memorialist of the mechanics of the Nazis' genocide, Hitler's model for the Holocaust was the Spanish Inquisition. Wiesenthal's basic argument was that the only evolution from Torquemada's thumbscrews to Auschwitz's ovens was technological. "No Jews would have survived in fifteenth-century Spain," he said, "if the Inquisition had had modern industrial methods at its disposal."

Arguably, other factors were involved in Iraq. But Hitler apparently was not alone in being inspired by the Inquisition. In his memoirs Henry Morgenthau, Sr., the American ambassador to the Ottoman Empire during the massacre of the Armenians in 1915, quoted Bedri Bey, Constantinople's police chief, as telling him that the government "studied reports of the Spanish Inquisition and other classic torture texts passionately and adopted the suggestions they discovered." For Wiesenthal, Hitler completed the circle: his anti-Semitism had deep roots in Roman Catholicism, especially the Inquisition, and he openly acknowledged his debt to the Turks. (No doubt Simon de Montfort's destruction of the Albigensian heretics in southwestern France at Rome's behest in the thirteenth century offers even earlier evidence of this thesis.) On the eve of unleashing World War II in August 1939, Hitler instructed his top generals about to invade Poland to "kill without pity all men, women and children of the Polish race. Who speaks nowadays about the extermination of the Armenians?"

Hitler and Saddam Hussein also shared a fascination for recording their handiwork, and a conviction they could act with impunity. "The Nazis kept records because they thought they could get away with it—and were proud of what they were doing," Wiesenthal said. The Germans were a meticulous people much given to following orders unquestioningly. "No German ever thought he could challenge Hitler," he said. "There was no question of questioning." I had provoked his remark by noting the penchant for scrupulous and often-macabre record-keeping that distinguished Saddam Hussein's elaborate and rival security forces. Not content with maintaining carefully cross-referenced written documents and photographs, they also kept confidential computerized data, tape recordings, and videotapes of their misdeeds. Wiesenthal sighed knowingly when I remarked that Communist East Germany's secret police, the Stasi, had provided its Iraqi counterparts with considerable technical assistance over the years.

Such was the Iraqi regime's self-confidence that no thought appeared to have been given to the possibility that such incriminating evidence could end up in its victims' hands. Whatever else was involved, such documents lent additional weight to Wiesenthal's insight about keeping up with new technologies.

As helpful as Wiesenthal's insights were, there was something quirkily Middle Eastern to the Iraqi refinements that escaped him. One videotape especially troubled me ever since Hoshyar Zibari had mentioned it one snowbound afternoon in February 1992 at KDP headquarters in Salahuddin, when he was explaining what Saddam Hussein had done to the Kurds. Thanks to a blizzard which discouraged the usual constant flow of visitors, Zibari for once had time to document for me the thoroughness of Iraqi secret-police operations. He began by telling me about his own family.* Before Saddam Hussein invaded Iran in September 1980 and touched off an eight-year war, Zibari's three brothers lived in the government stronghold of Mosul. They were not active in Kurdish nationalist politics (had they been, they would not have remained in Mosul), but Hoshyar had recently become a close collaborator of Massoud Barzani, the KDP leader.

That sealed their fate. The brothers received identical messages from the secret police: Hoshyar must stop working for the KDP. They protested they were law-abiding citizens and had no contact with, much less control over, him. The secret police called in one brother and made him drink a glass of orange juice, which turned out to be laced with thallium, or common rat poison. No Iraqis were allowed to treat him, but a clandestine KDP doctor saved his

* The "nationalist" Barzanis and the *jash* Zibaris were, and remain, traditional enemies despite Mullah Mustafa Barzani's dynastic marriage with a Zibari leader's daughter, which was designed to heal their often violent feuding. The marriage, by all accounts a most happy union, produced Massoud Barzani. Hoshyar Zibari is the exception: a Zibari who became a close Barzani collaborator.

life. When he recovered, the secret police summoned him again and had a male nurse give him a fatal injection. Later the two other brothers were called in together, reproached with Hoshyar's KDP activities, and killed in a "road accident" as they drove home.

Hoshyar then came to the tale of a videotape found by KDP *pesh merga* when they stormed the home of the former supreme Iraqi commander in Kurdistan in the brief week the Kurds held Kirkuk in March 1991. The video sequence showed a public execution with important Ba'ath Party cadres, other regime officials, and a large crowd in cheering attendance. First, the firing squad shot their five Kurdish victims, who were tied to stakes and blindfolded with their own checkered headdresses, and kept firing their AK-47s long after the Kurds were dead. Then an officer strode down the line of slumped corpses, administering final coups de grâce with a side arm. What amazed me even more was the presence of a second officer who followed the first, firing still more shots into the inert bodies. The videotape ended abruptly, but for all one knew every officer present followed suit.

The repetition brought to mind a description written by Freya Stark, that fine British connoisseur of the region, of the execution of Iraqi prime minister Nuri Said during the 1958 revolution, which ended Iraq's British-backed monarchy. Nuri Pasha tried to escape disguised as a woman, but he was caught by a Baghdad mob and put to death. The next night his enemies dug up fourteen bodies before they located and disinterred his, then forced motorists to drive over it repeatedly. Stark, who had been a good friend of Nuri Pasha's, remarked on "the savagery for which Iraq in her long history has ever been notorious." She mused on "the pendulum swing of murder, ancient and long familiar, which has made the pattern from the day when the first Ali [Mohamed's cousin and son-in-law, fourth caliph, and founder of Shi'ism, in A.D. 661] was stabbed in Kufa, and probably long before. Even the massacre of the Prophet's family is no novelty on that soil."

But was there something beyond the videotape's sheer repetitive horror that I did not fully comprehend? Why keep pumping bullets into cadavers? I'd been told the secret police delighted in making their victims' families pay for the bullets used in executions (as well as the coffins and transport costs) before releasing the bodies for burial. Was some macabre post-mortem shakedown involved? Hoshyar laughed at my confusion. What struck me as exceedingly odd behavior was for Iraqis perfectly in keeping with Saddam Hussein's governance. They all knew about his deliberately filmed purge of top Ba'ath officials soon after he seized total power in 1979. He had summoned an auditorium full of several hundred senior Ba'ath officials to hear a coup-plotter-turned-informer finger his fellow conspirators, allegedly out to seize power for themselves. With the mention of each conspirator's name a tearful Saddam Hussein ordered the man out of the room amid applause and exclamations of support. Guards seized each culprit and spirited him away. Saddam Hussein then obliged the surviving ministers and senior party officials to join the firing squad which executed the condemned men.

At work was a perverted form of male bonding, a pattern repeated throughout the chain of command: from the lowliest secret-police operative on up they shared responsibility in the executions, thus enforcing loyalty and subservience to Saddam Hussein. So the videotape I found odd provided physical proof that orders had been carried out, and no higher-up could question the efficiency of those involved. Such audiotapes and videotapes recording the regime at its most frightening were also useful in intimidating anyone less inclined to terror and cruelty.

The regime made copies of the 1979 episode, which were shown to selected Iraqi audiences, including the Kurdish army auxiliaries, the *jash*, as well as Kurds or Arabs in Ba'ath Party and other official posts. These vicious teaching tools dovetailed with evolving Ba'ath Party rule, a totalitarian system allowing Saddam Hussein and his extended family to rule in the name of the Sunni Arab minority centered in Tigris and Euphrates river towns such as his native Tikrit. The long war against Iran reinforced his already well established penchant for cruelty. The means he chose became ever coarser and extreme until finally he embraced poison gas and extermination as acceptable ways for settling scores, not just with foreign foes but with fellow Iraqis as well.

Saddam Hussein's incremental recourse to ever-greater violence should not have come as a surprise to the Kurds. His personal animus against them is easily dated over two decades, and he never hid his determination to get even with them. The Ba'ath Party's earlier intentions toward the Kurds is a matter of partisan dispute best left to future historians; its enemies point to an unbroken record of smashing all other Iraqi parties, but apologists for the regime have argued that immediately after its return to power in 1968 the Ba'ath Party was genuinely determined to share political power and oil wealth with the Kurds. Accommodation for all Iraqis—Sunni Arabs, Kurds, and the Shia Arab majority—made sense then, for the country was exhausted by a decade of near nonstop postrevolutionary turmoil following the monarchy's overthrow. The apologist school maintains that the Kurds' predilection for foreign alliances—specifically with Iran and Israel in the 1960s—skewed their judgment, causing them to raise their demands inordinately and ultimately persuading the Ba'ath to crush Kurdish nationalism rather than come to terms with it inside a federated Iraq.

In any case Saddam Hussein never forgot that in 1970 the Ba'ath Party was so weak that he personally felt obliged to negotiate the deal that granted the Kurds far-reaching autonomy. Such is the absence of consensus politics in Iraq—and elsewhere in the Middle East—that, as we have seen, the Iraqi government never genuinely sought to implement the agreement. Instead Saddam Hussein reneged on its terms when his regime regained strength, and tried to dilute the Kurds' claims to territory they considered rightfully theirs. Yet his methods—attempted assassination, the razing of villages, and collective deportation to the south—were within the harsh artisanal traditions that modern Iraq has inherited from Ottoman rule.

Within months of the agreement, for example, the regime tried to assassinate Idris, one of Mullah Mustafa Barzani's sons, in a shooting incident in which a driver was wounded. Then the government sent Barzani a crate of superb oranges, specially grown in the shade of palm trees alongside the Shatt al Arab: a prudent Mullah Mustafa tested one on a goat, which promptly died from poisoning.

On September 29, 1971, another effort was made to assassinate Barzani—in a bizarre plot known as the "case of the exploding mullahs." A delegation of Shia and Sunni divines planning to visit Barzani was enlisted by the regime to sound out his views; some of them were prevailed upon to strap tape recorders to their bodies "to catch his every word," but unbeknowst to them the recorders were packed with explosives. The secret police figured correctly that Barzani's well-known respect for clerics would keep his guards from frisking the visitors. As soon as the meeting started, agents doubling as the delegation's drivers detonated the charges by activating switches in their vehicles. The clerics were sent to their maker, and bits of flesh remained stuck to the ceiling and walls for days. Barzani escaped shaken but otherwise unhurt, thanks to the fortuitous presence of a tea server, who shielded him and was killed in the blast. In the confusion Barzani's guards, thinking their leader was dead, slaughtered a number of the clerics and retainers who had survived the explosion. One guest was gunned down in the toilet, as bullet holes in its door bore witness.

Over the years the Baghdad government rearranged administrative borders, kicked Kurds off strategic land located too close to the Kirkuk oil fields or the Iranian border, forced Kurds out of Kirkuk itself, and brought in Arabs to occupy their fertile farms and redress the population balance. The first of 4,240 Kurdish villages destroyed by the Ba'ath regime were razed right after Barzani's revolt collapsed in 1975; Saddam Hussein killed three of Barzani's sons (Luqman, Obaidullah, and Saber); and tens of thousands of Kurds were banished to the southern desert when they returned from Iran. More than two thousand Kurdish villages disappeared before 1987.

That was the seventh year of Saddam Hussein's war with Iran. At that point, he directed his military machine against the Kurds in a vengeful fury of operations that were deliberately planned to go virtually out of control. By the time the Kurds realized what was going on, it was too late. In December 1987, Massoud Barzani told me, "If this goes on, there will be no Kurds left in Kurdistan. Saddam's plan is to destroy us as a people. It's him or us. There's no other choice."

———

When Iraq's battle with Iran began in 1980, many Iraqi Kurds had not digested the lessons of the debacle five years earlier. In a series of wars over a generation they had come to terms incrementally with the ever more deadly arsenal at Baghdad's disposal—from highly maneuverable Hawker Hunter jets and napalm to helicopters, modern weapons that drastically reduced their mountains' protective value. More damaging still was the Kurdish inability to factor in risks. Iraqi Kurds, especially those loyal to Barzani's sons, saw the fighting only as an opportunity to get even and, as they so often had done in the past, they threw caution to the winds. "Better to live like a hawk for a day than like a hen all your life" was a Kurdish saying all too aptly illustrating their impulsive fatalism. The younger Barzanis took up arms against Baghdad once more without considering the repression sure to ensue if Iran lost and Saddam Hussein survived. Indeed, never in count-less hours of discussions at the time did I ever hear a Kurdish leader entertain the thought that the conflict might end on terms more inimical to their aspirations than the mutual exhaustion of Iran and Iraq. They neatly chose to overlook the Shah's well-established pattern of treachery and allied themselves with Aya-tollah Ruhollah Khomeini's Islamic Republic, despite its unbridled repression of Iran's own Kurds the previous year. In the summer after the Islamic revolution of February 1979, the new government rebuffed the Iranian Kurds' demands for autonomy and sought to crush them by force.

Kurdish territory was never the Iran-Iraq war's main theater of operations, but the *pesh merga* created the illusion of success for themselves by quickly "liberating" vast tracts of Kurdistan from the Turkish to the Iranian borders while the battles with Iran raged farther south. Iraqi Kurdistan contained the country's breadbasket and the major tributaries of the Tigris and other rivers, which is what, historically, made Iraq virtually alone of Arab countries self-sufficient in food and water. Kurdish collaboration with Iran in the north tied down many Iraqi troops that Saddam Hussein needed in the south, and at times it directly threatened strategic assets such as the Kirkuk oil fields and the Darbandikhan and Dukan dams, which supply Baghdad with water and electric power.

The regime's outlook radically changed as a result, with dire effect. In Saddam Hussein's eyes the *pesh merga* qualified as "saboteurs"—a word that in the Ba'ath vocabulary was to disqualify virtually all Kurds for Iraqi citizenship and, unbeknownst to them, place them beyond the pale. Whatever distinction existed between the *pesh merga* and noncombatant Kurds vanished. That most primitive of efforts to deny the very existence of an adversary was made: to reduce him to the status of nonperson. The regime also obliterated any of the restraints considered implicit in modern warfare. By the time the Iraqi army was in a position to settle the Kurds' hash, which, as we shall see, they began to do in April 1987 and continued throughout 1988, the high command boasted of using chemical weapons systematically, calling the operation a "struggle admired by the entire world" that rejected "all traitors who sold themselves cheaply to the covetous foreign enemy."

This ominous language, I discovered, was not without regional precedent: disturbing parallels existed between Baghdad's view of the Kurds as expendable nonpeople conniving with Iran, and the

Turkish leaders' attitude in exterminating the Armenians in 1915 on charges of collaborating with the Russian enemy. Enver Pasha, Turkey's War Minister, told Morgenthau, "You should understand that while we were fighting in the Dardanelles for our very existence, sacrificing thousands of men, we were not going to allow these people to stab us in the back." British intelligence later during World War I circulated a cipher telegram dated September 15, 1915, and purportedly captured from Talaat Pasha, Turkey's Interior Minister, by British forces in Syria: The government "has decided to destroy completely all Armenians living in Turkey," it said. "An end must be put to their existence, however cruel the measures taken may be . . . no regard must be paid to age or sex or to conscientous scruple."

Ali Hassan Majid, Saddam Hussein's first cousin and supreme commander in Kurdistan, thought in somewhat comparable terms. As soon as he took up his command as Secretary-General of the Ba'ath Northern Bureau on March 3, 1987, his ruthless efficiency surprised even the Kurds. Never before in their long struggle with Iraq had they been at the direct mercy of a single man entrusted with such life-and-death powers. In the past Saddam Hussein and his predecessors had never delegated overall authority for fear of encouraging potential rivals. Now Majid's authority was second only to his cousin's, and he had total power in civil, military, and security matters in northern Iraq. No longer could the Kurds hope to operate within the interstices of a totalitarian state, counting for survival on rivalry and jealousies among the intelligence and secret-police organizations, the ruling party, the armed forces, and the Kurdish auxiliaries. Majid exercised his power with unbridled gusto until he left Kurdistan on April 4, 1989. "The years 1987 and 1988," an Iraqi Kurdish intellectual lamented, "were the worst years for Kurdistan since Alexander the Great invaded" in 331 B.C. on his way to India. It was abundantly clear in listening to tapes captured by the *pesh merga*. Majid's telltale crude, often-obscene language, his oddly high-pitched voice, and his unmistakable regional accent all highlight the regime's systematic destruction of a people's heritage and way of life.

Majid immediately added a new twist to classic antiguerrilla doctrine by using chemical weapons to kill and terrorize the rural population of northern Iraq. To Kurds he became known as Ali Chemical. His tactics speeded up the systematic depopulation of the countryside and deprived the few remaining guerrillas of food and intelligence. Even before his arrival, rural Kurds had been uprooted and forced into easily policed "victory cities" along main roads close to the big towns. Majid accelerated the process, destroying the small hamlets and villages which since time immemorial were the bedrock of Iraqi Kurdish society. In a later stage, he rounded up, arrested, and sent to their deaths rural Kurds by the tens of thousands. Justifying the destruction of the Kurdish villages with a giant "no go" zone half the size of New England, Majid in one captured audiotape said in 1988, "If we don't act in this way the saboteurs' activities will never end, not for a million years."

Brushing aside the loss of production that the depopulation of Iraq's richest farmland entailed, he argued, "I don't want their wheat. We've been importing wheat for the last twenty years. Let's increase it for another five years." Much to the Kurds' chagrin, oil revenues, in no small part from Kurdistan, gave Saddam Hussein the wherewithal to pay for imported grain, and American greed made it easy: much of the wheat Iraq imported was subsidized American grain that the Reagan and Bush administrations uncritically made available to what became the powerful American wheat lobby's best export market. Thanks to Commodity Credit Corporation guarantees and subsidies, Iraq purchased $2.8 billion worth of wheat and in 1989 the Bush administration doubled the guaranteed CCC loans.

On another tape Ali Chemical justified the repeated use of poison gas against the Kurds in a harangue to Ba'ath cadres: "Who is going to say anything? The international community? Fuck them! The international community and those who listen to them." In early 1989, ruminating at a meeting with subordinates, he defended himself against potential critics who might dare question his wholesale execution of Kurdish men, women, and children in 1988: "Am I supposed to keep them in good shape? . . . No. I shall bury them with bulldozers," he said, as if recalling the terms of a debate about how to settle the Kurds' fate. "Where am I supposed to put all this enormous number of people? I started to distribute them among the governorates. I had to send the bulldozers hither and yon."

That was no hollow boast. A handful of survivors explained how tens of thousands of Kurds were executed at his behest, many of them women and children. When, much later, in the spring of 1991 the Kurds and the Iraqi government initiated a series of eventually sterile negotiations, somehow Massoud Barzani and the other Kurdish negotiators managed to control their emotions and deal with a notably nervous Majid as one of the government representatives. The Kurds told him that according to their calculations 182,000 Kurds had disappeared and were presumed dead, most of them in an unprecedented series of 1988 search-and-destroy operations known as al Anfal and directed principally against civilians. Majid jumped up in a rage and shouted. "What is this exaggerated figure of 182,000? It couldn't have been more than 100,000."* Pending eventual access to the most secret records in Baghdad, which may have kept track of the exact death toll, Kurdish injustice collectors tend to agree with Majid. On the basis of extensive interviews in Kurdistan and perusal of extant Iraqi documents, Shoresh Resoul, a meticulous Kurdish researcher, by the end of 1994 conservatively estimated that "between 60,000 and 110,000" died during Majid's Kurdish mandate. Amnesty International estimated that in Kurdistan and the rest of Iraq, apart from his period, "hundreds of thousands of other people have been victims of extrajudicial executions during the 1980s." Saddam Hussein's atrocities against the Kurds were "so grave," noted a U.N. report, and "of such massive nature that since the Second World War few parallels can be found."

Before Saddam Hussein invaded Kuwait in 1990 and threatened not lives but the Middle Eastern oil balance, Western governments consistently feigned ignorance to justify their lack of zeal in dealing with his human-rights violations during the Iran-Iraq war. Until then none of the various organs of the United Nations had issued a single statement criticizing Iraq's flagrant misbehavior, much less applied serious pressure on it to stop. Saddam Hussein's annexation of Kuwait, however, abruptly prompted outspoken condemnation of his human-rights record by an international community suddenly desperate to trick out with principle its determination to reassert control over Middle East oil. Rarely was there an acknowledgment that past indulgence of his excesses, especially those visited upon

---

* "At one point during the forty-two days I was involved in the negotiations," Adnan al-Mufti told me, "Ali Chemical got very nervous when I brought up the massive destruction of villages and the use of chemical weapons under his direction. 'If you are talking about Kurdistan you must start from the beginning, not just from my time,' he said, as if somehow the long history of Kurdish-Iraqi relations excused what he had done."

the Kurds, had encouraged him to think he could get away with Kuwait's annexation.

Once Kuwait was liberated, Iraq's human-rights abuses were forgotten yet again. They did not figure in the "mother of all resolutions" setting U.N. conditions for the cease-fire in April 1991. Nor did the Bush administration show enthusiasm for bringing Saddam Hussein to trial for war crimes or genocide, though for more than a decade serious human-rights organizations had kept careful book on his comprehensive destruction of Kurdish villages, extrajudicial executions, and other Ba'athist excesses.

But even by the savage standards of the Middle East, Saddam Hussein had shown he was in a league of his own. Right from its first battlefield deployment in 1983 against the human-wave assaults of Iranian infantry threatening to overwhelm Iraqi lines, Saddam Hussein's use of poison gas transgressed one of the world's last military taboos. For the record, Iraq was one of more than one hundred signatories to the 1925 Geneva Protocol banning the use of chemical weapons after the havoc they had wrought in World War I, but such treaty commitments meant nothing to Saddam Hussein, especially when he faced only regional foes.* At the time, the United Nations condemned Iraq—and, three years later, both Iraq *and* Iran—for using chemical weapons but took no further action: evidently the Iraqi regime believed itself justified in using any means at its disposal to prevent an Iranian victory in the south and central sectors.

But by 1988, it was obvious the tide of battle had turned definitively against Iran, and more than ever Kurdistan was a military sideshow. The palpable absence of any immediate provocation in no way deterred Saddam Hussein from resorting to chemical weapons against the Kurds, however. At that juncture Saddam Hussein unleashed his most terrifying use of chemical weapons yet, against noncombatant Kurdish citizens, and not just once but time and time again. The first attack occurred in April 1987. Over the next year and a half, his regime gassed at least sixty villages with impunity, and we cannot know what the foreign governments' lack

---

* Kenneth Timmerman, in *The New Republic*, January 20, 1996, wrote, on the basis of Pentagon and captured Iraqi documents, that Saddam Hussein had ordered front-line troops to use previously deployed chemical weapons against the American-led coalition allies in the Gulf War of 1991, but that his commanders had demurred.

of sustained public condemnation did to encourage him to continue.

Western governments finally were obliged to react when in August 1988 sixty thousand Iraqi Kurds crossed in panic into Turkey, fleeing these repeated chemical-weapons attacks. Even then, bent on preserving their lucrative markets in Iraq, these governments casuistically argued, on Saddam Hussein's behalf, that since the Geneva Protocol did not specifically mention a signatory's use of chemical weapons against its *own* population, the Kurds had no case to bring against the Baghdad regime. That muted international reaction also fitted neatly with a major justification for the West's pro-Iraqi policies: revolutionary Iran's much-discussed threat to the Middle East's oil supplies and political stability. Iraq's function as a bulwark against fundamentalist Iran warranted turning a blind eye to Saddam Hussein's excesses. For these reasons, the international community had earlier toned down protests against the growing file of human-rights abuses and the use of chemical weapons against Iranian troops.

Diplomats charting Iraqi affairs considered it a foregone conclusion that Saddam Hussein would exact exemplary punishment from Iraq's Kurds, civilians and guerrillas alike, for their alliance with Iran. William Eagleton, one of the State Department's few knowledgeable Kurdish specialists at the time, in 1986 used the phrase "cultural genocide" to predict the inexorable destruction of Kurdish society in Iraq. For once Saddam Hussein had used chemical weapons against the Iranians and gotten away with it, the likelihood grew that he would resort to gas to scourge the Kurds just as soon as the military situation allowed. There should have been no element of surprise. As the Kurds kept telling anyone who would listen, British, Dutch, French, German, Italian, Japanese, and Swiss firms had supplied the Iraqi government with the technology, chemicals, and, in some cases, technicians to turn outwardly innocent pesticide factories into chemical weapons plants.

Aside from the terror and illness that chemical weapons bestowed upon the Kurds, they were also cheap and efficient. Over the decades, in small and great wars, the Kurds had acquired a fearful reputation as warriors who regularly inflicted formidable losses on Arab troops. But using poison gas against their civilians was too much for the *pesh merga*: within days of the onset of the August 1988 gassing, Massoud Barzani issued an order as devastating as his father's farewell to arms thirteen years earlier. "Everything has ended; the rebellion is over," read his message suggesting surrender if civilian lives might be protected. "We cannot fight chemical weapons with bare hands. We just cannot fight on."* Gas was thus a cost-effective way of settling the Kurds' hash without risking Iraqi casualties at the end of a long and punishing war with Iran. (CIA estimates of the war dead put the toll for Iraq at 150,000 to 340,000 men, less than the 450,000 to 730,000 Iran lost but proportionately higher, since the population is roughly only a third that of its enemy's.)

Saddam Hussein also calculated correctly that the international community's moral qualms would be kept in check by a desire to share in rich reconstruction contracts in a country with oil reserves second only to Saudi Arabia's. Indeed in August 1988, the Turkish government had ample evidence of gas victims among the Kurdish refugees in its clinics and hospitals but found it politic to avoid saying so openly for fear of offending Baghdad: Turkey, a vulnerable neighbor, was owed billions of dollars by Iraq and feared the wrath of Saddam Hussein's accumulating arsenal, especially its surface-to-surface missiles.† The Arab League, confronted with the evidence, expressed its "total solidarity" with Iraq, reflecting both its members' traditional contempt for non-Arab minorities and their fear of a vengeful Saddam Hussein.

Only the United States spoke out forcibly. Secretary of State George Shultz said Iraqi use of such weapons was "unjustifiable and abhorrent." Citing intercepted Iraqi military communications, the Reagan administration specifically mentioned victims suffering from such classic chemical-weapons symptoms as blistering and

---

* KDP officials at the time estimated that 4,300 Kurds were killed while trying to reach the Turkish border, 2,400 of them, mostly women and children, near Kani Masi. I myself talked to Kurds who said that Iraqi troops effectively cordoned off a large area near the border, and as a result only those living north of the cordon easily reached safety.

† Three American doctors who succeeded in examining refugees at Diyarbakir and Mardin noted they had found "characteristic dermatological and lung lesions" (*The Wall Street Journal*, September 20, 1988), but Turkish authorities did all they could to prevent Amnesty International and the three Americans (representing Physicians for Human Rights) from gaining access to Turkish Red Crescent doctors and staff who had dealt with other refugees crossing the border. The authorities also tried to prevent Turkish journalists from talking to the doctors, provided false information about some of the refugees' whereabouts, and refused to provide medical reports of examinations conducted at the border. Amnesty International issued a statement complaining about this behavior.

oozing sores, dizzy spells, and periods of hallucination.* But the Reagan administration opposed sanctions proposed in the Senate that would punish this "campaign of genocide" by cutting off hundreds of millions of dollars' worth of U.S. soft loans and financial guarantees. Mindful that other nations might gain commercial advantage in the postwar Iraqi market, it was relieved when the scheme conveniently died in the congressional mill.

I've often wondered if the foreign press was guilty as well in going along with what effectively amounted to a conspiracy of silence about the use of chemical weapons against the Kurds. I regret that the Western press was not more successful in sparking an effective response. Kurdish officials told me and other Western journalists about the 1987 gassings within weeks of the attacks, and we duly reported them. That, with rare and honorable exceptions, was more than otherwise-excellent newspapers in the Arab world dared do. I recall taking an Arab newspaper editor friend to task for his refusal to deal with a subject he conceded was important but knew his owner would not countenance seeing in print. Such are the limits of an imperfect calling.

The Kurds did not help their cause. Saddam Hussein kept Iraqi Kurdistan off limits to the foreign press either by denying visas or by preventing journalists, whom the regime had after all admitted, from reaching Kurdistan. And the Kurds proved maddeningly inept. To no avail Massoud Barzani and Jalal Talabani repeatedly denounced the massive deliveries to Iraq of Western and Soviet war matériel and European sales of "insecticide" factories, the so-called dual-purpose plants that produced the mustard gas, yperite, and nerve agents used so extensively against the Kurds. Without access to Iraq to establish what had really happened, Western editors showed little interest. The Kurds, once so resourceful about smuggling journalists into Kurdistan in previous decades, now were incapable of sneaking them across from Turkey, Iran, or Syria. God knows I pleaded with Kurdish officials often enough, and I was not alone. But they were having troubles of their own. The best they could offer me in 1987, for instance, was a trip going from northeast Syria into Turkey and then into Iraq. Barzani's man in Damascus

---

* Sheila Austrian, the U.S. embassy spokesperson in Ankara at the time, told me in a telephone interview in Washington in December 1993 that the forceful U.S. stance was based solely on conversations with foreign correspondents conducted close to the border by her husband, the embassy political officer, Michael Austrian.

drew a detailed sketch complete with a river crossing, minefields, machine-gun nests—all to be completed at night. I demurred. "Can't really blame you," he replied. "We lost three men the last time we tried."

In desperation I suggested that the *pesh merga* buy dozens of cheap camcorders—secondhand, if necessary—to film what was happening inside Kurdistan, then distribute the footage abroad. For a wretchedly poor national liberation movement like the Kurds'—which used to salivate with jealousy when contemplating the Palestine Liberation Organization's overbrimming treasury— such a suggestion must have seemed a typically utopian solution from a well-meaning but ignorant Westerner. The Kurds did not act on my suggestion. In the event, the only major footage of chemical-weapons victims that reached an outside audience was shot a year later, in March 1988, when the Iranians flew Western correspondents by helicopter to record thousands of Kurdish civilians gassed to death in the Iraqi city of Halabjah, then briefly under Iranian control. (Various videotapes captured from Iraqi intelligence surfaced after the Kurds' uprising in 1991, showing gassed bodies and other graphic details. These videotapes were not shown widely, probably because they revealed the involvement of fellow Kurds—the *jash*—in these operations.)

In the age of the "global village," something as visually sickening as the plight of Halabjah's victims might have been expected to shock the most complacent into sustained, horrified action. At least after Halabjah, the outside world could not plead ignorance. But the obscene spectacle was not enough to stop Saddam Hussein or persuade the West to do more than issue pro forma condemnations. Naively the relatively few Kurds who at the time realized the extent of the Halabjah gassing hoped that outrage expressed abroad would protect the remaining Kurds left within Iraq. They vastly overestimated the foreign response. Saddam Hussein insisted that Halabjah was Iranian work, and barely five months later unleashed his last chemical attacks on the Kurds, which took place from August 25 to September 9, after the formal August 20 cease-fire effectively ended the Iran-Iraq conflict. These attacks were so strong that even honeybees on the Turkish side of the border died from them. It was as if Saddam Hussein was thumbing his nose at the international community for having sought so doggedly to end the war for him through diplomatic initiatives and clandestine arms deliveries.

But for the first time some of the new gas victims survived and managed to tell their tale after escaping across the border into Turkey. Confronted with their testimony, a shamefaced international community wrung its hands and organized a conference on chemical weapons to reaffirm the need to honor the Geneva Protocol's principles—in the future. At Saddam Hussein's insistence, France, who as the treaty's depositary convened the conference in Paris in January 1989, limited attendance to sovereign states, which barred the Kurds from confronting the Iraqis; in the person of Vice President Taha Moheiddin Maarouf, in November 1988 Iraq acknowledged it had deployed poison gas in Halabjah but denied any such utilization after the August cease-fire. During the Paris conference the French government took no chances: throughout the proceedings, held at UNESCO headquarters on the Left Bank, Kurdish protesters were kept safely on the far side of the Seine.

In September 1988 I had raced to Turkey to cover the arrival of the tens of thousands of stunned and terrorized Kurds fleeing the chemical attacks. Most of the actual victims had been cut off and captured by Iraqi blocking forces or too weakened by the gassing to make it to safety, but a few had managed to reach Turkey. I was offered a rare photograph of a badly gassed survivor; much to my stunned disappointment my foreign editor refused the $200 asking price for it—I must have dropped almost that much in special telephone slugs down a coin box in the middle of Turkish Kurdistan trying unsuccessfully to win him over by long-distance call. He argued that the survivors' testimony was sufficiently detailed and consistent to disqualify the Iraqi denials as preposterous. That sounded reasonable enough back in Washington, but my editor was a man who gave the impression of never having missed a hot meal in his life, and he had little empathy for the cruel and devious meanders of the Middle East. I had only myself to blame. Had I been smarter I would have bought the photograph outright and transmitted it to Washington without asking for authorization, counting on its obvious impact to get it into the paper willy-nilly.

My disappointment turned to rage when the Iraqi government predictably denied having used poison gas and brushed aside international demands for an impartial scientific on-site investigation. Allowing foreigners to conduct an inquiry would violate Iraqi sovereignty, Baghdad argued, and in a diplomatic pirouette challenged its critics to produce proof of the gassings. Saddam Hussein almost got away with it. Some two hundred foreign correspondents invited to visit Iraqi Kurdistan were taken on guided tours and predictably came up with no evidence of chemical-weapons use. The regime insinuated that such was the effect of Halabjah—which it was still blaming on Iran—that the use of crowd-control irritants had been enough to panic the Kurds in Turkey. But much to their minders' dismay, one group of correspondents unexpectedly stumbled on an army unit outfitted from tip to toe in elaborate chemical-warfare gear. Irrefutable scientific corroboration of the mustard-gas and nerve-agent use had to wait for years.*

Still, that chance encounter by reporters was a more extraordinary coincidence than was realized at the time. The handful of Western embassies in Baghdad actively on the lookout for such evidence never produced anything so damning, and not for lack of trying, whatever the Kurds thought. Iraqi officials trumpeted the glories of their military operations in Kurdistan—for example, even naming a post office and a natural-gas field after their campaign—without entering into the ugly details of what they were actually doing or allowing diplomats to visit the north to see for themselves. The self-serving official excuse was that the ban on travel was for the diplomats' "own security," since Kurdistan was a dangerous place because of the presence of Iranian troops and the *pesh merga.* So even at what passed for the best of times, suspicious Ba'ath officials made foreigners' contacts all but impossible with any Iraqis, especially with Kurds. In such circumstances the CIA was without assets and worthless. Other Western intelligence agencies were no better. Unimpeded access to rural Kurdistan was off-limits for diplomats, and heavy-handed secret police monitored the rare official trips to the countryside grudgingly approved by the Foreign Ministry.

American Ambassador April Glaspie and Haywood Rankin, the U.S. embassy's other Arabic-speaking officer at the time of the final al Anfal gas attacks in August 1988, did their utmost to get to Kurdistan to find out what had happened. Years later in Washington Glaspie told me that she finally bludgeoned her way into Kurdistan by invoking the need to visit the few Americans working on the

---

* Earth and other samples collected in 1993 at Birjinni, a village gassed in August 1988, revealed "degradation products of mustard gas and nerve agents" when analyzed at the British armed-forces Porton Down chemical-weapons laboratory. In October 1988, Gwynne Roberts, a British freelance journalist and veteran Kurdish expert, and a Kurdish guide had crossed clandestinely into Iraq from Turkey to collect earth samples, but Porton Down's analysis was then less clearcut.

giant Bechma dam for a joint Turkish-Yugoslav engineering company. The 284-foot-high dam was intended to provide irrigation
water and electricity, but it would also drown the Barzanis' home
village, Barzan, and its surrounding countryside, keeping the Barzanis in Badinan and the PUK in eastern and central Kurdistan
effectively separated. Glaspie blustered, threatening that if the
Iraqis did not give way, then their embassy's personnel in Washington would not be allowed to travel freely in the United States
—which, she knew, would mean the Iraqi secret-service agents
could not move around frightening and brutalizing Iraqis resident
in America.

Physically getting to Kurdistan did not guarantee gleaning information even when one found docile sources loyal to the Iraqi
regime. Rankin was declared persona non grata for visiting a solidly
pro-government Kurdish tribal leader. Speaking to diplomats was
a risky business for less well placed Kurds. On one occasion Ambassador Glaspie had managed to outsmart her secret-police escort
and sped ahead, but her tail soon caught up. She recalled her
dismay as she watched in her car's rearview mirror while secret
policemen grabbed a Kurd of whom she had just inquired where
she might purchase local honey. At other times she was reduced
to evaluating the destruction of villages from her car by checking
the careful notations that a New Zealand engineer, A. M. Hamilton,
had recorded in a book describing how he built the first strategic
military road through Iraqi Kurdistan under the British League of
Nations mandate in the 1920s and 1930s.

Even an experienced observer could be fooled. Abdul Rahman
Qassemlou, the Iranian Kurdish leader who enjoyed great freedom
of movement in Iraq and was also allowed access to Western embassies, was initially convinced by conversations with Iraqi Kurds
that the gas used in August 1988 was a nonlethal crowd-control
agent akin to Mace. The government was so completely in control
that in June 1989 Qassemlou had to travel deep into Kurdistan to
check out a report in *The Times* of London that the army had razed
Rania. It turned out not to be true: Rania was intact, and the razed
city, population 70,000, was nearby Qala Diza.

In fleeting conversations during her trips to Kurdistan, Ambassador Glaspie said, Kurds she met would readily recount their
efforts to talk Iraqi officials out of destroying their villages. In the
summer of 1989 she bulled her way into Amadiya, a mountaintop
town, by deliberately arriving on Thursday night and correctly

figuring the authorities would not dare do violence to the canons of Muslim hospitality by sending her away on the eve of the Friday holiday. No one would tell her what had happened, but one official at dinner remarked, "Two years ago you would have seen a necklace of lights [here] from all the surrounding villages." The only illuminated buildings she saw belonged to one of Saddam Hussein's palaces at nearby Sarsenk. Such understated explanations sufficed.

"Oddly, the Kurds I managed to see never mentioned mass murder or chemical-weapons attacks," she said. It seems incredible that they should not have known the facts. Were her interlocutors too frightened to speak of what had happened? Were they *jash* working for the regime? Or were they simply urban Kurds or those already living in the "victory city" shantytowns and not directly affected by the gas attacks and arrests in rural Kurdistan? Given arbitrary Ba'ath Party orders, Kurds urbanized by choice or force were spared the final mass destruction visited upon their rural cousins during al Anfal. Ambassador Glaspie recalled traveling westward from Sulaimaniyah in early September 1988, during another of the periodic Iraqi amnesties that had come into effect toward the end of the final al Anfal campaign, and coming across large groups of disconsolate women and children standing next to their meager bundled belongings on the roadside. "They were obviously without menfolk. I suspected the authorities meant me to see them." Saddam was not one to leave such encounters to chance. Families desperate for news of their relatives were left in the dark; in a page from the Nazis' *Nacht und Nebel* doctrine, designed to cast a fog of uncertainty about the status of prisoners, the regime deliberately withheld information about those it arrested. A captured document dated September 20, 1990, more than two years after al Anfal ended, stipulated that the phrase "We have no information about their fate" should replace the phrase "They were arrested during the victorious al Anfal operation and remain in detention."

So both a lot and a little were known. Yet no Iraqi Kurds worth their salt now believe that Western governments, especially the United States, could have ignored what was going on even if they had to take the Kurds' word for it. During his June 1988 visit to Washington, Talabani swore he gave three State Department officials more than enough detailed information about the use of poison gas and the massive destruction of Kurdish villages, as well as about his earlier negotiations with Saddam Hussein and why they failed, to spur any but a morally brain-dead administration to expose Baghdad's transgressions. U.S. embassy cables to the State Department (now in the public domain) were couched in the most general terms, reflecting the classic difficulty of obtaining corroboration of anything beyond bare-bones official communiqués. An April 19, 1988, cable estimated that 1.5 million Kurds had been forced into "victory cities," and between 700 and 1,000 villages were targeted for resettlement. U.S. spy satellites flying over Iraq pinpointed the damage. (That became evident with the distribution of maps used by U.S. forces during the liberation of Kuwait in 1991; military cartographers had marked the massive rural destruction by the word "destroyed" stamped on villages annihilated by Saddam Hussein.) An "unknown, but reportedly large number of Kurds have been placed in concentration camps located" near the borders with Jordan and Saudi Arabia. Kurdish officials I met in France and Syria at that time had no clearer ideas themselves where the uprooted Kurds were ending up. An embassy cable of August 15, 1988, ten days before the onset of the final use of poison gas against the Kurds, said, "Iran and the Kurds have accused the Iraqis of using chemical weapons in the operations."

By then all but the final damage was done. And what damage! I have visited more war zones than I can—or care to—recall, but the scale of destruction in Iraqi Kurdistan to me bespoke unusual dedication. I distinctly remember driving in October 1991 down deserted, unpaved back roads in the Jafati valley in Iraqi Kurdistan, listening to a grim Kurdish guide endowed with a photographic memory mechanically summon forth his reminiscences as a *pesh merga*—shelled in one place, bombed with poison gas a bit farther along, the fearful retreat across mountain-goat tracks leading off yet another hill meticulously pointed out. Outside the cities— Erbil, Duhok, and Sulaimaniyah—Iraqi Kurdistan that autumn was an empty place, aside from the hundreds and hundreds of tents of those who had fled their homes in the spring and now waited, in a precarious state of readiness, to rush back to the frontiers.

Over the years Iraqi army engineers equipped with bulldozers and explosives had flattened stone houses, ripped out water pipes, cemented over wells, torn out orchards, and razed power substations in a frenzy to obliterate. Across the length and breadth of Kurdistan, in plains, river bottoms, bald hills, and mountains, how was even a regiment of guides with similarly endowed memories to recall, much less resuscitate, this rural nation? How could one distinguish one leveled village from the ruins of dozens of others, one hulking Soviet-designed stone fort from its like a few miles down the road?

Much to its rage and embarrassment, the Iraqi government involuntarily answered those questions. Eighteen tons of Iraqi documents seized during the March 1991 uprising from Ba'ath Party and various rival secret-police archives offered a cornucopia of evidence about the regime's intentions, plans, and actions. Some were remarkably intact; most were crumpled, trampled, muddied, or partially burned by the Kurds who had burst into the hated secret-police buildings and seized them during the uprising. Transported for safekeeping to the United States thanks to the U.S. Senate's Foreign Relations Committee, Human Rights Watch, and the U.S. Air Force, the records, stored in the National Archives as official documents of the Congress, are still being translated, analyzed, and collated. To a striking degree, they bear out what Amnesty International, for example, had been saying for years when no Western government wanted to listen. They also corroborate extensive interviews carried out in Kurdistan by Kurds, Human Rights Watch, journalists, and others. For the first time in history, a regime's damning human-rights record was exposed by its own documents while it was still in power. Baghdad limply disowned the documents, repeatedly insisting they were fakes printed on stolen official stationery. These offhand denials—standard Iraqi rejoinders to all accusations of human-rights abuses—rang especially hollow this time. The sheer volume of more than four million pages of records gave a detailed insight into the bureaucracy of repression that allowed no such easy blanket disclaimer.

The team of human-rights specialists who worked on the documents were convinced they added up to a prima facie case of genocide—not just atrocities, war crimes, or crimes against humanity. But such are the niceties of international law that another government must formally press charges if Saddam Hussein's regime is to be brought to trial before the International Court of Justice in The Hague. Neither the United States nor any other Western nation demanded such a tribunal in the U.N. resolutions concerning Iraq. Saddam Hussein's loyalists in Iraq and elsewhere in the Arab world could be expected to dismiss any such approach as suspect "victors' justice," but a precedent existed: the extermination of the Armenians. In 1919 it was the defeated Ottomans' own military tribunal, under strong British pressure, that brought to trial and condemned the principal members of Turkey's government who were responsible for the Armenian genocide and other war crimes. Those trials "showed it was not impossible to expect the courts of a defeated country to avenge atrocities committed by their wartime leaders against other nationals."

The Iraqi regime's paper trail was undeniable. The researchers kept coming upon copies of the same damning documents in the records of often widely separated headquarters. In key cases the documents were issued after some of the more extreme practices had already begun. A prime example was the first use of poison gas against Kurdish fighters and noncombatants in April 1987, which reflected what was happening on the battlefield. Had Ayatollah Khomeini in Tehran not so stubbornly refused to stop the war and even increased his pressure in Kurdistan, Ali Chemical would likely not have received his sweeping orders. In less parlous times Saddam Hussein was not given to delegating total power, even to a Tikriti cousin.

In early 1987, after long hesitation, Talabani had finally thrown in his lot with Iran. A onetime *jash* in the days of Mullah Mustafa Barzani, he had founded the PUK on the ashes of the general's humiliating debacle in 1975 and had fought bruisingly with Barzani's sons in battles claiming hundreds of lives in both camps. So accommodation with the KDP took longer. For six years during the Iran-Iraq war, the PUK had refused to join the KDP in cooperating militarily with Tehran against Baghdad. (Indeed, in 1984 the PUK leader had negotiated with Baghdad.) Talabani's position was initially determined partly by prudence, partly by a determination to steal a march on his KDP rivals. He claimed to represent the better-educated urban elite and contested the tribal Barzanis' proprietary right to lead all Iraqi Kurds and the wisdom of another alliance with Tehran.

But PUK efforts to extract a better autonomy deal from the regime had come to nought. Turkey's opposition to any political accommodation with a neighboring country's Kurds, let alone its own, prompted its Foreign Minister to rush to Baghdad with an unambiguous message: the government must break off the new autonomy talks with the Kurds or Turkey would close down the trans-Turkey oil pipeline, then Iraq's only significant foreign-exchange earner (it also covered a third of Turkey's oil needs and generated $300 million in annual transit fees for Ankara).

In these dealings with Saddam Hussein, Talabani's wariness was well founded. The Iraqi leader had visited exemplary punishment on the KDP for helping Iran capture the border post of Hajj Omran, high in the Zagros Mountains, in July 1983. He rounded up between five thousand and eight thousand Barzani males—a few under ten, but most aged fifteen or more, including forty-two of Massoud's close relatives—and they were never seen again. A month later, he announced that "those people were severely punished and went to hell," a barely coded official description of the fate of tens of thousands of other "disappeared" Kurds. His vengeance against the Barzanis was nothing new, as we have seen.

This time the Barzani victims were not the fabled tribal fighters of yore. Surviving Barzani womenfolk and children were dumped destitute in various housing complexes along main roads in places like Qushtapa, on the highway between Erbil and Kirkuk. Some Kurds have concluded that the easy pickings of so many uncommitted and noncombatant Barzanis was definitive proof that the tradition of Barzani military toughness had been played out. Even more humiliating was the prostitution to which some of these women were reduced to survive. In Muslim society, dominated by notions of shame, their fate reinforced Saddam Hussein's cruel object lesson, and so, too, did the children born obviously out of wedlock after 1983. In shame and humiliation many surviving Barzani men abandoned their distinctive red-and-white headdress in favor of the black-and-white ones worn by all other tribesmen. For other Kurds their own impotence was all too clear.

Worse was to come, for the regime refined its cruelty by forcing ordinary Kurds to participate in its crimes. A Kurdish Army deserter I ran into in 1991 recounted the anguish and guilt he had borne for three years. Telling his tale of woe, even to a foreigner, was cathartic. In 1988 he served in an army unit actively involved in gassing fellow Kurds. He insisted he had no choice. Had he disobeyed orders, he kept saying, "I would have been summarily executed for disobedience and someone else would have done the dirty work anyhow."

If the *jash* felt such guilt, they rarely showed it. Entire tribes —Zibaris, Surchis, Baradosti, among others—had solid and long-standing *jash* credentials, for authorities from time immemorial, Ottoman, Persian, or their modern British and Arab successors, have used loyalist Kurds against Kurdish rebels. (That did not stop Ali Chemical from stating, in an audiotaped tirade, that if in theory "probably we will find some good ones" among the Kurds "we didn't find any, never.") Saddam Hussein manipulated *jash* commanders by paying them handsomely for each Kurd who joined the auxiliaries to avoid serving in the front lines against Iran. Recruits routinely had to bribe their way into *jash* ranks, which were used as scouts and cannon fodder against the *pesh merga* and rewarded with booty during army sweeps through Kurdish villages. Using *jash* also helped Baghdad, of course, by reducing the manpower pool for the *pesh merga*. Similarly, Baghdad's drawn-out negotiations with Talabani worked to its advantage by neutralizing the PUK, which was traditionally strong along the border with Iran.

When the talks with Baghdad collapsed, Talabani eventually turned to Tehran, which immediately applied pressure on him to make a peace with the KDP in the name of winning the war. It desperately wanted to reopen a Kurdish front in order to relieve pressure from the Iraqi army in the south. Meanwhile, in October 1986, Iranian soldiers and PUK *pesh merga* attacked Kirkuk's oil installations, crossing a red line by endangering this strategic asset. In January 1987, Iran staged yet another unnerving human-wave assault, this time against Fish Lake, in southern Iraq, which turned out to be their last such fanatical infantry onslaught (no one knew it at the time). By then Kurdistan was crawling with Iraqi army deserters and draft dodgers hiding in caves and ravines. Ali Chemical complained, "You can't go from Kirkuk to Erbil without an armored car." In March, as he took up his command, PUK and KDP *pesh merga* and Iranian troops were within eight miles of Rawanduz, a major northern Kurdish town well inside Iraq, and PUK *pesh merga* were picking up ground east of Sulaimaniyah in the Jafati valley.

Once decree 160, signed by Saddam Hussein on February 28, 1987, set out Ali Chemical's unlimited powers, his cousin lost no time in using them to the utmost. That decree was completed by two key documents that became standing orders. One, dated June 3, subjected "prohibited areas"—those under *pesh merga* control—to a total embargo on trade or personal movement with the rest of Iraq. Villages were to be destroyed and the population herded to the "victory cities." Within their jurisdiction, the armed forces "must kill any human being or animal present within these areas," read document 28/3650. "They are totally prohibited." The second document, number 4008, dated June 20, ordered commanders to "carry out random bombardments using artillery, helicopters and aircraft at all times of the day or night in order to kill the largest number of persons" in what amounted to a free-fire zone in the "prohibited areas" covering some one thousand villages. Kurds captured therein "shall be interrogated by the security services and those between the ages of 15 and 70 must be executed after any useful information has been obtained." *Jash* commanders (known as *mustashars*, or advisers) were authorized to keep loot taken from Kurds inside the prohibited areas—including cattle, sheep, women, and firearms, except for medium or heavy mounted weapons.

Completing Majid's methodically administered arsenal of decrees was a document effectively stripping Iraqi citizenship from any Kurd failing to take part in an October 1987 census. Since only those living in the government housing complexes were counted, the ruling excluded anyone remaining in their ordinary village homes or land inside the prohibited areas. They had failed to "return to national ranks" and thus were subject to "necessary measures," the regime's euphemism for extermination. (Unbeknownst to Kurdistan's small Assyrian Christian and Yazidi minorities, their refusal to be counted as Arabs in the census effectively made them nonpeople. That bureaucratic nicety was to cost them dearly. Despite their entreaties, Yazidis were not allowed to be considered Kurds for census purposes. On such grounds they were excluded in September 1988 from the "comprehensive and total" amnesty offered "all Kurds," yet another in a long series of trick pardons designed this time to lure naive Kurds back from the safety of exile in Turkey. Hundreds of returning Assyrians and Yazidis were arrested at the border, handcuffed, and driven off, never to be seen again.)

Within six weeks of taking office, Ali Chemical had acquired his nickname. On April 15, 1987, Iraqi aircraft dropped chemical weapons on the widely separated KDP and PUK military headquarters. The next day poison gas was dropped by aircraft and helicopters on Sheikh Wasan and Balisan, villages north of Sulaimaniyah, in the first of some sixty chemical attacks on civilian targets over the next eighteen months. They were the first Kurds confronted with clouds of chemical agents of often-differing hues, smelling variously of garlic, rotten apples, roses, mint, sweet melons, cucumbers, or perfume. Soon they complained of painfully swollen testicles or breasts. Others noticed blood in their urine. Many went temporarily blind or suffered from blurred vision or a yellowish discharge oozing from eyes or noses. Skin turned black or blistered. Some dropped dead almost immediately after fits of shivering or stumbling, hysterical laughter. Such quick deaths and clinical symptoms were associated not with mustard gas used wholesale but with sarin, a nerve agent developed, but never used in the field, by Nazi Germany.

In those first two gassed villages, more than 120 civilians died within an hour of exposure. Some two hundred survivors were taken first to Rania, then to Erbil, for medical care, where they were forced to say they had been gassed by Iranians. That did not suffice. Secret-police agents removed them at gunpoint from Erbil's general hospital, where they were being treated for burns and blindness, and took them to a secret-police jail, where the men were separated from the women and children and all were kept without food or medical care. Between 64 and 142 Kurds died there from untreated injuries suffered in the attack; some seventy men were taken away in buses and, like the Barzanis, never seen again. The surviving women and children were dumped on the plain outside Erbil and left to fend for themselves. A municipal morgue worker, ordered to pick up scores of dead, mostly children and the elderly, said he was told by a military intelligence official, "They are saboteurs, all saboteurs. We attacked with chemical weapons."

Such candor was unusual, since any official mention of chemical weapons was forbidden. But errors occurred, and very rare captured documents speak straightforwardly of "chemical strikes" or even of "special ammunition," the official euphemism for poison gas. In a taped harangue apparently referring to this first chemical attack, Ali Chemical alluded to Talabani's doomed offer to end his alliance with Iran if Iraq stopped its wholesale destruction of Kurdish villages, an offer which Talabani had conveyed via two released high-ranking Iraqi officers, sent with instructions to inform Saddam Hussein himself. "Talabani asked me to open a special channel of communication with him," Ali Chemical said on the tape. "That evening I went to Sulaimaniyah and hit them with special ammunition." In another captured audiotape, he bluntly told a *jash* gathering, "I cannot let your village stand because [what would happen if] I attack it with chemical weapons. Then your families will die. You must leave right now because I cannot tell you the same day that I am going to attack with chemical weapons."

Between April 21 and June 20, 1987, Majid destroyed more than seven hundred Kurdish villages, mostly in government-held areas and along main roads. Only urgent military requirements elsewhere interrupted a planned campaign against the prohibited areas still under *pesh merga* control. But by then Ali Chemical had experimented with chemical weapons against civilians, the disappearance of Kurdish men, mass deportations, transfer points, segregation by sex, deprivation of health care and food, firing squads, and mass graves. In an address to top Ba'ath cadres, he spelled out a "systematic military plan" designed to surround the *pesh merga* in a "small pocket and attack them with chemical weapons. I will not attack them with chemicals one day, but I will attack them with chemicals for fifteen days."

Thus in place and field-tested were all the bureaucratic and military powers of repression employed in the final assault on the Kurds, which started in February 1988. It was code-named Operation al Anfal, a name chosen in a curious nod to Islam on the part of the once militantly secular regime. Al Anfal is the eighth *sura*, or chapter, of the Koran, and it relates the triumph of 319 followers of the new Muslim faith over triple that number of unbelievers at the battle of Badr in A.D. 624. Al Anfal literally means "the spoils" and perhaps was thus entirely fitting for a military campaign of extermination and looting, which is what Ali Chemical's operations were about. Orders informed *jash* units that taking Kurdish goats, sheep, cattle, money, weapons (but not including heavy arms), even women, was *hallal*, or legal in religious terms.*

* The Iraqi regime's conversion to Islam and Islamic trappings was of recent vintage. Visitors to Iraq before the war with Iran remembered the Ba'ath Party's militant devotion to secular values. Some political analysts claimed that Michel Aflaq, the Syrian Christian who cofounded the Ba'ath Party in the 1950s and found an honored refuge in Baghdad, invented its lay ideology as a justification for allowing non-Muslim minorities to play a role in Middle East politics. But as the war against Iran's Islamic revolutionaries dragged on, an ever-cynical Saddam Hussein found it expedient to claim descent from the Prophet and have himself photographed in the humble garb of a pilgrim to Mecca. Al Anfal reads: "God revealed His will to the angels, saying: 'I shall be with you. Give courage to the believers. I shall cast terror into the hearts of the infidels. Strike off their heads, strike off the very tips of their fingers!' That was because they defied God and His apostle. He that defies God and His apostle shall be sternly punished by God. We said to them: 'Taste this. The scourge of the Fire awaits the unbelievers' " [A. Arberry translation].

Al Anfal was planned and its early stages executed at a time when the Iraqi regime was running scared, believing wrongly that the Iranians might launch yet another major winter offensive. It was also concerned, as we have seen, because the Kurds at long last were showing signs of overcoming their age-old penchant for dissension. By November, indeed, Tehran finally engineered a unity agreement between the KDP and the PUK, and the two rivals went hard at work on the formation of the Iraqi Kurdistan Front, initially involving three smaller parties as well. But by then the Iranian army was collapsing. By the winter of 1988 it was reeling from Iraq's terror tactics in the "war of the cities," which featured Scud missiles firing blindly at Tehran and other Iranian cities. Iran's undoing became undeniable by mid-April, when its troops abandoned Fao, the oil-exporting port on the Shatt al Arab whose conquest had marked their greatest victory on Iraqi soil.

The al Anfal campaign to clear rural Kurdistan of all inhabitants, guerrillas and noncombatants, got under way on February 23, 1988, with a major army thrust against PUK headquarters in the Jafati valley east of Sulaimaniyah, close to the Iranian border. Before the first operation ran its course on March 19, some of the overall campaign's distinguishing characteristics were obvious: massive deployment of force on the ground and in the air, destruction of villages, the use of gas, and trick amnesties enticing the naive into surrendering only to condemn them to disappearance and almost certain death.

Subsequent operations—there were eight in all, lasting as many months—added refinements: families were targeted and women and children arrested in giant search-and-destroy efforts designed to exterminate a people. Kurds were funneled into forts, the men separated from their womenfolk and children. Beaten, stripped to their undershorts, and ill fed, they never stayed long before disappearing, handcuffed, in convoys of filthy vehicles to killing fields hundreds of miles from the theater of operations. Their families went to the same fate at a more leisurely pace. A handful of survivors told the same basic tale: daylong drives without food or water to southern desert sites, where at dusk or in early evening they were forced out of their windowless vehicles, handcuffs removed for future use, wrists tied with string, then ordered to the brink of shallow trenches, where under the headlights of bulldozers they were shoved in and shot by troops firing automatic weapons.

The most devastating single Iraqi operation against the Kurds was not officially part of the al Anfal campaign, because its target was not rural Kurdistan but refugee-choked Halabjah, the government-held city close to the Iranian frontier and the strategic Darbandikhan dam. In mid-March PUK *pesh merga* helped Iranian revolutionary guards enter Halabjah, much to the dismay of the inhabitants, many of them government supporters. Tehran radio boasted of this victory, which it described as a reprisal for recent Iraqi chemical attacks on the Kurds. By March 15 Tehran radio reported that revolutionary guards were celebrating their victory inside the city of some fifty thousand residents. That same day Iraq ordered its civil servants out of Halabjah, increasing the foreboding of the remaining inhabitants. Captured Iraqi intelligence documents dated March 16 recommended the "escalation of military might and cruelty."

That very morning wave upon wave of clearly marked Iraqi aircraft dropped napalm and white phosphorus on Halabjah. The inhabitants sought refuge in large, primitive air-raid shelters. In midafternoon Iraqi planes returned to drop chemical weapons. Those still in the shelters desperately sought to caulk them with damp towels, applied wet cloths to their faces, and set fires to dissipate the gas. But many died in the shelters. Rescue workers intent on burying some four hundred bodies found in a cellar abandoned their efforts when heads, arms, and legs came apart in their hands. Those who survived the shelters were forced into the streets, where they were greeted with a latter-day version of Pompeii: frozen in death were thousands of fellow Kurds, some caught trying to protect their children in doorways, others slumped over the steering wheels of cars that had failed to carry them to safety, still more spread in grotesque postures all over the streets; others were stumbling around, laughing hysterically—telltale death throes of those doomed by sarin.

Shoresh Resoul, the careful Kurdish researcher, has conservatively estimated that at least 3,800 Kurds died in Halabjah; others claimed as many as 7,000 victims. Thousands of survivors fled through the mountains to Iran, where alerted medical teams were waiting with atropine to nullify the effects of sarin. Foreign journalists who came to Halabjah days later by Iranian helicopters recorded the carnage. At first Baghdad denied its use of chemical weapons and tried to blame Iran, but the captured Iraqi documents do not make this accusation. In rare violation of the standard orders not to mention the use of poison gas, a captured Iraqi military intelligence message dated April 11, 1988, refers to a videocassette on sale in Sulaimaniyah showing "the Iraqi chemical attack on Halabja." Despite this evidence, the U.S. Army War College in Carlisle, Pennsylvania, perversely insisted that both belligerents used gas against Halabjah on March 16.

For the *pesh merga* leadership, Halabjah was a terrible blow, vitiating the Iraqi Kurdistan Front, still in its formal gestation, and undermining its influence among everyday Kurds. Not for the first time alliance with Iran had proved disastrous. Soon after Halabjah I was in Damascus and had a somber, uncomfortable meeting with high-ranking Kurdish leaders I ran into. They disarmingly acknowledged their terrible error of judgment and the now-increasing likelihood that Iran would lose the war. Dr. Mahmoud Othman, a senior Socialist leader and General Barzani's old lieutenant, said, "People are scared and they are furious with us—and they're right to be." But he and the others retreated into a fatalistic acceptance of inevitable further punishment to come and spoke vaguely of urban guerrilla actions. "It looks like the 1975 debacle all over again," Othman said. After Halabjah, he told Iranian officials in Tehran that for Kurds the alliance meant "war until our annihilation." He added, "they were not so amused." Alone of the Iraqi Kurdish leaders he saw clearly that if Saddam Hussein won the war with Iran, "the situation will be very dangerous because he will come and wipe us out. For him we are insects."

The Kurdish leaders insisted they had entered into the Iranian connection without illusion and only because no real salvation could be found with the West, the Communist bloc, or the Arab world. It was the old Middle Eastern story—the enemy of my enemy is my friend. The Iraqi Kurds rarely progressed beyond that. Now the most they could muster by way of strategy was a refusal to embark on further joint military operations with Iran without a clear political undertaking. "No one lifted a finger to help," said a *pesh merga* cadre during a European tour. "Watching that television footage of Halabjah was like watching what happened to the Jews forty-five years ago."

It all rang hollow. The talk was a pipe dream, and the Kurdish leaders gave every impression of knowing it. After all, Talabani had gotten the message during the initial gas attack in 1987 and had offered to stop fighting then. And Ali Chemical had never relented. Indeed the regime was to continue to use chemical weapons even after the al Anfal campaign officially ended in September

1988. In Damascus that spring, after Halabjah, I had not understood why the *pesh merga* did not withdraw to the safety of Iran. Now, Resoul told me, "all Kurds knew some areas had been gassed, but if we gave up we feared worse awaited our people. The *pesh merga* mission changed from attacking Iraqis to trying to protect our people."

Such ambitions proved illusory, predictably. After the Iraqi recapture of Fao, the Iranians visibly weakened with every passing day. Additional Iraqi divisions were diverted from the southern and central sectors to Kurdistan for al Anfal operations. At one point Iraq fielded forty-six divisions, compared with a mere eight that had fought General Barzani in the 1970s. When in July Ayatollah Khomeini agreed to "drink the cup of poison" and accept the year-old U.N. cease-fire resolution, Iran did not bother to fulfill its promise to consult with the PUK before concluding what amounted to a separate peace.

Halabjah had other dire consequences for Kurds throughout the Middle East and in the diaspora beyond. If the international community could not prevent a Halabjah from happening—and would take no firm immediate action to help bring those responsible to justice—then, Kurds increasingly believed, they could count only on themselves. Once again they fell back on their ancestral byword: "The Kurds have no friends but the mountains." Deals, alliances, reliance on outside help, working within the system were all consigned to the ash heap of history. Enraged farmers, engineers, lawyers, truck drivers, doctors, and schoolteachers started talking the heady language of armed struggle.

Never mind that the Palestinians had gained critical mass and acceptance abroad only when they abandoned arms and violence in favor of a political settlement and the stones of the *intifada*. Interestingly, it was of scant importance to even educated Kurds to realize that the Palestinians' most important policy change in two generations was happening there and then. The Palestine Liberation Organization was credited with importance only because it had helped train members of the Kurdistan Workers Party (PKK), a service it provided for dozens of radical groups regardless of their position on the political spectrum. Whatever political savvy the Kurds had so dearly accumulated over a century was now as suspect as paper money in times of hyperinflation. What counted was that Halabjah was an unsurpassed recruiting sergeant for action—and the more violent the better.

Had I any doubts, they disappeared after a long evening in January 1991 spent listening to educated Kurds in Qamishli, a Syrian city smack on the border with Turkey and not far from Iraq. An Iraqi Kurdish friend in Damascus had arranged the meeting. My hosts were exquisitely polite. But these engineers and doctors answered my every objection to the PKK's excesses in Turkey with a single word: Halabjah. As they made clear, the immediate beneficiary of their determination to get even was the PKK.

At face value this was an odd choice. The PKK leader, Abdullah Öcalan, is a Turkish Kurd so culturally dispossessed that he expresses himself in Turkish, not Kurdish.* Apo—or "Uncle," as Öcalan likes to be called—styles himself an ideologue. Still, four hours spent interviewing him on March 16, 1991, in a safe house in Damascus left me only marginally the wiser about the ideological underpinnings of the PKK's fight for independence from Turkey. He described himself as a Marxist but not a Communist, and certainly not, as he put it, a "classic" or Soviet-style Communist. He was against Islam as it was practiced, but acknowledged religion's importance for many traditional, rural Kurds. (In the field the PKK has proved versatile, invoking Marxism to urban sophisticates, Islamic themes to more traditionally minded rural Kurds.) This son of a despised and failed peasant father shared the single-minded, blinkered devotion to violence I'd learned to identify over the years as a Middle Eastern cancer; I've seen it in Israeli zealots, Lebanese Christian warlords, and Iranian Islamic fundamentalists. The Turkish and United States governments considered Apo a terrorist, as did Western European states—with one notable exception: anything that weakened its traditional Turkish enemy was fine by Greece. "Apo's got a one-track mind and he's not very bright," remarked a Greek diplomat in Damascus who knew Apo well, "but he's very good at killing Turks."

Dressed in a surplus khaki British army sweater, Apo peppered his eclectic remarks with glancing references to Marx, Engels, Friedrich Nietzsche, the British historian Arnold Toynbee, the French philosopher Henri Bergson, and the sociologist Emile Durkheim. He said he'd read them all while studying political science at Ankara University on a government scholarship. That a

---

* Harvey Morris of *The Independent* (London) reported seeing Öcalan's portrait enjoying the place of honor alongside that of Syrian President Hafiz al-Assad during a visit to Qamishli a few months later.

boy raised on a hardscrabble farm near Urfa had gotten that far in itself was a tribute to the very Turkish political system he sought to shake off. Those who knew him at the university said he fixed on Kurdish nationalism only after he was rejected by genuinely left-wing radicals in the heady student politics of the late 1970s.

Apo's hesitation was the consequence of a half century during which the Turkish Republic systematically denied the existence of the Kurds' language, culture, and very identity. "The Turks make us live lower than animals," he said. Indeed, until Saddam Hussein's excesses, most Kurds traditionally saw Turkey as their worst enemy, given Ankara's heavy-handed suppression of one Kurdish revolt after another and its unbending assimilationist doctrine. "I had a lot of trouble accepting my true Kurdish identity," Apo told me. "To say I was a Kurd was to prepare myself for the worst difficulties in the world, to see doors close in my face."

Such doubts were now long behind Apo—unless lingering insecurity explained why he was much given to vainglorious boasting. "I am the strongest man in Kurdistan," he said without a trace of irony, "and the Kurdish people regard me as a prophet." He claimed his was the most important, indeed the only, authentic Kurdish political party because it would settle for nothing short of independence and owed nothing to any outside power. In his eyes dependence was the besetting sin of his rivals in Turkey, Iran, Iraq, and beyond.

But Apo was known to be a close friend of Jamil al-Assad, the Syrian President's brother. When challenged about Syria's support—and paradoxically Saddam Hussein's as well—he sought to bluster his way out of embarrassment with barely contained fury. I inadvertently touched a still-rawer nerve by asking if he was married and, if so, what role his wife played in the movement. My question was innocent. He was known for favoring equality between the sexes and indeed many of his recruits were young women, and I had asked about his wife as a stratagem to move on from his dense doctrinal ramblings. Instead I set him off on a long, largely incomprehensible, and very angry tirade, in which he accused his apparently middle-class wife of seeking to betray him to the Turkish authorities and of ordering some of the PKK's very acts of brutality which, he acknowledged, had caused problems.

The details made little sense to me, and without my knowing the background his remarks struck me as bordering on the paranoid. I had trespassed into a private garden which he preferred to forget. Whatever role his wife had played in his life and in the PKK was now expunged. That was clear. For several seconds after he finished, I wondered if I was in danger myself, but he abruptly changed the subject as if nothing had happened. His outburst and my unease combined to bring into focus something I had been trying to identify all evening: this thick-set man, with his black eyes, black hair, and black mustache, reminded me of Stalin, whose personality cult had been so carefully arranged with blow-brushed artistry.

Apo was a great believer in mental discipline and political indoctrination. In his boot camp in Lebanon's Beqaa valley, pride of place was reserved for ideological training. He considered the PKK's young volunteers from Turkey, Iraq, Iran, Syria, and the European diaspora as contemptibly damaged goods. Rough peasant boys, university students from Turkey, cultivated young women from as far away as Australia and Belgium—all submitted to what amounted to brainwashing. Apo never used that phrase during our meeting, but he made clear that months and months of indoctrination were far more important than learning basic guerrilla-warfare tactics or placing a high priority on physical endurance and living rough. That investment in ideology was all the more striking since, he offhandedly told me, "we can afford to lose" 70 percent of PKK recruits on the battlefield within a year of their completing training. Those were not odds to which he exposed himself: for all his tough talk, Apo was not one to lead from the front; he had fled Turkey soon after the Turkish army in 1980 staged its third coup in as many decades, and he had not returned since.

Yet it was his young followers' very willingness to kill—and to die fighting—that appealed to the successful professional men I met in Qamishli. As Turkish officials never tired of repeating, in insisting they were fighting terrorists, PKK tactics were cold-blooded to the extreme. The PKK targeted not just Turkish gendarmes but soldiers, special so-called "contra" commandos, and village guards, the local *jash*. Since the PKK started fighting for independence from Turkey in 1984, its followers also had a proven record of killing women and children and burning schools and assassinating teachers instructing young Kurds in Turkish. Apo unconvincingly blamed his followers' often bestial violence against fellow Kurds on the work of traitors within PKK ranks. But those men in Qamishli—and Kurds elsewhere—were not taken in by such self-serving arguments. They simply did not care.

They also seemed unperturbed by the severity of the Turkish security forces' repression. With every passing year, the PKK's war had gotten nastier. So had the retaliation of the Turkish army and security forces. In the conflict's first decade alone—and at an ever-accelerating pace—more than sixteen thousand Kurds died,* more than a thousand Kurdish villages were razed or forcibly abandoned, and hundreds of thousands of Kurdish villagers were forced to seek refuge in Diyarbakir or in Adana, Ankara, Istanbul, or Izmir in western Turkey. "After Halabja," Apo said, "we were stronger and had more recruits."

In February 1993, two years after meeting Apo, I walked four hours in bitter cold across crisp snow on narrow mountain paths to visit a PKK camp just inside Iraq's border with Iran that was training more young Kurds to fight against Turkey. I had no idea how—or even if—I would be received. In those two years much had changed. Kuwait had been liberated from Iraq's invasion by the American-led allied coalition. The Iraqi Kurds had revolted at the end of that war, been put down by Saddam's rump military, and fled to the mountains. They had taken advantage of allied air protection to conduct their first free elections for a regional assembly in May 1992. But the vacuum created by these tumultuous events also played into the hands of the PKK, and Apo turned northern Iraq into a major staging area for cross-border raids into Turkey. Escalating PKK operations against Turkey involved Apo in a side conflict with Iraqi *pesh merga* which cost hundreds of (mostly PKK) lives.

The Iraqi Kurds had tried in vain to avoid the clash. They had their hands full administering their ruined land under the overall U.N. economic embargo against Iraq and under Saddam Hussein's economic and administrative sanctions against the north imposed in October 1991. They wanted no trouble with Turkey, which was increasingly exercised over the PKK's cross-border raids. Nor did Iraqi Kurdish leaders relish the prospect of fighting fellow Kurds, and they tried with great patience to convince the PKK to stop using Iraq as a sanctuary. Such was Öcalan's arrogance that he paid no mind to these repeated warnings. For him all Kurdistan was one, and national borders were nonexistent. He felt justified in doing anything he wanted, and he had plenty of money, thanks to

---

* Turkish Kurdish sources estimated as many as twenty-three thousand died by the end of 1996.

the half-million Turkish Kurds in the European diaspora. He was also convinced that his reputation among ordinary Iraqi Kurds was so ascendant that Barzani and Talabani would not dare take up arms against the PKK. But the impoverished Iraqi Kurds had no choice but to attack the PKK: they were totally reliant on Turkey for their only sure access to the outside world—and for the "customs duties" they collected on illicit Iraqi diesel sales to Turkey to keep their ramshackle administration going.

At first Turkey tried to force the reluctant Iraqi Kurds to act by bombing their villages. Western military observers in northern Iraq believed that the Turkish pilots were flying too fast and too high to know whether their bombs were hitting PKK or Iraqi Kurds. But the signal was clear either way and scarcely a new tactic for the Turks. (Turkish warplanes had raided Barzani's bases in northwestern Iraq in 1986 in retaliation for PKK activity, with Prime Minister Turgut Özal openly stating in mid-August of that year, "Let this be a warning to those who shelter the rebels.") The PKK cross-border operations nonetheless continued until the Turks closed the border. Days after the Iraqi Kurds finally took on the PKK, the Turkish military intervened massively in northern Iraq as a blocking force, in a ham-handed operation that appeared to substantiate the PKK's argument about *pesh merga* subservience to Turks. This first of what became a series of Turkish incursions also embarrassed the United States, but out of solidarity with its NATO ally, it stood by idly, demonstrating the limits and ambiguity of the de facto Western protectorate in northern Iraq set up to shield Kurds from Saddam Hussein.

The PKK naively had figured that its grassroots support in Iraqi Kurdistan was so great that the *pesh merga* leaders would not dare fight back for fear of being associated with Turkish oppression of fellow Kurds. Apo either failed to understand the *pesh merga* predicament or thought he was in an unassailable position to exploit the tribulations he had created. He also counted on a special relationship with the PUK to split Iraqi Kurdish ranks, forgetting that the KDP controlled most of the border with Turkey. And if Barzani and Talabani accepted the PKK's use of Iraqi territory as a sanctuary, Apo and his thesis of "one Kurdistan" would only be strengthened at their expense. Apo appeared genuinely surprised in October 1992 when the KDP and the PUK cooperated closely in a bloody military campaign coordinated with Turkey that drove the PKK from the Turkish border. This explained why the PKK's only tolerated presence in Iraq, Apo's brother's training camp, was relocated far from Turkey. Lest the message be forgotten, Turkish jets bombed the camp from time to time.

It was to gauge the PKK mood that I embarked on my winter walk to this camp some one hundred miles south of the Turkish border. After a heavy overnight snowfall, I had set out at first light, figuring that if I got turned away by the PKK I could still get back by dusk to my starting point, where a *pesh merga* escort was waiting for me at a smuggler's market. It was not an easy trek, especially the first half, consisting of very steep hairpin turns. After two hours' steady hiking, my interpreter, Moayyad Yunis, and I, along with our *pesh merga* escort, reached the first PKK checkpoint, a tiny village called Zaleh, close to the Iranian frontier.

A young Syrian Kurd took my calling card as naturally as if he had been a butler in a turn-of-the-century Fifth Avenue town house. At my insistence he carefully noted my earlier meeting with Apo and disappeared. A good hour went by. I became fidgety. My loitering time was running out. Catch 22, I cursed. When it comes to protocol, Middle Eastern revolutionaries can be as serious sticklers as the Queen of England, and I had not warned the PKK of my arrival, for the good reason that there was no way I could have even had I wanted to.

Apparently surprised by such enterprise and by my no longer tender years, Apo's brother, Othman, waived my absence of invitation and received me over lunch. He wanted me to believe that his delay in bringing me in from the cold was due solely to radio difficulties reaching his brother in Syria to check me out. I had my doubts that he had bothered to waste radio communications on my case, or that Apo would have remembered me. Outwardly he was infinitely less scary than his older brother. I suppose a visit by an American reporter, with its promise of news from the outside world, must have broken the monotony of a snowbound winter.

Listening to brother Othman, I recognized a change of emphasis. The PKK had dropped some, but far from all, of its pretensions. Othman readily acknowledged that Apo had taken some hits. Perhaps because of his "miscalculations," as Othman put it, our luncheon conversation was less dogmatic than I had expected. In an aura of rapt devotion from the other Kurds present, Othman dispensed an amiable, half-baked version of Marxism, inspired perhaps by the collection of Stalin's speeches I had seen in a small office while waiting for final clearance. Two young women, packing pistols on their ample uniformed hips and grenades and ammunition magazines on their webbing, unsmilingly waited table. They were from Turkey. Also undergoing training were Kurds from Syria and Lebanon as well as from Iraq itself, Europe, and even Australia.

Othman enjoyed the relative comforts of a building which less than a decade earlier had been Jalal Talabani's clandestine headquarters. The 1,300 young volunteers, more than half of them women, lived rough in tents. Despite the cold, they wore running shoes. Involved was doubtless some imposed exercise in mortification of the flesh, for the PKK was flush, the Iranian border was next door, and Kurds since time immemorial have worn warm woolen winter footgear adapted to their harsh mountain climate. Halabjah was a constantly recurring theme in their conversation, invoked without my prompting to explain their allegiance to the PKK. They had become Apo's thoroughly indoctrinated creatures, the new PKK men and women.

Moayyad, my worldly and normally tolerant Iraqi Kurd interpreter, was so put off by the narrow-minded certainties of three young PKK recruits that he got into a bootless argument with them as we waited to see Othman. He was particularly angered by their disdain for honoring the terms of what had amounted to their surrender to the *pesh merga* only months earlier. They openly expressed contempt for the compromises the Iraqi Kurds accepted as the unavoidable price for maintaining a flimsy autonomy. The recruits said even now the PKK was sending men back to Turkey by bribing their way across the border into Iran and heading north before crossing back into Iraq. (I later learned that PKK money had bought off *pesh merga* checkpoints established to keep Apo's followers bottled up in Zaleh, so that they were able to drive straight back inside Iraq to the border area and resume their anti-Turkish operations.) That a Kurd as open-minded as Moayyad could lose his sweet reasonableness at eight thousand feet in a desolate valley in the dead of winter only convinced me that the PKK was a formidable force—and not just because the PKK trio so annoyingly kept proclaiming so.

After lunch Moayyad and I walked back whence we came, hurrying now before an early dusk caught us in the mountains. Our hike back was an ordeal. The snow had melted in the midday sun so we got our feet wet in the no-longer-frozen streams we had to cross. The trek was complicated by soft shoulders along the narrow paths, which we negotiated with great care for fear of setting off avalanches. At one point outside an abandoned village, we passed clumps of weather-beaten green, yellow, and black flags marking a martyrs' cemetery of Iraqi *pesh merga* who over the decades had fought and died for Kurdistan. The flags flapping wildly in the winter wind got me thinking about the Kurds' curious capriciousness, which made them seem at times more interested in the dead than the living. I did not think it was merely an Oriental sense of fate, or a certain callousness about individual suffering suffused in the unending marytrdom of Kurdistan.

Just a year earlier I had spent a disturbing stormy day with Teimour Abdullah, a slight, shy youth of sixteen who looked no more than thirteen or fourteen despite the shadow of a nascent mustache. I'd driven south from Sulaimaniyah in heavy snow and sleet and spent a frustrating hour before locating him in one of Saddam Hussein's ugly "victory cities" on the outskirts of Kalar, not far from the Iranian border. At the time he was thought to be the only survivor of al Anfal's death squads (a handful of others later materialized). With Saddam Hussein's hit men wandering around "free" Kurdistan virtually at will, his life was very much at risk, yet Teimour was living unprotected less than ten miles from the front lines of a regime whose inventive use of violent vengeance was legendary in the Middle East.

Previously he'd been brought to Sulaimaniyah on several occasions—wearing full *pesh merga* regalia, including the cummerbund, baggy pants, turban, and rifle—for interviews with foreign television networks. At first I thought it was that practiced experience—or perhaps the macho ethics of the Kurds—which accounted for his fluid, oddly dispassionate account of his travail. He kept warming his hands over the small kerosene drip stove that struggled unsuccessfully to heat the cold room. Sitting on a cushion and toying with his glass of tea, Teimour spoke in a high but very calm and steady voice, as if repeating a well-memorized chemistry lesson. On that April morning in 1988, he said, Iraqi soldiers fighting the *pesh merga* nearby arrived in his farming village on one of their periodic foraging expeditions. Instead of raiding houses and press-ganging draft-age men into the *jash*, Teimour said, "they lied to us." He, his parents, and three younger sisters were among six hundred villagers taken to the local army fort at Korotou, where other Kurds were rounded up and kept for ten days on bread and water in a large high-ceilinged hall. "We were afraid even then that they would kill us," he said, "because we knew that when you were taken away from your village, harm could come your way."

Then they were trucked east to a military base at Topzawa, outside Kirkuk. Able-bodied men were separated from the women and children under eighteen, forced to strip to their shorts, beaten, and eventually handcuffed and driven off in convoys to an unknown fate. Teimour's father and a group of other men disappeared in this fashion twenty days after their arrival in Topzawa. Teimour's own turn came ten days later when he, his mother, his sisters, and hundreds of other families were forced into some thirty vehicles and driven south all day nonstop. They were given nothing to eat or drink and were forced to relieve themselves inside the vehicles. They were not the first ones to have done so. At dusk the vehicles stopped. The Kurds were given some water. Then the journey continued for another hour. When the vehicles finally halted, it was already dark, but thanks to the headlights Teimour had time to survey the scene before they disembarked, forced to do so by armed soldiers who prevented them from running away.

Each vehicle had stopped next to a large shallow hole. Soldiers pushed the Kurds down the embankment. Even those who had wept in the vehicles were now silent. Sitting holding hands with his mother and his sisters, Teimour recalled, he thought he was going to die. "Nothing else was on my mind" as the minutes went by. After what seemed a half hour to Teimour, the soldiers opened fire. "For a long time they kept shooting at anyone who moved," he said. Wounded in the left shoulder by a bullet that exited from his right armpit, Teimour clambered out of the pit. An officer barked an order and Teimour was shoved back into the hole. A second bullet hit him, this time in the small of the back. The soldiers went to fetch a bulldozer to cover over the pit, and Teimour stood up. He saw an unwounded girl a bit older than he about six feet away across a mass of bleeding bodies.

"Come with me," he pleaded. "No, I am afraid of the soldiers," she said. Teimour's instinct for self-preservation prevailed. He waited until an army vehicle searching for eventual survivors with its headlights had driven by, then dragged himself out of the pit. He hid by carving himself a small hole in a mound of earth the bulldozers had piled up alongside the pits. Each time an army vehicle's headlights passed, Teimour made for the next pit and hid in the same fashion. After hiding near the fourth pit, he passed out. When he came to, the pits had been all filled in and the soldiers were still nearby. He saw a crossroads and took the newest-looking road and walked for two hours. Eventually dogs started barking and a bedouin emerged from a tent with a flashlight and took him by the hand.

"I was bleeding and I could not speak Arabic nor could he speak Kurdish," Teimour said. He made a sign that he was hungry, and he was fed. The bedouin washed his wounds. Three days later Teimour, dressed in Arab clothes, was driven to his benefactor's relatives in the city of Samawa. Sheltering Teimour put the lives of the bedouin and his family at risk in Saddam's Iraq, but the family did not stop there. Other relatives traveled hundreds of miles to purchase medicines and dressing in Baghdad so as not to arouse suspicion in Samawa. Over the next two and a half years Teimour never left the house in Samawa. He learned Arabic—to the point he forgot most of his Kurdish—and played with the family's children, who kept his existence secret.

One of the family's older boys was doing his military service in Zakho, the Kurdish city on the northwestern border with Turkey. He befriended a young Kurdish conscript and eventually entrusted him with a message for Teimour's uncle, which was delivered by the Kurd's father. Once again ordinary Kurds and Arabs were risking their lives for people they did not know. At first Teimour's uncle was convinced that he and the rest of the family were dead, but nonetheless he set out for Samawa with the cover story that he was trying to buy a secondhand tractor. That first time he failed to find Teimour. On the second attempt two of Teimour's uncles, accompanied by the family's soldier son and his young Kurdish friend, drove to Samawa, picked up Teimour, and drove him back to Kalar in the middle of the night. That was in September 1990, soon after Iraq invaded Kuwait. Police were still posted on every town and city street checking identities around the clock.

"I was delighted to see my uncles again," Teimour said, "but we were so afraid of informers that I could not attend school." In those final months of Ba'athist rule in northern Iraq, street-corner police posts kept close tabs on all residents. When the family heard that the secret police was looking for Teimour, the boy was taken to the safety of nearby mountains, where he worked as a goatherd. His family put it about that he'd gone to Baghdad to work in a restaurant. He returned to his uncle's home only after the liberation of Kuwait the following February. Now his uncle, three other men, and Teimour himself were all armed. But with the front lines with the Iraqi army so close—and Saddam's agents everywhere—"we are still afraid for him," his uncle said. It was still too dangerous to contact and thank the Samawa family, who continued to live in government-held territory. And it was also still too dangerous for Teimour to risk attending school, the only thing he really wanted to do. Abruptly looking up at the black-and-white photographs of his father and an assassinated uncle on the wall, Teimour said, "I am very sad. I never ask why I was the lucky one. I hurt and want to see a doctor," he added, mechanically pulling up his shirt to show the scars left by the bullets.

I was shaken by Teimour's account, and agitated by the insouciance of Kurdish leaders whose interest in him was apparently limited to the propaganda uses of his television appearances. My interpreter and I drove back north in silence. My upset must have been contagious, for my interpreter finally blurted out, "If I could I would have put Teimour on my back and taken him with me." I buttonholed Talabani, Barzani, and any other influential Kurd I came across to plead that Teimour, as al Anfal's sole survivor, should be removed from Saddam's reach and sent abroad for medical treatment and schooling. As a reporter and a foreigner to boot, it was really none of my business what the Kurds did or did not do. But I naively thought that eventually a case of genocide might be brought against Saddam's regime and that in such circumstances ensuring that Teimour remained alive was of capital importance.

I suppose I must have sounded somewhat hectoring. After hearing me out, Talabani took me by the arm. "There are hundreds of thousands of Teimours in Kurdistan," he said quietly. On the face of it he was wrong, of course. Carried to its logical extreme, such thinking wore smooth the rough edges of history called facts and obliterated any sense of pinpointed responsibility. That held for Saddam Hussein—and for that matter Talabani and Barzani—men who over the decades had been locked in often-perverse, ill-considered, and deadly power struggles. After all, bringing Saddam Hussein and his regime to book for their atrocities had lost none of its importance for the Kurds, and Teimour's testimony was crucial. But Talabani's remark was his way of telling me that all Iraqi Kurds had suffered and that they did not need the prompting of even a well-intentioned foreigner to understand the obvious.

I kept pondering that lesson. Two summers later, after yet another trip to Iraqi Kurdistan, I stopped on my way back to Turkey at Barzan, to look at the village's ruins. Singled out for destruction time and again—in Ottoman times, then by the British, the Iraqi monarchy, and various republican regimes—Barzan was used to having its rebellious ways marked for collective punishment. But by the time Saddam Hussein got through scourging the Kurds, Barzan was just another razed village among thousands, and a hardscrabble one at that. Thanks to a German charity, a hundred houses were being rebuilt, a start toward putting down roots of village life again.

Wandering around the ruins with two American friends on their first visit to Kurdistan, I came upon Abdelsalam Barzani under a tree sheltering him from the 115-degree heat. Named for an illustrious grandfather hanged by the Ottomans for conniving with the Russians on the eve of World War I, Abdelsalam had been a teacher of Arabic and English before returning to Barzan in 1991 after a long exile in Iran. He had been born here in 1939 and remembered a Barzan with Christians and Jews who had long since departed. He showed his visitors where Barzan's church, mosque, and synagogue had been grouped close to one another before explosives flattened them. "I can see in my mind's eye Isaac and his team of oxen plowing his field," he said, noting that unlike many places in the world, Kurdistan allowed Jews to own and work the land.

"We were all yearning to come back here," he said, explaining that his nine children—"all of them educated"—were spread out from Tehran to Orlando, Florida. But at least he was back, wasn't he? "We are skeptical," he said, "and we are afraid of the beast" —his way of describing Saddam Hussein and the uncertain state of affairs that Bush's unfinished war had created in Kurdistan. In fact, his entire life had been unsettled.

Mullah Mustafa Barzani and his much revered if eccentric elder brother, Sheikh Ahmed,* first launched Barzan into public prominence and serious trouble in the early 1930s. They had opposed a British plan to settle in Barzan and its environs Christian tribesmen from Hakkari, the high mountains due north across the nearby

---

* Abdelsalam Barzani recalled that one of Sheikh Ahmed's disciples once told him that when people criticized him for failing to fast or pray daily, he replied, "Do they say that only?" When I asked him if Sheikh Ahmed had founded a sect, Abdelsalam responded cagily, "There might be some truth to that assertion." He quoted from the Koran—"Pray that you might remember Me." He explained that "we put the stress on remembering only, not the praying. Some people say you have to pray five times a day, some say three times, but if He is in your mind He is there while you are sleeping, walking, working, whatever you are doing."

border with Turkey. In World War I the Hakkari Christians had fought alongside their Russian coreligionists against the Turks, been driven out of their mountains, and sought refuge in Iran around Lake Urmia, where the British recruited these mountain warriors as "Assyrian levies," in illustration of that classic colonial practice of using minorities to maintain law and order. Among other campaigns, the levies fought alongside Iraq's fledgling, British-commanded army against Kurdish rebels.

The levies eventually were abandoned, with dire consequences as a result of shifting British imperial priorities. After Britain finally secured the League of Nations' approval in 1926 for Kirkuk's oil, it sought to dampen Arab nationalism by transforming its League mandate into pro forma recognition of Iraq as a sovereign state in 1932. The transfer of power meant the end of British protection for the levies, who were no more loved by Iraq's Arabs than by its Kurds. The Kurds were also unhappy with what they correctly feared was the end of their dreams of autonomy, much less independence. Coupled with the ill-advised British settlement plan for the levies, the transfer of sovereignty helped to spark the Barzani brothers' first revolt.

In that more forgiving era the brothers and their followers were banished to southern Iraq and eventually allowed to settle under surveillance in Sulaimaniyah. Sheikh Ahmed was the Barzanis' religious and temporal leader, but it was Mullah Mustafa who escaped from Sulaimaniyah and raised the standard of revolt first in 1943, then again in 1945. The British, in the midst of fighting a world war, were not amused. They mounted an effective punitive expedition. As a boy Abdelsalam fled over the mountains with his uncles to Iran, where the Barzanis became the military mainstays of the short-lived Soviet-backed "Mahabad Republic."

In 1947, when Barzani struck out on his legendary retreat to the Soviet Union rather than return to Iraq to face charges of rebellion or accept exile in Iran, Abdelsalam's father followed him. But the boy, Sheikh Ahmed, most of the men, and all the families crossed back into Iraq and surrendered. Interned first in Kurdistan, the Barzanis were transferred to the southern Shia Muslim holy city of Kerbala, then sent to the port of Basra and later to Baghdad. In 1958 the revolutionary authorities who had overthrown the Iraqi monarchy freed Sheikh Ahmed, and immediately he helped to bring about the return of General Barzani and his followers from

Russia. Abdelsalam came back to Barzan; his father joined Barzani's revolt in 1961, fled to Iran in 1975, returned to Iraq, and was banished to the south.

In all Abdelsalam had lived only fourteen years in Barzan, and despite his bitterness with foreign meddling in Kurdish affairs, he blamed the errors of the Kurdish leaders for his people's fate. He grieved for his eight thousand fellow Barzanis who had disappeared in 1983. Putting himself in the shoes of Kurdish leaders the better to criticize them, he brushed aside suggestions that foreign alliances were responsible for the tragedy. "We have no one to blame but ourselves," he said. "What did we imagine Saddam would do when we were cooperating with his enemies and my people were living under his rule and we followed only our interests? He couldn't reach me when I was in Iran, but he could reach those within easy grasp and unfortunately their names were the same—they were called Barzani."

Allotted one of the simple houses rebuilt with German money, Fatima Mohamed Salih counted herself one of the lucky Barzanis. She'd been a baby with her exiled parents in Mahabad and later returned with them to Iraq; during the 1975 debacle she decided at the last minute not to flee again to Iran. "We didn't have any mules," she said, "and it was too far to walk to the border." With her family she was deported to the south. "The Kurds were divided up one family per village so we could not communicate," but after five years she and her family were allowed back in Kurdistan and sent to Qushtapa.

When Saddam Hussein rounded up the Barzani men without warning that early morning in July 1983, her husband was off seeing a doctor and managed subsequently to save his life by hiding. But their eleven-year-old son disappeared. "They told us the men were needed for a meeting and would be back in three days," she recalled. "No one was fooled. Women who tried to defend their men were shot for their trouble. They sent the police to beat us and cut water and electricity. They kept coming back for two months checking that no men had survived and told us, 'You should die here.'" All told, she had lost "about three hundred" members of her extended family, though two sons and five daughters had survived. As soon as she could in 1991, she moved back to Barzan, where she had lived in a tent for two harsh winters. "All the vineyards and orchards were destroyed, and we had no oxen to farm with," she said. Her hands were torn by thorns she'd been clearing to prepare for the apples, figs, vegetables, pomegranates, and pistachios she was determined to grow again. "In the past the Barzanis suffered more than other Kurds," she said. "This time it was everyone—everyone suffered."

9

Turkey's Social Earthquake

Ankara might be able to drain the sea, but it will not be able to catch the fish.

YAŞAR KEMAL

Only a state as slavishly faithful to the ossified letter of its founding dogma could have backed itself into a corner as totally as Turkey did in this final decade of the twentieth century. In an ironic boomerang effect, the Kurds, who were among the Turkish Republic's first victims, now after seven decades found themselves in the forefront undermining the increasingly creaky system that Mustafa Kemal Ataturk had put in place. In turn, the government's failure to come to meaningful terms with even the simplest Kurdish cultural, economic, and political aspirations helped compromise what many Turks hoped would be their best chance in centuries for greater decentralization and secular democracy, for growing wealth and increased influence. All these hopes evaporated as successive governments after 1984 failed to end a burgeoning and ever more expensive civil war in Turkish Kurdistan.

Yet on paper Turkey's chances never looked better. With the demise of the Cold War and the collapse of the Soviet Union, Turkey, for the first time in two hundred years, was not threatened by a more powerful Russian neighbor. But still the dividends failed to materialize, and equally empty were Turkey's dreams of glory and wealth in the Turkic central Asian republics at long last freed from Moscow's grip. Lulled by rigid devotion to its outward signs of secular democracy, its front-line membership in the North Atlantic alliance, and its participation in various European institutions, republican Turkey kept on trumpeting its Western proclivities as proof of its fidelity to Ataturk's vision of modernity. But with the passage of time Kemalism became less a modern concept than an aging reflection of foreign ideologies, borrowed from the French and Russian revolutions and from Mussolini's corporate state, which had so influenced Ataturk in the years after the foundation of the Turkish Republic in 1923.

Ritual official genuflection to increasingly hollow institutions was disavowed at the ballot box. Whatever its imperfections, Turkey remained (in between military coups) a formal democracy that respected the notion of free, open, and multiparty elections—a capital difference when compared to Iran, Iraq, and Syria, where other large groups of Kurds lived. But in the December 1995 legislative elections, 46 percent of Turkey's registered voters in effect wasted their votes, abstaining (despite a legal obligation to participate), spoiling ballots, voting for Islamist candidates or for small parties eliminated by a requirement that they win 10 percent of the nationwide poll. The mainstream newspaper *Hürriyet* somberly concluded that for the first time the Turks were demonstrating opposition to Ataturk's ideology and republican institutions. Doomsday disillusionment with the electoral process was such that an establishment journalist concluded, "In Turkey it's not the elected government which governs but the state, a state controlled by occult forces who for its own salvation and that of the 'official ideological system' bestow crumbs on sham governments."

Early in November 1996 a seemingly banal road accident on a remote highway one hundred miles southwest of Istanbul so illustrated this point that not even the most unquestioning patriot could deny the pervasive rot in Turkey's establishment. Killed outright were a former beauty queen, her gangland protector (wanted by Interpol for breaking out of a Swiss jail where he was incarcerated for drug trafficking), and a senior security official long involved in notorious anti-guerrilla operations in Turkish Kurdistan. The only survivor was Sedat Bucak, a Kurdish feudal landlord and member of parliament, who ran a private army of *jash* for the government which, it turned out, broke its own accounting rules by paying him more than $1 million a month directly. Bucak's doctor said his client was suffering from short-term memory loss, which fortuitously prevented him from recalling anything very useful. But within days, this odd quartet's friend Interior Minister Mehmet Agar was forced to resign. The Turkish media kept uncovering scandal after scandal for months, starting with the mobster Abdullah Catli's guns, silencers, diplomatic passport, official gun license, and half a dozen identity papers under various aliases. Among the highlights was the allegation that Catli had been an official government killer for more than a decade, despite his unsavory role in arranging the 1978 jailbreak of Mehmet Ali Agca, the man who later tried to assassinate the Pope. There was always one common denominator: the infiltration of organized crime in the army, security forces, government, and parliament, which variously condoned drug running, extrajudicial murder, and large-scale corruption for the happy few inside this state-within-a-state. Taken together, they constituted the heart of the so-called war party, which masked its cupidity with Kemalist patriotism to refuse any political solution to the Kurdish question. Particularly upsetting to Kemalists was the showing of the Islamic party called Refah, or Welfare, which emerged as the country's biggest single party, its 21 percent of the vote exactly three times greater than its showing in the 1987 elections. In 1994 Refah captured major municipalities, including Ankara, Istanbul, and Izmir.

Many Kurds voted for Refah to punish the mainstream secular parties they held responsible for their plight. They were also impressed by Refah's promises to end the war against them and to authorize the use of Kurdish on radio and television and in schools. So fearful was the government of Refah's drawing power that a month before the elections, Hadep, the acronym for the latest legal Kurdish party called People's Democracy, was authorized to run candidates, as a way of cutting into the Islamist vote among Kurds. Despite more than a decade of war and repression, the campaign was lively in Turkish Kurdistan. Kurdish women abandoned their traditional backseat in politics and for the first time showed up in massive numbers at political rallies in Diyarbakir and other Kurdish cities and towns to press demands for the end of the violence.*

* Despite the last-minute approval of Hadep slates, Refah polled 27 percent of the vote in the Kurdish provinces, its second-best showing nationwide, and came in either first or second there. But in the Kurdish heartland Hadep did exceptionally well in Hakkari, with 54 percent of the vote, and in Diyarbakir, with 37 percent, where voters believed that a Hadep vote showed support for Kurdish identity. But in the cities of western Turkey it failed badly. Explanations for that poor performance, 4.17 percent nationwide, varied: lack of registration of many displaced Kurds, a last-minute campaign, a desire not to waste votes

Something else was new. Big business, the part of modern Turkey determined to break out of the bureaucratic Kemalist straitjacket and propel the country to less rigid governance, for the first time said straight out that the war against the Kurds should end. In 1995 the main employers' association commissioned a study showing that Kurds wanted not independence, as the PKK and the state kept on insisting was their objective, but equal political rights as first-class citizens in Kurdish provinces, which were entitled to long-overdue investment. Why the business community finally found the courage to speak out—or, rather, why it remained cowed so long—is not clear, but enlightened self-interest was served by forcing the political debate into the open.

Turkey's new entrepreneurial successes in banking, textiles, and the manufacture of everything from cars to refrigerators was becoming threatened by the dead hand of an unimaginative government unable to settle a long war. But even the business community lacked consistency. It was so frightened by the prospect of Refah's coming into power that it joined forces with the military once the election results were known. Under unrelenting pressure from big business and the Turkish army—rival forces that were united in opposition to Refah participation in government—the two mainstream right-of-center secular parties, the Motherland Party of Mesut Yilmaz and Tansu Çiller's True Path Party, formed a shaky minority coalition after two months of bickering. Few Turks expected its awkward rotating-leadership provisions to last throughout the five-year life of the current parliament, much less provide the forceful, imaginative guidance required to solve the Kurdish conflict or Turkey's other major problems, for that matter.

For that reason, many Turks and Kurds were profoundly skeptical when the new coalition government early on announced what sounded like a radical change in Kurdish policy. Soon after assuming office, Yilmaz, the first rotating Prime Minister, in March 1996 marked Nowruz, the Kurdish New Year, which Kemalists in recent years had "turkified" for their own purposes, by vaguely promising "a new approach" involving an end to nine years of emergency rule in Turkish Kurdistan. "We have concluded," he told the Grand Na-

---

(the 10 percent threshold seemed out of reach), and fears about Hadep's apparent support for the PKK and its electoral alliance with small, left-wing Turkish parties. The upshot was that many Kurds, especially in the east and southeast, thought they had been deprived of genuine representation in parliament.

tional Assembly, as Turkey's parliament is formally called, "that the problem can be solved only by peaceful, not military, means." He was far from being the first Turkish leader to mouth such promises upon assuming office. And his intentions to lift the ban on the use of Kurdish and end emergency rule in Turkish Kurdistan did not mean the government was willing to negotiate an end to the conflict.

In the event, the coalition collapsed in June with the Refah leader Necmettin Erbakan exacting revenge for being frozen out of power. Precipitating the fall of the government was Refah's accusation that just before the 1995 elections Çiller, Turkey's first female Prime Minister, had pocketed $6.5 million in government slush funds. Such had become the mores of Turkish politics that Erbakan and Çiller nonetheless soon formed a government together, which for the first time since 1923 ensconced an openly Islamist politician as Prime Minister of the lay Turkish state. Çiller abruptly dropped her much-publicized role as the self-proclaimed bulwark against Islam in politics, a position she had assiduously bragged about in Washington and other Western capitals. Erbakan's apparent willingness to water down previous policy positions about the Kurds, the state itself, and other bedrock issues was dictated by the need to disarm the army's well-advertised suspicions.

Such caution was understandable. Symbols are important in politics, but they often discourage healthy experimentation. Ataturk's hallowed interest in the French Revolution helped to explain Turkey's unending penchant for Jacobinism, the belief in a centralized lay state uniting disparate peoples in the cult of the nation even at the expense of their own cultures, languages, religions, and other particularities. After World War I, Jacobinism seemed just the formula for turning Turkey's back on the disgraced Ottoman imperial tradition, when the Treaty of Sèvres stipulated rump Anatolia's dismemberment by Greeks, Italians, Armenians, and even Kurds. That treaty, and earlier Christian missionary interference in nineteenth-century Ottoman affairs, created such paranoia among Turks that they often denounced the American-led protection of Iraq's Kurds from Saddam Hussein as a modern-day version of the old plot to carve up Turkey.

Yet over the years, in a classic case of hardening of the political arteries, the omnipresent compulsory statues and portraits of Kemal Ataturk throughout Turkey had, ironically, come to symbolize the state's reluctance to accept the changes in his doctrines that alone could ensure the future of a system identified with his name. Caught in political gridlock, long unwilling to privatize money-losing state corporations or to decentralize a grotesquely corrupt and inefficient political and administrative system, Turkey resorted to violence in dealing with the Kurds. After nearly a half century of Kurdish submission, small guerrilla operations launched in 1984 by Abdullah Öcalan and his Kurdistan Workers Party from bases in Syria and then Iraq and Iran spread gradually throughout the Kurdish eastern and southeastern provinces from the first target areas along the frontiers. PKK guerrillas ruthlessly indulged in terror to intimidate and kill landowners, schoolteachers, and other pillars of the establishment, as well as ordinary Kurds, including significant numbers of women and children in *jash* families. Taking a page from many another cash-strapped belligerent, the PKK also became more and more involved in heroin-smuggling operations in Western Europe to generate funds.*

Starting in 1987, first ten, then thirteen contiguous provinces in eastern and southeastern Turkey were declared under emergency rule—tantamount to the martial law that had obtained in the same area from 1925 to 1950, then from 1960 to 1963, and again from 1970 to 1974. By 1990 a super-governor in Diyarbakir was empowered to ban publications and seize Kurdish printing presses even elsewhere in Turkey, displace civil servants, evacuate villages, and deport Kurds at will. With rare exceptions, only the super-governor's bare-bones official versions of events appeared in the naturally chauvinist Turkish press, which needed little encouragement to accept such self-censorship, especially when threatened with seizure of its printing plants. (With similarly rare exceptions, Western media coverage was no better.) Despite cos-

* Kurdistan has long been a smuggler's paradise, with both Yüksekova in Turkey and Zakho in Iraq as only the best-known centers. Before the Iranian revolution in 1979, arms passed across northern Iraqi Kurdistan on their way to help overthrow the Shah. In the late 1980s and, especially, the 1990s, heroin smuggled from Iran and farther east crossed Turkey and ended up with PKK wholesalers in the Netherlands after passing through intermediaries thanks to well-greased palms along the way, according to Western European police officials. The PKK involvement in drugs was scarcely innovative. Among random and far from exhaustive examples, the British "opened up" a reluctant China to trade in the mid-nineteenth century in what are known as the "opium wars" by forcing the Chinese to buy much of their opium production in India: France financed part of its costs for the Indochina conflict in 1945–54 by dabbling in drugs; the United States was accused of following suit during its Vietnam war in 1963–74.

metic changes in Turkey's draconian judicial system, carried out under Western pressure in 1992, virtually none of the reforms was applicable to the emergency-rule zone, where police and officially protected vigilantes tortured and killed with impunity, according to local human-rights campaigners, Amnesty International, Human Rights Watch, and the annual State Department worldwide reports on human rights. Thousands of suspects were brought before State Security Courts, the spiritual descendants of the harshly punitive Independence Tribunals that Ataturk set up after Sheikh Said's revolt in 1925.

In the early 1990s, casualties in the conflict between Turks and Kurds doubled from year to year. By 1994 some four thousand schools in Kurdistan were closed, either by PKK operatives who targeted teachers as purveyors of a hated Turkish culture or because the government found few teachers willing to risk their lives. By the end of 1994 the fighting and the insecurity had emptied more than 2,600 hamlets and villages,* sending some two million rural Kurds into cities near and far, where no meaningful provision was made for their well-being. The dispossessed provided a ready reservoir of PKK recruits. Their massive presence in Turkey's southern and western cities also sharpened tensions, for the Kurds complained of discrimination in obtaining houses, jobs, even places in schools for their children. Desultory schemes were announced, aping Saddam Hussein's roadside concentration-camp "victory cities," but they never materialized, for lack of funds. Turkey was no Iraq sitting on top of the world's second-largest proven oil reserves.

By early 1994 the conflict was costing as much as $8.2 billion a year, amounting to about 20 percent of Turkey's budget and almost twice its annual deficit, according to former Minister of State Ali Savki Erek. In operations privately compared to the American war effort in Vietnam, planes, helicopters, tanks, and artillery were deployed against lightly equipped Kurdish insurgents who never

---

* The exact number remains a military secret. Separate estimates by Kurdish human-rights activists, Kurdish politicians, Turkish academics, and Western sources, including diplomats, vary widely. Interior Minister Nahit Mentese, briefing parliament on June 27, 1995, spoke of 2,200 fully or partially emptied villages, 19,000 civilian and military casualties, and 2,000 mystery killings. Official statistics covering operations through 1994 and released in July 1995 acknowledged the evacuation of 2,660 villages. In February 1996, I was given estimates ranging from 2,700 to 3,300 villages. Part of the discrepancy is due to differing appreciations of rural Kurdish society, with its tradition of small, separated groups of hamlets considered part of larger villages.

numbered more than six thousand, including support troops, according to Turkish official estimates. War expenses, estimated at a total of $40 billion since the start, had abruptly ballooned in 1993 with a major beefing up of security forces in Kurdistan, and with 300,000 men serving there, key army and gendarmerie units in Thrace and along the Aegean Sea were skeletonized. Taking another leaf from Saddam Hussein's book, the government began to recruit "village guards," the Turkish equivalent of the *jash*. By 1995 as many as sixty thousand *jash* were earning as much as $200 a month—a princely salary in economically underdeveloped Kurdistan—and often terrorizing their Kurdish neighbors with impunity, in inevitable settlement of old scores conveniently blamed on the PKK. Failure to join the village guards—repugnant to many Kurds aware of the inherent risk of civil strife—was often judged prima facie proof of pro-PKK sentiments and grounds for destroying and/or evacuating villages.

Some 3,200 Kurds disappeared in 1993 and 1994 in so-called mystery killings, which foreign and Turkish human-rights activists nonetheless often linked with officially protected death squads. Kurdish politicians and party activists, human-rights activists, journalists, teachers, and other members of the intelligentsia were frequent targets. Virtually none of these cases was properly investigated, much less brought to court, nor were their perpetrators punished. Because of a governmental effort to intimidate, lawyers defending Kurds accused of political crimes were themselves frequently convicted of similar offenses—such as encouraging "separatist propaganda"—and sentenced to long prison terms.

In a tired replay of the folly committed by Israel and many Arab states in dealing with left-wingers, Turkey encouraged an Islamic extremist group called Hezbollah (but without links to a similarly named Iranian group) to assassinate suspected PKK members and often even ordinary Kurds. (The security forces found it expedient to rein in the Hezbollah abruptly in 1994, arresting hundreds of its acolytes and conveniently blaming their violence on a previously unpublicized split within its ranks. But no explanation was forthcoming, for example, on the long-tolerated operations of a Hezbollah prison-and-torture center only sixty yards from a police station in Batman in which hundreds of victims died.) Although the army was the self-styled "guardian of the secular republic," it was in the forefront of this pro-Islamic policy, begun under the military governments after the army coup in 1980 and featuring state-financed religious instruction in schools and the construction of hundreds of new mosques. Year after year Amnesty International, the U.S. State Department's annual human-rights report, Human Rights Watch, and many Turkish and other groups provided stacks of carefully documented chapter and verse on human-rights abuses. They ranged from routine torture, such as anal and vaginal rape, the ancient practice of beating on the soles of the feet, known as *falaka*, and arbitrary arrest, to less violent forms of public humiliation, such as one case in 1989 in which soldiers forced a village headman to eat animal manure in a stable.

Given that Turkey's penal code excluded cases in the emergency-rule area—and the appeals courts were reluctant to consider the few cases that did go to trial—the only recourse for victims was the Council of Europe's Commission of Human Rights. As a member of the Council of Europe, Turkey was obliged by treaty to accept its jurisdiction, but the commission agreed to investigate only a small fraction of incidents submitted to it. Decisions often took years, especially if the country involved refused the arbitration and took its case to the Council of Europe's court. (For example, the excrement case was settled five years later with an award to the victim of 300,000 French francs.) Inevitably, Turkish Kurds compared their fate to that which Saddam Hussein meted out to the Kurds of Iraq. Turkish napalm certainly killed fewer Kurds than Iraqi chemical weapons or Saddam Hussein's al Anfal campaign of willful extermination, but both states carried out village evacuations on a massive scale and indulged in wholesale human-rights violations. Even the U.S. State Department acknowledged the similarities. Asked in 1996 how the destruction of Kurdish homes in Turkey differed from that in Iraqi Kurdistan, John Kornblum, Deputy Assistant Secretary of State, replied: "If you're in a village, there's no difference whatsoever."

So thoroughgoing were abuses in the region of Tunceli in the autumn of 1994 that Azimet Köylüoğlu, the State Minister for Human Rights, blurted out embarrassing official confirmation of the security forces' excesses, which private human-rights campaigners had long laid at their door. "Acts of terrorism in other regions are done by the PKK; in Tunceli it is state terrorism," he said. "In Tunceli it is the state that is evacuating and burning villages. In the southeast there are 2 million people left homeless. The evacuated villagers must be given food and shelter." They weren't, in any meaningful manner. But Köylüoğlu's remarks were precedent-setting, even if he fancifully implied that the PKK was responsible for all other acts of terrorism in Turkish Kurdistan. No senior official before or since acknowledged as much. Indeed, his underfunded ministry purposely had been set up in 1992 to mollify growing European and American criticism of Turkey's human-rights record without embarrassing the government.

Tunceli, inhabited by Zaza-speaking Kurds of the Alevi faith, was no ordinary Kurdish province. A region of high mountains and deep valleys, remote even by Kurdish standards, Tunceli—or Dersim, as it was called before the Turks changed Kurdish names wholesale—was brought under government control only in 1937–38. Its very isolation had bred a long-established indifference to central government, and a concomitant disdain for paying taxes provided Ataturk with the pretext to break this last bastion of opposition to his governance. Since republican Turkey's archives remain sealed, few verifiable details are known, but Dersim even today summons forth for some Kurds unproven but ugly rumors about the use of poison gas.

No one disputes that the military operations that subjugated Dersim were so fiercely repressive that Kurdish nationalism in Turkey remained quiescent for nearly half a century thereafter. Seven years earlier, Ismet Inönü, an ethnic Kurd and Ataturk's right-hand man and immediate successor as president, left no doubt about the republic's determination. Although Kurdish himself, Inönü warned that "only the Turkish nation is entitled to claim ethnic and national rights in this country. No other element has any such right." That simple thought became the bedrock of republican indoctrination, and indeed Inönü was put in charge of the Dersim campaign.

Sabiha Gökcen, Ataturk's adopted daughter and an early Turkish aviatrix, for example, fifty years after bombing the Dersim rebels recalled having no regrets, then or since. "This was necessary for the protection and viability of the young Republic," she explained in defending the virtually unquestioned republican notions of secular modernity against what passed for the obscurantist Muslim religious influences which were alleged to motivate the Kurdish forces. "It was a mission Ataturk assigned me and I fulfilled it." Men, women, and children were walled up in caves and burned to death. Deliberately set forest fires killed others who had sought refuge there. (That practice was repeated in 1994; ironically, the area had been turned into a national park to preserve its trees.)

The Dersim Kurds fought until their ammunition was exhausted. Villages were destroyed wholesale, and survivors were deported by the thousands in fulfillment of what Turkish newspapers of the day headlined, in hortatory paraphrased emulation of Cato's famous exhortation to raze Carthage, *"Delenda est Dersimo."*

For the most part the European mainstream readily accepted the Kemalist view of a modernizing crusade.* Kurds expelled from Dersim were allowed home only in 1946, when special emergency regulations were lifted. Two years later a Turkish reporter visited the region and wrote, "If you speak to [the people] of government, they translate it immediately as tax collectors and policemen" because there are "no schools, no doctors. We give the people of Dersim nothing; we only take. We have no right to carry on treating them like this."

A half century later Minister Köylüoğlu's iconoclastic remarks produced no lasting effect. Nor did the village evacuation policy stop, although by 1995 the rhythm of evacuations, mystery killings, and state prosecutions in Turkish Kurdistan slackened, perhaps because the state was running out of victims. The minister himself was banned from visiting the evacuated Tunceli villages in 1994. The army also prevented hawkish Prime Minister Çiller from seeing for herself. Questioned by aggrieved villagers complaining that army helicopters had fired on residents and their homes, she took refuge in surrealistic denial. The gunships must have been Afghan, Armenian, or Russian, certainly not Turkish, she argued. A despairing American diplomat detailed to jawbone Turkish officials about correcting human-rights abuses concluded after several years' soul-destroying effort, "Turkey is its own worst enemy." But Çiller was not alone in indulging in denial.

Turkey's NATO allies watched the war in Turkish Kurdistan in dismay, but did not intervene to stop a conflict that made a mockery of Turkey's claims to be a reliable front-line ally and regional bulwark. To be sure, occasionally Germany temporarily suspended its arms deliveries, as in 1993, after Turkey was discovered using German-donated weapons against the Kurds. But by and large the

---

* There were a few exceptions. Basile Nikitine, a former tsarist Russian diplomat in the region and an authority on the Kurds, in a letter to *The Times* of London on July 16, 1937, took issue with the newspaper's headline swallowing the Kemalist justification for the Dersim conflict, "Those Who Object to Education, A Revolt Suppressed by Troops." He wrote, "It is an error to suppose that the Kurds object to education; what they are resisting is turkification."

policy of turning a blind eye was in force. In Iraq the West had been unable or unwilling to pressure a notorious dictator about his mistreatment of the Kurds for reasons of commercial rivalry and the geostrategic containment of Iran. And the NATO alliance failed to take effective action with a democratically elected government to protect Turkey's Kurds—out of geostrategic interests, deference to an ally, and reasons of commercial rivalry.

Back in June 1992 I had had my first inkling of the repression's quickening pace during a trip to southeastern Turkey with two young English reporters. We drove east from Diyarbakir through the PKK heartland, a wide loop of plateaus and mountains stretching eastward to Lice, Batman (Turkey's oil capital, notorious for "mystery killings"), Silvan, Siirt, Şirnak, Uludere (where many Iraqi Kurds had sought shelter in 1991), then west back along the borders with Iraq and Syria to Silopi, Cizre, Midyat, Idil, and Nusaybin before heading north for Mardin and Diyarbakir again. I'd arranged with Kurdish friends in Ankara to provide an interpreter. He turned out to be a young man with cursory English and boundless devotion to the PKK and Öcalan's Marxist visions. Deciphering his remarks was sometimes difficult, but they confirmed that blind faith which I'd seen so often in wars propelling the young to self-sacrifice. His naïveté was an irresistible target for somewhat sadistic teasing on my part. He made clear he thought me a hopeless imperialist, a word that elsewhere in the Middle East had gone out of fashion with the Soviet Union's collapse. Our exchanges helped keep down my anxiety, for I was worried about what would happen to him if we got into serious trouble with Turkey's security forces, which happened often with foreign and Turkish journalists, diplomats, human-rights representatives, and those few Kurdish politicians who still dared to moved around within the emergency-rule area. At worst we risked expulsion and perhaps a beating, but he was risking his life for helping nosy foreigners embarrass the republic. For the most part roads were bad, the frequent checkpoints tense, and the general atmosphere at best sullen. But to our astonishment we were able to go anywhere we wanted, a major stroke of luck.

Our interpreter had the knack of winning over the Kurds we purposely interviewed at random, often on little-traveled back roads where we figured we had not been followed and thus were less likely to get people in trouble for talking to us. Near Eruh, where the PKK's first military operation, against a gendarmerie post, had taken place on August 15, 1984, a farmer complained about the guerrillas and the security forces, especially the so-called special teams whose members often wore civilian clothes, sported earrings, and were feared as the cruelest of the cruel.

More enlightening than the standard lament about being trapped in the escalating violence was his blank stare when we asked him how to get to the next town. We kept repeating the question until we realized that few Kurds used the place-names that the Turks over the years had decreed should replace the original Kurdish designations. (I later learned Armenian and Arab names had also been expunged, except on official highway or waterworks maps, where notions of practicality took precedence over ideology.) With such gimmicks, plus the genuinely appreciated installation of electricity and telephones, the Turks had changed Kurdistan outwardly, but not the Kurds. Their only seeming, if still major, interest in Turkey was getting a fair share of government investments, since they had a taste of what Ankara could do for them if it wanted. What the little people we talked to hadn't yet grasped was that the state was even then gearing up to smash them more thoroughly than ever before.

You had to go back to the slaughter and deportations of the Ottomans and Safavids in the sixteenth century to have an idea what was coming the Kurds' way. "Our parents who survived the Sheikh Said repression kept warning us the state was cruel, but this was the cruelest time" was how Ahmet Türk years later appraised the repression for me. Scion of an important Kurdish tribal family and a veteran member of parliament, Turk's own father had belatedly joined that 1925 rebellion. In the repression his father's life was spared by pure fluke. "Before, people directly involved in an uprising were punished, or bunches of tribal leaders to cripple the leadership, but this time ordinary people who had nothing to do with armed conflict were punished for not taking the state's side. In the past the aim was to suppress a rebellion; this time to suppress a people and its identity, its personality."

The PKK was asking for it, God knows, and showed early signs of being intoxicated with its own success. From 1990 on, pro-PKK demonstrations, shop closings, and overt propaganda had led to fierce reprisals by Turkey's armed forces. In the nationalist stronghold of Şirnak, just weeks before a major army rampage emptied the town, frightened young men encountered in back streets told us in whispers of government vigilantes and troops shooting at random. Only official buildings had been spared (invalidating government charges that a PKK attack had been responsible for the massive damage). We considered ourselves lucky to have talked our way into the town, long off limits to foreigners, especially journalists, and ran into a bizarre pro-government ceremony of men, women, and children at the inevitable Ataturk statue. The participants—local village guards, their families, and a band of sorts—self-consciously went through the motions of a formal show of loyalty to the republic. I latched onto the local *vali*, or governor, and kept badgering him to receive us until he nervously agreed. I rode back to his office in his car surrounded by armed bodyguards. Once behind his desk, he listened to our questions, then babbled on for ten minutes or so. Then, abruptly, he ordered us out of town. He was not in a reasoning mood. We went.

In midafternoon a few days later we drove into the square in front of the city hall in Nusaybin, the Turkish town that shares the border with its twin, Qamishli, in Syria. We had had a long, hot drive and sought refreshment at an outdoor café on the square. Our arrival stopped the raucous conversations we'd overheard as we were parking, and we sat down among a dozen stony-faced men. Most sported visible handguns, some in shoulder holsters. Our attempts to strike up conversation failed. They had no experience with foreign journalists and no desire to start with us.

We crossed the square and were graciously received by the local magistrate in the municipal building. Nusaybin was notorious for its numerous mystery killings. The victims were sometimes understandable targets—Kurdish political activists, local distributors, or reporters for a pro-Kurdish newspaper printed in Istanbul—sometimes gratuitous nobodies whose corpses were left in the streets as reminders of state power. How come, we asked, no one ever seemed to get arrested for these political murders? Why were charges of "widespread and systematic torture," in Amnesty International's words, never investigated? Simple, replied the meticulously polite magistrate, a man in his midthirties. With great patience he explained that Turkey's old penal code—and the recently adopted, and much ballyhooed, reformed version—did not apply to the emergency-rule region. Decisions to prosecute state employees were left to the supergovernor in Diyarbakir, who in practice deferred to the regional military commander, who as a matter of course took no action. But surely the often-repeated charges that policemen, soldiers, gendarmes, and "special teams" systematically violated human rights on a massive scale were besmirching the state's reputation? He raised and spread his hands as if to say that he was only applying the law, and in the middle of a war why would anyone in authority find it expedient to go beyond the letter of the law.

He somehow reminded me of Turkish civil servants described two generations ago by a Western visitor as lonely men carrying out the republic's civilizing writ in "wildest Kurdistan": teachers instructing the Kurdish savages, soldiers maintaining law and order, or magistrates applying its stern ordinances, drinking hard at night, and fighting off scorpions lurking in the bedding. Something else suddenly came to mind as I listened to him: law 1850, conferring total impunity for a six-month period in 1930 on anyone taking part in the repression of the Ararat rebels. On our way out we paid a courtesy call on the *kaymakam*, or prefect, who assured us all was calm in Nusaybin and had been for three months.

We went back to the outdoor café for a beer. The taciturn armed men must have been drinking steadily since we last saw them. They were more communicative, though not more friendly. They told us to get out of town before dark. We had no intention of following their advice, since we would never make it to Mardin, the next city with a hotel, before dusk, and we were not about to tempt fate by traveling after nightfall. In any case, we were tired and already had decided to spend the night in Nusaybin. We ate dinner in a cheap restaurant and went back to an even cheaper hotel to sleep.

Shortly after ten p.m. we heard a loud explosion followed by the sound of automatic weapons fire. I went out onto the landing, trying to dope out where the shooting was coming from, and was all but crushed by a dozen half-naked men rushing down the stairs, strapping on weapons as they went. We went out to visit the purported scene of some of the shooting, the turn-of-the-century railway station the Germans had built for their never-completed Berlin-to-Baghdad line. So much for the government's claims of peace in its Wild East. When we returned to Diyarbakir, we discovered that only hours before a young reporter, our interpreter's close friend, had been shot and killed in the center of the city on his way to work.

When I returned to Diyarbakir almost four years later, the evidence of rural repression—and urban calm—was everywhere. Such was the pace of village evacuation that the population of

Turkish Kurdistan's unofficial capital had ballooned from 380,000 to 1.5 million since 1990. Most of the displaced newcomers from the countryside had no steady work. They survived thanks to the generosity of fellow Kurds, since state aid was virtually nonexistent. A lawyer who handled human-rights cases and was constantly hassled for his trouble gingerly took me on a tour of the ever-expanding slums surrounding the ancient city on the Tigris. First stop was the "450 buildings," a four-story housing complex originally built on Diyarbakir's outskirts to house rural victims of a 1976 earthquake. The residents were the lucky ones, displaced villagers with a solid roof over their heads. But most were unemployed, trudging along muddy, unpaved lanes with the aimless stare of uprooted peasants everywhere. Snot-nosed children played near piles of sticks and branches stacked high for firewood outside the various entrances. Completing the rural setting were occasional donkeys and goats, which the refugees had managed to save when forced from their village homes. Savoring the irony, my guide explained that these Kurdish victims of the Turkish state's village-evacuation campaign had replaced Kurdish victims of Saddam Hussein's repression: Iraqi Kurds who had survived Saddam Hussein's chemical warfare in August 1988 and fled to Turkey had been parked in the "450 buildings" until they had finally gone home to Iraq in 1991.

We drove closer to town on winding back lanes through a hilly neighborhood of jerry-built one-story dwellings in a shantytown innocent of running water and electricity. Suddenly we were overlooking spanking-new, well-appointed, but yet-unoccupied apartment buildings complete with paved access roads and parking lots. None of this had existed during my last visit and I expressed surprise at such relatively lavish new construction, which I had also seen in the city center and other outskirts. Who in Kurdistan could possibly afford such housing? "They're for the families of the gendarmes, soldiers, secret police, and other security forces brought in for the war," my guide explained. An engineer friend good at figures scratched a few numbers in a notebook. "With just over half the money the state laid out for four thousand housing units such as these in Diyarbakir," he announced, "two thousand two hundred evacuated villages could be made livable again and each displaced family provided with an ox, a cow, two lambs, and two goats." Refugees I talked to said they longed to return to their villages but knew the security forces would not agree. At least they had the consolation of being near their villages if the war ended or the authorities relented. And here they were safe from the assimilating pressures to forget their own language and customs that awaited the Kurds who fled farther afield into western and southern Turkey.

My lawyer guide had been threatened so often he was careful to be home at six p.m. But for less prominent targets, city life had become less tense and dangerous thanks to the security forces. I walked around Diyarbakir, with its ancient dark basalt walls, morning, noon, and night and found people going about their business or pleasure at all hours. In the past, pedestrians had been off the streets well before dusk. Now there were also far fewer police and gendarme patrols. Had the state uprooted the PKK infrastructure or simply driven it underground? I spent what previously would have been a nervous-making late afternoon insistently searching for the Zia Gökalp museum, which after much trouble I found in a back street not far from the central market. Gökalp was born here in 1876 of Kurdish stock to a father who was a minor city official. Self-taught, an impassioned poet and eclectic professor of sociology, he became a leading ideologue for militant Turkish nationalism.

Influenced by Emile Durkheim and other French as well as German thinkers, Gökalp rose to prominence under the Young Turks in the years before World War I. But it was in *The Principles of Turkism*, published in 1920, that he provided Ataturk with key arguments to justify a strong, lay, centralized power intolerant of minorities and determined to "turkify" them. "A nation is not a racial or ethnic or geographic or political or volitional group," he argued, "but one composed of individuals who share a common language, religion, morality or aesthetics, that is to say, who have received the same education." Gökalp died in 1924, before Ataturk got around to applying his ideas with such terrible consequences for the Kurds.

Like many Kurds who prominently served the Turkish Republic, Gökalp refused to consider himself Kurdish. This denial contrasted with the Ottomans' view that their far-flung empire's Christian, Jewish, and Muslim subjects were Ottomans who did not have to repudiate their mother tongues, ethnic origins, or cultural specificities. "I would not hesitate to believe that I am a Turk even if I had discovered that my grandfathers came from the Kurdish or Arab areas," Gökalp maintained, "because I learned through my sociological studies that nationality is based on upbringing."

For years I'd seen the sign at a major crossroads indicating the general direction of the museum. I hoped the visit would help me decipher what struck me as a curious denial of his own Kurdish roots in the name of an all-encompassing Turkish nationalism. There were examples galore, not just Gökalp or Inönü or, a generation later, another Kurdish general named Cemal Gürsel, who became president, leading the first of three army coups, seizing power in 1960, and warning potential Kurdish nationalists that "the army will not hesitate to bombard towns and villages; there will be such a bloodbath . . ."

What struck me when I finally located Gökalp's museum was the very ordinariness of the place, built around a small courtyard and deserted but for a half-dozen chickens. I wandered alone around the freshly painted building only to be told by its lackadaisical caretaker that the museum was "under repair." Indeed, except for the obligatory head of Ataturk gracing all public premises in Turkey, the half-dozen rooms and their glass display cases were empty. I was disappointed at first, but now I am not so sure I had not found the answer I was looking for.

As NATO's senior partner, the United States was inevitably of central importance in Turkey. Even after the end of the Cold War, Turkey for years occupied third place in the list of recipients of American foreign aid, albeit well behind Israel and Egypt. In 1994, the year of the worst repression in its Kurdish provinces, Turkey was the biggest single importer of American military hardware and thus the world's largest arms purchaser. Its arsenal, 80 percent American, included M-60 tanks, F-16 fighter-bombers, Cobra gunships, and Blackhawk "slick" helicopters, all of which were eventually used against the Kurds. The Pentagon consistently pushed Turkey to buy ever more American weapons, except for briefly holding up antipersonnel cluster-bomb units. Washington was embarrassed when human-rights groups revealed that Turkish F-16s had bombed villages and inflicted civilian casualties, but by invoking a loophole, the Pentagon made sure that the Clinton administration did not suspend arms deliveries, as required by a law designed for just such cases of misused weaponry. First things first. Several thousand American troops still manned NATO intelligence-gathering equipment and installations dotted around Turkey and once considered vital in the Cold War, especially after the Islamic revolution in Iran had closed even more valuable listening posts near the Caspian Sea in 1979.

But at no point was this military presence, dating back to the 1950s, ever utilized for developing an insight into Turkey's Kurdish plight. American troops were under strict orders not to talk politics with their notoriously thin-skinned Turkish counterparts. I know, because since the mid-1980s I regularly asked American officers serving in Turkey about Kurdistan, where several key American installations were located. My astonishment at their total lack of interest never ceased. Their attitude struck me as a mindless rerun of the attitude I had observed among their military and diplomatic counterparts at the U.S. embassy in Tehran in the 1970s, officers who with disastrous consequences for American national interests deliberately shied away from trying to understand the opposition to the Shah out of deference to him.

Over the years successive American administrations changed the justifications for tolerating Turkey's repression of its Kurds. In the 1950s, the Baghdad Pact (rebaptized CENTO when Iraq dropped out following the overthrow of the monarchy in 1958) amounted to Western approval of anti-Kurd animus, enshrined in the Saadabad Treaty of 1937. Nationalism, especially among minorities, was as suspect in the "pro-Western" Middle East confrontation states along the Iron Curtain as it was in the Soviet empire. With the waning of the Cold War and the rise of Khomeini's Iran, Turkey was promoted to being a secular gendarme, helping to keep its unruly Islamic neighbors in line for Western interests. The messy conclusion to the Gulf War in 1991 made the United States a virtual prisoner of Ankara and of Washington's own often-contradictory policy interests. Baldly stated, Washington needed Turkey's agreement to use Incirlik air base, near Adana, to run air patrols protecting the Iraqi Kurds and its own still-tarnished reputation. In return, it looked the other way at Ankara's increasing repression of its own Kurds.

That air-cover policy, code-named Provide Comfort, or, sometimes, Poised Hammer, was unpopular with virtually all mainstream Turkish politicians, who illogically had convinced themselves that the United States was purposely aiding and abetting a PKK sanctuary in northern Iraq. (Only the influential Turkish General Staff was realistic enough to prefer Provide Comfort to a rerun of millions of defenseless Iraqi Kurds jamming up against Turkey's border, and it quietly prevailed on successive governments to renew the arrangement.) For decades the United States had gone along with the Turks' official "mountain Turk" dogma denying the Kurds' very existence, and now it also steadfastly accepted the contention that the PKK was a terrorist organization pure and simple. Still, the PKK's success in turning Turkish repression to its own nationalist ends and extending its political influence among Kurds doubtless did worry Washington and other Western capitals.

Many Turkish Kurds who genuinely feared and opposed PKK tactics on human-rights grounds, and who understood the cycle of government repression against ordinary Kurds that they triggered, nevertheless acknowledged Öcalan's importance. Single-handedly, he had resurrected the long-denied Kurdish identity. But Washington never did more than wring its diplomatic hands. Successive Assistant Secretaries of State for Human Rights visited Turkey and denounced abuses by both government and guerrillas. Yet the United States perpetually preferred to see the Turkish glass half full when many Turks themselves knew it was at best half empty and leaking. The U.S. government encouraged missions from Washington to push for criminal-procedure reforms and less brutal interrogation methods that would obviate confessions based on torture. And despite mounting evidence of uncorrected abuse, American officials placed hopes in improved police training and forensic techniques, or in the creation of a (powerless) Human Rights Ministry and other cosmetic changes that many in Turkey considered either humbug or as interference in their domestic affairs. Their stress was always on the benefits of such reforms for all Turks, not just Kurds. But the United States, fearful of the Turks' notorious chauvinism and dependent on Turkey's cooperation in other policy initiatives, took no overt action to favor a political solution for ending the deadly civil war so detrimental to Turkey's well-being.

American-Turkish relations were shot through with such contradictions. Because of its PKK problem, Ankara was ambivalent in dealing with Iraq's Kurds, who even when they later fell to fighting among themselves in 1994 remained an essential factor in Washington's policy to topple Saddam Hussein (or at least to go through the motions of seeming to do so). Turkey's own policy was hardly consistent. Ankara made no secret of its unhappiness with the Iraqi Kurds' regional parliament and government, denounced as an embryonic state that Turkey feared as a precedent for its own

Kurds and said it would not tolerate; yet it began giving them some $13 million a year for food and other necessities, allowed the KDP and PUK to open liaison offices in Ankara, and, despite U.N. economic sanctions banning all humanitarian exchanges with Iraq, tolerated the thriving black market in bootleg Iraqi diesel fuel, which helped Iraq's Kurds pay salaries and other expenses.

Those gestures sailed close to Turkey's dealing with something that for all intents and purposes resembled a state. Yet Turkey also tried to resume diplomatic and economic relations with Saddam Hussein, in the hope that somehow he would reassert control over Iraq's Kurdish region and thus deprive the PKK of sanctuary. Never mind that Saddam Hussein in the past had his own reasons for helping the PKK cause problems for Turkey: such contradictions were played down. And Turkey, by invading northern Iraq more and more frequently in the name of smashing PKK bases and guerrillas there, exacerbated the already-tense relations between rival Iraqi Kurdish militias. All these moves, likely to increase Baghdad's influence in northern Iraq, were scarcely to Washington's liking.

Nor, given the Clinton administration's dual-containment policy for ostracizing and isolating Iraq and Iran, was Iran's newly open and influential role in Iraqi Kurdistan, starting in 1994. But in a neat international division of labor, European governments openly criticized the Turkish military incursions into northern Iraq, while the United States waffled in public and told its critics it was working to greater effect behind the scenes (always an American favorite). Senior State Department officials from time to time wrung their hands in public, allowing piously that repression alone would not end the war against the PKK.

Thus did Washington and Ankara become deeply involved in ambitious and complicated regional tradeoffs without apparent connections to the Kurds which nonetheless impinged on them. The diplomatic juggling might arguably have made sense if the party involved had been an established European ally. But little mind seemed to have been paid to the potentially debilitating effects of such multifaceted policies on Turkey, no powerhouse, but a country beset by poor-to-bad relations with most, if not all, of its eight neighbors, quite apart from the Kurdish conflict. The Clinton administration nevertheless enlisted Turkey as the regional centerpiece for its dual containment. It also swallowed its misgivings about the revamped Saadabad-style meetings at which Iran's,

Syria's, and Turkey's foreign ministers—powers Washington would have just as soon kept apart—regularly expressed their animosity to all things Kurdish. (These demonstrations of formal diplomatic solidarity did not stop Syria, Iran, and Iraq from offering sanctuary to the PKK for military operations against Turkey.)

Theirs was an elementary case of payback, using Turkish Kurds as messengers for "plausible deniability." Turkey baited the trap. Such was its disdain for the Ottomans' former Arab colonies that it dealt with Iraq and Syria as if bilateral relations with them concerned strictly security problems divorced from the higher sphere of diplomacy governing intercourse with other foreign powers. The results were disastrous, though few Turkish officials did more than complain that they "lived in a tough neighborhood," as if to excuse their lack of diplomatic imagination and initiative.

Nowhere were the results more costly than in the Southeast Anatolia Project, better known by its Turkish initials as GAP. In the 1980s Turkey had bulled ahead unilaterally with this overly ambitious irrigation and development project harnessing the Tigris and Euphrates rivers. In the absence of clear-cut international law, Turkey argued that since the two rivers rose within its borders it need not take into consideration any neighboring nations' demands for water-sharing, despite their vital dependence on the quality and regularity of the flows. By way of dismissing their complaints, Ankara insisted that its neighbors were receiving a steady water supply for the first time thanks to its new dams. Intermittent three-power water-sharing negotiations remained largely inconclusive. The International Monetary Fund, the World Bank, and other international and private foreign investors refused financing for fear of entanglement in such a sensitive dispute and on the grounds that Turkey had not first ironed things out with Iraq and Syria. That was the limit of Western disapproval.* International experts estimated that upon eventual completion of the Turkish plans, Syria might receive only 40 percent of its traditional flow of the Euphrates water and Iraq 20 percent. In February 1996, as Turkey's politicians were thrashing around trying to put together a government, its armed forces unilaterally signed a military training agreement with

---

* GAP was advertised as providing massive employment for Kurds, but in fact it did not do so significantly. Even if GAP had been completed as its planners had dreamed, it is doubtful that uneducated and unskilled Kurds in southeastern Turkey, where unemployment and underdevelopment were most severe, would have been hired for it anyhow, since the land was locally owned.

Israel: this tit-for-tat riposte to Syria's backing for the PKK reincarnated Israel's old periphery policy, although this time the Jewish state was using Turkey to pressure both its old enemy Syria and its erstwhile ally Iran.

As the Kurdish problem came to complicate the region's politics, the Clinton administration became more dependent than ever on Turkey, for domestic American political reasons. After the November 1995 Dayton accords, which ended forty-three months of fighting in Bosnia, Washington turned to Ankara to solve a major problem that risked bedeviling President Clinton's reelection chances in 1996. The administration judged it politically risky to keep American troops in Bosnia for more than a year, much less undertake directly the potentially even more time-consuming training of the Muslims' fledgling army, designed to fend off Croats and Serbs. Yet that training was a high domestic American political priority. Washington decided that Turkey, a former but sufficiently distant imperial power in the Balkans, could be decked out as a friendly, pro-Western, moderate Muslim NATO partner and handle the training mission admirably.

Turkey was pleased to be elevated to such major-league status and to stake out a claim for the future. In public no one mentioned the ironies of Turkey, a state involved in crushing the identity of its Kurdish minority, helping Bosnia's beleaguered Muslims to survive against proponents of "greater" Croatia and Serbia. (Ataturk had turned his back on the Islamic world and had left Turkish communities stranded in the Ottoman Empire's former colonies, but Turkey in the 1980s claimed there was nothing inconsistent in its repression of its own Kurds and its defense of Turkish minorities in Bulgaria, Greece, and Cyprus.) Especially attractive in the Bosnian training program was the likelihood of IOU's to be cashed in later, especially if NATO allies got pushy about the Kurds or any other dodgy aspect of Turkish policy. For the first time Turkey risked becoming part and parcel of American domestic politics, a potentially dangerous development for foreign-policy formulation, as American diplomats knew only too well from dealing over the years with the powerful Greek and Israeli lobbies at home.

How complicated American relations with Turkey had become in so few years! All through the Reagan years, the American ambassador in Ankara had been the Vienna-born Robert Strausz-Hupé, a political appointee and onetime teacher of political science at the University of Pennsylvania. He was well into his eighties when, ten years ago or so, I badgered him about the United States' apparent nonchalance toward mounting Turkish human-rights abuses, especially in Kurdistan. Even then, Western human-rights advocates were questioning the wisdom of supplying Turkey with massive amounts of arms likely to be used in a civil conflict. (Later, in 1996, they vainly tried to persuade the State Department to invoke an American law, article 502 B of the Foreign Assistance Act, specifically banning weapons deliveries to countries with a record of consistent human-rights abuses, except under special waiver provisions which, *mirabile dictu*, were always granted.) Strausz-Hupé got my drift. But his main job was keeping the Turks revved up against Reagan's "evil empire" Russians in that last, tense period of Cold War confrontation. He offered a few desultory comments about letting the Europeans carry the human-rights ball and retreated into that classic old-man's gambit: he fell asleep, and tiptoeing aides ushered me out of his office lest he wake. Those were still the years of official Turkish silence about their "mountain Turks." In an act of utter daring, a left-wing magazine, *Yeni Gundem*, in 1987 devoted an entire issue to the proposition that Kurdistan was Turkey's number-one problem, which could only be solved politically. Among the contributors were safely retired senior military and civilian establishment figures who had served in southeastern Turkey and Kendal Nezan, the self-exiled director of the Kurdish Institute of Paris, whose very name was anathema in official Ankara. Predictably, the issue was seized, but only after remaining on sale for six days. That was considered akin to official indulgence.

———

A year or so later, I confronted Kaya Toperi, Özal's press spokesman, in his Ankara office. I'd known him for years, and he had been kind enough to arrange an interview at short notice in Diyarbakir with the supergovernor, a particularly tough nut who received me with scarcely concealed ill grace and refused to answer my questions with any semblance of reality. I knew Toperi well enough to warn him that such stonewalling was childishly self-defeating. I also filled him in on the excesses I had witnessed. Surely, I argued, Turkey had better things to do than jail Kurds for selling cassettes of their music or singing in their own language, unless giving the PKK a helping hand was perversely the government's intention. I didn't go into the security forces' grosser behavior. Judging by his squirming reaction, I didn't have to.

If my random interviews in the countryside were a reliable yardstick, I said, harassing civilians and burning villages risked alienating Kurds. In their vast majority, those I had talked to did not demand independence, then still the PKK's main demand, nor did they share Apo's fascination with Marxism. They just wanted to be treated like first-class citizens, with basic respect for their culture and a fair share of state development investments in their long-neglected region. Over the years I'd watched Third World insurgencies by the dozen and failed to understand why a supposedly Westernized country and NATO member seemed to be so perversely misreading the all too obvious signals. Surely the Turks were smart enough to realize that government repression served only to swell rebel ranks. I kept up my criticism until I feared Toperi would ask me to leave, despite our long friendship. When I stopped, in an almost inaudible whisper Toperi confided, "I know, I know. But it's the army, and only Özal knows how to deal with them."

What Toperi was telling me was that Özal—the most imaginative and iconoclastic Turkish politician since Ataturk himself, the man entrusted by the generals to head an ostensibly civilian government after their putsch in 1980, the third in as many decades—was not in total charge, although he had been democratically elected in 1983. In and by itself the remark was revealing, but hardly shocking. After all, Ataturk scuttled the Ottoman system and founded his republic in 1923 thanks to the army. Other states relied on an administration, a middle class, a feudal system, or other forms of support, but the army had created the Turkish Republic, an initially weak state that feared for its territorial integrity contested by Christians, in the form of invading Greeks in the west and Armenians in the east out to avenge Ottoman massacres and reclaim their historic lands. And Ataturk's officer corps served as the ultimate bulwark of an essentially top-to-bottom system designed to modernize the backward Anatolian heartland by ripping it loose from its Islamic roots and turning it westward once and for all, whether its inhabitants liked it or not.

Sheikh Said's religion-tinged Kurdish revolt in 1925 confirmed the regime's authoritarian streak. So did another uprising in 1930, which curiously combined Kurds and their erstwhile victims, the

Armenians, and ended disastrously when Reza Shah of Iran allowed Turkish troops to enter Iranian territory and surround the insurgents on Mount Ararat. (His treachery was echoed forty-five years later by his son, Shah Mohamed Reza Pahlavi, when in 1975 he ditched General Barzani.) Along with the Dersim campaign, these events kept alive official suspicions of Kurdish nationalism in the great stretches of eastern and southeastern Turkey, which remained under martial law until 1950 and off-limits to potentially nosy foreigners until 1965.

Before, during, and especially after the Cold War, Turkey's armed forces kept the Kurdish card up their sleeve to justify their preeminence in Turkish public life, just in case the nation's eight often-rambunctious neighbors were not enough. Had not Kurds been involved in all but one of the eighteen revolts between the two world wars? Whatever the military caste's inner doubts over the years about winning its longest war, the conflict with the PKK certainly kept it busy and at the very center of politics. Its chosen instrument, the National Security Council, was nominally presided over by the President of the Republic, who from 1989 to 1993 was Özal. With the possible exception of Özal himself, military figures—the general heading the Turkish General Staff and the uniformed commanders of the army, air force, navy, and gendarmerie—all counted for more than the civilians, who also included the Prime Minister and the defense, foreign, and interior ministers. The NSC was the most influential institution in Turkey; the chief of the General Staff constitutionally outranks the Defense Minister and other members of the government.

Özal's relationship with the army that had launched his executive career was complicated, at times even disdainful, as when he scandalized Turks by showing up at a parade in shorts. Indeed, such unpredictability was one of his principal arms in his battle not just with the military but with all the Kemalist vestal virgins, ever ready to invoke Ataturk's sacred memory to thwart opening up Turkish society. Özal's trailblazing decisions—welcoming Iraqi Kurdish refugees, relegalizing the spoken use of Kurdish in 1991, and especially dealing with Iraqi Kurdish leaders that same spring—demonstrated he could apply imagination to Turkish politics even at the price of disconcerting the generals. "Özal was thinking about the Kurds as about many of Turkey's other major problems," a long-serving Western diplomat remarked, "in ways this society could not even imagine, much less digest."

Unlike most Turkish politicians, Özal was not systematically paralyzed with fear of the armed forces. Mehmet Ali Birand, the television and newspaper star who caused a major scandal in 1988 by becoming the first Turkish establishment journalist to interview Öcalan, credited Özal with "allowing people like me to act under his shadow" to pry open debate on the Kurdish issue. Süleyman Demirel, Özal's longtime rival and successor as Prime Minister and President, never forgot that he had twice been overthrown by the army in earlier decades, and was widely believed to be so terrified of another coup that, in one journalist's words, at the very thought "he shits in his pants, the military can smell it, and they take all kinds of advantage of him."

But Özal's deportment with the military was less forthright than his admirers chose to remember with the passage of time. He effectively surrendered responsibility for the emergency-rule area after a hundred or so Kurdish civilians were killed in one-sided clashes with security forces during the March 1992 Nowruz celebrations marking the Kurdish New Year. That August the security forces stormed the town of Şirnak, acting, apparently, on unfounded rumors of a guerrilla presence inside the town near the Iraqi border; they inflicted heavy material damage and sent its twenty thousand residents fleeing for their lives.

To give the security forces their head did not seem to be a policy that produced the desired results. By early 1993, the pace of death and destruction in Turkish Kurdistan reached new heights. No longer did even Kemalist stalwarts deny that the war was the country's number-one problem, debilitating for everyone. Then, out of the blue for the first time since 1984, a small glimmer of hope appeared: at the prodding of Jalal Talabani, Öcalan on March 17 announced that the PKK was inaugurating a nearly monthlong unilateral truce to take effect on March 21. Öcalan had proposed a cease-fire involving Turkey once before, in 1990, but this time he took the initiative, promising that his guerrillas would fight only in self-defense. And Talabani told a Turkish newspaper four days earlier that Öcalan was ready to jettison armed struggle and terrorism in favor of a negotiated settlement for less than independence; Kurdish members of Turkey's parliament could negotiate in Öcalan's name if he was an unacceptable interlocutor, he added.

In Turkey many Western diplomats believed that the PKK was enlarging its political and military influence. The PKK arrogantly warned Western tourists to obtain PKK visas from its European offices before traveling in southeastern Turkey. Civilians, and often security forces, too, dared not venture out after dark in Kurdish towns and cities, much less in the countryside. But Turks, more hawkish, who for months had been claiming that the PKK was riven with strife and Öcalan was losing influence inside it, now argued that Öcalan's offer of a cease-fire meant that the PKK was beaten in the field and should not be allowed to recoup politically. A dovish minority saw a chance to explore an opening. Özal's relationship with the armed forces instantly became crucial, despite his climb-down the year before. Among Turkish politicians only he was credited with possessing the vision, the taste for precedent-breaking experimentation, and political skills needed to devise a formula to end the war acceptable to all sides.

Through Turkish reporters in touch with Öcalan in Lebanon, Özal had been tipped off that the cease-fire was in the offing. He was initially skeptical, believing that Syria, Öcalan's main backer, would sabotage such a gesture rather than risk losing the PKK as a lever in its long-running quarrel over the Euphrates water. But within days Özal warmed to the challenge. He even sketched out a plan of sorts to Genciz Çandar, the journalist who had helped set up the meeting with the Iraqi Kurds in 1991 and now had just returned from a private meeting with Öcalan. Receiving Çandar for four hours in the dead of night in Ankara, Özal favored a far-reaching but gradual amnesty: at first, rank-and-file guerrillas accused of no specific crimes would be pardoned and allowed to take part in Turkish public life, then their leaders after a two-year wait, and perhaps senior commanders and even Öcalan himself after five years.

What stumped Özal was how to win approval from a parliament and government dominated by hawks who even then were announcing that the state "would never negotiate" with terrorists. "The military are less of a worry than the civilian politicians," Özal confided breezily, "because they are in the front lines and know what it's like to be shot at." He was also convinced he could win over General Doğan Güreş, the hard-line head of the General Staff, archly boasting that as President he had the power to extend Güreş's term in office by a further year. Such optimism was not shared by all Kurds. Some questioned his—or any civilian's—ability to influence, much less bring around, the Turkish armed forces. The parliamentarian Ahmet Türk said Özal told him at about the same time, "I'm determined to try to influence the top generals to accept a peaceful solution." Türk concluded then and there that Özal believed he was far from assured of success, since "by saying he was trying to develop good relations with the military that meant real power was not in his hands."

In discussing his options Özal insisted that the state must not be seen to be hurrying to deal with the PKK. They were not to be put on the same footing. The state must "stop playing second fiddle" to Öcalan and regain the initiative. Ramadan, the Muslim month of fasting, was about to end and Özal found it useful to do nothing until after the ensuing holiday week. Coincidentally, Nowruz fell during the same period, and passed without bloodletting, thanks to Öcalan's orders and Özal's instructions to the armed forces.

When Çandar talked to Özal again on April 15, in the plane flying back to Ankara after an extended presidential visit to the former Soviet Central Asian republics, it was to tell him that Öcalan would agree on the following day to prolong the unilateral cease-fire unconditionally. Özal was pleased, but said, "I am afraid these idiots will ruin everything." Çandar asked who the idiots were. "The government" was Özal's grumbled response. He had ruled out their participation in devising a settlement and intimated he was thinking of sidestepping them with some form of presidential amnesty approved by the constitutional court. "Once I'm back in Ankara, I have to do something, and fast," Özal said, "because if we miss this chance the situation will get much worse." He agreed to meet Çandar in Istanbul two days later for a brainstorming session.

But the President died of a heart attack on April 17. His last meeting on the evening of April 16 was with Demirel, who succeeded him as President a month later. Turkish politicians became so involved in the frenzy of presidential succession that no serious mind was given to the PKK cease-fire, much less Öcalan's now-scaled-down demands. Whether Öcalan was ready to negotiate was not tested, nor has it been since. When dealing with the Kurdish issue, Turks do not negotiate, from strength or weakness, if they can avoid it. A handful of veteran establishment journalists, who remain the only obvious bridge between the combatants, doubt that Turkish secret agents maintain back-channel communications with Öcalan.

Why Öcalan went along with Talabani's cease-fire suggestion is still unclear. Perhaps he had realized that the cost of continuing the armed struggle was about to escalate dramatically. He had told Çandar in March that he wanted the unilateral cease-fire to end the government's policy of "razing villages and transferring the population." That indicated the PKK was hurting, but Öcalan's proven pain threshold was notoriously high. "I know we cannot win against the army, but we can extract a very high price," he added, expressing standard national-liberation-movement logic about exhausting a stronger adversary. He had also mused about becoming a mainstream political player in Turkey, without explaining how he would manage such a major transmogrification.

Ahmet Türk returned from his meeting in Lebanon with Öcalan a month later, convinced that Apo now realized that "imperialism was no paper tiger" but that the PKK leader was still far from being a mature politician. Significantly, Öcalan's published demands no longer included self-determination: in renewing the cease-fire in mid-April, he lowered his political sights to "cultural freedoms and the right to broadcast in Kurdish," abolition of the village guards, lifting of the emergency regulations, and "recognition of the political rights of the Kurdish organization." Turkish moderates had asked for no more.

Whatever Öcalan's real state of mind, he was genuinely taken aback by Özal's death. In 1991, he had stated, "If anyone is going to find a way to solve our problem, Özal will." Now, overlooking the perpetually overweight Özal's history of heart disease, he told Kurdish parliamentarians visiting him in Lebanon at Özal's behest that he believed the Turkish President had been poisoned to prevent him from making peace, an idea entirely in keeping with his often-paranoid views.

With no sign of any Turkish willingness to reciprocate Öcalan's offers, the cease-fire broke down. PKK guerrillas stopped a bus near Bingöl on May 24 and killed thirty-two unarmed Turkish soldiers on leave and four civilians. The next month Öcalan declared the cease-fire officially over. The PKK staged anti-Turkish acts of violence in Europe and against centers of the $4 billion-a-year tourist industry in southern Turkey. These repeated acts of violence got the PKK banned and its offices closed in both France and Germany, but its operations continued underground. In Turkish Kurdistan fighting resumed with ever-greater intensity, as security forces targeted the PKK strongholds of Lice and Kulp near Diyarbakir.

Many Kurds and Turks still share Öcalan's conviction that Özal was just about to devise a successful political formula for ending the war, though no hard evidence supports that view. But to everyone's increasing despair, no one remotely capable of stopping the conflict was—or is—on Turkey's horizon, much less in power and secure enough to take meaningful action. Had Özal lived, some Turks who knew him believe, he would have been no pushover for the Kurds. Birand, for example, saw him often and says, "If Özal were handling the situation today, he would settle the conflict in a way which gave the Kurds less than they thought they should have."

That was certainly my impression when I last interviewed Özal on January 6, 1993. His proposed solution for the Kurdish problem then was a mixture of assimilation and economics, rather than political or even cultural accommodation. Time and patience were needed, he argued. Twenty years earlier, "90 percent of Kurds lived in the east and southeast, now only 60 to 65 percent live east of Ankara," he said, "and in another twenty years only 15 to 20 percent will remain there." That appeared to be the sum total of his thinking, or at least what he chose to share with me. Turkish statistics are always subject to caution, and to this day I have no idea whether his percentages corresponded to reality. Özal was basically arguing that in the Kurdish east and southeast there were too many Kurds on too little arable land.

Like the earnest World Bank economist he had once been, Özal had tried development economics. He had brought electricity and telephones to the smallest Kurdish hamlet in the mid-1980s to provide infrastructure and attract badly needed investment to the long-neglected region. The government had also unilaterally launched a wildly ambitious, controversial scheme, GAP, the $32 billion project that exhausted the treasury and caused serious problems with Iraq and Syria, which backed the PKK in retaliation. In any event the fighting had compromised hopes that economic development alone could solve Turkey's Kurdish problem.

So without ever explicitly saying so, Özal led me to deduce that the Kurds would be "turkified" willy-nilly by moving them west. With roughly only a third of Turkey's 13 to 15 million Kurds left in historic Kurdistan by his calculation—and their numbers there likely to diminish—most of them would soon simply forget tongue, culture, identity, and especially virulent nationalism. His own grandmother was a Kurd who spoke no Turkish, he had told delighted Iraqi Kurds when Turkey gave asylum to them in 1988. Once Turks got over their shock from that revelation, they could only observe further that Özal was an eminently Turkish President of the Republic—speaking no Kurdish.

He slid over the essential: the changing nature of the exodus. Initially Kurdish migration had been voluntary and driven by economics, part of a larger movement of Anatolian peasants to the country's western cities. Now the armed forces were deliberately provoking wholesale village evacuations. Skipping over the war's depredations, Özal instead bubbled with can-do enthusiasm about giving Kurds jobs on Turkey's western and southern coastlines. It was part of his larger dream of integrated Black Sea economic cooperation. His onward-and-upward spiel had little to do with reality. But fair enough. After all, he was talking to an American journalist, so why not put the best face on a bad situation?

Half a year later it came to light that only a month after I'd seen him Özal had written a dour six-page letter to Demirel, describing the PKK's growing influence on the increasingly disaffected Turkish Kurds. "The Turkish republic is facing the greatest threat yet. A social earthquake could cut one part of Turkey from the rest, and we could all be buried beneath it." His odd epistolary solution was to open up public discussion of the problem and to deport 200,000 Kurds from areas the armed forces considered vulnerable, a policy that had already begun. Whether or not he realized it, displacing so many more Kurds had the perverse result of ensconcing PKK sympathizers and militants not just in Kurdistan but in Turkey's cities.

Displacing Kurds by the tens of thousands could at best solve a temporary military problem, but it held little hope of achieving what Özal had said was the goal. His thinking took no account of realities on the ground. The earlier, more gradual emigration had made assimilation easier, true: Kurds found more or less plentiful, though often menial, jobs and educated their children in Turkish schools. But the war had dumped Kurds pell-mell into the cities and grubby suburbs, where they formed distinct islands of Kurdish rural life impervious to the surrounding society and its assimilating processes. Turkish employers made a specific practice of not hiring Kurds. All too often the funerals of Turkish soldiers killed in the fighting touched off ugly clashes with displaced Kurds.

Whatever Özal's intentions or abilities to bring them to fruition might have been, he had acted as a brake limiting the security forces' penchant for destruction. Once he was dead, his successors abdicated their responsibilities in the conduct of the war to the armed forces. Long before he replaced Özal as President, Demirel had forgotten his recognition of "Kurdish reality" and his promises to turn Turkey's notorious police stations into structures "with glass walls." Those phrases, uttered within weeks of his legislative election victory in November 1991, had set off wild hopes among Kurds and Western embassies, but they soon were dashed. From the start of his third term as Prime Minister, Demirel showed himself a pliant tool of the armed forces, pledged to destroy the remaining guerrillas root and branch before reassessing Kurdish policy. He was not about to go on his travels again.

His elevation to the presidency changed that determination not at all. Tansu Çiller, his handpicked successor as Prime Minister, initially indicated interest in studying the "Basque model," Turkey's political code word for political decentralization as practiced in Spain. She discussed details with Spanish Prime Minister Felipe González, and toyed with authorizing Kurdish language radio and television broadcasts at long last. But a single session with Demirel and the Turkish General Staff turned her into an enthusiastic hawk, insisting that reforms would have to wait until terrorism was crushed. Without a political base of her own, she found that allying herself totally with the armed forces boosted her public-opinion poll ratings mightily, which in turn helped this American-trained economist survive her disastrous mismanagement of Turkey's finances. The military budget more than doubled, contributing heavily to Turkey's record 124 percent inflation in 1994, when the country's normally high-performance economy went into reverse with a 6 percent decline in gross national product.

Çiller's trajectory illustrated the political bankruptcy of mainstream Turkish politicians. She needed no great persuasion to junk what had passed for principles. In her headlong desire to please she further devalued the civilian government's claims to legitimacy, unwittingly preparing the justification for yet another military intervention, if hardliners in the armed forces were eventually to scapegoat their bloody repression in Kurdistan. She was the perfect "useful idiot." She showed no discernible sign of discomfort with any form of repression. Village evacuations, disappearances, mystery killings all increased dramatically in her first two years in office. Record numbers of journalists covering the Kurdish situation disappeared, were killed, or ended up facing the ultra-Kemalist State

Security Courts by the hundreds on catch-all charges of spreading separatist propaganda or worse.* So did their publishers and intellectuals incautious enough to criticize government actions. Ismail Beşikçi, a maverick Turkish sociologist who was first imprisoned for defending Kurdish rights in 1971, was sentenced to more than two hundred years in jail for persevering in his outspoken beliefs. Even Yaşar Kemal, the country's most revered novelist, who is of Kurdish stock, writes in Turkish, and is a perennial Nobel Prize nominee, was hauled before the State Security Court at the age of seventy-one: he came a cropper with the Kemalist hardliners for protesting against the treatment of the Kurds in an essay published in the German news magazine *Der Spiegel*, specifically charging systematic oppression "to kill the Kurdish language and culture since the founding of the republic." Given a twenty-month suspended sentence in March 1996 for "inciting the people to hatred and enmity and making separatist propaganda," he said, "There is no democracy in this country, no law."

Any such washing of Turkey's dirty Kurdish linen abroad—especially testimony at U.S. Congressional hearings, Washington's Carnegie Endowment for Peace, the European Parliament, or the Council of Europe—all but guaranteed prosecution, often before the State Security Court. By mid-1994 Çiller dissolved the Kurds' Democracy Party, sending half a dozen of its members of parliament scampering for European asylum, and arresting, putting on trial, and condemning to long prison sentences six others who stood their ground or were not fleet enough of foot, effectively ending the often-sophomoric but nonetheless first freely chosen Kurdish representation in Turkey in seventy years. It was as if the government and parliament had never recovered from its initial shock of hearing Leyla Zana, an attractive young *pasionaria*, take her oath of office in Kurdish as well as Turkish.

If Çiller had qualms about silencing the last safety valve of legal Kurdish political expression in Turkey, she never let on. In the United States the photogenic Prime Minister's command of American English on television made her a favorite of the media, agog

* The New York-based Committee to Protect Journalists, in its annual survey for 1995, said that Turkey had the world's highest number of journalists in jail—fifty-three—mostly for running afoul of the government over coverage of Kurdish matters. "Turkey surpasses such totalitarian regimes as China and Syria in its willingness to throw journalists in jail," said Kati Marton, who heads the CPJ. She asked the government to abolish the 1991 antiterrorist law often used to suppress the press.

with a blond woman running a Muslim country, and no one questioned the wisdom of her policies.* Thanks to her bravura performances, the Turkish armed forces were able to regain the initiative, even pacify large stretches of previously PKK-held territory, but without ever succeeding in stamping out the Kurds' rebellion.

———

In Istanbul, so swollen with refugees that it is now by far the world's biggest Kurdish city, the Erik family one blustery day in February 1996 took me into their home. They lived at the end of a muddy street in Kanarya, a slum twenty minutes beyond the airport with sixty-five thousand other recent arrivals from the countryside, two-thirds of them Kurds. The extended family—four brothers and more than thirty people of all ages—was virtually invisible as far as the Turkish state was concerned. Like many Kurds forced from their homes in the east and southeast, they had been in trouble with the law. Two brothers said they had been tortured and jailed on suspicion of aiding the PKK back in their mountain plateau village near Şirnak, a notorious nationalist stronghold close to the Iraqi-Syrian borders.

The eldest brother, Abdurrahman, forty-one, said his problems began with his arrest the same August day the PKK launched its first military operation in Eruh, about sixty miles from his village. He said he'd had nothing to do with the attack but was tortured for 193 days on unjustified suspicion of PKK membership, then sentenced to seven years in jail "for refusing to serve in the village guards," as he put it. He volunteered matter-of-factly that he had a son with the PKK. His own arrest had triggered that of his younger brother Khalit, who had been doing military service outside the Kurdish provinces, a standard army practice. Khalit, thirty-five, said he had been tortured for one out of the five months he spent in military jail, then arrested subsequently "about ten times"— he'd lost track of the exact number. The Turkish secret police had tried vainly to recruit him as an informer.

Security forces kept returning to their village, burning selected houses, often with domestic animals inside, and finally the family

---

* In December 1993, I tried to interest an editor at *The New Yorker* in an article on Turkey and its problems. He initially seemed enthusiastic, but soon made clear he meant only a profile of the Prime Minister, and a positive one at that. He had watched her on television during her visit to Washington and readily admitted he had fallen under her spell.

got the message: they left in 1993 in dribs and drabs for Kanarya, where a brother-in-law had preceded them. The women and children had traveled by bus, the men hitched rides with truck drivers "because that way was cheaper and there were fewer security checks." No one in the family was officially registered as a Kanarya resident. As was the case with many such dispersed Kurds, the adults thus could not vote. But the brothers, who did almost all the talking, were vociferous supporters of Hadep, because, in Abdurrahman's words, "the party stood for Kurdish identity even if we will never be allowed to have the independent state we deserve . . . At least Kurds should be given equal rights and a fair share of investments," he said, echoing the lowest-common-denominator demand that even Kurds opposed to the PKK make.

Without proper papers, neither he nor anyone in the family could work legally. But they were enterprising and always found black-market jobs in construction and other ill-paid trades where papers were not required nor questions asked. A bribe here and there so far kept the police away from the door. The family had no legal title to the crowded one-story house. The construction entrepreneur who hired two of the brothers had helped them build the house in lieu of pay. Some of the children attended school, thanks to a Turkish friend who claimed they were hers and registered them under her name.

Pride of place in the Eriks' rug-covered living room, lit with jury-rigged electricity purloined from the street, was reserved for the television set. Every evening the family watched Med-TV, the PKK satellite television station which began broadcasting from abroad in 1994 and drew ever-larger audiences despite increasingly outraged official Turkish efforts to close it down. (Thanks to "Apo TV's" amazingly sophisticated legal structure in five Western European countries, only in the summer of 1996 did Turkey unravel its interlocking cross-border operations and persuade the concerned governments to pull the plug on it. Even so, its resourceful backers soon managed to get the service back on the air.) The brothers had ponied up almost two hundred dollars to buy the decoder needed to unscramble the propaganda and cultural programs beamed in Kurmanji, Sorani, Zaza, Arabic, and Turkish. They had taken special care to camouflage the external antenna and decoder, just in case the police decided to crack down.

Was that enough, watching Kurdish television programs? The brothers and their dependents kept saying they dreamed constantly of returning to their village. Khalit, who alone of the brothers had graduated from secondary school, had no doubts about the worth of going into opposition. "I've lost more than a hundred friends, including more than twenty from my high school," he said. "Yes, it was worth it." There was no hesitation whatsoever in his voice.

A similar absolute conviction that their cause was just was the strongest impression that a young Turkish reporter for Agence France-Presse, Kadri Gürsel, retained after twenty-six days unintentionally spent with the PKK, mostly not far from the Eriks' village near Şirnak. Gürsel relived for me his misadventure on March 31, 1995, when, driving back at night along the international highway from covering Operation Steel, Turkey's 37,000-man invasion of northern Iraq, he was captured at a roadblock organized by young PKK women guerrillas armed with Kalashnikovs near Nusaybin.

He and his traveling companion, a Reuters photographer, had only themselves to blame. They knew the road after dark was considered dangerous, but they were in a hurry. They were well treated by the PKK but kept constantly on the move, mostly at night, to avoid detection. After surviving an army ambush, mortar rounds landing nearby, and helicopters hovering directly overhead, they came to fear the Turkish forces more than the PKK. The illiterate women guerrillas spoke only Kurdish; except for a handful of Iraqis and Syrians, the PKK men spoke Turkish and readily struck up conversations with the journalists, whose tenderfoot ways earned them the teasing nickname of "two tulip bouquets" in walkie-talkie exchanges.

The commanders—better educated, with seven or eight years in the field—talked about Marxism; the less schooled troopers were interested only in Kurdish nationalism. All of them wanted to build one Kurdish state uniting Kurds everywhere and counted on the cost of the trouble they were inflicting in men, money, and matériel to bring Turkey to the negotiating table. They frequently invoked the Americans' defeat in Vietnam as an example of what they hoped to achieve. Few of the rank and file had served more than a year or two, a not negligible survival rate given the enormous means at the Turkish state's disposal for killing them. They made no secret of their own heavy losses. The journalists trekked through some twenty-five villages abandoned or destroyed during the previous year, proof of the security forces' success in draining the population pond and depriving the revolutionary fish of sustenance.

Indeed, eating had become an obsession for the pasty-faced guerrillas, whose pale white-and-yellow fingernails betrayed their anemia. Most of the time they gave the village guards a wide berth, but from time to time they would attack flocks of sheep protected by *jash*, and in one instance killed eight guards to obtain mutton. Most of the time the guerrillas survived on rice, pasta, and tea, replenished from stashes in caves. At one point they took refuge in a cave littered with empty cans of sardines, herring, tuna, olive oil, and soft drinks which had served as a major supply depot. A guerrilla nostalgically recalled when such supplies, as well as fresh salad, olives, and cheese, arrived regularly and "we were as rich as the state." The only outward sign of collective depression that the journalists discerned was when the sugar ran out. Illness and weakness of any kind, including homesickness, were considered poor form and treated with disdain and contempt.

Gürsel was left with an overwhelming impression of determination—and of missed opportunities. Many of the Kurds in the sixty-member unit were young men who had completed high school, looked for work long and hard in Diyarbakir and other cities, and only when they found no jobs decided to join the PKK and fight the system that had let them down. "I think for anyone but them it would be very hard to survive for long in such conditions," Gürsel told me. "But they have an energy, call it an obsession or a faith, of their own. I think they are very strong militarily. They are quicksilver, invincible, because theirs is another dimension of reality." His testimony dovetailed with what Öcalan had told me in Damascus about the basic training he dispensed to his recruits: it was the indoctrination, not the physical conditioning, that counted most.

To my astonishment, I heard somewhat similar arguments in the chambers of the parliamentary office of Kamran Inan in Ankara. If the Kemalist system was in such dire straits, said this arch-establishment Kurd, it was the fault of successive governments, which had not invested enough in education, jobs, and roads in the east and southeast for young Kurds, who thus "became kindling for the terrorists" of the PKK. "What is the PKK," he asked, "except a bunch of young men who finished high school, failed to get accepted at universities, felt they could not go back to the farm, and couldn't find jobs?" The war was primed by young Kurds faced with a bleak future at home and realizing that Kurdish migration to western and southern cities was reaching a saturation point. His analysis was accurate enough, but frankly I had not expected to hear it from him, particularly expressed with such vehemence.

I had known Inan for more than a decade and had written him off as a Kurdish Uncle Tom. In the past I had thought I understood his thinking, but obviously I hadn't, or times were changing. A true-blue establishment republican, Inan in the old days could be counted on to expound the Kemalist line with great clarity, as became this law graduate of the University of Geneva, former diplomat, ex-minister of state, presidential candidate, and long-serving member of both houses of parliament. Over the years I had interviewed him repeatedly, especially about the GAP irrigation-and-power-generation scheme, his pet project when he was Minister of Energy and Natural Resources. A more conflicted man would have been hard to imagine.

Inan's Kurdish roots were a most delicate subject for this scion of a distinguished family of Naqshabandi divines, whose mother was an Armenian survivor of the 1915 massacres. He had been born in 1929 in a railway cattle car transporting his family from their home in the eastern province of Bitlis into internal exile in western Turkey. Following repeated Kurdish revolts, such banishment became common practice; the Kemalists deported prominent Kurdish clerics and tribal chiefs whether or not they had actually taken part in the uprisings. (Iskan Azizoğlu, a charming former member of parliament from Diyarbakir, owes his first name, meaning "resettlement," to the fact he was born in 1939 during his family's banishment from the eastern city of Silvan in 1925–47.) The idea was to leave the Kurds without leadership. The deported got off easily compared to the hundreds of Kurdish intellectuals who were sewn up in sacks and drowned in Lake Van on suspicion of backing the Ararat uprising of 1930. Harsh as internal banishment was, it was also less draconian than Ataturk's stated preference for deporting all Kurds to surrounding countries, a policy never carried out only because of lack of funds.*

---

* During a visit to Ankara in November 1926, Henry Dobbs, the British High Commissioner in Baghdad, was told by Foreign Minister Tewfik Rushdi Bey that the government "had concluded that the Kurds could never be assimilated and must be expelled. Modern Turkey was founded on hecatombs of dead and must continue to be ruthless. She had got rid of the Greeks and the Armenians and her next move would be to get rid of the Kurds." Rushdi Bey justified the Kurds' expulsion by their "hopeless mentality," and said Turkey needed their fertile land and could not trust them on the frontiers. "Turkey will never take them back" once expelled, Dobbs quoted him as saying.

After 1950, Inan and other well-born Kurds had prospered despite their families' travail, an accomplishment many among them as well as many Turks chose to celebrate as proof of the republic's rough impartiality. Inan became the quintessential servant of Turkey, not of the Kurds of Bitlis province, whom he nonetheless represented in the upper or lower house for decades. Like many establishment Kurds who prospered under the republican system, he sublimated the tensions born of loyalty to Kemalism and to his own ancestry, and on previous occasions when I had mentioned the question he had danced away without providing a clear answer. This time, when I asked him straight out whether he was a Kurd or a Turk, he replied, "That is a question I never ask myself. As a *seyyid*, a descendant of the Prophet, I suppose I should be considered an Arab."

The pirouette was perhaps too neatly executed. Yet, as his remarks about the PKK's attractions demonstrated, a man of greater nuances than in the past boldly emerged. He certainly still had no use for the PKK, strong enough in his Hizan district to have prevented him for years from returning home, much less campaigning there in person. (Such were the abiding Naqshabandi influences that he was reelected anyhow.) But he was furious with the system, especially so because his beloved GAP had had its funding cut for four years running. Paying for both guns and butter was too much for Turkey's economy. Even in better times GAP's costs had added hugely to the enormous budget deficit, and now these cuts were a sign of the escalating cost of the Kurdish war. Indeed even GAP's first section of irrigation farming—earmarked not for Kurds but for Arabs of the Harran plains, abutting the Syrian border—was not functioning, because money was lacking for the final mile of giant reinforced concrete pipes.

Inan berated the mindlessness of Ankara's civil servants. He once asked a group of them working on government development projects if they had been to Western Europe. All but two or three raised their hands. "When I asked how many had visited the east and southeast, only one hand went up," he said in disgust. "They didn't know their own country. They devised their plans here in Ankara, and no wonder development projects failed," he said. He mentioned an Italian engineer who returned to Ankara from visiting a site in eastern Turkey chosen for a factory (this was long before the fighting began) and ever so politely asked if the Turkish designers and engineers had done likewise, for their plans failed to take into account the harsh climate and other local factors. "No one was willing to go take a look," Inan said.

Inan also suggested that the Kurds were almost more sinned against than sinning—a new claim. He seemed downright proud of them, although he ritually faulted them for many of Turkey's problems because "they always ally themselves with the country's enemies." He boasted about the Kurds' key, though officially unmentioned, role in helping Ataturk in the years before the republic's founding: "The Kurds created the republic and fought for Ataturk against the French, the British, the Greeks and Armenians," he said. "In Ataturk's speech marking the republic's tenth anniversary in 1933, most of the leaders whose names he cited were Kurdish." It was as if he was under the spell of a truth serum. He now had the bit between his teeth. Between "250 and 300" members of the 550-seat parliament, he insisted, were "of Kurdish origin even if elected from Istanbul," a standard distinction he and others of his ilk often invoked to explain how assimilation made good republicans of all citizens no matter where they came from.

The Inan I had known in the past was in good company in suspending, some might say even anesthetizing, his Kurdish sensitivities. But now I was taken aback. I'd never before heard a figure even half that large. Inan seemed to be suggesting that Kurds had some special political gift that got them elected out of all proportion to their numbers. I pushed my luck. I asked, did he agree with those who predicted that ethnic Kurds would outnumber ethnic Turks by the middle of the next century? "Not at all impossible, given their higher birthrate," he replied. This was yet a further deviation from the Kemalist taboo on breaking down ethnic population statistics.

10

Dog's Breakfast

My conversations with Inan and other Turkish Kurds had preoccupied me for a good part of early 1996. But indeed all year, and especially in the last weeks of the summer, increasingly jittery Kurds kept telephoning me from all over Iraqi Kurdistan, London, and Washington to warn of impending disaster. Exactly eight years earlier some of the same callers had alerted me to Saddam Hussein's gassing of Badinan, his way of celebrating the cease-fire ending the fighting in the Iran-Iraq war. This time they were fretting about an implacable and long-simmering feud between Massoud Barzani's KDP and Jalal Talabani's PUK that seemed hell-bent on squandering what little remained of the Kurds' best chance for achieving durable self-government in the twentieth century. But not even the most inventive of my callers could foresee the rival warlords' ever more debilitating thrusts and counterthrusts, which all but succeeded in expunging the Iraqi Kurds' dwindling capital of sympathy abroad. In the next months, guerrillas conducted a kind of roller-skating war, in which first the KDP, then the PUK lunged across great swaths of the same territory, to the confusion and shame of many everyday Kurds who were mindful that their onetime nationalist heroes risked becoming cat's-paws for their respective Iraqi and Iranian backers.

Day after day in late August, Saddam Hussein concentrated tens of thousands of his best troops—Republican Guards, plus hundreds of tanks and artillery pieces—just south of the 36th parallel marking the limit of the sketchy "no go" area in northern Iraq that was patrolled by American, British, and French war planes. I for one was not surprised. When I'd been in Kurdistan in February, I'd heard persistent rumors that Barzani had been negotiating with Saddam for months. Had he not purchased several dozen tanks and armored cars from Baghdad during the winter? With the clarity of despair my callers now pinned ever-diminishing hopes on the Clinton administration's willingness to use air power to prevent the worst—by which they clearly meant the joint operation that to their horror did indeed begin to unfold before dawn on August 31 and swiftly compromised the tattered remnants of Iraqi Kurdish nationalism and Desert Storm's tarnished claims of victory.

Back in 1988 I had rushed from Martha's Vineyard to the Turkish border, with the *Post*'s blessing, to report on the plight of Kurdish survivors of Iraq's gas attacks. Now my editor was decidedly uninterested, despite my repeated pestering with updated information about ever more detailed evidence of Iraq's offensive intentions. Nor, more ominously, apparently was the Clinton administration interested in the undeniable threat to Erbil, the Kurds' unofficial capital in Iraq, a mere dozen miles north of the buildup. It reassuringly insisted it was monitoring the situation as it had many other past Iraqi threats which had fizzled.* Washington seemed smugly convinced that a boxed-in Saddam Hussein was loath to jeopardize the laboriously negotiated oil-for-food deal which within weeks would allow Iraq to sell $2 billion worth of crude oil every six months.

Whatever Washington's real intentions, Middle Easterners believed that the United States government had opted for the calculated risk of doing nothing during a presidential campaign season. But from the administration's point of view, there was little that could be done. There were simply too many players—Iran, Syria, Turkey, Turkey's Kurdish rebels, Saddam Hussein, and the two feuding Iraqi Kurdish warlords—for Washington to control, especially on the cheap. Intervening against Saddam Hussein's military thrust was a no-win proposition of siding with one Kurdish faction beholden to Iran against another allied with Iraq. Through-

---

* When the Erbil crisis blew up a week or so later, the only Ankara-based diplomat available who still traveled frequently to Iraqi Kurdistan (and became point man in the subsequent window-dressing negotiations) was the Britisher Frank Baker.

out much of the previous year, in a series of meetings in Kurdistan and Ireland the administration had tried and failed to reconcile Talabani and Barzani, but their blood-stained rivalry stretched back to the 1960s, and it ignored Washington's insistence that American support would depend on unity in the Kurdish camp. (The KDP and PUK believed, rightly or wrongly, that the United States was only lukewarm in its peacemaking efforts, since it failed to produce the few million dollars to bankroll a buffer force that they both had accepted.)

Instead, some four thousand Kurds, mostly civilians, died in the mayhem by the summer of 1996, and thousands more were killed over the next two months. Once-vibrant public support in the West waned, and Iraqi Kurds were no longer welcome in Western corridors of power. (At one point in 1995 an American negotiator, frustrated by Kurdish inflexibility, had confided, "If I didn't understand beforehand why the Kurds never had a state of their own, now I can see why.") American strategic interest in Iraqi Kurdistan also dwindled. The leaders' feud undermined the effectiveness of the Iraqi National Congress, the CIA-financed opposition umbrella group based in Kurdistan and dedicated to overthrowing Saddam Hussein and to inaugurating democracy in Iraq.

Washington's conflicting regional interests nonetheless dictated that the United States maintain a minimal presence in northern Iraq, despite these recurring temptations to wash American hands of the Kurds and their problems. The principal concern was Turkey. Since April 1991 it had been especially important to defend Iraqi Kurds—if necessary, even against their leaders—if only to ensure that Saddam Hussein not panic millions of them to the Turkish border again; after all, it had been at President Özal's persistent behest that the procrastinating President Bush had finally rescued the Iraqi Kurds from the mountains. Only later had the United States decided to use the vacuum created in resettling the Kurds as a forward base to help in building an anti–Saddam Hussein opposition. And the initial impetus for financing the united, pro-democratic opposition which became the Iraqi National Congress was provided not by a reluctant Bush administration but, in late 1991, by the Congress, determined to get rid of Saddam. This support was always tempered by the desire to avoid giving umbrage to the supersensitive Turks, suspicious to the point of paranoia about their inability to end their own Kurdish rebellion.

Turkey, not to mention Iran and Syria as well as Iraq itself, was

always fearful that the United States might be secretly encouraging
a Kurdish state in Iraq. In other words, the Turks wanted it both
ways: nothing smacking of a Kurdish state in Iraq, but Western,
essentially American, protection from trouble at the border caused
by an unpredictable Saddam Hussein. Thus, Western policy was
to keep Iraqi Kurdistan on a tight economic leash, which mollified
the Turks but produced massive unemployment and distress in
northern Iraq, and exacerbated the tensions between Barzani and
Talabani. In a moribund economy, toting a Kalashnikov became
the easiest way to make a living.

American policy in the power vacuum of northern Iraq descended to the level of the lowest common denominator to deal
with all these contradictory considerations: balancing the divergent
Iraqi Kurds, keeping the Turks on board, maintaining the INC as
an opposition focal point against Saddam Hussein. The policy was
brought under further stress by Iranian, and occasional Syrian,
maneuvers. Such was the uncomfortable irresolution that Washington had inherited when the Bush administration pushed the
pause button and did not finish the job in 1991. It proved ever
more difficult after American air cover was withdrawn from a maverick CIA scheme for using Kurds to prime an Iraqi army uprising
in March 1995; already at daggers drawn with Talabani, Barzani
smelled a rat and withdrew at the last moment. The incident estranged the KDP and INC and marked a further deterioration in
relations between the two Kurdish leaders. No wonder the United
States resigned itself to living with the uneasy Kurdish cease-fire
that its diplomats had crafted that summer in Ireland. (The arrangements never solidified, partly because of the Kurdish leaders'
bad faith, partly for want of $2 million to pay neutral Kurds and
other opposition forces to monitor a durable settlement. The missing money, some said, had fallen victim to the penny-wise pound-
foolish budget war between President Clinton and the Republican-
controlled Congress, which briefly shut down the federal government in early 1996. Others claimed that Washington believed the
Kurds themselves should pony up at least half the bill as earnest.)

The theoretical solution was simple enough, if ever elusive: Talabani would relinquish control of Erbil and allow the Kurdish
regional government and parliament there to function anew; in
return, Barzani would resume payment of the PUK share of taxes
levied on the lucrative sanctions-busting trade across Kurdish territory of Iraqi diesel fuel illegally sold to Turkey. Talabani's growing

reliance on Iran for trade and transit, which was dictated by geography as long as Barzani controlled the only road to Turkey, would wither, if not entirely disappear. Thus the old status quo could be achieved anew.

Washington was trapped in what might be called a policy of avoidance, which is always doomed to unravel sooner or later. Only in mid-August 1996, when serious fighting between the KDP and PUK erupted for the first time in more than a year, did the Clinton administration recognize that the situation was getting out of control and stir its stumps in public. On August 27, Robert H. Pelletreau, Assistant Secretary of State for Near Eastern Affairs, telephoned both warlords and won their approval for yet another reconciliation effort: a London meeting was scheduled for the end of the month. But by then it was too late, and fighting resumed the very next day. The whole jerry-built scheme for protecting the Kurds was about to collapse. The administration failed to appreciate that the rival Kurdish leaders' unquenchable mutual suspicion and hatred at last had reached the point of no return.

Economic privation imposed by Baghdad and the West itself—plus incursions great and small by Iranians, Turks, and Iraqis—had perverted the very notion of "safe haven" for the Iraqi Kurds, that notion invented by the allies in 1991 to woo Kurdish refugees down from the mountains and relieve pressure on Turkey to take them in. In such circumstances, the benefits of gaining statehood by stealth, as the Iraqi Kurds' anomalous status was sometimes described, paled. Both Barzani and Talabani had convinced themselves that their very survival was at stake, and both fell back into that traditional Kurdish trap—craven reliance on rival states. Barzani's fateful talks with Saddam Hussein and Talabani's with the Iranian government had begun in June.

A final alert at the end of July took the form of a three-day Iranian military incursion deep into Iraqi Kurdistan by "nearly two thousand" revolutionary guards, according to the KDP, their ostensible target the headquarters of the much-weakened guerrillas of the Kurdistan Democratic Party of Iran, located a good eighty miles inside Iraq near Koisanjaq. Constantly pushed farther back from the border over the years, these guerrillas were no longer a threat to Iran, so the Iranians' real purpose surely lay elsewhere. Barzani was convinced they had gone in to give heavy weapons to Talabani, who for months had openly boasted that an uprising against the KDP was in the offing and that the PUK would aid it. But the incursion also demonstrated the Iranians' freedom of movement in northern Iraq, where for years the Turkish army and its PKK quarry had also come and gone at will. More important still, it underscored the hollowness of the American administration's pretentious dual-containment policy designed to isolate and ostracize both Iran and Iraq. Barzani publicly demanded that Washington identify the aggressor, as stipulated in the negotiations in Ireland. Instead Washington's reaction was decidedly muted.

Thus was the stage set for one of the stranger decisions in Kurdish history—so replete with seemingly logic-defying throws of the dice. Convinced that he enjoyed solid backing from the Iranian government, Talabani became insolent and, as so often in the past, too clever by half. He would not listen to outside advice. Iran had overreached most visibly. And in saying that the only way Barzani would see Erbil was "through binoculars" from the KDP mountain resort headquarters of Salahuddin, Talabani taunted his rival once too often.

When Talabani launched a major offensive near the border with Iran on August 17, it coincided with the fiftieth anniversary of the KDP's founding and Massoud Barzani's own fiftieth birthday. Day after day the KDP denounced Iran for providing the PUK with artillery and helicopter support, accused it of helping PUK forces cross Iranian territory, and clamored for the American government to condemn Iran and Talabani. It was not lost on the Kurds that indeed the Iranians had given Barzani exactly the same kind of assistance earlier in the feuding, and that traditionally the KDP had been Tehran's favored Kurdish faction in Iraq. In the final week of August, as Pelletreau prepared to meet both Kurdish groups in London, a KDP background paper again beseeched the State Department, the National Security Council, the CIA, and anyone else in Washington who would listen to issue a "clear warning" against Iranian "meddling." It also wanted the administration to "warn the Iraqis, too"—a curious new twist. After all, Talabani had lately monopolized warnings about connivance between Barzani and Saddam Hussein. The KDP paper left little to the imagination. The Iraqi military buildup, it said, meant that the Iraqis were "poised to intervene and reassert their control of the north" in the name of opposing Iran. With the United States and Iraq's neighbors unwilling to take even political action against this, the KDP warned, "the only option left is the Iraqis who are salivating to balance Iranian influence and come back to the north. If that happens the KDP will not stop them." Barzani himself in a telephone call that week sought to persuade Pelletreau that the fighting was "not a Kurdish issue" to be sidestepped but Iranian aggression. "I cannot withstand this pressure," he said. "If you do not do something I may seek help from the Iraqis."

But the United States was still determined to avoid taking sides in the quarrel. With KDP positions collapsing along the strategic Hamilton Road in the mountainous northeast, thanks to Iranian artillery support for the PUK, Barzani became convinced that his forces were faced with annihilation unless he made what his closest advisers described as a deal with the devil. Blanking out Saddam Hussein's murder of three of his brothers, more than eight thousand clansmen, and tens of thousands of ordinary Iraqi Kurds, Barzani now asked the Iraqi ruler for military help to drive the PUK out of Erbil. The KDP background paper at best had been disingenuous: not only did the "KDP not stop" the Iraqis but, as the Iraqis later disclosed to Barzani's embarrassment, he had already asked for their military aid as early as August 22.

At least that was what Iraqi Deputy Prime Minister Tarik Aziz claimed in revealing, mischievously, that Barzani on that day had sent a letter to Saddam Hussein addressed as "Your Excellency," imploring him to "interfere to help us ease the foreign threat" from Iran. To what degree Barzani and his inner circle weighed the possible consequences of their act—or indeed exactly when they took their fateful decision—was not clear to most Iraqi Kurds. What was clear was that the KDP publicly played Pelletreau for a fool, appearing to string him along by attending a meeting in London on August 30 and duplicitously agreeing to another meeting for the next day, when the Erbil operation was actually supposed to start. But even discounting the KDP warnings in Washington, the administration could scarcely have harbored illusions, in light of the daily more ominous aerial and satellite photographic intelligence documenting the Iraqi buildup.

In seeking to understand the KDP's motives, it may be easy to conclude that Barzani hated Talabani more than he feared Saddam Hussein, or to write off the matter as further corroboration of the old Middle East saw—"the enemy of my enemy is my friend." But there was more to Barzani's decision than that. After all, a terrible stigma attached to the idea of collaborating with the Kurds' single most implacable enemy in the twentieth century. In fact, other bits of unpleasant history were important, too. Massoud Barzani had never forgotten Kissinger's treachery in 1975, had never totally recovered from the humiliation of his years of enforced exile, which he blamed on the United States. And he had certainly understood the ambiguities that in 1991 had saved the Kurds. Thereafter he never stopped worrying about American constancy, despite re-iterated promises—some of them said to be in writing—from U.S. officials ranging from Brent Scowcroft and James Baker in the Bush administration to Vice President Al Gore and Clinton's National Security Adviser Anthony Lake.

Scowcroft, who is now retired, curiously reinforced such Kurdish doubts by acknowledging to the press, "We recognized that the seemingly attractive goal of getting rid of Saddam would not solve our problems, or even necessarily serve our interests. So we pur-sued the kind of inelegant, messy alternative that is all too often the only one available in the real world . . . Had we continued the war and overthrown Saddam, we might be worse off today," he argued, for it would have created a "gaping power vacuum in the Persian Gulf for Iran to fill" and committed American troops to occupation duty indefinitely.

Barzani was also determined not to go into exile ever again. Still ringing in my ears are his words during the Easter Sunday debacle in 1991, as he exhorted unheeding fellow Kurds not to panic and "flee into exile and become refugees like the Armenians." That bedrock desire to stay put in Iraq at almost any cost helps to explain why he stood his ground and tried to negotiate with Saddam Hus-sein until January 1992, when even he had concluded there was no hope. Such reasoning in no way tarnished his nationalist cre-dentials. Up in the mountains in January 1991 he had insisted to me that the Kurds had every right to an independent country for themselves, before explaining that the repressive nature of the surrounding states was unlikely to make that ultimate goal possible for a good century.

He had briefly overcome his reservations about American mo-tives in July 1992, during his visit to Washington, when he signed on in good faith to American plans for using the Iraqi National Congress to overthrow Saddam Hussein. But he came to resent American inflexibility in the U.N.'s sanctions committee when they refused any relief for the Kurds, who labored under the U.N.'s general embargo and Saddam's own economic blockade. Economic problems also sharpened his differences with Talabani. It was not Barzani's fault alone if Saddam Hussein remained in power: if he shared blame for the feuding with Talabani and for compromising the opposition, he also felt entitled to wonder whether the result did not privately please Washington. Over the years, as homegrown Islamic fundamentalists threatened Saudi Arabia and other key gulf allies, American ardor—and theirs—for toppling Saddam Hussein seemed to have waned. Perhaps the Americans were less serious about it than they let on.

That being the case, wasn't Washington indulging in a rerun of Kissinger's game: using the Kurds to weaken but not to overthrow the regime in Baghdad? Barzani was not the only Kurd to wonder if that was what Washington's dual containment really meant. In any case, the real problem Iraqi Kurds faced in the future, remarked a senior American diplomat to me, was not Saddam but "the 'nice' Sunni Arab general likely to take his place. What happens when the international community describes him as a new Thomas Jefferson and he decides to exercise Iraqi sovereignty throughout the country?" the diplomat asked. "Congress and the administration will face some tough decisions."

If the Americans, their Western allies, the Kurds, and the opposition were beset by such soul-searching anguish, Saddam Hussein was not. To be sure, the Iraqis' oil-for-food deal was delayed—only until December it turned out—but that hurt ordinary Iraqis, not their ruler, his family, the pampered Republican Guards, or the security services that kept his regime in power. When he finally decided to move in the hours before dawn on Saturday, August 31, he struck with characteristic decisiveness. In a textbook demonstration of overwhelming force, Saddam Hussein deployed 300 artillery pieces, more than 350 tanks, and between 30,000 and 40,000 troops, mostly Republican Guards. The gamble paid off. Despite the no-fly zone above the 36th parallel, allied aircraft did not intervene. In the next few days, Defense Secretary William Perry described what was going on as a "Kurdish civil war," to justify the administration's decision, and President Clinton excused the failure to take action by insisting that the U.S. ability to control Iraqi events was "limited." At least, the administration consoled itself, its do-nothing policy in Kurdistan would have an undeserved dividend: it would remove Iran's increasingly nettlesome influence from northern Iraq. But even that consolation was to prove but temporary.

By midafternoon of Day One, Saddam Hussein had achieved his primary objectives with little actual fighting, and the Iraqi flag flew over the regional parliament, the government building, and radio and television premises in Erbil. Under covering fire from Iraqi tanks and artillery, the KDP attacked and routed the lightly armed PUK forces, who put up little resistance. Saddam's revitalized army and secret police concentrated on their high-priority goal: rolling up the CIA-financed Iraqi opposition, a heteroclite collection of Shia Arab, Assyrian, Turkoman, and other groups located in Erbil and its Christian suburb of Enkawa. The CIA got its own men out just in time, though it abandoned a small fortune in state-of-the-art electronics and opposition files.

Left in the lurch were the Kurds who worked for American offices in Erbil, long-standing promises that the United States had a detailed evacuation plan for them having turned out to be hogwash. Hundreds of opposition militants, many of them Iraqi army deserters in INC ranks who knew they could expect no mercy from Saddam Hussein, were killed while fighting, executed on the spot, or arrested, the latter as often as not meaning torture, then guaranteed execution. Iraqi secret police, sometimes dressed in Kurdish kit, systematically hunted down their prey thanks to accurate information pinpointing their homes or offices. Terrified survivors had to fend for themselves, and they were convinced that Iraqi secret-police agents would arrest or kill them from one moment to the next. From Barzani on down, senior KDP officials seemed unashamed about the betrayal of their theoretical allies in the Iraqi National Congress, and Perry's "civil war" gambit was economical with the truth, since it deliberately overlooked the INC's plight, as the leaders of more than two hundred INC agents, who had escaped from Erbil and were holed up in a Salahuddin hotel, confirmed to me. This debacle of a CIA scheme—compared by some connoisseurs of treacherous abandonments of local help to what happened in Saigon in 1975 or at the Bay of Pigs in 1961—scarcely encouraged future opposition attempts to unseat Saddam Hussein or, indeed, any form of collaboration in undercover operations anywhere in the Middle East, for that matter.

The damage Saddam Hussein inflicted did not stop there. America's inaction exposed the emptiness of the carefully constructed fiction that the Western powers were protecting Iraq's 3.5 million Kurds spread over seventeen thousand square miles. True, since mid-April 1991, allied war planes had patrolled the no-fly zone north of the 36th parallel, but the United States had rapidly withdrawn its ground troops three months later; in the post-Vietnam, post-Cold War period the world's only superpower had no stomach for a muscular foreign policy that actually risked its ruinously expensive armed forces in combat. To make its northern-Iraq policy credible, Washington had relied instead on threats of air power against Saddam Hussein's vital interests—by implication this meant Iraq's painstakingly reconstructed oil installations. But in reality, the American retaliation for the Iraqi action in Erbil was military targets, Saddam Hussein's quickly repaired air-defense systems, which were now singled out for attack by pilotless cruise missiles.

All these events in the autumn of 1996 focused attention on the purposely fuzzied details of the old 1991 Operation Provide Comfort, which wags now took to calling Operation Provide Illusions. The formal allied commitment to protect Kurds on the ground had in fact never extended beyond the safe haven, a small triangle in northwestern Iraq which did not even reach as far south as Duhok. Moreover, the Iraqi opposition was convinced that under relentless Turkish pressure, in order to keep the air umbrella at all, the United States and its allies had been forced in 1995 to curtail its mission, severely limiting the war planes' offensive role. Now that Iraqi armor had moved north of the 36th parallel, the whole pretense collapsed; every Kurd felt that what Saddam Hussein had done with impunity he could do again.

CIA Director John Deutch put his finger on the real worry when he noted that despite the subsequent withdrawal of Iraqi soldiers, "it is clear that there are Iraqi intelligence and security personnel in the region." Even more exposed were Kurds south of the 36th parallel, those living in Sulaimaniyah or, further afield, in Kalar and Kifri, who had never enjoyed the allied air umbrella's reassuring protection. In the past, when pressed about these southernmost Kurds, diplomats breezily insisted that U.N. Security Council resolution 688, the first international document mentioning the Kurds since the ill-fated Treaty of Sèvres, could be invoked to provide protection.

The conclusions that the United States drew from Iraqi's military presence in Erbil were pessimistic and far-reaching. Iraqi strategists had expected swift American retaliation against the Republican Guards, though perhaps not until after their withdrawal from Erbil, to avoid appearing to take sides in the KDP-PUK feud. But no such thing occurred. Since it was judged bootless to strike at Saddam Hussein in Kurdistan, the administration shifted the focus of retaliation farther south, amid convenient but unsubstantiated suggestions that his real aim was Kuwaiti and Saudi Arabian oil fields rather than damaging coalition credibility or extending his sovereignty in the north. Administration spokesmen tried to play down American responsibility for protecting Iraqi Kurds, condemned Barzani's and Talabani's mindless behavior, and subliminally suggested that the United States morally could now wash its hands of the future of ordinary Kurds because of their leaders' errors.

The State Department spokesman, Nicholas Burns, brushed aside any notion that American shortcomings or penny-pinching indifference had contributed to the crisis. "If there's any responsibility it's with the two Kurdish groups for the outbreak of fighting, not with the United States," he said. "We gave the Kurds every opportunity for five years. We gave them political protection, we gave them economic and humanitarian assistance; we gave them a security zone in the north where they could run their own affairs in a highly autonomous way. And the Kurds failed to meet the great historic opportunity for the Kurdish people."

Immediate events on the ground did nothing to discourage suggestions that northern Iraq was a write-off in Washington's view. Hours before the first wave of retaliatory American cruise missiles were dispatched on September 3 against air-defense installations in government-held territory, the Pentagon ordered the evacuation of the Military Coordination Center in Zakho, just across the Khabur River from Turkey. I arrived at that center to find an empty building guarded by confused Kurds. Of course, the MCC had long since lost the key function it performed in 1991 under Colonel Richard Naab, its first American commander, who enjoyed comparing his negotiations with the recently defeated Iraqi army to "dealing with Hitler." Since then, the Turks had first insinuated an officer onto the American, British, French, and Dutch MCC team, then had become co-commanders as the price for allowing the air umbrella to operate from Incirlik. Such was the Turks' paranoid conviction that the MCC was helping Turkish Kurd guerrillas of the PKK in northern Iraq that they virtually paralyzed its operations. When in April 1994 a U.S. Air Force error resulted in shooting down two American helicopters transporting key Kurds and MCC officers, for all intents and purposes the MCC mission ceased, much to the regret of the Kurds, who were convinced that the very presence of Western officers somehow would have cowed

Barzani and Talabani into stopping their feuding. The administration did successfully ward off Turkish demands for transferring its operation just across the border to Silopi, and just weeks before the Erbil episode, Turkey agreed to renew the air umbrella until the end of the year, but its government betrayed its pro-Iraqi bent by vitiating its effectiveness: Incirlik was no longer to be available for retaliatory air strikes. Some Kurds said the Turks kept the planes from carrying bombs and, in some circumstances, even ammunition.

The MCC's abrupt pullout was the first overt signal that the United States no longer considered Iraqi Kurdistan safe from what Burns later described as Saddam Hussein's "security goons." (The KDP acted surprised; this was its first public recognition that the outside world did not agree with its constantly repeated claim that its collaboraton with the Iraqis was an isolated, limited, and now completed operation in Erbil.) The State Department's Office of Foreign Disaster Assistance, which had disbursed more than $795 million in American food and other aid to the Kurds since 1991, now also departed. Within weeks several hundred MCC guards and staffers, OFDA employees, and some two thousand members of their extended families were moved first to Turkey, then to the Pacific island of Guam to await eventual entry to the United States, conveniently out of sight until after the American elections in November. (In mid-October seven hundred INC men and their families finally followed. I had raised an alarm about their plight about five weeks before, by interviewing these frightened men while they were still stuck in Barzani's headquarters at Salahuddin, which helped them reach the border town of Zakho.)

The American decisions prompted the very few Western nongovernmental organizations still dispensing aid to the Kurds to follow suit. By the end of November another 5,000 Kurdish relief workers and their families were flown to Guam on their way to the United States in a move that salved the administration's conscience but deprived Iraqi Kurdistan of many of its ablest men and women. These nongovernmental organizations were part and parcel of American policy, and their workers, consistently denied Iraqi visas, knew all along that they would face prolonged imprisonment if captured by the Iraqi authorities. Ten days after the capture of Erbil, the Iraqi government turned up the pressure. Without warning the KDP, ever more embarrassed by Baghdad's efforts to publicize their connections, Saddam Hussein lifted his ill-conceived blockade of the north, which he had imposed five years before. He had stopped paying Iraqi civil servants in the north, cut off fuel and food deliveries, and otherwise sought to bring the Kurds to their knees. In lifting the blockade Baghdad now also announced what turned out to be bogus appointments of secret-police chiefs for three Kurdish governorates. Initially, the blockade had done much to buoy Kurdish nationalism, but it had also caused real economic suffering. Now its abrupt abrogation meant that travel between government-held territory and Kurdistan was unrestricted for everyone, including the dreaded secret police, and the terms of the new amnesty offer specifically excluded Kurds who worked for humanitarian relief organizations. These stipulations sobered even those Kurds who were delighted that they could now buy gasoline and, especially, kerosene for heating, at just 1 percent of the previous black-market price. Even within Barzani's headquarters in Salahuddin, old friends confided to me their fears about secret-police penetration and anxiously asked if the Americans and their allies would renew the air umbrella into 1997. It was, in fact, renewed at Christmas, although, at Turkish insistence, it was no longer called Operation Provide Comfort, was apparently totally restricted to aerial reconnaissance, and France had pointedly withdrawn its aircraft from the operation. The new restrictions confirmed the Iraqi Kurds' worst fears.

Ordinary Kurds knew full well that Saddam Hussein's deal with Barzani had rent the fraying coalition which Bush had stitched together in 1990. Two of the participants, France and Russia, both owed billions of dollars by Iraq for over a decade and hopeful of lucrative future oil and trade deals, now took their distance from the United States in the Security Council. The French pointedly refused to join their American and British allies in extending the southern no-fly zone from the 32nd to the 33rd parallel, and recommended direct political negotiations between the KDP and Saddam, scarcely advice that Washington wanted to hear. America's major allies in the Arab world (with the notable exception of Kuwait, still traumatized by Iraq's occupation) were also unenthusiastic about the cruise-missile retaliation so far from Erbil. Voices were heard suggesting that Saddam Hussein had violated no international law in reasserting his authority in northern Iraq. Saudi Arabia, where twice American servicemen had been attacked in less than a year, was not the only Arab state worried that close ties with Washington could become a hangman's noose in the hands of anti-Western Islamist opponents: no Saudi bases were made available for Washington's riposte.

In Ankara, the embarrassed Islamist Prime Minister, Necmettin Erbakan, who had only recently dispatched two ministers to Baghdad on a fence-mending mission, went to ground for three critical weeks. Foreign Minister Tansu Çiller and the all-powerful Turkish General Staff took advantage of his eclipse to announce plans for establishing in northern Iraq a near carbon copy of Israel's self-proclaimed "security zone" in southern Lebanon, hinting that they feared the PKK would take advantage of the increased instability in northern Iraq. But their motives were far from clear: diplomats noted that an eventually restored Iraqi government presence along the border with Turkey would put Saddam Hussein in a perfect position to retaliate for Turkey's allowing Washington to use its bases during 1991.

In the event, the security-zone plan was quietly shelved. Turkey, which after all had conducted largely fruitless incursions big and small in northern Iraq for the past five years without ever succeeding in uprooting the PKK presence there, backed down, and the confusion in its policy became all the clearer when Çiller in late September suggested it would not mind if Iraqi troops returned to the border and indicated Saddam Hussein had been so informed. When the State Department protested, Çiller unconvincingly insisted that no policy difference existed between Ankara and Washington.

Inside Kurdistan an odd schizophrenia obtained. I was able to move around with surprising ease. On September 5 old KDP friends even produced a special pass authorizing me to cross their lines to visit Talabani, who was holed up at his Qala Chowlan headquarters in the mountains between Sulaimaniyah and the nearby Iranian border. A senior KDP official apologized for making me drive the long way around, explaining, "The direct road is out because we started another offensive nearby this morning to prevent Talabani from trying to retake Erbil." By the time Hugh Pope of *The Independent* of London and I reached PUK territory, Kurds reported to us that dozens of ambulances crammed with wounded had preceded us on the road south to Sulaimaniyah. At his mountain retreat we were received as long-lost family by Talabani and Hero, his wife, who had made a miraculous escape under heavy fire from their now thoroughly trashed residence outside Erbil.

But Talabani was long on rhetoric and short on facts when he questioned him about the renewed fighting. He criticized the Americans for disregarding his warnings and for not stopping Saddam Hussein's forces when they advanced on Erbil. "They missed a golden opportunity to hit four Republican Guard divisions in Erbil," he said. "Had they done so, that would have been the end of Saddam Hussein." He blamed France for vetoing allied air strikes and swore to accept help "from the devil himself." Punching the air with a cigar, he said, "I will not commit suicide," and insisted he was determined to fight on against "Mr. Barzani not as a Kurd but as a traitor." At one point, when Talabani inadvertently left the door open while using his satellite telephone to call the State Department in hopes of talking to Pelletreau or Robert Deutch (the head of Northern Gulf Affairs, who had negotiated the stillborn compromise agreement in Ireland), we heard his end of the conversation as he was told they were in meetings or otherwise not available; he settled for an underling who must have opened the conversation with "How are you doing?" or a similarly bland salutation. "I am not well," he said, doubtless thinking we were out of earshot.

The remark was an accurate evaluation of the PUK's collapsing fortunes. Just three days later the KDP swept fifty miles east of Erbil and captured the commanding heights of Haibat Sultan east of Koisanjaq, without meeting major PUK opposition and with no Iraqi troops involved, despite Talabani's charge that Saddam Hussein was aiding the KDP again, this time with everything from heavy artillery and tanks to poison gas. If anything this chemical-weapons accusation further demoralized the PUK forces routed in Erbil, and few physical signs of combat of any kind were visible along the road on Sunday; the PUK had retreated, apparently all the way to its other stronghold, in Sulaimaniyah.

The next day Kurt Schork of Reuters and I were at a key crossroads a few miles farther east with KDP *pesh merga* awaiting their orders. At midmorning it was already boiling hot. Suddenly, a young man in the back of a pickup shouted, "Who wants two free seats going for Sulaimaniyah?" and two *pesh merga* jumped aboard. With that the KDP started dashing pell-mell down the road to the Dukan dam, a nominal military objective since the PUK at the hydroelectric plant there had cut off power to all of the Erbil governorate in reprisal for losing Erbil itself.

The KDP's disorderly column of perhaps five thousand men of all ages rode in a motley of requisitioned trucks, buses, and private cars. Schork, who had survived almost a year in Kurdistan in 1991–92 before moving to Sarajevo to cover the Bosnian war, worried like a good infantryman about their disdain for elementary military caution, and so did I. But Schork kept us near the head of the column, where the most determined troops were constantly encouraged to keep pressing ahead by two senior KDP cadres, Roj Nuri Shaways and Fadil Mirani, a onetime used-car salesman in Nashville. "Mam Jalal's on the run," they kept saying, "so let's not miss this chance to finish him off."

We passed a deserted restaurant where I'd lunched only days before on the way to see Talabani. Down the road automatic weapons fire erupted from steep hills on the east. The KDP only then sent out flankers and brought up a Dushka, a heavy machine gun mounted on a pickup. Each side lost a *pesh merga* carted off in the back of a pickup. The column pressed ahead. A half hour later Schork, I, the driver, and a Kurdish interpreter were pinned down by the roadside by a PUK rifleman firing single shots close enough for us to hear them whistling overhead. The KDP had all scampered for cover. Schork waited in vain for the firing to subside, then lost patience. Abruptly he jumped in the car, motioned for us to follow, and, with the mastery of a Prohibition getaway-car wheelman, reversed at high speed until we were out of trouble. But I felt a sharp pain in the middle of my back: for an instant I thought I'd been wounded, and was furious with myself for being in this most dubious of battles.

It turned out to be a wasp sting, and in fact there was little fighting. Multiple rocket launchers and heavy antiaircraft guns mounted on heavy trucks occasionally fired up into the mountains, either silencing the PUK or driving them from their positions. Schork kept muttering, "A single mortar squad could make mincemeat of this bunch." Someone in the PUK eventually had the same idea: we were uncomfortably caught in the open when a dozen or so mortar rounds bracketed the road, wounding a half-dozen KDP *pesh merga*, who then awaited evacuation to the rear in stoic silence. The KDP lost a half-dozen men during the day and by late afternoon had covered more than twenty miles, capturing Dukan only to discover that the previous day the PUK had removed the computer programs controlling the dam's power generation.

A smiling Barzani showed up and sat under shade trees with his principal lieutenants. The KDP was certainly not going to stop here at Dukan, if indeed Barzani had ever intended to limit his offensive against a demoralized foe. The next day, he now confided, his forces in Halabjah, near the Iranian border, would march on Sulaimaniyah to show the world that Talabani was lying when he charged that Iraqi troops were involved in the fresh fighting. I'd made arrangements with the dam's well-mannered chief engineer for us to spend the night at his place, and when we showed up, the KDP top brass was already drinking scotch on his carefully manicured lawn overlooking the dam's reservoir. Our host insisted we stay anyhow to share the celebratory fish dinner.

Around nine p.m. a messenger arrived with news that Sulaimaniyah had fallen at dusk. The Halabjah troops had jumped the gun and captured the city without a fight. We slept under the stars on the engineer's lawn, and when we awoke at six a.m., the KDP had moved on to complete the occupation of Sulaimaniyah. We made for the border, driving in the last miles past PUK stragglers headed on foot for Iran and middle-class Kurds who'd fled to the mountains forty-eight hours earlier and were now returning to Sulaimaniyah. Many were fed up waiting at the border crossings the Iranians refused to open. In a mini-rerun of the 1991 mass exodus, cars, trucks, tractors, and buses were piled up waiting for a change of mind.

Three well-dressed young Kurds encountered by the side of the road at the mountain town of Penjwin were trying to decide what to do. All spoke excellent English; the man worked for an international relief organization, and his two sisters taught at Sulaimaniyah University. They had fled two days earlier when the PUK started pulling out of the city, horrified by what the elder sister kept calling "Massoud's treachery" and the "threat of renewed Ba'athist rule" which, they were convinced, it automatically entailed. They were scared stiff of what lay ahead at home. Then why not go to Iran? "We did that in 1991 and stayed six weeks. The Iranians were even worse than Saddam Hussein."

———

That despairing evaluation expressed the mood of many Kurds after a quarter century of Iraqi punishment and five years of turmoil. Indeed, how Kurds kept up their spirits for so long required a suspension of disbelief. From the start, anything smacking of developing a viable economy had been vetoed by the Western allies on the grounds (never publicly stated) that Turkey would then accuse Washington, London, and Paris of encouraging incipient Kurdish statehood. Syria, Iran, and Iraq were of course also delighted with keeping the Iraqi Kurds on short rations. Officially, the Iraqi Kurds were told that making exceptions for them would only play into Baghdad's hands, allowing its allies to ask for similar leniency for itself.

The U.N. sanctions committee refused to allow the importation of fuel or spare parts to keep northern Iraq's few factories running. Also vetoed was machinery to build a small refinery to process the piddling oil production that remained in Kurdish hands. Turkey even prevented a British de-mining organization from bringing in technical equipment for fear it would somehow help the PKK rather than remove the millions of mines left behind after the Iran-Iraq war. Yet all this respect for rules in no way prevented major breaches of the sanctions. Thus, the West's upside-down reasoning allowed the Kurds to sell wheat to Iraq, levy taxes on the lucrative diesel-fuel trade between the governments of Iraq and Turkey, and even pay dollars for Iraqi-provided electricity. But they were not authorized to import missing parts worth four thousand dollars to fix the Duhok telephone switchboard.

For years, the pure euphoria of being out from under Saddam's terror had somehow kept many Kurds going. The first free Kurdish elections, held in northern Iraq in May 1992, created such a genuine outpouring of pride and joy that Iraqi Kurds long bore hardship without complaint. Neither before nor since have I ever seen Kurds so happy. But perversely this only sharpened the differences between Barzani and Talabani. The elections had been called mainly because Barzani had come to the end of the road in his long negotiations with Baghdad, and he wanted the legitimacy of the ballot box before concluding a deal. Meanwhile Talabani had been upping the ante, demanding an ill-defined federalism as a way of embarrassing Barzani into going beyond the never fully implemented 1970 autonomy agreement between his father and Saddam Hussein. In the voting (marred by imported German ink, which turned out not to be indelible, as advertised), Barzani and Talabani each was convinced he had won and accused the other of fraud. (The smaller parties were eliminated for failing to meet a 7 percent minimum threshold. Had they won seats, some Kurds agree that they could have avoided the subsequent fighting by acting as a buffer.)

Fighting between the two major leaders was only narrowly avoided at two stormy meetings, thanks to an awkward compromise announced on the third day after the vote. Many Kurds sickened by the subsequent violence later became convinced that without the compromise fighting would have broken out there and then, but the public mood in fact was euphoric. Whatever their past problems or second thoughts about the future, delighted *pesh merga* from both main militias manned joint checkpoints that they had deliberately festooned with KDP yellow and PUK green.

Also helping to save the day then had been pressure from outside, especially from the United States, as ever in favor of elections on principle, but too nervous to be officially represented on election day for fear of appearing to favor Kurdish separatism. (Colonel Naab returned from retirement and at an election-day feast thrown by Talabani waited for allied warplanes to fly over to announce: "That's John Major and Hajji Bush casting their votes.") Finally the KDP and PUK accepted a power-sharing agreement: the KDP gave up a seat to allow each big party to have fifty seats; Barzani and Talabani tacitly shelved the runoff vote for the post of leader, in which the KDP chief was ahead but short of the required 50 percent for a first-round victory. If anything, the election winner was Talabani, who had campaigned against making any deal with Saddam and in favor of federalism as a step beyond the 1970 agreement's autonomy.

These partisan considerations were obscured, especially in the months after the regional parliament and government began to function in July 1992. But by January 1993 people said that the fifty-fifty arrangement had become a formula for gridlock. A KDP minister automatically had to have a PUK deputy and a PUK minister a KDP assistant. "Soon the ridiculous system was so out of control," a friend said, "that it was enforced right down to the tea servers." Subsequent repercussions, especially after sporadic fighting began in 1994, were more serious. During the visit I made to northern Iraq in February 1996, friends unburdened themselves of their frustrations. "Ordinary Kurds in KDP-controlled territory hate Barzani," my friend Moayyad Yunis said, "and in PUK-controlled areas they hate Talabani."

Public esteem for the KDP and PUK slipped so much that Kurds who had lined up by the thousands in 1992 to donate blood for victims of a car bomb planted by the Iraqis now turned a deaf ear to televised appeals for donors for the militiamen wounded in internecine fighting. Ticking off high prices, tolls at checkpoints, and other taxes, Moayyad said, "Everyone with five hundred dollars in his pocket is trying to leave—if not himself, then his son—to earn money to send home to the family." Hardest hit were the urban Kurds, for survival meant going back to the land. Many returned to the ruins of their old villages, now rebuilt with American and other Western aid. Hundreds of vitally needed doctors, engineers, professors, and other professionals who had rallied to the nationalist cause were now reduced to selling off their belongings; soon they lost heart and went abroad.

Particularly grating was the militias' habit of arbitrarily kicking people out of their homes. Not even Saddam Hussein had seized private property in the cities, preferring as he did to concentrate his terror on the more difficult-to-control countryside. "It is an outrage," wrote Amnesty International, "that the Kurds—having suffered gross human rights violations for so long at the hands of the Iraqi government forces—should once again have to endure such abuses, only this time at the hands of their own political leaders." That was in June 1994.

The Amnesty International report issued the following February held the KDP and PUK "fully responsible" for most of the abuses, ranging from torture and arbitrary arrest to deliberate killing of political opponents, peaceful demonstrators, and rival militiamen captured in battle. The "abandonment of fundamental human rights principles to which the Kurdish leadership had publicly committed itself," Amnesty said, was "all the more regrettable since these were the same principles which the Iraqi government itself consistently failed to uphold, and the consequences of which have meant endless torment and suffering for Iraq's Kurds." Such excesses naturally troubled Western human-rights activists. In another sphere, Human Rights Watch had for some time been working to interest certain governments in bringing Iraq to the International Court of Justice on charges of genocide. Once-high hopes of applying the "right to interfere" to other crises also faded, and "safe haven" became a dirty word: the "humanitarian aid zone" established by French troops in southwestern Rwanda in July 1994 came too late to save Tutsi lives and served principally to protect Hutu thugs; in Bosnia in the U.N.-protected "safe area" of Srebrenica thousands of Muslims were slaughtered by Bosnian Serb soldiers in 1995.

In Kurdistan it was not as if Barzani and Talabani were oblivious to what was happening around them. In fact, neither sought to hide the abuses. "Our fighting and the human-rights violations have done incalculable damage to the Kurdish cause," Barzani told me in February 1996. "I am so ashamed to see foreign friends that I hesitated before agreeing to receive you." I had no reason to doubt Barzani's sincerity. But something had gone very much wrong over the years in Kurdistan, so much so that even the most disarming confession at this time sounded like trite lip service. It was easy enough for the leaders to blame each other and the outside world, and for the outside world to blame them, but the offhand and often mindless violence seemed never to end. The Kurds' critics have long maintained that their violence is genetic. But the Kurds as well as other Iraqis all bear the mark of nearly three decades of corrupting Ba'ath Party rule. Repression, terror, totalitarian rule have scarred them all, but no group more than the Kurds.

Over the years the handful of Kurds who fought alongside Barzani, Talabani, and other nationalist leaders were holed up in some of the world's most forbidding terrain. When the *pesh merga* gained control of the Kurdish cities in 1991 for the first time, they were by and large untutored and lacked experience in administration, finance, or anything but guerrilla warfare and political indoctrination. They expressed shock at the disappearance of Kurdish values, which they had idealized in the mountains. By that they often meant the end of traditional rural society eradicated by Saddam Hussein's massive destruction of their village life and replaced by the characterless "victory cities," offering instead electricity, police surveillance, and Ba'ath indoctrination in schools. Kurds educated abroad and aware of contemporary trends elsewhere either never returned for more than fleeting visits or often turned into the worst of carpetbaggers.

During my visit to Erbil in February 1996 I asked Moayyad what had gone so wrong. He reminded me that years before I had told him of a meeting with Nizar Hamdoon, a senior Iraqi official who served with great efficiency as Saddam Hussein's ambassador to Washington during the war with Iran and was currently the ambassador at the United Nations. "He told you that within a year the Kurds would be on their knees praying for Saddam to return," Moayyad recalled. "That was in 1992. I was profoundly shocked at the time."

And now, I asked?

"I have a recurring dream," he replied sheepishly. "Saddam returns, drives out the Kurdish militias, and then goes back to Baghdad so decent Kurds can get on with their lives." He let his remark sink in. "Don't get me wrong," he said. "I'm proud to be Kurdish, to have my own government. No Kurd really wants to go back to Saddam. But I think that dream means that Kurds have suffered a lot from this fifty-fifty militia government and have gained next to nothing." I'd tried Moayyad's dream out on senior KDP and PUK officials, half hoping they would get angry and offer a reasoned defense of their rule. Instead they just shrugged. One asked, "What else can we do?"

A very similar evaluation apparently was at play less than three weeks after the Erbil operation when Pelletreau met Barzani in Ankara. At this inconclusive encounter, each side was visibly interested in damage control, as well as trying to figure out the other's longer-term intentions. Both needed a decent interval. The administration, with almost two months before the November presidential election, wanted to allay impressions that all was irremediably lost, for Washington critics were giving congressional testimony comparing the situation to President Kennedy's Bay of Pigs fiasco in Cuba in 1961. At the State Department, Burns now described Barzani as someone "very important in northern Iraq," hinting that the administration might yet be persuaded that an Iraqi Kurdistan run efficiently by one Kurd would simplify things. A cynical Western diplomat in Ankara at the time remarked, "Barzani gobbled up all of Kurdistan with Saddam's help, and now he wants us to hold his hand again."

Barzani needed to reassure the Iraqi Kurds that the Americans had not concluded he had sold out to Saddam. His aides let it be known he would again welcome a close working relationship if Washington would provide heavy weapons and guarantees of a kind no Western government so far had ever seen fit to vouchsafe; if not, they hinted, Barzani would take up the negotiations with Baghdad broken off in 1992. Barzani was trying to put his best foot forward. He announced new elections to give a stamp of legitimacy that his advisers thought necessary to justify such an eventual course, and Barzani himself quickly sought to win over critics with a general amnesty for all his foes, including Talabani. He released his prize PUK prisoner, Fouad Mazoum (the first Kurdish Prime Minister in 1992), with a message for PUK leaders in exile in Iran offering reconciliation and the right to contest the elections. Parliament was reconvened with 69 of its 105 members in attendance. A new—KDP—Prime Minister was appointed.

But could Barzani, who had sworn he wanted to turn Kurdistan into "a citadel of democracy and pluralism," break off his alliance with Iraq if he wanted to? Would the United States send the MCC back as a sign of renewed faith in him, or refuse on grounds that its allied officers and newly hired local guards might end up having to be extracted for fear of falling victim to Saddam's secret police? Could the United States justify renewing the air umbrella into 1997? Would Turkey now realize that this air cover was in its own interest and lobby on its behalf?

Some, but not all, of these questions became redundant barely six weeks after Erbil, when Talabani's revitalized PUK stormed out of the Iranian border area and chased the KDP almost all the way back to the Iraqi-protected capital. The rapidity of this October comeback surprised Talabani's critics, even if Iran had provided arms, ammunition, and key artillery support in the series of border battles that demoralized the KDP and got it to abandon Sulaimaniyah. Within days the KDP counterattacked, in a forlorn effort to reclaim its hold on all of the north, but it only lost hundreds of fighters. (The PUK was said to carry out retaliatory killings when its forces recaptured temporarily abandoned territory, and the KDP likewise, testimony to the efficiency of Kurdish security and assassination squads and the pervasive influence of Saddam's own baleful models.) Massoud Barzani's claims to being King of Kurdistan evaporated, leaving Iraqi Kurdistan insecurely divided into spheres of influence, with Iran predominant in the east and Barzani increasingly dependent on Iraq in the west. At the very end of October Pelletreau was back in Ankara negotiating a cease-fire between middle-level KDP and PUK representatives, hoping to salvage some American influence from the ruins. But in the absence of their leaders, the talks were considered little more than window dressing. (Pelletreau returned to Turkey in January 1997 for further inconclusive talks with the Iraqi Kurds.)

As I completed perfunctory Kurdish formalities at the border before leaving Iraq and crossing back into Turkey in mid-September, my eye caught a sign: "Welcome to Iraqi Kurdistan." I wondered if I really would be welcome if I ever chose to return or was allowed to. In years past Barzani and Talabani separately had insisted I hire a carload of armed *pesh merga* to guard against Iraqi agents who would be only too delighted to bag a Western reporter and collect a reputed $7,000 bounty for killing Westerners. And the Turks had made it increasingly difficult for foreign correspondents to cross their border with Iraq. If Iran or Iraq really ended up controlling the north, would old Western friends be encouraged to visit? Would I take that risk, much less chance, to cover an always-possible proxy war between Iran and Iraq or indeed Turkey? Would I want to? Reporters are not supposed to take sides, and I had done my best not to when writing about the Iraqi Kurds. A story is a story is a story.

Yet, I confess, the gambler in me was rooting for the Kurds to make something of the situation they'd inherited in 1991. The fact was, they hadn't—never mind the reasons, not all of their doing by any account. Still, in the little over five years since I first crossed into Iraq under Kurdish control, the United Nations had taken in a dozen or so new states, many once vassals of the now-defunct Soviet empire and some relatively close by in Central Asia and the Caucasus. Not only was statehood hard to imagine now for the Kurds, but so was the less impossible dream of autonomy. They didn't even have U.N. observer status. Even the Palestinians had that. Kurdish leaders who had once passed for being reasonable men were either dead or compromised. The survivors I once thought I knew and liked best—Barzani and Talabani—were now seized by some atavistic penchant for self-destruction, defying rational analysis even by some of their most loyal followers. Most everyone I met in Kurdistan was terrified and felt powerless. By default Turkey now curiously seemed the best hope for Kurdish nationalism, less because of the PKK's dogged, if declining, battlefield performance than because of its success in revitalizing a long-dormant sense of identity among Turkish Kurds.

In the Iraqi border city of Zakho late the night before my departure, a frightened Kurdish doctor who had worked for a foreign-aid organization accosted me in a mobile phone shop next to the Baghdad Hotel. He was sure that because of that job he would be targeted by Iraq's secret police if he went home to Sulaimaniyah. Or that was his story. Would I help him get out of Iraq by hiring him? I tried to explain that any document I signed stood little chance of being honored by American officials processing would-be refugees. This didn't draw much water. I tried to be polite, but I was dead-tired and probably wasn't as understanding as I should have been. I wasn't telling him anything he didn't know. But here was a foreigner—an American, he judged by my accent—and maybe he would get lucky. Like many another Kurd he was just another sinner in the hands of an angry God. So many Kurds I'd known over the years died violent deaths. He was just another Kurd who wanted to live.

I thought of my friend Abdul Rahman Qassemlou, the worldly Iranian Kurd gunned down in a fifth-floor Vienna apartment on July 13, 1989, by an Iranian secret-police hit squad posing as high-level political negotiators. For a smart man he'd been plain dumb. He'd bamboozled himself into thinking, right after Ayatollah Ruhollah Khomeini's death, that Tehran wanted to make peace with Iran's Kurds. Normally a stickler for security, he was lured to his death like an amateur, incautiously dispensing with bodyguards provided by Talabani in previous rounds of secret negotiations in December 1988 and January 1989. Only two days earlier we had finished a bottle of scotch at my home in Paris celebrating his first visa for the United States, granted after years of his being blacklisted as a supposedly subversive Marxist agent. The Cold War— with its unreviewed prejudices—was ending. He'd also helped enlighten the American embassy in Baghdad about mistreatment of Iraqi Kurds. Maybe he'd stop being Kurdish enough.

Yet until he let his guard down, Qassemlou always struck me as the only Kurd with enough moxie to cut a decent deal with all comers. His understanding of the world's workings and his friendships and ties with politicians, journalists, and academics in Europe and beyond gave him a pragmatic dimension that Barzani, Öcalan, Talabani, or Turkey's fledgling Kurdish parliamentarians lacked. Some Kurds swore that had he survived he would have furthered the political agenda for all Kurds. Now he was just another Kurdish martyr.

Now Mohamed Jaafari Sahraroudi, the Iranian intelligence officer who masterminded—and participated in—Qassemlou's assassination, had started showing up in Iraqi Kurdistan. He had become a key negotiator with Talabani, who for decades had gloried in his close friendship with Qassemlou. (The KDP later produced documents purporting that Talabani, to please Sahraroudi and his masters, had arrested Qassemlou's followers when they tried to infiltrate into Iran in 1994. If the story was true, the arrests were simply variations on a theme, since three decades earlier Mullah Mustafa Barzani had delivered Iranian Kurdish nationalists to the Shah.) No thinking Kurd thought the choice of Sahraroudi was coincidental when Iran decided to improve relations with Talabani: it was the kind of attention to detail for which Iranians through the ages have been famous.

Was it also due to Iran's growing influence with the PUK that by the summer of 1996 the wall overlooking Sulaimaniyah's main traffic circle had altered its portrait gallery of the good, the great, and the sacrificed among this century's Kurdish natonalist leaders? Since I'd last visited the city in 1993, the gallery of martyrs had changed with all the suspect subtlety of an airbrush artist in the Kremlin's palmiest days. Gone without trace was Qassemlou's likeness. Also volatilized was that of Mullah Mustafa Barzani. I debated whether his disappearance reflected the spiteful personal revenge of Talabani or some twist in Iranian Islamic ideology I'd somehow failed to follow. For the time being only Qazi Mohamed, and a minor local martyr, looked out from the wall. I was puzzled to see the likeness of Qazi Mohamed, the ill-fated leader of the ephemeral "Mahabad Republic." But with the demise of the Shah and of the Cold War, were Qazi Mohamed's nationalist credentials now deemed unassailable, protected by some unwritten regional statute of limitations? Or was it just a question of time before even that trace of Kurdish nationalism was expunged?

William Eagleton, at the end of his history of the Mahabad Republic, concluded that the Kurds who fought for General Barzani in the 1960s were in some cases "sustained by little more than the old Kurdish tradition of *shar chaktira la bekariya* (fighting is better than idleness)." That certainly went a long way toward explaining the mindless events that had brought me back to Sulaimaniyah in the 1990s. At least this time the United States had repeatedly dispatched an assistant secretary of state to deal with the Kurds, rather than stonewalling them from Washington, as Kissinger had done. Was it progress of a sort? Or, more likely, was it containing the damage sustained by a foiled policy, being unable to unseat Saddam Hussein or arrange a Palestinian-Israeli peace, part of the unspoken bargain to win Arab support for Desert Storm?

Eagleton also argued: "It can be predicted for the future, as we know from the past, that the Kurds in their distant mountains and separated valleys will at times be forgotten or ignored. Then, moved by resolve or temerity, some of the characters of 1946, and others, younger and perhaps unknown in Mahabad, will be heard of once again." All I could hope was that still-younger and wiser Kurds would somehow salvage something from the wreckage of what had seemed such an auspicious chance for renewal. But many Kurds feared that a new period of repression by neighboring states was looming in the immediate future, neighbors who shared, if nothing else, a deep-seated hatred of Kurds and Kurdish nationalism. Kurds, perhaps too pessimistically, took Western abandonment for granted, if not now, then down the road.

What, I wondered, sitting in a senior State Department office in Washington in late October, would these decent folk make of the officer's vehement insistence that the air umbrella protecting Kurdistan would be maintained even if only the United States alone wanted it. My diplomat friend spoke of Iraq and the Kurds as being the "Lebanon of the nineties," with all the weariness that long, violent, and messy conflict in the Levant elicited. Somehow I doubt that the prediction of eternal resurrection will come true in what remains of my working lifetime. May I be pardoned an old reporter's selfish regret, for I would sorely like to be there to chronicle their struggle.

Notes

1 / "Have You Notified Your Next of Kin?"

5 assassination of their leaders in Iran: See Siyamend Othman, "Contribution historique à l'étude du Parti Demokrati Kurdistan-i-Iraq, 1946–1970," unpublished doctoral thesis, Ecoles des Hautes Etudes en Sciences Sociales, Paris, 1985, p. 115; and David Fromkin, *A Peace to End All Peace: The Fall of the Ottoman Empire and the Creation of the Modern Middle East*, New York, 1989, p. 422.

2 / After Such Knowledge, What Forgiveness?

12 "a thousand sighs": René Mauriés, *Le Kurdistan ou la mort*, Paris, 1967, p. 1.
17 population growth figures: David McDowall, *A Modern History of the Kurds*, London, 1996, p. 441.
17 The estimates represent a rough averaging of statistics from various governments and Kurdish nationalists themselves. All are subject to caution. By way of comparison, League of Nations officials in 1925 estimated some 3 million Kurds lived half in Turkey, 700,000 in Iran, 500,000 in Iraq, and 300,000 in Syria. Accompanying the San Francisco map twenty years later were doubtlessly inflated population claims of 9 million. Among the minimalists, William Lynn Westermann in *Foreign Affairs* (July 1946) counted only 2,419,000 Kurds—700,000 each in Iran and Turkey, 419,000 in Iraq, 125,000 in the Soviet Union, and 100,000 in Syria. Martin van Bruinessen, a recognized authority, estimated the breakdown in 1970 as 5.7 million in Turkey, 4–4.5 million in Iran, 2–2.25 million in Iraq, 500,000 in Syria, and 60,000–100,000 in the Soviet Union. David McDowall in *The Kurds; A Nation Denied*, London, 1992, p. 12, estimated the total Kurdish population at 22.6 million—10.8 million in Turkey, or 19 percent of the country's 57 million citizens; 4.1 million in Iraq, or 23 percent of 18 million, 5.5 million in Iran, or 10 percent of 55 million; 1 million in Syria, or 8 percent of 12.5 million,

half a million in the former Soviet Union; and 700,000 elsewhere, largely in Western Europe.

18 "mountainous irrelevancy": See Mehrdad R. Izady, *The Kurds: A Concise Handbook*, Washington and London, 1992, p. 41.

18 "nearly 400,000 dead": Ibid.

18 700,000 "of whom all but half perished": Sureya Bedr Khan, *The Kurdish Case Against Turkey*, Princeton, 1929, pp. 33–34, quoted in Arshak Safrastian, *Kurds and Kurdistan*, London, 1948, p. 76. Other sources put the Kurdish death toll during the war at 700,000. See Kendal Nezan, in Gérard Chaliand, *A People Without a Country*.

18 "Kurdistan was a land": Izady, *The Kurds*, p. 59.

19 "Reconstruction of Kurdish history": Ibid., p. 23.

20 "the Kurds can present": Westermann, in *Foreign Affairs* (July 1946).

21 Xenophon, *Anabasis*, IV 1–3.

26 Their numbers are dwindling, and suggested statistics: Izady, *The Kurds*, pp. 145–58.

28 feuding: Martin van Bruinessen, in *Middle East Report* (July-August 1986).

3 / Suckered

33 Malraux: *Les Noyers de l'Altenburg*, Paris, 1945.

39 "If you have forgotten": *The Washington Post*, January 25, 1991.

40 some four hundred Ba'ath . . . agents: Interview with Hoshyar Zibari, Salahuddin, February 20, 1992. A higher figure—seven hundred—is given by Kanan Makiya, *Cruelty and Silence: War, Tyranny, Uprising and the Arab World*, New York, 1993.

40 "what was done in Halabja": Quoted in Makiya, *Cruelty and Silence*, p. 89.

41 some three thousand men: Interview with Newsherwan Mustafa Amin, London, November 23, 1991.

41 "One second": Gwynne Roberts (television documentary),"A Dream Betrayed," April 1991, Channel 4, London, quoted in Makiya, *Cruelty and Silence*, p. 89.

41 "the result of seventy years of struggle": News conference, Erbil, March 24, 1991; see *The Washington Post*, March 27, 1991.

47 "I simply could not imagine": Interview with Newsherwan Mustafa Amin, London, November 23, 1991.

47 "number of Iraqi tanks": *The New York Times*, March 25, 1991.

47 "we could have": *The New York Times*, March 27, 1991.

47 open to question: in an account in *The Independent on Sunday*, December 8, 1991, John Bulloch quoted General Colin Powell, Chairman of the Joint Chiefs of Staff, telling a fellow general on August 5, 1991, "I'm just thinking about the end game. How do we finally deal with Iraq? We can't leave them with nothing. We have nothing to balance Iran. It would look best to me if we allowed them an army of 100,000 with something like 1,000 tanks."

48 Five years later: Public Broadcasting Corporation interview with David Frost as reported by the *Los Angeles Times*, reprinted in the *International Herald Tribune*, January 16, 1996. Bush said he should have sought Saddam's personal ouster, acknowledging, "I miscalculated" because "I thought he'd be gone."

53 hundreds of thousands of Turkish Kurds: Colonel François Buchwalter, former French military attaché in Turkey, estimated that as many as 400,000 to 700,000 Kurds fled. Interview with author, Paris, November 11, 1991.

4 / Died and Gone to Heaven

58 "Why," he wondered, "is there such enthusiasm": Interview with an Elysée Palace official who insisted on anonymity, Paris, November 13, 1991.

59 "historic guilt complex": Interview with David Gore-Booth, Foreign and Commonwealth Office, London, November 28, 1991.

60 "The children are beautiful": Telephone interview with Alan Pizzey, Rome, July 14, 1991.

60 Eric Rouleau: Interview with Rouleau, Paris, June 16, 1994.

61 sale of Hawker Hunter jets: Interview with Ambassador Bernard Dorin, French embassy, London, November 27, 1991.

62 Galbraith's Easter Sunday escape: Interview with Peter Galbraith, Washington, D.C., July 29, 1991.

63 "would have been political suicide": Telephone interview with U.S. Ambassador Morton Abramowitz, Washington, D.C., August 8, 1991.

63 "magic phrase": Interview with Patrice Paoli, Quai d' Orsay, Paris, November 2, 1991.

63 "threats to international peace and security": Interview with Turkish Ambassador Tungay Uzçeri, NATO headquarters, Brussels, October 22, 1991.

63 *refoulement:* Five years later, in the wake of the controversial forced repatriation of Hutu refugees from Tanzania and Zaire to their native Rwanda, a refugee expert cited the decision to keep the Kurds inside Iraq in 1991 rather than letting them enter Turkey as "the beginning of the end of classical asylum" as understood for most of the second half of the twentieth century. By that was meant the notion that had held sway from the end of World War II and the Cold War. During that period refugees were given international status in third countries rather than being provided protection and assistance in their own countries. *The New York Times,* December 22, 1996.

64 Bush administration's initial displeasure with safe-haven scheme: Interview with Uzçeri, October 22, 1991. Uzçeri said, "When Özal first told Baker about the safe-haven idea, Baker was flabbergasted and hinted the U.S. would not go along with what he considered a dangerous and unorthodox plan. He made clear Washington was just interested in disengaging its troops, not committing forces to northern Iraq."

64 "In voting to send humanitarian aid": Mario Bettati, professor of International Affairs, Université Paris-Sud, in a *Washington Post* op-ed-page article April 14, 1991.

64 Rouleau's influence on Abramowitz and dispatch of American diplomats to the border: Interview with Marc Grossman, U.S. embassy, Ankara, October 2, 1991.

65 "you had to move quickly": Telephone interview with Abramowitz, August 8, 1991.

65 "knew of the ambassador's refugee work": cited in interview with Grossman, October 2, 1991.

65 "throwing popcorn at pigeons": Anne Devroy and Molly Moore, *The Washington Post,* reprinted in the *International Herald Tribune,* April 15, 1991.

66 importance of Baker visit: Interview with Abramowitz, August 8, 1991.

66 "Perhaps the best-invested twelve minutes": Cited by Don Krumm, chief refugee coordinator attached to the Ankara embassy, in an interview with the author, Geneva, October 31, 1991.

67 only a military operation: Interview with Jane Howard, Foreign and Commonwealth Office, London, July 21, 1991.

67 use of C-130s: Victor Tanner, "A Unique Operation, Lessons Learned, 1991," a report

by Intertect, Frederick Cuny's consulting firm advising U.S. armed forces during Operation Provide Comfort.

68 "terrible weeks when there was no one": Interview with Gore-Booth, London, November 28, 1991.

68 death toll figures: Centers for Disease Control, Mortality and Morbidity Weekly Report, July 5, 1991, vol. 40, no. 26, for the Turkish border; telephone interview with U.N. High Commissioner for Refugees, Geneva, December 14, 1993, for the figures in Iran. The more alarmist claims were made by an anonymous U.S. official to the press in early April—"1,000 people a day are dying and we were all being held responsible" —and by a U.N. official in Iran suggesting two thousand daily deaths there. The mortality declined, according to the CDC, because the most vulnerable categories, infants and the aged, died off quickly, and also thanks to the rapid intervention of Green Beret medics along the Turkish border who improved hygiene, provided clean water, and handed out oral rehydration salts.

69 "neither a single dollar": Interview with Jalal Talabani, Erbil, February 12, 1996.

69 "never losing an opportunity": David Broder of *The Washington Post* in the *International Herald Tribune*, April 10, 1991.

69 "cut his winnings": William Safire of *The New York Times* in the *International Herald Tribune*, April 2, 1991.

71 British officials . . . did not have the impression: Interviews with British diplomats who requested anonymity, London, Foreign and Commonwealth Office, July 23, 1991.

72 slowly raising his eyes: Interview with an official who requested anonymity, December 21, 1990.

72 "It is not easy": Interview with Richard Haass, Washington, D.C., December 19, 1991. Five years later, Haass, now out of the government, disarmingly said, "I was wrong" about his encouraging the administration's footdragging once the Kurdish refugees fled to the mountains, and his failing to think of the possible political repercussions inside Iraq after the liberation of Kuwait and the likelihood of a Kurdish uprising. Interview, Washington, D.C., December 20, 1996.

73 "The Kurds did not ask our advice": Interview with a bureaucrat who requested anonymity, State Department, Washington, D.C., July 28, 1991.

73 "a hostile population": Interview with Phebe Marr, Washington, D.C., July 28, 1991.

75 locked into place: Devroy and Moore, *The Washington Post*, reprinted in the *International Herald Tribune*, April 15, 1991, reported that the decisions were taken in the fall of 1990.

76 "If you talked to Baker": Interview with senior U.S. diplomat closely associated with Baker, who spoke on condition of anonymity.

78 "10,000 lives": In the event only twenty-eight allied troops were killed in the fighting, according to General H. Norman Schwarzkopf, *It Doesn't Take a Hero*, New York and London, 1992, p. 564. U.S. losses were 148 dead, of whom 38 were killed by friendly fire, according to Theodore Draper in *The New York Review of Books*, January 30, 1992, p 42.

79 a string of scandals: The International Atomic Energy Agency on February 13, 1996, said that more than a dozen European companies had been in the race to supply Iraq with weapons, weapons that were probably used against Western forces during the war in 1991. This announcement was made just before the publication of the Scott report investigating the British government's "deliberate failure" to inform Parliament of arms sales after the Iran-Iraq war for fear that such sales would be "politically

inconvenient." Similarly, in 1992 the House Energy and Commerce Investigation and Oversight Subcommittee heard testimony from administration officials about American policy toward Iraq: *The New York Times*, on March 8, 1992, quoted Gary Milhollin, director of the Wisconsin Project on Nuclear Arms Control, as saying, "Between 1985 and 1990, the U.S. Department of Commerce approved export licenses for $1.5 billion of strategically sensitive exports to Iraq. Many were for direct delivery to nuclear weapons, chemical weapons and missile sites." All quoted in *Middle East International*, no. 520, March 1, 1996.

80 an Iraqi central bank source: Information supplied on condition of anonymity by a prominent Kurdish exile with excellent connections with the bank; interview with author, Paris, September 25, 1988.

80 "the Europeans would sell more": Interview with a State Department official who worked in the Gulf during the 1980s and spoke on condition of anonymity, December 21, 1991.

81 "left Iraq with a million-man army": Schwarzkopf, *It Doesn't Take a Hero*, p. 346.

82 "NEA was simply too bruised": Interview with an NEA staffer who spoke on condition of anonymity, Washington, D.C., December 22, 1993.

83 "We worked on intuition": Robert D. Kaplan, *The Arabists: The Romance of an American Elite*, New York, 1992, p. 274.

85 It was left to a retired Kurdish specialist: Interview with William Eagleton, Vienna, January 2, 1992.

86 "He did not pose a threat to us": Cited by Devroy and Moore of *The Washington Post*, in the *International Herald Tribune*, April 15, 1991.

89 Talabani at the State Department: Interview with an NEA diplomat who spoke on condition of anonymity, Washington, D.C., December 21, 1992.

89 rumors of a . . . presidential executive order: Telephone conversation with Shibli Mallat, Professor, School of Oriental and African Studies, London, February 15, 1995.

91 "Your questions were more interesting": Conversation with Kaya Toperi, Ankara, January 30, 1991.

92 "I read three hundred to four hundred pages": Interview with Turgut Özal, Presidential Palace, Ankara, January 6, 1993.

92 "things I have not yet been thinking about": Telephone conversation with Kamran Karadaghi, London, February 2, 1994.

92 Çandar's trip to London: Telephone interview with Çandar, Istanbul, October 15, 1991.

93 "Please, please, please": Interview with Karadaghi, London, November 29, 1991.

94 "Iraqi troops would have been on the move": Interview with Pat Theros, deputy chief of mission, U.S. embassy, Amman, May 14, 1991.

94 "laughed and asked what had gotten into me": Interview with Abramowitz, August 8, 1991.

95 the first Turkish-Kurdish meeting: Talabani said afterward that "the most significant result . . . [was] Turkey's lifting its objection to the establishment of direct relations between the Kurdish front and the United States." See Michael M. Gunter, *The Kurds of Iraq: Tragedy and Hope*, New York, 1992, p. 51. Also, Interview with Uzçeri, NATO headquarters, Brussels, October 22, 1991. Uzçeri recalled that the Turkish General Staff accurately estimated that the rump Iraqi military could make short shrift of the lightly armed Kurds, although perhaps not the "single armored battalion" that was mentioned as sufficient.

95 sent . . . information to a Kurdish-American dentist: Interview with Peter Galbraith, Zagreb, June 30, 1993.

96 Richard Schifter . . . backed out: Interview with Kendal Nezan, president of the Kurdish Institute, Paris, February 18, 1994. Nezan had been at the State Department meetings.

96 "Whatever the justifications": Telephone interview with Zalway Khaledzeh, Washington, D.C., December 21, 1993. In his November 21, 1991, testimony before the Senate Foreign Relations Committee hearings considering his confirmation as ambassador to Finland, John Kelly at first insisted that the State Department had received the Kurds despite the record. Closely questioned by Senators Claiborne Pell and Alan Cranston, he was finally obliged to concede that the Kurds had been received at the State Department on April 21, but not before. For further details of State Department policy, see "Civil War in Iraq," Committee on Foreign Relations, United States Senate Staff Report, 1991.

96 "Our policy is to get rid of Saddam Hussein": Cited in "Civil War in Iraq."

97 "Washington was in total confusion": Interview with Frederick Cuny, Paris, December 10, 1991.

97 50,000 to 100,000 Iraqi refugees: Interview with an NEA official speaking on condition of anonymity, Washington, D.C., July 28, 1991.

98 "We didn't know diddly": Interview with an NEA official speaking on condition of anonymity, Washington, D.C., December 22, 1993.

98 "Saudi officials proposed": "Civil War in Iraq."

99 no reason for him to stay: Telephone conversation with Karadaghi, February 8, 1994.

99 "We never made any promises": Cited by Devroy and Moore in the *International Herald Tribune*, April 15, 1991.

99 March 3 meeting: Schwarzkopf, *It Doesn't Take a Hero*, p. 600.

100 "I dare say": Baker on *Meet The Press*, March 17, 1991, and reported in newspapers the following day.

101 "don't approve of what Saddam Hussein is doing": Joseph Fitchett, cited in the *International Herald Tribune*, March 27, 1991.

101 "opening Pandora's box": Christine Moss Helms, quoted in *The International Herald Tribune*, March 20, 1991.

101 "Frankly, we wanted to wait": Cited by Devroy and Moore in the *International Herald Tribune*, April 15, 1991.

101 In that dark night: Accounts of the collapse from Barzani and Talabani, Iraqi Kurdistan, April 1991.

102 Sabrakhan Gring's story: Interview with Gring, Rania, April 29, 1991.

105 "Your role is to plead": Interview with Kendal Nezan, Paris, March 8, 1996.

105 "You can say all the deaths": Interview with Talabani, Rania, Iraqi Kurdistan, April 29, 1991.

106 "Back in Washington they kept wanting": Interview with Don Krumm, Geneva, October 31, 1991.

107 "If you can get the Iraqis to let you into Duhok": Interview with Cuny, Paris, December 10, 1991.

108 "policy requiring constant management": NEA official speaking on condition of anonymity, Washington, D.C., December 22, 1993.

108 "For the last forty years": Ibid.

109 "Don't you see": Interview with American diplomat who requested anonymity, Zakho, Iraq, June 23, 1991.

109 estimates by Zibari and Sami Abderrahman: Interviews with Zibari and Sami Abderrahman, Salahuddin, February 10 and 11, 1996.

5 / Alchemy: Gold Coins into Horseshoes

112 "The Kurdish nationalist struggle": David McDowall, *The Kurds: A Nation Denied*, London, 1992, p. 20.

112 "famous for their fighting qualities": Sir Mark Sykes, "The Kurdish Tribes of the Ottoman Empire," *The Journal of the Royal Anthropological Institute of Great Britain and Ireland*, vol. XXXVIII, January 28, 1908.

112 suckled in prison: Dana Adams Schmidt, *Journey Among Brave Men*, Boston, 1964, p. 138.

113 "even jump off the edge": Martin van Bruinessen, *Agha, Sheikh, and State*, Utrecht University, 1978, p. 311.

113 "Everyone in the Barzani family": Interview with Sami Abderrahman, Rawanduz, October 10, 1991.

115 "I can keep [the rest]": Quoted by René Mauriés, *Le Kurdistan ou la mort*, Paris, 1967, p. 158.

115 "And what about justice?": Interview with Haim Levakov, Tel Aviv, October 1991.

116 Emir Nizar's trick: Basile Nikitine, *Les Kurdes: Etude sociologique et historique*, Paris, 1956, p. 188.

117 Simko's cruelty: Archie Roosevelt, *For Lust of Knowing: Memoirs of an Intelligence Officer*, Boston, 1988, p. 251. During World War I Simko treacherously ambushed and killed Mar Shimun Benyamin, the Christian Assyrians' spiritual leader, then over ninety, and drank his blood in a blind rage. Simko's record of excesses greatly embarrassed the Kurds. A Kurdish historian said his "record of atrocities . . . places him alongside such historical villains as Attila the Hun," who nonetheless to this day remains a hero to the Turks, if quite the opposite to Kurds and Westerners. Mehrdad R. Izady, *The Kurds: A Concise Handbook*, Washington and London, 1992, p. 57.

117 Obaidullah's letter: British government Blue Book, Turkey, 5, 1881, quoted in Derk Kinnane, *The Kurds and Kurdistan*, London, 1964, p. 24.

117 "merely nominal outside the larger towns": Ely Bannister Soane, *To Mesopotamia and Kurdistan in Disguise*, London, 1926, p. xii.

118 Lord Curzon: Quoted by Wilson N. Howell, "The Soviet Union and the Kurds: A Study of a National Minority," unpublished Ph.D. thesis, University of Virginia, 1965, p. 143.

120 "the discovery of oil": CIA document, "Den of Spies: The Kurdish Problem in Perspective," research paper, June 30, 1979.

120 Kirkuk's community mix: This is a bone of contention. Some sources claim Turkomans constituted a plurality, if not the majority, with a quarter Kurd and smaller Arab, Christian, and Jewish colonies.

120 75 percent of Iraq's oil: *Financial Times*, August 20, 1974, quoted in Gérard Chaliand, *A People Without a Country*, London, 1980, Brooklyn, 1993, p. 161. With increasing production from the Basra fields, Kirkuk's oil production decreased proportionally.

120 "Sèvres had been humiliating": Quoted in Chaliand, *A People Without a Country*, p. 49.

121 between 40,000 and 250,000 peasants: McDowall, *The Kurds: A Nation Denied*, p. 37.

121 perhaps a million: Basile Nikitine claims that a million Kurds alone were deported in the immediate wake of the Sheikh Said rebellion's collapse; *Les Kurdes*, p. 134.

121 so strong were Kurdish feelings: Sir Arnold Wilson, *Mesopotamia 1917–1920*, quoted in Chaliand, *A People Without a Country*, p. 191. Wilson, chief British political officer in Baghdad at the time, noted, "The Kurds wish neither to continue under the Turkish government nor to be placed under the control of the Iraqi government . . . In southern Kurdistan four out of five people supported Sheikh Mahmoud's plan to set up an independent Kurdistan."

122 A British military intelligence report: Public Record Office, Kew, England, 453340 e2199, July 14, 1945.

122–23 Mahmoud's government and subsequent British statement: C. J. Edmonds, *Kurds, Turks and Arabs: Politics, Travel and Research in Northeast Iraq, 1919–1925*, London, 1957, p. 301.

123 British High Commissioner: In correspondence with the Secretary of State for the Colonies, the British High Commissioner, B. H. Bourdillon, on February 10, 1926, also said, "I admit that up till the spring of 1923 it appeared it might be necessary to grant the Kurdish districts of Iraq some form of local autonomy. The eviction of the Turkish garrison from Rowanduz at the end of April 1923 produced a profound change in the situation." Public Record Office, Kew, England, FO 371/11460 132121.

123 Ataturk's deal with Britain: van Bruinessen, *Agha, Sheikh, and State*, p. 363.

124 Iraqi Prime Minister's warning: McDowall, *The Kurds: A Nation Denied*, p. 84.

124 British frustration: "In the end the British public would be shocked by the sight of British airplanes bombing the tribesmen of the Euphrates or Kurdistan to enforce tyrannical or mistaken decrees hatched among the intrigues of Baghdad coffee houses." Public Record Office, Kew, England, secret report, cabinet 24/201, copy 28, p. 338, February 1929.

124 Sheikh Mahmoud's letter: March 3, 1931, to the League of Nations, cited in Nikitine, *Les Kurdes*, p. 300.

126 "That the primitive Barzanis": William Eagleton, Jr., *The Kurdish Republic of 1946*, London, 1963, p. 50.

126 thousands of educated Kurds: Ismet Sherif Vanly estimated that 100,000 urban Kurds fled to Free Kurdistan between March 11 and 15, 1974, just before hostilities resumed. See Chaliand, *A People Without a Country*, p. 165.

126 government-provided pittance: "If the Iraqi government had behaved with more generosity and understanding in this individual case, it would have saved many lives, much government prestige and sums of money, a thousand fold greater than a small increase in the Mullah's allowance," Roosevelt, *For Lust of Knowing*, p. 149.

127 American critic: Eagleton, *The Kurdish Republic*, pp. 50–54 on Barzani and pp. 102–26 on retreat.

127 "Kurdish nationalist feeling": Interview with Mohsin Dizai, London, November 28, 1991.

127 emerging from fields of wildflowers: Interview with Sami Abderrahman, Rawanduz, October 10, 1991.

127–28 Mahabad details: Eagleton, *The Kurdish Republic*, and Archie Roosevelt, Jr., "The Kurdish Republic," *The Middle East Journal*, vol. I, no. 3, July 1947.

130 Barzani's treason charge: Interview with Abdul Rahman Qassemlou, Paris, September 30, 1988.

132 KDPI men . . . handed over to the Iranian government: Ibid.

132 "The Kurds have not been defeated": Cited in Eagleton, *The Kurdish Republic*, pp. 113ff.

133 Barzani's meeting to harangue his men: Interview with Sami Abderrahman, Rawanduz, October 10, 1991.

133 veteran's recollections of retreat: Michel Hegener, in *NRC-Handelsblad*, August 2, 1991. The exact numbers of men in the retreat and its duration are not clear. Barzani himself told Dana Adams Schmidt that 496 men participated in a fifty-three-day retreat.

134 Talabani and Barzani in Moscow: Interview with Jalal Talabani, Erbil, January 19, 1992.

135 report prepared by the President's national security adviser: 00229-1951, cited in "Den of Spies," p. 92.

135 "I am not a Communist": Mauriés, *Le Kurdistan*, p. 153. In 1962 he told Dana Adams Schmidt the same thing.

135 Barzani and visitors: Interview with Talabani, Erbil, February 11, 1996.

136 "halcyon period": Interview with Ambassador Anthony Parsons, London, November 21, 1991.

139 hopes of independence: Interview with Ismet Sharif Vanly, Lausanne, October 31, 1991; interview with Abderrahman, Rawanduz, October 10, 1991.

140 1,270 villages destroyed: Robert D. Kaplan, *The Arabists: The Romance of an American Elite*, New York, 1992, p. 251.

140 seven thousand Communists: Marion Farouk-Sluglett and Peter Sluglett, *Iraq Since 1958: From Revolution to Dictatorship*, London 1987, quoted in John Bulloch and Harvey Morris, *No Friends but the Mountains: The Tragic History of the Kurds*, New York, 1992, p. 124.

141 "military promenade": Mauriés, *Le Kurdistan*, p. 167.

141 "Jalal Talabani is a traitor": See Iraqi army telegram, quoted in Mauriés, *Le Kurdistan*, p. 141.

141 "agent for everybody": See Edmund Ghareeb, *The Kurdish Question in Iraq*, Syracuse, 1981, p. 181.

142 economic data: Chaliand, *A People Without a Country*, pp. 159–60.

143 "a ruse": Izady, *The Kurds*, p. 68.

143 Obaidullah: Statement to Ghareeb, July 19, 1974, cited in Ghareeb, *The Kurdish Question*, p. 155. Obaidullah was assassinated by the Iraqis early in the Iran-Iraq war, after an argument with Saddam Hussein in which he defended Mullah Mustafa by imprudently saying that at least he knew who his father was. (Saddam Hussein's paternity was a subject of controversy, especially among his adversaries.)

143 "The Iraqi Kurds have nothing": Interview with Qassemlou, Paris, September 30, 1988.

143 the Kurds' army: See McDowall, *The Kurds*, p. 95.

144 "Barzani was like a God to us": Interview with Ahmed Bamarni, Talabani's representative in Paris, Paris, September 25, 1986.

6 / Kissinger: Missionary Work Among a Hill Tribe

145 "absolute purgatory": Asadollah Alam, *The Shah and I: The Confidential Diary of Iran's Royal Court, 1969–1977*, London and New York, 1992, p. 224.

146 When Amir Aslan Afshar: William Shawcross, *The Shah's Last Ride: The Fate of an Ally*, New York and London, 1988, p. 164.

147 "Once we anointed [the Shah]": George W. Ball, "Issues and Implications of the Iranian Crisis," December 1978.

147 That was the phrase: *The Pike Committee Report*, Nottingham, 1977, pp. 195–98, 212–16.

147 forty-three-page briefing book: Department of State, "Visit of Richard Nixon to the Empire of Iran," May 1972, National Security Archive, Washington, Document 00767. Some four pages were blacked out when this document—originally marked in parts "secret" but mostly "confidential"—was declassified. Their context does not not suggest that the excisions dealt with the Kurds.

147 a key intelligence officer in Israel: David Kimche, *The Last Option—After Nasser, Arafat and Saddam Hussein: The Quest for Peace in the Middle East*, London, 1991, p. 194.

148 Barzani and Carolan: Interview with Ahmad Chalabi, London, August 10, 1996.

148 so hush-hush: See Tad Szulc, *The Illusion of Power: Foreign Policy in the Nixon Years*, New York, 1978, pp. 582–85.

149 "we did not know much": Interview with Henry Kissinger, Martha's Vineyard, Massachusetts, August 23, 1992.

149 "we knew plenty about the Kurds": Interview with Richard Helms, Washington, D.C., December 21, 1991.

149 "the Kurds were just part": Interview with Morris Draper, Washington, D.C., December 18, 1991.

149 Footnote: Interview with Chalabi, London, August 10, 1996.

150 Even before the deal was concluded: Alam, *The Shah and I*, p. 129.

151 The day after Nixon flew home: Ibid., p. 225.

151 "Our perfectly clear strategy": Interview with Kissinger, August 23, 1992.

151 Golda Meir . . . made one of her periodic incognito visits: Alam, *The Shah and I*, p. 215.

151 The entire U.S. outlay . . . was only $16 million: Kimche, *The Last Option*, p. 194, notes that "American aid made its way to the Kurds via Teheran, though not in the substantial manner which we had expected."

151–52 pocketed a percentage of the aid: Letter from Siyamend Othman to the author, January 27, 1993.

152 Washington stonewalled: Interview with Thomas Carolan, Istanbul, October 5, 1991.

153 "He told us very clearly": Interview with Mahmoud Othman, Sulaimaniyah, October 9, 1991.

154 "In his heart of hearts": Interview with Sami Abderrahman, Rawanduz, October 10, 1991.

154 Roosevelt-Barzani meeting: Archie Roosevelt, Jr., *For Lust of Knowing: Memoirs of an Intelligence Officer*, Boston, 1988, p. 284.

155 Other Kurds: Interview with Abdul Rahman Qassemlou, Paris, July 6, 1989.

155 "they would either have opposed it": Barzani, letter to congressmen and senators, February 24, 1977.

155 "contrary to American interests": Barzani, letter to President Jimmy Carter, February 9, 1977.

156 "The U.S. government did not give us any formal assurances": As cited in interview with Jim Hoagland, Paris, November 5, 1991.

156–57 his older brother: Interview with Sami Abderrahman, Rawanduz, October 10, 1991.

157 "believed nothing was done": Interview with Mohsin Dizai, London, November 26, 1991.

157 "General Barzani just thought": Interview with Dr. Mahmoud Othman, Sulaimaniyah, October 12, 1991.

157 "Indeed, it was inconceivable": Siyamend Othman, letter to the author, January 27, 1994.

157 On the eve of renewed fighting: Interview with Sami Abderrahman, Rawanduz, October 10, 1991.

157 "honor-bound": Barzani, letter to President Jimmy Carter, February 9, 1977.

158 "hope I end up in Peking": As cited in an interview with Mohamed Dosky, Washington, D.C., July 27, 1991.

158 "I don't know what difference" Interview with Kissinger, August 23, 1992.

158 "big boy": Interview with Helms, Washington, D.C., December 21, 1991.

158 Grechko in Baghdad: See William Safire, *Safire's Washington*, New York, 1980, p. 85, quoting his own *New York Times* column of February 12, 1976.

158 "We're stronger than you believe" and "If there is war": Elaine Sciolino, *The Outlaw State: Saddam Hussein's Quest for Power and the Gulf Crisis*, New York, 1991, pp. 277–78.

159 the British and the Shatt: Britain feared that if Iran remained neutral in a future war Iran might refuse passage of British warships to Basra. See Kimche, *The Last Option*, p. 193.

159 "If we were to find ourselves": Sciolino, *The Outlaw State*, pp. 277–78.

159 "more than once": Karadaghi, cited in Gérard Chaliand, *A People Without a Country*, p. 226.

159 their very existence was a tap: Interview with Eric Rouleau, Paris, October 23, 1993.

160 Rapiers at border and Iranian artillery: Alam, *The Shah and I*, p. 418.

160 "belatedly, we realized": Barzani's letter to President Carter, February 9, 1977.

161 By September 1974: Alam, *The Shah and I*, pp. 387 and 391.

161 "fighting like lions": Ibid., p. 411.

161 for weeks . . . he was kept waiting: Interview with Dizai, London, November 28, 1991.

161–62 intrigue in Amman and Cairo: Interview with Dizai, London, November 28, 1991; and with Chalabi, August 10, 1996.

162 Barzani letter to Kissinger, January 22, 1975: Interview with Dosky, Washington, D.C., July 27, 1991.

162 Kissinger had long since "known everything": Interview with Mahmoud Othman, Sulaimaniyah, October 9, 1991.

162 "my dear general" letter: Cited in interview with Dosky, Washington, D.C., July 27, 1991.

163 "always an option" and other quotations: Interview with William E. Colby, Washington, D.C., December 21, 1991.

163 "I thought Washington would be pleased": Interview with Helms, Washington, D.C., December 21, 1991.

163 "was for us that rarest": Kissinger, *White House Years*, New York, 1979, p. 1261.

163 "Iran, like ourselves": *The Pike Committee Report*.

164 "stunned" and "He did not ask our opinion": Interview with Kissinger, August 23, 1992.

164 Interview with Chalabi: London, August 10, 1996.

164 the Shah and others: Anthony Parsons, former British ambassador to Iran and Under-

secretary for the Middle East at the Foreign Office in the middle 1970s, said Kurdish resistance had virtually ended in the winter of 1974–75 and "the Shah had to settle or have a real war with Iraq." Interview with Parsons, London, November 21, 1991.

164 "the Kurdish affair and its tragic outcome": Kissinger, *White House Years*, p. 1261.

164 "decision in 1975": Ibid., p. 1265.

165 when Chalabi warned Barzani: interview, December 4, 1986.

165 "sovereign decision to make": Kissinger, *White House Years*, p. 1261.

165 "four to six weeks": Interview with Kissinger, August 23, 1992.

166 "our hearts bleed": Cited in *The Pike Committee Report*, pp. 215–16.

166 "Covert action:" *The Pike Committee Report*, p. 198.

166 The weakness of his position: Interview with Dizai, London, November 28, 1991.

166 "Is headquarters in touch?": *The Pike Committee Report*.

167 "most successful": Alam, *The Shah and I*, pp. 417–18.

168 "This is the end for us": Interview with Dizai, London, November 28, 1991.

169 "so very angry": Interview with Dizai, London, November 26, 1991.

169 The Shah delayed his audience: Kamran Karadaghi cited in Gérard Chaliand, *A People Without a Country: The Kurds and Kurdistan*, p. 215.

170 "What are we going to tell our people?": Interview with Mahmoud Othman, Sulaimaniyah, October 9, 1991.

170 "I know, because I have seen official Iraqi documents": Interview with Dizai, London, November 26, 1991.

170 "I replied that": Alam, *The Shah and I*, p. 419.

170 "You can surrender": As cited in interview with Jim Hoagland, Paris, November 5, 1991.

171 Cornered and dispirited: Ismet Sharif Vanly, in Chaliand, *A People Without a Country*, p. 173.

171 "unmistakable note of farewell": Karadaghi in Chaliand, *A People Without a Country*, p. 215.

171 "leave one of your sons": Interview with Sami Abderrahman, Rawanduz, October 10, 1991.

171 "to no avail": Ismet Sharif Vanly, in Chaliand, *A People Without a Country*, p. 198n.

171 "This is going to hurt Barzani a lot": Interview with Dizai, London, November 28, 1991.

171 "Had Barzani stayed on": Interview with senior Kurdish leader who insisted on anonymity, Shaqlawa, October 11, 1991.

172 "I can think of no other example": Ismet Sharif Vanly, in Chaliand, *A People Without a Country*, p. 177.

173 Issa Swar's death: Interview with Hoshyar Zibari, Salahuddin, January 18, 1992.

173 Details of Iraqi retribution: Karadaghi, in Chaliand, *A People Without a Country*, p. 216.

173 "cultural genocide": Interview with William Eagleton, Vienna, January 2, 1992.

174 "if senior Americans": Cited in *The Pike Committee Report*.

174 assuming Hoagland was an official: Interview with Hoagland, Paris, November 5, 1991.

174 To his fury: Interview with Dosky, Washington, D.C., July 27, 1991.

176 "we certainly would have made some effort": Interview with Colby, Washington, D.C., December 21, 1991.

176 "You murdered": Interview with Dosky, Washington, D.C., July 27, 1991.

177 Haim Levakov: Interview with Haim Levakov, Tel Aviv, October 20, 1991.

177 Draper thought: Interview with Draper, Washington, D.C., December 18, 1991.

177 the Shah sent a telegram: Interview with Dosky, July 27, 1991.

177 "It was like having the Chinese": Interview with Draper, Washington, D.C., December 18, 1991.

178 Kissinger was so determined: James A. Bill, *The Eagle and the Lion*, New Haven, Connecticut, 1988, p. 219.

178 "Do you have any choice?": Cited by Kissinger, *White House Years*, p. 1265.

178 Barzani was delighted: Interview with Dizai, London, November 28, 1991.

178 "had his friends": Interview with Draper, December 18, 1991.

179 "Look at what happened": Cited in interview with Dosky, July 27, 1991.

179 "I am not afraid": Cited in Roosevelt, *For Lust of Knowing*, p. 284.

180 "Are you afraid": Ibid., p. 288.

182 the ordinarily outwardly composed foreign-policy specialist: Interview with Kissinger, August 23, 1992.

7 / The Blind Beggar: Ecumenical Arbaeen

183 Details on the *arbaeen*: Interviews with Haim Levakov, Menachem Navot, and Tsuri Saguy, Tel Aviv, October 1991.

184 a senior Mossad officer: Interview with Aluf Hareven, Jerusalem, October 17, 1991.

185 "The Anglo-Saxons are always falling": Cited in Archie Roosevelt, Jr., *For Lust of Knowing: Memoirs of an Intelligence Officer*, Boston, 1988, p. 205.

185 "Put a Kurd atop a mountain": Interview with Saguy, Tel Aviv, October 18, 1991.

185 Occasional hardheaded dissenters: See Ian Black and Benny Morris, *Israel's Secret War: The Untold Story of Israeli Intelligence*, London, 1991, pp. 77–78.

185 "periphery policy": See Black and Morris, *Israel's Secret War*, and Dan Raviv and Yossi Melman, *Every Spy a Prince: The Complete History of Israel's Intelligence Community*, Boston, 1991, p. 21.

186 "feared a too powerful": David Kimche, *The Last Option—After Nasser, Arafat and Saddam Hussein: The Quest for Peace in the Middle East*, London, 1991, p. 190.

187 Bedir Khan: Black and Morris, *Israel's Secret War*, and interview with Joyce Blau, Paris, January 1, 1993. In his *"Diary of Major Noel on Special Duty in Kurdistan,"* published in London in 1920, Bedir Khan notes that the family was so well known as troublemakers to the Ottomans that "there is a special group for the Bedir Khans in the Turkish special cyphers."

189 journalist . . . to Kurdistan: Interview with Ibrahim Ahmad, Sutton, Surrey, England, November 25, 1991. Another version says that two Israeli agents posing as West German journalists were involved; see Siyamend Othman, "Contribution historique à l'étude du Parti Dimokrati Kurdistan-i-Iraq, 1946–1970," doctoral thesis, Ecole des Hautes Etudes en Sciences Sociales, Paris, 1985.

189 "the Israelis were small potatoes": Interview with Siyamend Othman, London, November 24, 1991.

189 "the blind beggar": Interview with Kamran Karadaghi, foreign editor of *Al Hayat*, London, November 29, 1991.

189 "looked older": Interview with Navot, Tel Aviv, October 18, 1991.

190 twenty thousand dollars: Interview with Navot, Tel Aviv, October 18, 1991.

190 A visiting foreign journalist: Interview with Alex Efty of the Associated Press, Nicosia, October 21, 1991.

191 "on anything they wanted advice on": Telephone interview with Amatzia Baram, Israel, October 15, 1991.

191 incident involving Eric Rouleau: Interview with Levakov, Tel Aviv, October 20, 1991.

191 an Israeli officer . . . deliberately revealed his identity: *An Nur*, the Ahmed-Talabani faction newspaper published in Baghdad during the split with Barzani, disclosed this and other details concerning Barzani's Israeli ties on January 29, 1969.

192 "the Kurds knew the terrain": Interview with Levakov, October 20, 1991.

192 "Every man a sharpshooter": Interview with Saguy, Ramat Gam, Israel, October 18, 1991.

192 "built for battle": Interview with Saguy, October 18, 1991.

192 So many people have claimed credit: Siyamend Othman, letter to the author, January 27, 1993.

192–93 account of Hendrin battle and Barzani's reaction: Interview with Saguy, October 18, 1991.

193 casualty figures: René Mauriés, *Le Kurdistan ou la mort*, Paris, 1967.

193 conversation between Saguy and General Aharon Yariv: Conversation with Saguy, as cited in interview with Saguy, October 18, 1991.

194 pilot defection: Raviv and Melman, *Every Spy a Prince*, pp. 141–43.

194 With the Shah's blessing: Asadollah Alam, *The Shah and I: The Confidential Diary of Iran's Royal Court, 1969–1977*, London 1991, and New York 1992, pp. 41, 83, and 84.

194 Kirkuk operation: Interviews with Levakov and Sami Abderrahman, Rawanduz, October 5, 1991.

195 "We are a problem for them": Interview with Navot, Tel Aviv, October 18, 1991.

196 "All the officials": Interview with Ismet Sharif Vanly, Lausanne, October 31, 1991.

196 "You got rid of de Gaulle and Nixon": Matti Golan, *Shimon Peres*, London, p. 150. During his visits, Barzani especially enjoyed renewing his long-standing friendship with an immigrant Kurdish Jew who had bought bread for his troops during the retreat from Iran to the Soviet Union in 1947.

196 Mossad's Kimche also claimed credit for Israel: Kimche, *The Last Option*, p. 194, hints that Israel helped in that radical policy change. "Kissinger had been kept informed of the Iranian-Israeli effort to encourage and strengthen the Kurdish insurgents. He was persuaded to join with us and support the Kurds against the advice of the State Department professionals, led by Morris Draper, who argued that America had nothing to gain from such a venture. Kissinger decided otherwise."

197 there was desultory talk: William Safire, *Safire's Washington*, New York, 1980, p. 83, argued in a column first published on February 5, 1976, that the Kurds were "willing to launch an attack of their own that would have won them their freedom as well as taken some pressure off the Israelis," but Kissinger thwarted them. "On October 16, [1973], he ordered intelligence chief William Colby to send this message to the Kurds: 'We do not repeat not repeat consider it advisable for you to undertake the offensive military action that ["another government," says the Pike Committee, meaning Israel] has suggested to you.' "

197 "was not much for it": Interview with Mahmoud Othman, Sulaimaniyah, October 8, 1991.

197 in his memoirs: Henry A. Kissinger, *White House Years*, New York, 1979, p. 1265.

197 "chewed to pieces": Interview with Kissinger, Martha's Vineyard, August 23, 1992.

197 "impression that Israelis": Interview with Kissinger, August 23, 1992.

197 "I've no desire to have the Kurds": cited in Alam, *The Shah and I*, p. 327.

198 (which proved unreliable): Interview with Saguy, October 18, 1991.

198 a reinforced tank company: Telephone conversation with Karadaghi, January 28, 1994.

198 Saguy . . . taken aback: Interview with Saguy, October 18, 1991.

198 treachery in *pesh merga* ranks: Telephone conversation with Karadaghi, January 28, 1994.

199 abrupt withdrawal of two and a half battalions, invoking routine rotation: Kimche, *The Last Option*, p. 195.

199 Acting on sudden orders from SAVAK: Interview with Uri Lubrani, Ministry of Defense, Tel Aviv, October 18, 1991.

199 was taken aback: Ibid.

199 A senior Iranian official: See Kimche, *The Last Option*, p. 195.

200 Key Kurds have acknowledged: Kamran Karadaghi, in a telephone conversation of January 28, 1994, said that Mahmoud Othman, then General Barzani's closest adviser, acknowledged that the leadership knew of contacts between the Iraqi and Iranian foreign ministers. "It was our fault" for not realizing that contacts which had been going on for months were on the verge of producing a solid agreement."

200 Kimche has denied: Kimche, *The Last Option*, p. 195.

200 but an Israeli historian: Telephone interview with Ofra Bengio, at the Dayan Center, Tel Aviv University; Israel, October 17, 1991.

200 Mullah Mustafa would change the subject: Interview with Morris Draper, Washington, D.C., December 18, 1991.

201 William Safire: Column in the *International Herald Tribune*, April 2, 1991. Similar indifference noted by the White House spokesman Marlin Fitzwater (reported April 6–7) and Joseph Fitchett (reported April 10, 1991, *International Herald Tribune*).

201 "The closer you get": Interview with William E. Colby, Washington, D.C., December 20, 1991.

201 Telephone conversation with Karadaghi, Paris, January 28, 1993. Frederick Cuny, consultant to American troops involved in returning Kurdish refugees to their homes, said he bumped into three men speaking Hebrew near the Kurdish city of Diyana but was unable to ascertain what they were doing there. Interview, Paris, December 13, 1991.

202 "simple people in the region": Interview with Lubrani, October 18, 1991.

8 / Ali Chemical

203 Simon Wiesenthal: Interview with Wiesenthal, Vienna, September 3, 1994.

204 the Armenian massacre: As many as 1,396,000 Armenians died in the slaughter, according to Lord Bryce, quoted in Howard M. Sacher, *The Emergence of the Middle East, 1914–1924*, New York, pp. 106–7. Kurdish nationalists are convinced that as many as 700,000 Turkish Kurds also died, either at the hands of Ottoman troops or from starvation and mass deportation. For other testimony about Kurdish involvement in the slaughter, see U.S. Consuls J. B. Jackson and Leslie A. Davis, quoted in Henry Morgenthau, *Ambassador Morgenthau's Story*, Garden City, New York, 1918, pp. 263, 273, 276, 383, 386.

205 "intent to destroy": "Bureaucracy of Repression: The Iraqi Government in Its Own Words," Human Rights Watch/Middle East, New York, February 1994, p. x, notes that although "no single master plan to exterminate the Kurds" has been found, it was "confident that the evidence is sufficiently strong to prove a case of genocidal intent

on the part of the Iraqi government." The U.N. Convention on the Prevention and Punishment of the Crime of Genocide was signed in December 1948 and entered into force in 1951. Iraq signed it in 1959.

205 "studied reports of the Spanish Inquisition": See Morgenthau, *Ambassador Morgenthau's Story*, p. 266. Doubt has been cast on the authenticity of this—and other— Morgenthau assertions. Heath W. Lowry, in *The Story Behind Ambassador Morgenthau's Story*, Istanbul, 1990, argues that the memoirs were American propaganda written with official State Department benediction after the United States declared war against the Ottomans in 1917. He suggests that Morgenthau's closest collaborators both in Constantinople and in preparing his memoirs upon his return to the United States were Armenians who had every reason to blacken the Ottomans' reputation by invoking a link with the Inquisition.

205 "kill without pity": Cited in letter from Haik Arslanian, *International Herald Tribune*, October 20, 1993.

206 computerized data: Azad Awny, a Kurd who escaped from jail in Baghdad during an American air raid in January 1991, said the bombs which jarred open his cell destroyed the computer record center in a building inside the prison compound. Interview with Awny, Erbil, March 22, 1991.

206 Stasi: See *"Disappearances" and Political Killings: Human Rights Crises of the 1990s: A Manual for Action*, Amnesty International, London, 1994, p. 18.

206 his own family: Interview with Hoshyar Zibari, Salahuddin, February 12, 1992.

206 The secret police: Rat poison was much favored by the Iraqi dirty-tricks agents. In an interview in Paris, February 1, 1991, Dr. Mahmoud Othman and Adnan al-Mufti recounted their misadventure: On November 24, 1987, Othman, deputy leader of the Socialist party, his assistant, Adnan al-Mufti, and another colleague survived yogurt laced with thallium and served at lunch by the pretty Kurdish wife of a senior Talabani bodyguard. She, unbeknownst to Othman and his companions, had agreed to work for the secret police in order to gain the release from prison of her husband. Three other Kurds died after vomiting and terrible suffering. (Among the other symptoms were heartburn, blistered feet, and, later, hair loss.) Othman's medical training helped him diagnose the malady. He remained in Iraq, but three other seriously ill men were spirited across the Iranian border on donkeys and then driven by ambulance to Tehran for treatment. Thanks to Amnesty International, a liquid antidote, Prussian blue, was rushed from Germany and stabilized their condition. The U.N. High Commissioner for Refugees arranged for them to leave Iran for London, where Amnesty International organized further treatment. The *pesh merga* smuggled the antidote into Iraq for Othman. The Iraqis who had blackmailed the poisoner released her husband on condition that both work for them. During the Kurds' 1991 uprising, she was arrested in Sulaimaniyah, tried, condemned to death, and executed. Her husband was executed separately.

207 "the savagery for which Iraq": Freya Stark, *Dust in the Lion's Paw*, London, 1962, pp. 141–42. Talcott Seelye, an American diplomat with long experience in the Arab world, similarly remarked, "The Iraqis are prone to violence and extraordinary bestiality that is not fully explained by the artificiality of their state." Quoted by Robert D. Kaplan, *The Arabists: The Romance of an American Elite*, New York, 1992, p. 252.

208 perverted form of male bonding: An Iraqi security officer who fled to Saudi Arabia said that on several occasions in 1985 and 1986 he and other senior security officials were summoned to feasts in Iraq's Tharthar desert. After dining and drinking beer or whiskey,

they were given weapons and each time ordered to shoot several hundred bound and blindfolded prisoners. The victims fell into previously dug trenches, and bulldozers covered over their bodies. Interview with Ahmad Chalabi, Iraqi National Council, London, August 10, 1996.

210 4,240 Kurdish villages: Telephone interview with Shoresh Resoul, London, November 19, 1994. In 1961, the Iraqi air force had "destroyed no less than 1,270 villages." Kaplan, *The Arabists*, p. 251.

210 "If this goes on": Interview with Massoud Barzani, Damascus, December 3, 1987.

211 "struggle admired by the entire world": "Genocide in Iraq: The Anfal Campaign Against the Kurds," Middle East Watch, New York, p. 111.

212 in the Dardanelles; Morgenthau, *Ambassador Morgenthau's Story*, p. 196.

213 "If we don't act": "Genocide in Iraq," p. 347.

213 "I don't want their wheat": Ibid., p. 346.

213 "Who is going to say anything?": Ibid., p. 349.

213 "Am I supposed": Ibid., p. 352.

214 "What is this exaggerated figure": Cited in interview with Adnan al-Mufti, Paris, October 28, 1991.

214 "between 60,000 and 110,000": Telephone interview with Shoresh Resoul, November 19, 1994.

214 "hundreds of thousands": *"Disappearances" and Political Killings: Human Rights Crises of the 1990s: A Manual for Action*, Amnesty International, 1994, p. 17, discusses the difficulty of putting exact numbers on extrajudicial executions, "but it can be estimated that, in addition to those of the 'disappeared' who were executed or otherwise killed, hundreds of thousands of other people have been victims of extrajudicial executions during the 1980s."

214 "so grave": *National Geographic*, vol. 182, no. 2, August 1992, p. 46.

215 at least sixty villages: "Genocide in Iraq," p. 359.

218 "campaign of genocide": Interview with William Eagleton, Washington, D.C., December 1986.

218 Barzani's man: Interview with Ghazi Zibari, Damascus, May 6, 1987.

220 Vice President Taha Moheiddin Maarouf: In the *International Herald Tribune*, November 8–9, 1988.

221 Glaspie told me: Interview with April Glaspie, Washington, D.C., December 22, 1994.

221 "degradation products": "Genocide in Iraq," p. xxix.

223 "We have no information": "Bureaucracy of Repression: The Iraqi Government in Its Own Words," Human Rights Watch/Middle East, New York, 1994.

223 During his June 1988 visit: Interview with Jalal Talabani, Paris, September 21, 1988.

225 Baghdad limply disowned: "Bureaucracy of Repression: The Iraqi Government in Its Own Words," Human Rights Watch, New York, 1994, p. 23, contests the forgery charge in great detail. While noting that so far no "single master plan" has been uncovered, its authors said the evidence "spread over an enormous number of files," and "however fragmentary, displays a remarkable consistency, and the tiny bits of evidence in fact turn out to constitute so many small pieces in a gigantic jigsaw puzzle."

225 the niceties of international law: Telephone interview with Resoul, London, November 19, 1994.

226 "showed it was not impossible": Istvan Deak, "Misjudgment at Nuremberg," *The New York Review of Books*, vol. XL, no. 16, October 7, 1993.

228 "probably we will find": "Genocide in Iraq," p. 353.

228 "You can't go from Kirkuk": Ibid., p. 34.
230 "They are saboteurs": Ibid., p. 68.
230 two released high-ranking Iraqi officers: Telephone interview with Resoul, London, November 19, 1994.
230 "Talabani asked me": "Genocide in Iraq," p. 349.
233 at least 3,800 Kurds died: Telephone interview with Resoul, London, November 19, 1994.
234 Despite this evidence: This argument is repeated by Stephen C. Pelletiere, in *The Iran-Iraq War: Chaos in a Vacuum*, New York, 1992. The Carlisle accusation that Iran gassed the Halabjah Kurds was based on the fact that blue lips were observed on some cadavers, and only cyanide gas, which Iraq was not believed to possess, was deemed capable of provoking that condition. But on May 23, 1993, Middle East Watch interviewed Dr. Howard Hu, professor at the Harvard School of Public Health, who maintained that blue lips could also be caused by acetylcholinesterase inhibitors, nerve agents which cause respiratory paralysis. See "Genocide in Iraq," p. 26.
234 "People are scared": Interview with Dr. Mahmoud Othman, Damascus, April 23, 1988.
235 "all Kurds knew": Telephone interview with Resoul, London, November 19, 1994.
247 much revered, if eccentric, elder brother: Interview with Abdelsalam Barzani, Barzan, Iraq, June 23, 1993.
249 one of the lucky Barzanis: Interview with Fatima Mohamed Salih, Barzan, Iraq, June 23, 1993.

9 / Turkey's Social Earthquake

252 "occult forces": Understood as a code word for the armed forces and security services; comment by Yavuz Gökmen, *Hürriyet*, December 23, 1995.
257–58 war expenditures: See *Turkish Daily News*, January 21, March 25, and June 16, 1994. In February 1996 Western diplomats in Ankara whom I interviewed estimated that Turkey in fact could be spending in excess of $10 billion.
258 300,000 men: Estimate by Mesut Yilmaz, while in opposition, *Hürriyet*, August 16, 1995.
258 Some 3,200 Kurds disappeared: *Milliyet* in December 1994 reported 3,240 such murders, all but a relative handful of which occurred in the Kurdish provinces.
259 "If you're in a village": *60 Minutes*, January 14, 1996.
259 "Acts of terrorism": cited in *Cumhuriyet*, October 11, 1994.
260 Dersim . . . poison gas: An official Turkish military historian in the early 1970s published a carefully pruned, bare-bones, single-volume account of all Kurdish uprisings between the two world wars, but his book was soon withdrawn from circulation. No meaningful casualty figures were provided. But a French authority estimated that as many as 40,000 Dersimi Kurds died, a possible exaggeration. Lucien Rambout, *Les Kurdes et le droit*, Paris, 1947, p. 39.
260 "only the Turkish nation": Quoted in *Milliyet*, July 31, 1930. The Justice Minister was even clearer: "Those who are not of pure Turkish stock can have only one right in this country, the right to be servants and slaves."
260 "This was necessary": Cited in interview with Reuters correspondent Hidir Gojtas, Ankara, February 8, 1996.
261 raze Carthage: "For some weeks the Turkish press extolled the conquest of Dersim

and shouted the paean: Dersim is no more—*delenda est Dersimo.*" Arshak Safrastian, *Kurds and Kurdistan*, London, 1948, p. 86. Safrastian was a British vice consul in Bitlis before World War I and, despite his Armenian background and the 1915 Armenian massacres, remained a friend of the Kurds.

261 "If you speak": Osman Mete, *Son Posta*, April 1948, quoted by Kendal Nezan in Gérard Chaliand, *A People Without a Country*, London, 1980, p. 72.

263 "Our parents who survived": Interview with Ahmet Türk, Ankara, February 8, 1996.

267 Gökalp's remarks: First from *The Principles of Turkism*, Ankara, 1920; second from *Kucuk Mecmua*, no. 28, Diyarbakir, 1923, quoted in *Pan-Turkism in Turkey, A Study in Irredentism*, by Jacob M. Landau, London, 1981.

276 Özal's relationship with the military: In 1991 Özal angrily told the army: "You're perfect for fomenting coups and building apartments for officers, but that's all," *Les Cahiers de l'Orient* 1993, Paris, p. 15.

276 "Özal was thinking": Interview with a Western diplomat who spoke on condition of anonymity, Ankara, February 7, 1996.

277 "allowing people like me": Interview with Mehmet Ali Birand, Istanbul, February 5, 1996.

277 Nowruz celebrations: "The Turkish military and police forces were directly responsible for about every casualty that took place during Nowruz," Helsinki Watch, vol. 4, no. 9, June 1992. The government's junior partners in the Social Democratic People's Party denounced the "excessive use of force by the security forces," noting that there were no known government casualties.

278 Özal and Çandar: Interview with Genciz Çandar, Istanbul, February 18, 1996.

279 "I'm determined to try": Interview with Ahmet Türk, Ankara, February 8, 1996.

281 "If Özal were handling the situation": Interview with Birand, Istanbul, February 5, 1996.

282 Özal letter: *The Independent* (London), November 13, 1993.

284 "Turkey surpasses such totalitarian regimes": *The New York Times*, March 15, 1996.

285 into their home: Interview with the Erik family, Istanbul, February 7, 1996.

287 his misadventure: Interview with Kadri Gürsel, Istanbul, February 5, 1996.

288 Illness and weakness: Iraqi Kurds fighting the PKK in 1992 reported that the PKK killed their own wounded rather than allow them to be captured; interview with author, Erbil, January 14, 1993.

288 "became kindling": Interview with Kamran Inan, Ankara, February 8, 1996.

289 "had concluded that the Kurds": British Public Record Office, Kew, Document FO 371/11557.

10 / Dog's Breakfast

294 "If I didn't understand": conversation with Ahmad Chalabi, London, September 27, 1995.

295 $2 million: Barzani and Talabani at one point offered to share half the costs, leaving only $1 million to be provided by Washington. Telephone interview with Hoshyar Zibari, London, October 27, 1996.

295 Iraqi diesel fuel: Various Kurdish sources in 1996 estimated the daily take at anywhere from $150,000 to $200,000, a senior State Department official at as much as $250,000; Washington, D.C., October 30, 1996.

297 He would not listen: "For months to no avail I warned Talabani to stop taunting, goading, and humiliating Massoud. I also told him that if things soured, Iran would not help until the PUK was driven back to the border and totally dependent on Tehran." Conversation with Chalabi, September 27, 1995.

297 KDP paper and Barzani-Pelletreau telephone conversation: Interview with Zibari, London, September 21, 1996.

298 Iraqi military aid: Tanks used against Erbil were reported leaving Saddam Hussein's hometown of Tikrit as early as August 12, which would suggest that planning for the Erbil operation went into high gear soon after Iran's incursion in July, and that serious talks between Barzani and Baghdad began a month earlier. Telephone interview with Chalabi, Washington, D.C., September 15, 1996.

299 promises . . . in writing: In 1992 in Washington, trying to convince both the KDP and PUK leaders to join the INC, Scowcroft told Barzani, when he recalled Kissinger's treachery, "We will not abandon you." Baker made a written commitment to that effect. Interview with Zibari, Salahuddin, February 5, 1996. Gore, the highest-ranking American official ever to call unequivocally for Saddam Hussein's overthrow, and Lake reiterated American protection for the Kurds and Shia: Paul Wolfowitz, testimony before the Senate Committee on Foreign Relations Near East and South Asia Sub-committee, September 19, 1996.

299 Scowcroft: *Newsweek*, September 23, 1996.

300 300 artillery pieces, etc.: John Deutch, Director, CIA, testimony before the Senate Select Committee on Intelligence, September 19, 1996.

300 "Kurdish civil war": Perry, cited in the *International Herald Tribune*, September 9, 1996.

301 hogwash: The Americans had promised their Kurdish employees an evacuation plan for years but never followed through; interview with Moayyad Yunis, February 6, 1996.

301 unashamed about the betrayal: Sami Abderrahman argued that the KDP did evacuate INC people in territory it controlled but "was not responsible for people in Talabani's area," meaning Erbil and Enkawa; news conference, Salahuddin, September 12, 1966.

301 Bay of Pigs: Paul Wolfowitz, testimony, before the Senate Foreign Relations Committee on the Near East and South Asia, September 19, 1996.

302 "it is clear": Deutch, testimony before Senate Select Committee on Intelligence.

303 "If there's any responsibility": *International Herald Tribune*, September 12, 1996.

303 MCC: For what it's worth, senior KDP and PUK officials separately insisted that the MCC could have stopped the internecine fighting "then and there" by merely showing up and lecturing Barzani and Talabani; interviews in Iraqi Kurdistan, February 1996.

304 $795 million: Nearly $583 million was disbursed in fiscal year 1991, subsequent yearly amounts constantly dropping from $71 million to $22.4 million in 1996; Fact Sheet #96-60, U.S. Agency for International Development, September 5, 1996.

305 bogus appointments: Interview with Zibari, London, September 21, 1996.

306 unconvincingly insisted: Çiller, quoted in *The New York Times*, September 21, 1996.

312 "It is an outrage": Amnesty Report, "Iraq Human Rights Abuses in Iraqi Kurdistan Since 1991," February 1995.

312 charges of genocide: Human Rights Watch, after studying captured Iraqi documents transferred to the United States, approached various governments in hopes they would take the lead in bringing such genocide charges against Iraq in the International Court

of Justice at The Hague, Memorandum from Kenneth Roth, Executive Director, September 30, 1994.

312 "Our fighting": Interview with Barzani, Salahuddin, February 13, 1996.

314 "Barzani gobbled up": *The Daily Telegraph*, September 18, 1996.

318 Eagleton also argued: William Eagleton, *The Kurdish Republic of 1946*, London; 1963, pp. 131–32.

Bibliography

Adamson, David. *The Kurdish War.* London, 1964.

Alam, Asadollah. *The Shah and I: The Confidential Diary of Iran's Royal Court, 1969–1977.* New York, 1992.

Amnesty International. *Getting Away with Murder: Political Killings and "Disappearances" in the 1990s.* London, 1990.

———. "Human Rights Abuses in Iraqi Kurdistan Since 1991." London, 1995.

———. "Iraq: Human Rights Violations Since the Uprising." London, 1991.

———. "Iraq: The Need for Further United Nations Action to Protect Human Rights." London, 1991.

———. "Turkey: Brutal and Systematic Abuse of Human Rights." London, 1989.

Bell, Gertrude. *The Desert and the Sown.* London, 1907.

Black, Ian, and Benny Morris. *Israel's Secret War: The Untold Story of Israeli Intelligence.* London, 1991.

Bois, Thomas. *The Kurds.* Beirut, 1965.

Bulloch, John, and Harvey Morris. *No Friends but the Mountains: The Tragic History of the Kurds.* New York, 1992.

Chaliand, Gérard. *A People Without a Country.* London, 1980, and Brooklyn, 1993.

"Civil War in Iraq." Committee on Foreign Relations, United States Senate, Staff Report, 1991.

Cockburn, Andrew, and Leslie Cockburn. *Dangerous Liaison: The Inside Story of the U.S.–Israeli Covert Relationship.* New York, 1992.

Dersimi, Nouri. *Le Dersim dans l'histoire du Kurdistan.* Aleppo, 1952.

Driver, G. R. *Kurds and Kurdistan.* Mount Carmel, 1919.

Eagleton, William, Jr. *An Introduction to Kurdish Rugs and Other Weavings.* Buckhurst, Essex, England, 1988.

———. *The Kurdish Republic of 1946.* London, 1963.

Edmonds, C. J. *Kurds, Turks and Arabs: Politics, Travel and Research in Northeast Iraq, 1919–1925.* London, 1957.

Farouk-Sluglett, Marion, and Peter Sluglett. *Iraq Since 1958: From Revolution to Dictatorship.* London, 1987 and 1990.

Fromkin, David. *A Peace to End All Peace: The Fall of the Ottoman Empire and the Creation of the Modern Middle East.* New York, 1989.

Galbraith, Peter W. "The United States and the Kurds." Remarks delivered to the H. John Heinz III School of Public Policy and Management, Pittsburgh, November 5, 1992.

Ghareeb, Edmund. *The Kurdish Question in Iraq.* Syracuse, 1981.

Ghassemlou, Abdul Rahman. *Kurdistan and the Kurds.* London, 1980.

Gordon, Michael, and Bernard E. Trainor. *The Generals' War: The Inside Story of the Conflict in the Gulf.* Boston and New York, 1995.

Gunter, Michael. *The Kurds in Turkey.* Boulder, Colorado, 1990.

———. *The Kurds of Iraq: Tragedy and Hope.* New York, 1992.

Hamilton, Archibald M. *Road Through Kurdistan.* London, 1937.

Hay, W. R. *Two Years in Kurdistan.* London, 1921.

Hourani, Albert. *A History of the Arab Peoples.* Cambridge, Massachusetts, 1992.

Howell, Wilson N. "The Soviet Union and the Kurds: A Study of a National Minority." Unpublished Ph.D. thesis, University of Virginia, 1965.

Human Rights Watch. "Bureaucracy of Repression: The Iraqi Government in Its Own Words." New York, 1994.

———. "Landmines: A Deadly Legacy." New York, 1993.

"Incontournable Turquie." *Les Cahiers de l'Orient.* Paris, 1993.

Izady, Mehrdad R. *The Kurds: A Concise Handbook.* Washington and London, 1992.

Kaplan, Robert D. *The Arabists: The Romance of an American Elite.* New York, 1992.

al-Khalil, Samir. *Republic of Fear.* London and New York, 1990.

Kimche, David. *The Last Option—After Nasser, Arafat and Saddam Hussein: The Quest for Peace in the Middle East.* London, 1991.

Kinnane, Derk. *The Kurds and Kurdistan.* London, 1964.

Kinross, Lord. *Ataturk: The Rebirth of a Nation.* London, 1964.

Kutschera, C. *Le Mouvement national kurde.* Paris, 1979.

Laurie, Thomas. *Dr. Grant and the Mountain Nestorians.* Boston, 1853.

Lowry, Heath W. *The Story Behind Ambassador Morgenthau's Story.* Istanbul, 1990.

Makiya, Kanan (Samir al-Khalil). *Cruelty and Silence: War, Tyranny, Uprising and the Arab World.* New York, 1993.

Mauriés, René. *Le Kurdistan ou la mort.* Paris, 1967.

McDowall, David. *The Kurds: A Nation Denied.* London, 1992.

———. *A Modern History of the Kurds.* London, 1996.

Middle East Watch. "The Anfal Campaign in Iraqi Kurdistan: The Destruction of Koreme." 1993.

———. "Endless Torment: The 1991 Uprising in Iraq and Its Aftermath." 1992.

———. "Genocide in Iraq: The Anfal Campaign Against the Kurds." New York, 1993.

———. "Hidden Death: Land Mines and Civilian Casualties in Iraqi Kurdistan." October 1992.

———. "Human Rights in Iraq." 1990.

———. "Kurds Massacred: Turkish Forces Kill Scores of Peaceful Demonstrators." 1992.

———. "Unquiet Graves: The Search for the Disappeared in Iraqi Kurdistan." 1992.

More, Christiane. *Les Kurdes aujourd'hui: Mouvement nationale et partis politiques.* Paris, 1984.

Morgenthau, Henry. *Ambassador Morgenthau's Story.* Garden City, New York, 1918.

National Security Archive. *"Iran 1977–1980."* Previously classified documents from Department of State and other government agencies.

Nikitine, Basile. *Les Kurdes: Etude sociologique et historique.* Paris, 1956.

Othman, Siyamend. *"Contribution historique à l'étude du Parti Demokrati Kurdistan-i-Iraq 1946–1970."* Ecole des Hautes Etudes en Sciences Sociales, Paris, 1985.

Pelletiere, Stephen C. *The Kurds: An Unstable Element in the Gulf.* Boulder and London, 1984.

Pichon, Jean. *Les Origines orientales de la guerre: 1921, le partage du Proche Orient.* Paris, 1938.

Raviv, Dan, and Yossi Melman. *Every Spy a Prince: The Complete History of Israel's Intelligence Community.* Boston, 1991.

Reza. *Les Chants brulés.* Bern, 1995.

Roosevelt, Archie. *For Lust of Knowing: Memoirs of an Intelligence Officer.* Boston, 1988.

Roux, Georges. *Ancient Iraq.* London, 1964.

Safire, William. *Safire's Washington.* New York, 1980.

Safrastian, Arshak. *Kurds and Kurdistan.* London, 1948.

Schmidt, Dana Adams. *Journey Among Brave Men.* Boston, 1964.

Sciolino, Elaine. *The Outlaw State: Saddam Hussein's Quest for Power and the Gulf Crisis.* New York, 1991.

Shawcross, William. *The Shah's Last Ride: The Fate of an Ally.* New York and London, 1988.

Soane, Ely Bannister. *To Mesopotamia and Kurdistan in Disguise.* London, 1912. 2d edition, 1926.

Stark, Freya. *Letters:* Vol. I, *The Furnace and the Coup, 1914–1930,* London, 1974. Vol. II, *The Open Door, 1930–1935,* London, 1975.

Sykes, Mark. *The Caliph's Last Heritage: The History of the Turkish Empire.* New York, 1973, rpt. of 1915 London edition.

———. *"The Kurdish Tribes of the Ottoman Empire."* *The Journal of the Royal Anthropological Institute of Great Britain and Ireland,* vol. XXXVIII, January 28, 1908.

Thesiger, Wilfred. *Desert, Marsh and Mountain: The World of a Nomad.* London, 1979.

Trollope, Anthony. *Can You Forgive Her?* London, 1982.

Turkey Human Rights Report, 1994. Ankara, September 1995.

United Nations, Economic and Social Council, report on Human Rights in Iraq, 1992, 1993, 1994.

United Nations, General Assembly, Situation of Human Rights in Iraq, Max van der Stoel, Special Rapporteur to the Commission of Human Rights, 1991, 1992, 1993.

van Bruinessen, Martin. *Agha, Sheikh, and State.* Utrecht University, 1978.

Westlake, Bruce. *The Arab Bureau: British Policy in the Middle East, 1916–1920.* University Park, Pennsylvania, 1992.

Winstone, H.V.F. *Gertrude Bell.* New York, 1978.

Xenophon. *The Persian Expedition.* Trans. Jeremy Antrich and Stephen Usher. Exeter, England, 1978.

Zaza, Nourredine. *Ma Vie de Kurde.* Geneva, 1993.

Index